Emergence

The Journey of a Young British Muslim Living in an Age of Extremism

by

Damir Rafi

UTOPIA INTERNATIONAL LTD

Emergence: The Journey of a Young British Muslim Living in an Age of Extremism

Damir Rafi

Published in the United Kingdom by Utopia Press

ISBN 9781097865963

Version1.0

"We are not going in circles, we are going upwards. The path is a spiral; we have already climbed many steps."

Herman Hesse, Siddhartha

Contents:

1. Introduction

On 22nd March 2017, a British Muslim, Khalid Masood drove a car into pedestrians outside the Palace of Westminster in London, in a devastating terrorist attack which killed five people and injured more than 50. Then, exactly two months later, Salman Abedi, a 22-year-old man detonated a home-made bomb in Manchester Arena following an Ariana Grande concert. CCTV footage from this incident was played widely across TV networks across Europe and highlighted the fear, trauma and devastation that those at the Arena experienced.

Incidents such as these, in which Muslim men commit atrocities, citing religious justification for their acts, have been all too prevalent in Europe and the wider world over the past two decades. Each instance in which such an attack occurs, wherever in the world it may take place, provides a stern test to the tolerance and compassion of wider society. *'Those Muslims again,'* becomes the overriding subliminal thought process in increasingly large numbers of people, until before long, every Muslim displaying any aspect of their faith becomes scrutinised and viewed through a lens of suspicion. A middle-aged woman wearing a hijab, a young man with an average-sized beard, even a group of Muslims speaking in Arabic, Urdu or any other foreign language becomes a subconsciously perceived threat to our individual or collective safety.

We do not want to think like this. When time and time again however we see the same headlines, the same "AllahoAkbar" screeched before blood is shed, our confidence in other cultures and faiths and belief systems becomes increasingly challenged.

A couple of weeks after the Manchester Arena bombing and a few days after yet another atrocity – the London Bridge attacks - I wrote an article for the *Independent Online* entitled *"I'm a British Muslim man of the same age as the London and Manchester terrorists – and I know why we turned out so different.*[1] *"* In this piece, I highlighted the importance of strong education and mentoring within Muslim communities – such that potentially extremist beliefs could be challenged and nipped in the bud. Moreover, I suggested solutions to radicalisation and terrorism, such as more government monitoring of mosques, particularly those linked to the Saudi government, which often practise Wahhabism, a creed which promotes militant and extremist views. The article ended with a guarantee – that at the vigils and commemoration ceremonies, many of which had already taken place at the time of writing, hundreds or even thousands of Muslims would be present, standing shoulder to shoulder with those of all other faiths and none – condemning Islamist terrorism and indeed atrocities of all kinds.

I myself attended one of these commemorations. Hosted by London Mayor Sadiq Khan, a sombre vigil was held in Potter's Park on the evening of June 6th. Together with a large group of my Muslim friends we coordinated and arrived wearing T-Shirts with *"I'm A Muslim"* written on them and holding banners and placards with messages such as "Love for all, Hatred for None," and "Muslims for Peace." Throughout the evening, locals who had been personally affected by the attacks and other Londoners who joined the vigil chatted to us, took photos with us and thanked us for standing with them in solidarity.

At one point, a tall, burly man with an interest in theology came and began discussing religion with me in an animated but friendly manner. After a couple of minutes, I looked to my right and noticed a group of strangers watching our conversation with concern. I turned towards them and as I did so one of them came nearer to me and whispered *"Are you alright? He's not bothering you at all?"* It was then that I realised that the group had congregated to ensure

8

that I was safe – that I as a young Muslim male was not being harassed or abused for the actions of Khuram Butt, Rachid Redouane and Youssef Zaghba, the terrorists of the same age group as myself, who had inflicted so much hurt upon the people of London. I thought at the time that even in their anguish, they still maintained decency, humanity and empathy for others, rather than turning to bitterness and xenophobia. This spirit of understanding and compassion is one that is enduring in many people, regardless of the trials and sufferings that they face.

A couple of days after my article had been published in the *Independent*, I woke to find dozens of private Facebook messages in my inbox. Intrigued, I opened them and was stunned to find the same message, written over and over again, in different words by different people across the world. The message was this: We were on the brink of turning to hostility and anger and this article reminded us that there are good Muslims out there, even though our televisions for the past month have only shown us evil ones. Among my favourites was a message from a lady living in Hertfordshire, which read:

"I just read your article about how to prevent radicalisation of young British Muslims. Thank you, you have given me hope at a time I have been feeling quite scared for the future of the world. There is a lot of negativity about Islam and I don't know what to believe as a white British lady living in monoculture Hertfordshire. There is a lot of anger and fear among my neighbours and much internal conflict as these acts of violence are pushing tolerance to its limit. Your article has helped me so I just wanted to say thank you."

The experiences from the vigils I attended and social media messages I received taught me that there exists within the hearts and minds of much of the British public and wider global society, a yearning to accept and love and trust others. However there also exists a simultaneous reluctant suspicion and fear of the unknown – especially Islam today. Is Islam as an ideology really responsible for the actions of madmen and terrorists who bring fear and atrocity to

9

the shores of Britain? Are Muslim extremists perverting Islam or are they in fact practising it in its purest form? If they are, what does that teach us about how we should interact with Muslims in everyday society?

The truth is that most people have little idea how to accurately answer these fundamental questions. Much of the population navigate through a hectic, busy life with family, work and social commitments, just about able to keep up with current affairs via a quick glance at a newspaper during a bus or train journey. In reality few people, unless they possess a natural, deep interest in the subject, are able to easily find the time to study holy books, or theological texts. However, in the current age, Islam is used as a weapon to divide society, both by Muslim extremists who declare a 'jihad' on the West and by far-right extremists who seek to burn Qurans and rip hijabs off unsuspecting females. As such, understanding the philosophy, theology and basic tenets of Islam arguably becomes of substantial importance in order to maintain the very fabric of society. Without a basic knowledge of the faith, those who use it as a weapon to divide people may begin to succeed. This has already started to happen throughout Europe. Islamic face coverings have been banned in a number of countries in recent years, including Belgium, France and Bulgaria. Such a ban, in reality, serves no useful purpose in preventing radicalisation or extremism. By using the sadness and hurt that the nation feels after terrorist attacks to justify victimising ordinary innocent Muslims, social cohesion and interfaith harmony is likely to become increasingly strained.

The theology and philosophy of Islam is not a secret. However, its reality has become obscured through media portrayal of Muslims, through the confusing web of Internet information, and most importantly through heinous acts of some Muslims themselves.

This book is designed to open a door and help the reader understand Islam with reference and applicability to modern times, relatable to contemporary world events. It will read not like a theological textbook but a reflection of my life as a British Muslim growing up in turbulent times. Whilst we as ordinary individuals cannot singlehandedly control or reduce the frequency of terrorist atrocities, we can play a part in controlling our responses to them. My hope is that this book can provide a spark, ultimately through which discriminatory attitudes and laws targeted against Muslims, based on misunderstandings of the religion, may be replaced by renewed mutual respect and empathy, and that interfaith harmony and pluralism can prevail across our societies.

2. Connection

There is a glow here.

It is dim at first, barely perceivable like a fading dream, despite the picturesque lake glimmering like glass and reflecting the starlit sky, the birds warbling in the trees and the gentle murmurs of the wind.

Though I live amidst the peace and stillness of nature, in a uniquely serene location for University accommodation to be situated, the glow comes not from the beauty of the surroundings but from meeting those around me, fellow first year students as apprehensive as I was, and connecting with them.

It takes me two weeks and after that time I grow to know the routines, the patterns of behaviour of those who live around me. I am the first to leave my flat each morning, entering the outdoors at a time when most bedroom curtains are still closed, beaten only by the first specks of light trickling into the sky from the east. I wait for any of the other medical students in my block to join me. There are four of us in total. James from flat number twenty, a mature-looking individual, active, sporty, a smooth long face with a stern and serious expression but always a twinkle of humour in his eye. Hassan from number twenty-four, late teens, a large individual, round glasses, soft beard, always with a childlike, jovial demeanour. Almost always however it is Holly who for better or for worse wins the race to walk with me each morning. Silky brown hair, shiny nails, a soothing

12

northern accent, we traipse together to medical school ready for our early morning lectures.

We relate to each other easily. Both having led reasonably comfortable childhoods with close family units, we now struggle with our newfound independence, our new lives. We leave our accommodation complex, with the tranquillity of the velvet grass landscape well behind us, and into the concrete world. The sun is still waking up, with often the moon still visible, appearing high and white over the city, slowly disappearing as the roads and pavements start to spring into life. We walk past taxis drifting past us, traffic lights slowly changing colour, buses stopping for passengers and as we turn the corner we see massive detached houses with in-out driveways or well-maintained front gardens. Some of our University lecturers live here, we later learn. On our last stretch of the journey the pavement is narrow and Holly slips behind me, the two of us walking in single file to make way for those hurrying in the opposite direction; early-morning joggers or dog walkers or men in suits rushing to catch their trains to the city centre. Our stroll is no more than fifteen minutes, but before long, walking the same journey each day back and forth, we grow to develop a bond, a connection, a much-needed mutual empathy during these challenging times, these new beginnings.

I am in the same seminar group as Hassan and for three hours each day we sit together, trying to get our heads round the muscles of the neck or the course of the splenic artery or the histology of the nephron. His friendliness makes me comfortable, despite the depth and complexity of information we are trying to learn. Hassan is a bright student, capable of grasping concepts quicker than me. Often I spend hours the night before a session preparing notes and pre-reading, while he simply breezes in without any preparation and catches up with my knowledge within a matter of moments. He quickly becomes a friend, a companion, who makes otherwise tedious anatomy sessions bearable and thus whose company I grow to value deeply.

13

It is in the evenings that I mostly spend time with James. At least once a week, we head to the 'Hub,' the central point of our accommodation complex, and play table tennis together, with streams of students passing us as they make their way to the cafeteria for dinner. We are competitive and I laugh as we engage in lengthy rallies, with James' usually serious expression transforming into visible joy and enjoyment. Occasionally we even earn applause from passers-by. Around six-thirty, without fail, Holly arrives at the hub too with her flatmates, dressed casually and looking relaxed, hoping it's not burger night at the canteen since she hates the burgers there. She gives me a wave, mouthing to me "meet you outside same time tomorrow morning?" as I smile and nod back at her.

There is a glow here.

It is dim at first, barely perceptible, but when I find others with whom I feel connection, then before long that glow becomes more of a brightness and the brightness becomes a radiance, an illumination.

It was during this month, October, that I first climbed up to the highest part of my university campus for the first time. A month into my new, independent existence, I looked out at the buildings, the greenery, the medical school, with the clock tower imprinted upon the centre of my vision, the defining image of my view.

Despite the friends I had made early on, university was nonetheless proving a more difficult challenge than I had envisaged. Coming out of seven years of grammar school, same people, same routines, I now found myself for the first time outside my comfort zone.

I was battling not simply my social inadequacies, my study habits and my attempted new-found independence, but also against my own self. Wondering what kind of life I should live and how to juggle the various contradictory influences in my life. Wondering what was more important, my familial culture or my current circumstance.

Deliberating over whether the rules that my faith and upbringing taught were made to be followed, or intended to be inevitably broken. Pondering over how to live life in a way as to get the most out of it and most importantly, seeking the answer to the question of who I really was and the kind of person I wanted to ultimately become.

November Year 1:

A taxi pulls over just outside my block of flats, its engine screeching to a halt and jolting me awake from my sleep. I look out of the window of my ground floor accommodation and see the door open and a single person clamber out of the vehicle. It is my flatmate Callum, unusually smartly dressed in a white shirt and an unknotted tie hanging loose around his shoulders, who trudges towards our front door as the taxi immediately drives away, out of sight.

I live in a flat of four. There is Callum, a thick-accented Liverpudlian international-relations student, Alex, a jolly Southerner studying chemistry and Andy, who spends so much time playing American football that I rarely see him. I can't even remember what he studies. I have not gelled with any of my flatmates, probably due to a combination of my own social ineptitude, our habits of prioritising other people to spend time with and the fact that all three of them have vastly different characters and interests to me.

For most students, the first months of university have so far been a storm of parties, club-nights and fancy-dress events. While the three of them have grasped the freshers opportunities with both hands, full on, with no compromise, I have largely been watching from afar, wondering from time to time if I should join in. I have a naturally reserved demeanour, and am happy to have a few close friends rather than hundreds of superficial ones. However, the first stages of university are the time, it seems, to meet as many people as is physically possible and party with them as if you've known them your whole life. I don't drink, I don't smoke or do drugs, I don't get with girls in the way they do. I have left the comfort of my family and old friends behind, many miles away, realising that independent life is a challenge. It is now close to midnight and as Callum knocks on the front door of my flat I leave my room to open it. He barely acknowledges me, looking slightly dejected as he trudges inside. I follow him to the kitchen.

"I thought you were on a night out?" I ask him. As they had done every day this week, all my flatmates had left the flat around 8pm to go for drinks elsewhere, before heading off to whichever club was hosting that night's entertainment. Callum, the most enthusiastic party-goer of them all, looks at me and, with a shrug, explained: "I wasn't feeling it." Curious, I stick around in the kitchen waiting for him to tell me what in particular had happened to cause his evening to end so prematurely. He doesn't elaborate.

"Are you OK?" I ask him, slightly concerned. Callum is the kind of person who I had never previously encountered. He has a poor relationship with his parents and describes university as the perfect way of escaping their company. He is obsessed with his body image, with a passion for gymming and drinking protein-shakes. His enormous biceps are his most precious possession, if you can call them that. He is a passionate clubbing enthusiast and has already seemingly made dozens of friends on the various nights-out which he's religiously attended – hence my surprise at seeing him back so early on this Wednesday evening.

"Am I OK?" he asks me with a sigh. "Do you know what OK means?"

Taken aback by the question, my answer is stuttering. "Yes, I do know I think."

"Well what does it mean then?"

My panic at his slightly odd question causes me to reply abruptly. "You tell me."

He comes a step nearer to me then, close enough for me to see the scar on the left side of his forehead, the contours of his jawline, the light brown hairs on his cheeks and chin. He is the same age as me, but due to his light facial hair, his physical bulkiness and his tall stature he appears at least five years older.

"Everybody tells you they're ok don't they? They all go around walking the streets, telling the world they're fine, but you know what they really are?"

For someone who wants to come across as a 'tough-guy,' I am taken aback by his show of weakness, of vulnerability.

"They're swans, that's what they are."

I wonder if he is a bit drunk.

He sighs again as he comes even closer, which I hadn't really thought was possible. His dark eyes are now boring into me and I can smell his alcohol-tinged breath against my cheek. His voice becomes more excitable now.

"Graceful on the outside, but under the surface they're desperately kicking, trying to stay afloat, knowing that if they don't maintain this disguise they'll be looked down upon, if they don't keep their desperations hidden, if they don't hide their helplessness, if they don't…"

I step back at this point, surprised by his poetic outburst, as his voice trails away. Not knowing how to react, I instead decide to change the subject, in an attempt to lift his mood. It works. We engage in lighter conversation for the next half hour before I return to my bedroom.

I keep an eye on Callum over the next few days, concerned that his drunken outpouring, which remains fresh in my mind, is reflective of his inner state. He continues exuberantly going out at night, enjoying the university scene, but every so often, when I see him during the day, his eyes betray a sense of anxiety, of insecurity. We all feel like this at some point, particularly during these difficult

17

stages of life. For me, in order to combat these feelings, my mind tries to go someplace else, somewhere deeper, in an attempt to transcend the mundanity of everyday life.

I sometimes think that there are two realities. One is that of consumerism, of materialism, while the other is that of spirituality. Perhaps it is impossible to truly belong in both. Embrace spirituality and one must abandon the love of the world. Become enamoured by material pleasures and desires and the spiritual world grows ever more distant. Sitting on the bridge between the worlds, belonging everywhere yet nowhere, as I feel, is not a good place to be.

December Year 1:

I stand in front of a mirror, fastening the buttons of my clean long-sleeved white shirt. I pick up my bow tie, looping it around my collar, making sure it is tied adequately, adjusted properly, straight. I hear murmured voices outside my window, footsteps growing increasingly louder. Hassan and James and two other medics are waiting for me to emerge, waiting for the taxi to arrive. As I exit my flat, with a quick nod to Callum as we pass each other in the hallway, a sudden gust of wind greets me as I step outside to wait with my friends. It is a cold Friday evening, the frigid winter air making our smart evening attire inadequate, the biting wind hitting our skins and reddening our noses. We are en route to one of the poshest conference halls in the city for the most eagerly anticipated event of the semester– the university ball. It starts early – before 7pm the first of a three-course meal is served, followed by a short speech from a head of department, or student union president, or someone or other. I don't really listen. We sit, chatting contently and comfortably, as if we have known each other for years.

It doesn't take long before a posh evening out descends into a drunken club night. Music blaring from the front stage, people dancing madly, freely, the air no longer immersed with the subtle

18

smell of braised lamb and roasted vegetables but with an overwhelming stench of alcohol. People's disinhibition leads many to greet me joyfully. I respond in kind, knowing full well that the next day we may pass each other on campus with barely a nod of acknowledgment. James doesn't drink either, but he enjoys and embraces the chaos of the evening more than I do. It is only just past 10pm, someone throws up near me and I take this as my cue to leave.

I wake up late the next morning. Opening the curtains of my bedroom I catch sight of my flatmate Alex outside, walking to the accommodation hub with his washing bag, murmuring a song to himself, seemingly lost in his own thoughts. There is no one else in my view. It is a crisp morning, the world quiet and still, the winter sun shining high, birds sailing through the air like ships. My mind wanders to those who must have been out until the early hours, for whom such nights out are a regular occurrence. Such people, the majority of my university friends, are free, in some ways. Working hard during the days and during the nights, or on weekends, attaining the reward of losing themselves, their worries, concerns, inhibitions disappearing for a few hours. Amidst the glamour of the world finding transcendence beyond the humdrum of routine life.

My own upbringing, my belief system however teaches me something different. That alcohol, gambling, drugs and clubs are to be avoided. To be truly free, it teaches, requires discipline, sacrifices and a different kind of journey. On the opposite end of the bridge I think of people I have encountered - spiritual people, religious people, who seem equally free, contented within their own selves. I am teetering in the middle of that bridge, neither free to fulfil my desire for escapism with alcohol nor with faith. This is my dilemma.

I start to try to unravel the unknown, to understand how my own belief system attempts to create a harmonious society and a contented individual.

19

For many practising young Muslims, this is the predicament they face. The world is as technologically and materialistically as advanced as it has ever been, yet society is still not happy. Religion to many seems outdated and irrelevant. Despite this Islam still provides a perspective on social affairs, applicable to today, which is in some aspects vastly different from the West's. However, it claims that through following its teachings, it can satiate one's thirst for lasting satisfaction in a way that no worldly pleasure can.

What really are these Islamic perspectives, however? Despite its potential flaws, living in a liberal Western society with shared freedoms, that had provided me with vast opportunities over the course of my childhood and early adulthood, was something I never took for granted. Muslim societies across the world undoubtedly enable far fewer freedoms. I wondered whether the inherent teachings of Islam were to blame for this.

My university journey led me to compare these differing ways of life, from Western societies to modern-day Muslim societies to idealistic 'Islamic' societies, in an attempt to decide for myself in which direction I should travel on my allegorical bridge.

I quickly realised that this journey consisted of two components. The first was to ascertain the best path to follow as an individual. It was driven by my own internal state of mind. Is a religious philosophy a help or a hindrance to securing a sense of inner peace and contentment? The second was to establish the most beneficial philosophy for society at large. This aspect of my journey was sparked by the constant media spotlight on Islam, most notably terrorist attacks committed by Muslims across Europe and also throughout other parts of the globe. Do the ongoing troubles of the Muslim world exist as a result of the theological teachings of the religion, or a perverted concept of faith? Extending this, are the philosophies of Islam and the West compatible, or antithetical? On the surface, given the widespread perceptions prevalent across the West that Islam is an illiberal, intolerant, even aggressive religion, with harsh 'Sharia laws' and poor treatment of women, adhering to the teachings of Islam whilst integrating into Western society may seem impossible to some. I see-sawed between these two strands over the course of my university life. My conclusions, shaped by experience, my research and my spiritual practices, proved both revealing and significant.

My first firm area of solid investigation was with regards the Islamic standpoint on freedom of speech and thought. Throughout my years as a university student, I found that free-flowing discussion with all kinds of people, of different faiths and backgrounds and cultures, was one of things I lived for most. How are such freedoms being interpreted and applied today, and is the concept of liberalism compatible with a truly Islamic vision of society?

3. Islam and Liberalism

In November 2017, Tim Farron, who had recently quit as leader of the UK Liberal Democrat Party, wrote an article for the Guardian entitled *"Liberalism has eaten itself- it isn't very liberal anymore²."* *"When a liberal turns out to be an evangelical Christian, people are surprised or confused,"* he begins. *"If you are one of those...then you are a victim...of liberalism's comprehensive triumph - where the main loser has been...liberalism."* Farron argues in this article that though much of the country would describe themselves as 'liberal,' including members of the Conservative Party and right-wing press, the very concept of liberalism has been undermined by the constant condemnation and abuse that we give each other. Many who claim to be liberals, Farron argues, in fact are not. *"People talk about shared values today,"* he writes. *"But when they do, what they mean is: 'These are my values - and I am going to act as though they are also yours and will demonstrate contempt for you if you depart from them.'"*

This article resonated with me. According to Oxford Dictionaries, to be liberal means to be *willing to respect or accept behaviour or opinions different from one's own; open to new ideas.* Over the past couple of centuries liberal thought has created great successes for society - it has enabled people of all different races, genders and belief systems to live side by side in peace and harmony. Such thought has enabled the abolition of slavery, the establishment of freedom of religion and civil rights for women and black people. It has allowed the flourishing of new ideas and perspectives in society which in turn has contributed to great scientific and technological advancements. However, recently liberalism has taken a turn for the worse, as Tim Farron himself discovered.

Throughout the 2017 General Election Campaign, many of Farron's radio and television interviews were dominated by journalists asking him whether he considered homosexuality and abortion as sins, to which he initially repeatedly refused to provide a definitive answer. Eventually, due to continued pressure he finally caved, stating in a Channel 4 interview that he did not consider gay sex a sin. The following year, he expressed his regret for the comments he made, stating that he felt pressured by his party to 'foolishly and wrongly' make a statement that was 'not right.'

Interestingly, in the Commons Farron continuously voted in favour of gay marriage – first in the 2013 Marriage (Same Sex Couples) Bill and then in 2014 in a Bill on the topic of extending the right to gay marriage to Armed Forces personnel outside the United Kingdom. During the election campaign, Farron was keen to try to highlight that he was in fact a true liberal – being able to support and defend the rights of others despite holding an alternative viewpoint himself. Despite this, he eventually resigned. In his resignation speech, he talked of the fact that it was impossible to be a political leader and a committed Christian and that he had been treated with suspicion because of his faith. *"We are kidding ourselves if we think we yet live in a tolerant, liberal society,"* Farron stated.

In a 2017 interview on ITV's *Good Morning Britain*, prominent Conservative politician Jacob Rees-Mogg affirmed his personal belief that same-sex marriage and abortion were wrong. When asked whether he was taking a political risk by conveying these views, he responded by saying that his own party, oddly, were more tolerant of religious faith than other parties which professed to be liberal. *"The Lib-Dems pretend that they're liberal, but they could not cope with having a Christian as their leader,"* he remarked.

The mark of a healthy society is being able to live alongside those who profess different beliefs and opinions without resorting to censorship or abuse. To compel people to think in a certain way, or to have particular specific perspectives, is not conducive to the creation of interesting, expressive, free-thinking citizens. Critics of religious beliefs, political philosophies or social trends should all be entitled to convey their perspectives so long there is no direct incitement to violence or hatred. Currently, vast numbers of people are accused of hate speech simply because their views go against the prevailing liberal philosophy. This includes critics of Islam. Maryam Namazie, a human rights campaigner and prominent opposer of Islam and Sharia law, was prevented from speaking at Warwick University in 2015 because of concerns that her speech was 'highly inflammatory.' The university student union stated that external speakers 'must seek to avoid insulting other faiths or groups.'

The points that Namazie raises, though antithetical to the beliefs of most Muslims, are both interesting and require intellectual responses. Simply shutting her up, or labelling her an 'Islamophobe,' does nothing to actually counter her arguments. As prominent clinical psychologist Jordan Peterson argues, *"Making hate speech go away does not make hate go away. It drives it underground, where it festers invisibly. If you want to know where the haters are, then let them talk."*

We are in danger of ironically letting our own pro-tolerance attitudes lead us to shut down debate with those whom we perceive to be less tolerant than ourselves. This is a problem, as it can ultimately lead to hatred rankling in people's hearts, without them being able to properly express their views such that they can be challenged. This is especially true of Islam. In a 2017 poll, it was found that a quarter of English people believe that Islam is a dangerous religion that incites violence, with more than four in ten people admitting to being suspicious of Muslims. In our current climate it is quite possible, even likely, that those who feel this way also feel anxious or scared to express their worries and fears relating to Islam without being criticized for 'Islamophobia.' It is also plausible that allowing them the freedom to express their views could help to allay their fears and enable bridges to be built between different sections of society. Necessary and important discussions can be generated and mutual empathy increased through understanding the perspectives of others.

Challenging ideas and philosophies are something to be encouraged in a healthy society, however this does not mean that freedom of speech should be an absolute freedom. Just as with any freedom, limits exist in order to protect society from potential adverse consequences. For example, the principle of confidentiality exists between doctors and patients. Despite 'freedom of speech,' doctors are duty-bound to protect the confidentiality of those they care for and not disclose patient information without consent.

Though freedom to express genuine differences of opinion should never be censored or curtailed, there is nonetheless a difference between speech intended to challenge ideas and speech intended simply to abuse. Maryam Namazie aimed, through her proposed talk at Warwick University, to share ideas and though those ideas may have made certain students uncomfortable, those students should not have an inalienable right to not be offended. Sometimes, legitimate criticism can lead to people becoming offended and in a healthy society, the right to level intellectual criticism is of importance, even if offence is caused inadvertently.

However, another category of speech is that which is done for the very purpose of offending. In September 2012, French newspaper Charlie Hebdo published a series of cartoons of the Prophet Muhammad, including caricatures depicting the Prophet as naked and in a wheelchair[3]. In preceding years, Danish newspaper Jyllands-Posten came under scrutiny for cartoons including ones depicting the Prophet with a bomb and the Prophet as a dog[4].

Whilst some described these cartoons as 'satirical,' in reality many of them cannot be described as such. Satire is the use of humour, irony or wit to highlight the absurdity of another's position. It requires a high degree of intelligence to be satirical – framing an argument in a humorous way in order to make a particular point. Charlie Hebdo's cartoons did not even attempt to convey legitimate criticism, rather they aimed simply to abuse and denigrate the beliefs of others. Abuse, unlike satire, does not require intelligence. If, through cartoons, Charlie Hebdo had aimed to level arguments against Islamic teaching, or criticise it in a tangible manner, then even if people were offended by it, it would serve as a useful piece of intellectual discourse which could be responded to. However there is no way to intelligently respond to compromising drawings of the Prophet Muhammad, because the drawings themselves were not intelligent pieces of work.

Responding to a similar kind of controversy, the publication of cartoons of the Prophet Muhammad in a Danish magazine in 2006, an Independent editorial[5] wrote a piece which concluded:

"However much we should strive to limit offence, there must never be a situation in which people have a legal right not to be offended. But these are questions that must be viewed through the prism of a diverse society and one in which we each bear a responsibility to consider the implications of what we say, write and depict. We should be pleased that Britain is developing into a country where tolerance - rather than the right to offend - is valued most highly."

In other words, a freedom in and of itself does not tell you how it should be used. Simply possessing a freedom is no praiseworthy thing, rather it is the exercise of that freedom which determines the quality of the society. The piece argues that in order to protect the social cohesion and harmony of society, an element of self-censorship is required. Gratuitously abusing others simply because we feel like it does nothing to help the cause of society and in fact undermines the benefits of freedom of speech. However, the article also highlights that this responsibility should be a moral one, rather than a legal one. When offensive material which serves no intellectual purpose is published, the population as a whole should stand up against such attempts to fracture the peace of society and condemn such publications. This already occurs with many

26

instances of purposefully offensive speech. For example, Holocaust denial, often used as an insidious form of antisemitism, is always roundly condemned by the vast majority of peace-loving citizens, because of the way it is used to gratuitously abuse Jewish people. For the sake of consistency, society should ensure that those of all religious and ethnic groups are protected from this kind of abuse of freedom of speech.

Contextualising the Charlie Hebdo cartoons is also important. At the time they were published, Muslims in France were suffering under a barrage of persecution, hate crimes, verbal abuse and governmental legislation banning garments which were integral to the identity of many Muslim women. The ban on face-covering was passed by the French Parliament in September 2010, which made it illegal to wear face-covering veils or other masks in public places[6]. Since the implementation of this law, several clashes have been reported between police and Muslim women, who for religious reasons have refused to remove their veils. In April 2018 in Toulouse, a woman refused to remove her veil and was taken into police custody, ultimately leading to rioting associated with this incident, during which 11 vehicles were set afire. Such an incident highlights the current tension existing between law enforcement agencies and Muslims. Hate crimes against Muslims have been steadily increasing in France since 2010, as well as the scale of violence against them, with recent attacks including arson and grenade throwing. A 2012 poll conducted by Ifop found that 42% of French people felt that Muslims posed a threat to 'national identity,' and in a 2014 study, three-quarters of those surveyed associated negative connotations with Islam[7].

Muslims constitute around 3% of the population of France and over recent years negative attitudes towards them have increased significantly. Since this is the case, it can be argued that that acts of Charlie Hebdo in caricaturing the Prophet in the manner they did, only served to deliberately provoke an already demonised and downtrodden minority. If the ruling classes continually abuse a marginal population group, at some stage it surely becomes propaganda.

Freedom of speech is a means to an end, not an end in itself. The ultimate purpose of it is to enable a peaceful, harmonious and socially cohesive society. Our words must be placed in context to the nature of society at the time. Though legal restrictions should not be placed on offensive speech, unless it directly incites to violence, we have a moral responsibility to ensure that our actions do not create unnecessary divisions and thereby fracture societal peace.

On 7th January 2015, two Muslim gunmen entered the Charlie Hebdo headquarters in Paris and opened fire, killing twelve people and wounding eleven, yelling phrases such as *'The Prophet is avenged.'* The gunmen were later identified as Chérif Kouachi and Said Kouachi, two brothers in their early thirties[8].

The attack received immediate condemnation from governments across the world. Leaders including Vladimir Putin, Barack Obama, Angela Merkel, Benjamin Netanyahu and David Cameron produced strongly-worded statements of outrage and denunciation. Muslim governments across the world responded in the same vein. Countries including Saudi Arabia, Iran, Lebanon, Morocco and Qatar offered their condemnation, as did Islamic organisations such as the Muslim Council of Britain and the Union of Islamic Organisations of France. Both the Hamas government and the Palestinian Liberation Organisation also denounced the attacks, stating that *'differences of opinion and thought cannot justify murder.'* A tiny minority of extremist Muslim preachers, such as notorious British radical Anjem Choudary supported the attack, however the vast outpouring of immediate support for Charlie Hebdo by prominent Muslim organisations and governments across the world conveyed the point that the actions of the killers were in no way representative of their views.

The Quran speaks extensively on the concept of freed   ᴗ.
as well as the kind of speech it expects from its adhε
Islam endorses the notion of freedom of expression, ιτ αιѕν ᴗᴗ
its followers to restrict harmful or hurtful speech. *"Allah likes not
the uttering of unseemly speech in public, except on the part of one
who is being wronged (4:49)".* As well as forbidding evil speech, it
repeatedly encourages virtuous talk, especially towards others. The
theme of *"And speak to men kindly... (2:84)"* is regularly affirmed
throughout the Quran.

Blasphemy, defined as hostile contemptuous statements against
religion – for example against God, his Prophets, or the
fundamentals of Islam – with the direct intention of hurting the
sentiments of Muslims, is considered an offence according to
Islamic teaching. However, despite this, the Quran makes clear that
no punishment should be meted out by any human being towards
those engaging in blasphemous talk or activity. According to the
Quran, it is the sole responsibility of God to punish or forgive
blasphemy. The Quran states *"...and you shall surely hear many
hurtful things from those who were given the Book before you and
from those who set up equals to God. But if you show fortitude and
act righteously, that indeed is a matter of strong determination."*
Even if blasphemous behaviour hurts one's feelings, Islam's solution
is very clear: *"...and those who suppress anger...and Allah loves
those who do good (3:135)."* Forgiveness and suppression of anger
is emphasised as the correct and Islamic response to all forms of
offensive speech.

The clearest practical advice for a Muslim in how to approach
situations in which their feelings are harmed is given in Chapter
Four of the Quran. Such advice flies in the face of those who
condone violence as a legitimate response to cartoons of the
Prophet. *"...when you hear the Signs of Allah being denied and
mocked at, sit not with them until they engage in a talk other than
that; for in that case you would be like them... (4:141)."* The proper
response, according to Islam is simply to move away from the

29

ource of offence and not to take part, such that one's own behaviour remains pure.

Islam encourages debate and dialogue and embraces the diversity of thought that humans possess. Whatever one's opinions, both the Quran and the example of the Prophet Muhammad testify to the importance of respectful discourse.

Linked to this issue is that of apostasy – in other words leaving the faith. Many anti-Islam proponents raise the accusation that Islamic Law dictates that anyone who leaves Islam should be given the death penalty. To provide evidence for their claim, many cite the example of Muslim governments in the world today. Sudan, Saudi Arabia, Iran, Pakistan, Yemen and Afghanistan all have harsh apostasy laws, which they claim are grounded in Islamic philosophy. However, when searching for Quranic justification for this claim, none can be found. This is even admitted by high-profile Islam critic Sam Harris, who states: *"Interestingly, [the penalty for apostasy] isn't spelled out in the Quran."*

The reason the punishment for apostasy isn't written in the Quran is that there isn't one. An individual's faith is in all circumstances between himself and God. Apostasy in mentioned numerous times in the Quran but never is it mentioned alongside any kind of punishment. In fact, punishment is specifically forbidden. In one place, referring to the people of his time, God tells the Prophet Muhammad, *"So if they submit (i.e. properly accept Islam), then indeed they follow the right way; and if they turn back, then upon you is only the delivery of the message (i.e. it is not for you to enforce the belief upon others) (3:20)."* On several occasions, the Quran clearly sets out the remit that the Prophet Muhammad possessed – *"Thou art only a Warner (35:24)."* His role was to advise others as to the benefits of embracing Islam, not to compel others to accept it.

A further clear piece of evidence against the argument that Islam endorses death for apostasy comes from Chapter 4 of the Quran. In verse 138 it states: *"Those who believe, then disbelieve, then again believe, then disbelieve and then increase in disbelief, Allah will never forgive them nor will He guide them to the way."* Evidently, as stated, if Islam allows individuals to freely believe and disbelieve as many times as they like, then there is no possible way that it could sanction death as a punishment for apostasy, as then those 'guilty' would have been put to death the first time they apostatised, before they could *'again believe, then disbelieve.'*

Though as a religion, Islam seeks to increase its adherents' moral and spiritual status, thus encouraging kindness in speech and steadfastness in faith, it prescribes no worldly punishment for breaching these rules. Like the Independent editorial article, Islam agrees with the concept of each of us exercising moral responsibility in ensuring that our words do not tear apart the fabric of our society. Likewise, Islam encourages Muslims to reflect upon their faith and ensure that morality and righteousness is applied when considering whether to leave the faith. In both these instances, no punitive legal measures are condoned, rather the Quran categorically forbids enforcing punishments for either of these acts. Islam's real attitude, in summary, towards blasphemy and apostasy demonstrates its liberal, tolerant, pluralistic attitude towards freedom of thought, speech and expression.

In July 2018, Donald Trump visited the UK for his first official visit as US President. He was met with widespread protests and in London alone, tens of thousands of people marched through the streets decrying his visit and his divisive views. I attended the march late in the day as the protesters made their way to Trafalgar Square for the centrepiece of the organised action. Though I was pleased by the general sentiments of the occasion – anti-racism, anti-xenophobia, anti-misogynism, the event nonetheless left a bad taste. Amidst the numerous benign banners, there were some bearing distasteful messages. Placards of naked cartoon Trumps and Putins, messages of abuse aimed at the US President, even posters bearing insults at right-wingers in general. The protest highlighted to me the enormous level of division and polarisation existing in today's world. It also demonstrated the sad reality that in people's passion, ugliness can ensue, often despite the fact that the values they initially sought to defend are worthwhile and just in themselves. The end result of such rage is ultimately always negative. People become poor at listening, at seeking to understand the perspectives of others. They become blind, only seeing their own views as true and this becomes accentuated by the social media echo chamber. Before long, much of society becomes dogmatic in their approach to life. Their combination of anger and discontentment, coupled with the conviction that their principles and solutions are the correct ones, causes liberalism itself to go out the window.

Islam is a faith which aims for its followers to develop a complete and total certainty in its reality, urging them to strive in spirituality and intellect in order to experience the metaphorical fire of contentment and conviction. However despite this, it expects its adherents to respect the views of others so deeply that a truly pluralistic society can be maintained. The Quranic principle of *'for you your religion and for me mine,'* is a statement of true liberalism, a far cry from the forced conversions, blasphemy laws and barbaric punishments we see in some Muslim-majority nations today.

Islam encouraged me to think freely, to accept or reject it as I so wished. But it was here that the harder questions came into fruition. Was it worth starting my own personal voyage into the depths of religion and spirituality? Did I have enough reason to, enough initial evidence? Could faith really help me, or did it simply constitute an ancient, tired approach to understanding the world?

4. A World Beyond

My internal spiritual mind is like a window, which I carry with me always. At first the glass is murky, misty, as I begin to search for the kind of life worth living, the kinds of personal values worth protecting. Through the haze I see an isolated road with only the concrete greyness, the watching trees and the encompassing silence of the starlit darkness. This is the path where I begin, a lonely path, but soon I find myself metaphorically climbing to the top of snow-capped mountains, crawling across glaciers of ice, plunging into seas of coral – trying to find the perfect view. At times it seems as close as my fingertips, at others as far away as the moon.

At one point during my early university days I thought back to a conversation I had had a few years earlier with a school friend. We were talking about the various rules and constraints of my religion. *"I can't drink, or do drugs, or have sex before marriage,"* was the essence of the conversation. I remember my friend frowning and incredulously asking me, *"So basically you can't have any fun at all as a teenager?"* I paused then, realising I had never thought of my own situation in the bleak manner which he had just conveyed. Now, as I entered University these thoughts kept coming back into my mind. *"Do I belong to a faith which inhibits and restrains me for no real reason? Am I being disadvantaged by following a belief system that I'm not even certain is true? Is there any point of swimming against the tide, when everyone else seems to be flying exuberantly though the water in the opposite direction?"*

The biggest issue for me was certainty. Following rules and laws from old texts seemed pointless unless I could be certain of God's existence and the truth of whichever religion I chose. Was it worth forgoing some of the adventures of growing up for the sake of a hazy inference or an idealistic hope or solely a source of comfort? Probably not. Though if there was a way of attaining certainty in God's existence and I attained it, then I knew that I would happily follow whatever rules were ordained, even if they required sacrifices on my part.

January Year 1:

Time floats away like a dream. Christmas holidays come and go, and we are back, January exams over, scurrying across campus for lunch with James, our heads bowed to escape the biting winds hitting our faces. Despite the revision, my four-week break was restful and enjoyable. For James, as he was about to tell me, it was upsetting but transformative. I walk myself almost out of breath, finally reaching the central cafeteria on University square. We join the queue for a sandwich. I buy a Southern fried chicken wrap and find us a table, as he waits for his to be toasted.

James has two pieces of news for me, on this, the first week back from holidays. My girlfriend broke up with me, is his first. I react with surprise and genuine sadness – he had had a three-year strong relationship with Lauren, a girl I had never met but through his descriptions had seemed perfect for him – kind, affable, intelligent. The break-up had taken James completely by surprise too, he had intended to spend Christmas Eve with her family and had already bought her and even her brother a gift. I ask him how he is doing, five weeks on and he tells me his second life development.

"You know who the most mentally strong person was in human history?"

I shrug, thinking we are drifting towards a more light-hearted subject, perhaps sport. I sit back on my chair, intenseness over.

"Tiger Woods?"

He looks at me sternly, leaning forward, still with a serious expression.

"No."

"Who then?"

"Jesus."

I look at him, perplexed, a part of me wondering whether he is talking about the footballer or about Christ. We had never discussed religion and I knew he possessed little interest. Until now, evidently. I wait for him to explain.

"Jesus was persecuted and beaten and oppressed and sentenced to crucifixion and yet told his disciples not to let their hearts be troubled. He told them that following him was the way to attain true life, that the world hated him because of his purity. He lived in a tiny Palestinian village and yet said to his followers to take heart, "for I have overcome the world."

James pauses, thinking of how best to explain the point he is trying to make.

"Even though he suffered so much, he still had total inner peace. How good must it be to feel like that?"

"Are you a Christian now?" *I ask him, still confused as to exactly what's going on.*

"No," *he tells me.* "I've just been reading and watching videos...I just thought since you have a religion, you might understand a bit..."

Little did James know that the exact same thought processes had been reverberating in my mind ever since I started university, perhaps in even a more dramatic way, since it was over the past months that I developed the realisation that I lived a life in which I had everything that the world had to offer but that in this world, even everything is not quite enough. No pleasure in this world, however wonderful it may seem, is ever unlimited. Eventually, I thought, despite the initial high, there is always something lurking not far behind. This is the inevitability of betrayal, of bitterness, of deception. This is a force that follows behind everything when one gets too engrossed in the world. It is a power that one can never escape from despite the illusions that one tries to create to avoid it. It is something that steals even the greatest of worldly memories and turns them into nightmares and depressions. I figured that perhaps in reality, it is the fire that appears like water and that water that appears like fire. Jump in the pit that appears to be fire and it will satiate your thirst and cool you. Jump in the pit that appears like water and it will destroy your insides and burn you.

I was in many ways an introspective, reflective person and had a spiritual desire that needed to be fulfilled. But how best to fulfil this desire? Some of my friends who felt it too decided to go travelling in an attempt to satisfy their souls. I considered this briefly before university started – taking a gap year to see the world. The experiences I would undergo and the people I'd meet might teach me who I really was. I could encounter different perspectives and ways of life, which might lead me to realisations about the world, about myself.

Now however I started to think that there was a better way to find myself. Travel was magnificent, it broadens one's horizons and opens one's mind. Such experiences could help me to decide who I could be in theory, but it could only be through enduring perseverance and striving that might truly enable me to develop a lasting peace, contentment in my own skin, in the company of my own thoughts. After all, I thought, the answers to life's big questions could not be found at the top of a mountain or in the depths of a beautiful ocean. Beauty and wonders could be found there, but the beauty of enduring inner peace required experiences that originated from beyond the places that we could physically travel. Don't travel to find yourself, I reflected. Find yourself and then travel.

The fact that I didn't gel with my flatmates meant that I often had evenings to myself and I started to utilise them to discover the spiritual world, through reading, through videos and through prayer. Jesus, as well as all other holy religious personages, provided a complete instruction manual in finding oneself. Such figures from the past suggest that the process involves a spiritual journey of purification. It was in my moments of quiet reflection, of wondering how to attain happiness when I seemingly had everything I needed to make myself content, that I decided to follow this manual. It might come with thorns and hurdles and obstacles. But ultimately it could divert my course. I hoped that I would no longer be consumed by the black hole of the world, but would be taken instead somewhere else entirely, to a spiritual universe as yet inaccessible to my senses.

During the early stages of my reading, I learnt that there are three kinds of knowledge that it is possible for man to acquire. The first is through inference. If a person sees smoke rising from a distance he infers, quite legitimately, that there is likely to be a fire. He is probably correct, however there may be other less obvious reasons for the smoke being there. The second, stronger kind of knowledge is through sight. If the person proceeds towards the fire and sees it with his own eyes, he would conclude, with a high level of certainty that it is indeed there. This kind of knowledge is highly likely to be accurate and reliable, however even in this instance it is possible that his eyes could be deceiving him and that which appears to be a fire could instead be something else, like artificial electric flames. The third kind of knowledge is that of experience. The person who having seen the fire then jumps into it and becomes burned by its flames, can now say in complete certainty that the fire exists. This is the highest and most certain form of knowledge. Religion, particularly Islam, urges people to climb the ladder of knowledge, ascending from inference to sight to immersion, in order to discover absolute proof of God's existence.

The teleological argument, or argument from design, was popularised in recent centuries by William Paley, who likened the universe to a watch with many interrelated parts coming together to fulfil a grander purpose. The Quran, revealed in the 7th Century to the Prophet Muhammad (more on this later) urges its readers to reflect upon this very principle – that every aspect of creation contains the invisible signature of a Designer. Could blind processes, it asks, be responsible for forging the wonders that we see around us? Moreover, are these wonders all ultimately part of no grand objective or design? Is it possible that from an eternal nothingness the magnificence of the heavens and the earth could emerge, which will eventually all perish into an eternal nothingness once more?

Our inference tells us that just as we assume every building or vehicle or piece of technology has been designed by a conscious mind, so it should be the case that the source of natural wonders, which are far greater, should be designed by an even greater consciousness. Going further, it suggests that our lives are therefore not simply accidental vain happenings in an unintended universe, but possess a meaning for which we must search. The evidence of design in our universe is like seeing the smoke from a distance. It acts as a stepping stone, to further ponder over our lives and motivates us to approach the smoke to try and see the fire for ourselves.

As I mentioned, however, if inference was the strongest form of evidence for God's existence then I wasn't too interested. How could I truly find satisfaction in something that I wasn't completely certain was really there? My days in my early months of university were mainly spent on university campus – attending lectures and seminars, winding down in the cafeteria, working in the library. My free evenings were spent figuring out religion. I would watch videos and read books relating to theology, philosophy and arguments for and against God's existence. Then I would pray. I needed to try and see the fire and I knew that if there was to be a way then this would be it.

I was born a Muslim and so from a young age I would pray in a very specific way. Islamic prayer essentially consists of a series of physical postures, from standing to bowing to prostrating to sitting. This repeats a number of times and during each position, prescribed prayers from the Quran in Arabic are recited, with opportunity to also offer prayers in one's own language.

The philosophy of this method of prayer is as follows: our physical movements or actions have an impact upon our internal thoughts and feelings. This is a universal rule. For example, if someone was to make an effort to try and make tears come from their eyes, the harder they tried, the more they would find that somewhat bizarrely they would start to feel sad, even if they didn't before. Similarly if one was to spend a day when their chest puffed out and their head held high, they would most likely feel more internally confident than they would if they walked with shoulders slumped and shuffled steps. In the context of prayer therefore, the act of bowing towards God creates the internal state of obedience and the act of prostrating creates the feeling of love for God, in the hope and expectation that prayers will be answered. Other religious texts, especially the Bible, also make reference to the Prophets (such as Jesus) praying in various positions, most notably prostrating in supplication during difficult times.

As a medical student who was first aid trained, I was aware of the concept of 'Shake and Shout.' Essentially, when someone appears to be unconscious the foremost method of ascertaining whether they are really awake is to shake their shoulders and simultaneously ask them loudly to open their eyes if they are conscious. The same concept can be applied to the quest of finding God. If God really existed and was alive then logically speaking he should respond in an unambiguous way to the sincere prayers of those seeking to find Him. Moreover, the Quran speaks clearly of God being responsive. Addressing the Prophet Muhammad, the Quran states: *"And when My servants ask thee about Me, say: 'I am near. I answer the prayer of the supplicant when he prays to Me. So they should hearken to me and believe in Me, that they may follow the right way.'"*

Muslims are taught to pray five times in a day – once in the morning between dawn and sunrise, twice in the afternoon and twice in the evening. Such a task may seem arduous; however, the goal of Islam is to develop a deep love for God and establish communion with Him– and so just as speaking five times a day to one's spouse doesn't seem unreasonable to anyone - similarly taking a few minutes at various points to communicate with God becomes more pleasurable than laborious. At least, in theory that is the case when love for God has been established truly in a person's heart – and when the fire begins to become visible.

Prayer is a serene experience, performed either individually or in congregation and designed to be beneficial for both physical and spiritual health. It reduces anxiety, worry and residual anger. Every prayer ends with the worshipper looking towards those on their right-hand side and saying the words *"May the peace and blessings of God be upon you,"* and then doing the same on their left side.

I found some success and satisfaction through my prayers. After some intense months, during which I even woke regularly for lengthy optional night prayers, I started to become glad that I hadn't been completely lured by the attraction of worldly pleasures and giving in to all the temptations around me. A fire started to glow inside my heart.

Indeed, my individual spiritual journey was gathering pace but fear of Islam throughout the world was only growing year by year, day by day.

5. Cherries in the Desert

Just uttering the words 'Sharia law,' is enough to terrify many people. Over recent years Sharia has become synonymous with bloodthirsty and barbaric punishments such as stoning and the dismemberment of limbs. It has attained such a reputation that even world leaders and prominent politicians have expressed their own condemnations. In 2015, during his Presidential campaign, Ben Carson insisted that a practicing Muslim should never become President of the United States[10]. Carson declared that he would never advocate a Muslim for President *"if they are not willing to reject sharia and all the portions of it that are talked about in the Quran."*

Indeed, whenever Islam and its compatibility with the West are discussed, Sharia law is always high on the list of factors which supposedly renders Islam and the West at odds. According to a 2018 YouGov survey of over 10,300 UK citizens, 32% of respondents believed that certain areas of Britain were almost exclusively Muslim and dominated by Sharia law[11]. In a 2016 survey described by the media as a 'shock poll,' it was found that over 40% of UK Muslims supported 'aspects' of Sharia law[12]. None of the articles which reported this poll described which 'aspects' these were, nor did they attempt to explain the meaning of Sharia law.

In reality, Sharia law, a term used today to invoke fear into people's hearts, is one which is both misused and profoundly misunderstood. The literal meaning of the word 'Sharia,' is 'a path to life-giving water.' Far from just referring to punishments, Sharia constitutes a complete guide upon which all Muslims are advised to follow. The first step in following a religion is to believe in the existence of a Deity, a Creator, a God. Islam seeks to provide clear signs and evidence of this. The Quran refers to the beauties and wise-design of nature, the universe and the human body. It then gives the examples of Prophets of God and other God-fearing individuals, both male and female, throughout history. It then urges readers to follow in the footsteps of the spiritual models of the past and claims that through the worship of God, with resilience and effort and determination, each person can themselves find proof of His existence. Sharia Law follows on from this. It presupposes that the individual believes in God and has accepted that the purpose of human existence is to worship Him, through prayer and good deeds and actions and also that morality is defined by following God's laws and commandments.

There are five main branches of Sharia – worship, beliefs, personal morality, transactions and contracts, and punishments. In other words, it provides a complete guide for a Muslim on how to live a moral life and best contribute to society. Thus, the 'punishments' aspect of Sharia is both vastly overinflated and overemphasised by the media. Every nation has its own 'Sharia,' – its code of life aiming to enable its citizens to live in the best manner possible and provide a suitable balance between individual freedom and societal peace. While some governments throughout history have been cruel and oppressive through the implementation of their 'Sharia,' others have found more success. Islam does not specifically advise any form of government. Rather it urges its followers to elect those who are most beneficent. The defining verse in this regard reads as follows:

"Allah commands you to make over the trusts to those best fitted to discharge them and that when you judge between the people, you do it with justice. Excellent indeed is that with which Allah admonishes you. Allah is All-Hearing, All-Seeing." (4:59)

The key point to this verse is that religion is not mentioned at all. Rather, Islam promotes both religious tolerance and complete pluralism. Far from attempting to enforce religious creeds, laws or perspectives, Sharia law in fact promotes secularism, with equal rights for all citizens regardless of faith. True justice, as declared in this verse, can thus only be achieved through a complete separation of religion and politics. To compel a non-Muslim to follow Islamic laws would be a breach of justice and thus violate the very principles of Islam.

In 626 AD, the Prophet Muhammad, who was at that time the ruler of Medina, gave a letter to the Christian monks of St Catherine's monastery. His words, which are preserved to this day, serve as evidence of the true teachings which he endorsed for his followers. The letter reads:

"This is a message from Muhammad, son of Abdullah, as a covenant to those who adopt Christianity, near and far, we are with them. Verily I, the servants, the helpers and my followers defend them, because Christians are my citizens; and by Allah! I hold out against anything that displeases them. No compulsion is to be on them. Neither are their judges to be removed from their jobs nor their monks from their monasteries.

No one is to destroy a house of their religion, to damage it, or to carry anything from it to the Muslims' houses. Should anyone take any of these, he would spoil God's covenant and disobey His Prophet. Verily, they are my allies and have my secure charter against all that they hate.

No one is to force them to travel or to oblige them to fight. The Muslims are to fight for them. If a female Christian is married to a Muslim, it is not to take place without her approval. She is not to be prevented from visiting her church to pray.

Their churches are to be respected. They are neither to be prevented from repairing them nor the sacredness of their covenants. No one of the nation of (Muslims) is to disobey the covenant till the Last Day (end of the world).[13] *"*

The original form of this letter can be found at the Royal treasury in Constantinople in Turkey. St Catherine Monastery preserves a copy, which is on display.

From a theological standpoint, the heinous ways in which some Muslim leaders and governments behave today can in no way be used as valid arguments that Islam preaches barbarity and intolerance. Rather, to ascertain what Islam teaches requires analysing the original sources and the original followers and Founder. The Prophet Muhammad created the first notion of an 'Islamic state,' but it was the antithesis of what groups such as Daesh (also known as ISIS) represents in the modern age. A true Islamic state is one in which Muslim citizens are prepared to not only live in peace with those of other faiths, but be willing to fight and die to safeguard their rights.

But what of the so-called punishments themselves that Islam supposedly advocates? This, for many, is the crux of the issue. Does Islam give permission for men to beat their wives? Are stoning or beheading legitimate Islamic punishments? As with all issues, simply touching the surface is not enough. A deeper understanding is required to ascertain the true nature of punishment under Sharia law. Each issue can be tackled in turn.

One particular verse, famous for the apparent license for men to strike their wives, when read properly, in fact does the opposite. Chapter 4 verse 34 reads:
"And as for those (wives) on whose part you fear disobedience, admonish them and keep away from them in their beds and chastise them..."
Whilst difficult to translate from its original, richer Arabic form, the verse essentially refers to a circumstance in which the wife commits a major offence against the husband – whether that be having an affair,

44

taking money, betraying his secrets or physically abusing him. Referring to men specifically, it devises a solution as to how to resolve a conflict situation. It gives three progressive, escalating steps. The first is verbally admonish the wife, essentially in an attempt to resolve the conflict though dialogue. If this fails, the verse advises separating beds, for a period of up to four months. The purpose of this is to reduce the chances of violence significantly – by encouraging the man to separate himself from a situation which he may find emotionally difficult to internally deal with. The temporary separation between the two individuals serves to enable both to reflect and promotes eventual reconciliation.

If both these steps fail, the verse then mentions the third option – 'chastisement' – which is a translation of the Arabic word *'daraba.'* Interestingly, the word has numerous meanings, including 'to heal,' and 'to separate.' Some have argued therefore that this word in context has nothing to do with violence at all. However, even if it does, then the clear rule – as per the linguistics of the verse and the commandments of the Prophet Muhammad, is that there should be no mark on the woman's body. Essentially, this commandment eliminates all possibility of domestic violence, since to strike anyone in a painful way without even a chance of leaving a mark is difficult, if not impossible. The purpose of this stepwise approach is to channel a man's anger in order to prevent physical abuse. For physically natured men, for whom their natural inclination would be to become violent towards their wives, this verse provides a restriction, not a permission for them to engage in aggressive acts. The preventative nature of Islamic teaching means that peaceful reconciliation or eventual divorce are the only real options. This perspective is validated by the behaviour of the Prophet Muhammad, whose purpose as a Prophet was to be a model for his followers. According to his wife Aishah: *"The Messenger of Allah never beat any of his servants, or wives and his hand never hit anything."* Moreover, when asked by a companion how Muslim men should treat their wives, one of his foremost instructions was *"do not beat them and do not make them miserable."* Later in the same chapter, there is a similar verse which provides advice to women as to what they should do if they have been wronged by their husbands. Again, reconciliation is promoted, but failing this it advises them to initiate a divorce as a last resort.

There is no Islamic basis for either stoning or beheading. The only time stoning is mentioned in the Quran is in instances where Prophets and their followers had to face such punishments themselves by their opponents.

There are two main physical punishments described in the Quran. The first is 'lashes,' which are mentioned in the Quran as a legitimate punishment for public lewd sexual indecency. This is a crime in the UK for which the culprit can be sentenced to up to two years in prison. In order for anyone to even be tried of such a crime, it requires four morally upright, trustworthy witnesses to have actually observed the act taking place. Though the concept of lashes may sound harsh, they are intended to be painful to the skin but cause no lasting damage. Islamic teachings explain that the arm should not be raised to whip, only the forearm, thus limiting the amount of discomfort that can be caused. Given that the equivalent punishment to this crime in the UK is a prison sentence of up to two years, one could argue that the lashes are more lenient, despite perhaps still serving as a greater deterrent.

The second type of physical punishment mentioned in the Quran, which causes extensive controversy, is the cutting of hands for stealing. *"And as for the man who steals and the woman who steals, cut off their hands in retribution of their offence as an exemplary punishment..."* (5:39).

There are two ways in which this verse can be taken – literally or metaphorically. The expression for 'cutting hands' in Arabic is an idiomatic one, and is used in another place in the Quran when referring to the reaction of the ladies of the court when seeing the handsomeness of Joseph. In their awe of his good looks, they metaphorically 'cut their hands.' The same expression can also mean 'preventing someone from doing something.' In other words, when referring to thieves, 'cutting their hands,' can mean to prevent them from having the means to steal, for example through imprisonment.

However, according to widespread opinion, the term can also be used in in its literal sense. This is a punishment which, firstly, if to be used at all, is reserved only for the most severe and persistent offenders, not simply those who steal, for example, out of desperate hunger. Secondly, the punishment exists more as a deterrent than an actual penalty to be implemented. This is because of the underlying philosophy of Sharia itself. Before any types of punishments can be implemented, Islam insists on first creating a moral, reformed society in which such crimes are exceedingly rare. In the context of such a society, firstly there would be very few individuals who would commit theft on a grand scale. Secondly, even if such people did exist, then the proposed punishments would serve as a suitably strong deterrent.

The issue is most eloquently conveyed by the late Mirza Tahir Ahmad, who summed it up as follows:

"...the system of evidence as proposed by Islam, is so strict and so deeply bonded with the sense of morality that a witness is required to hold certain values. In any immoral society...where witnesses can be bought or influenced...where the moral standard unfortunately to our detriment is very low, Islamic laws cannot be implemented. It is wrong to implement any law in the name of Islam before preparing that atmosphere. It would be like trying to plant a cherry in the heart of the desert. The atmosphere in the desert is not promotive to the growth of cherries....So, Islam not only speaks of laws. It's a religion. So, it speaks of the preparation for the implementation of laws as well. This is why according to Islam the Prophets first attend to the moral values of the country. They transform the society, raise the standard to a high degree. Then to maintain that standard and to safeguard its values, some stern measures are taken which are very

seldom applied in reality. But the society in bargain is much happier and safe.[14] "

Theft is a serious offence. It can cause individuals and whole societies to live in fear and destitution. Thus, the threat of a severe punishment, given to hardened criminals, is perhaps preferable to the suffering of innocent people.

Islamic law in general is not harsh. It is only the misconceptions which circulate that create fear in people's hearts. Many of the so-called punishments which are dished out by cruel Muslim governments today have no religious basis at all, but are implemented under the guise of piety for the purpose of oppressing minorities or dissidents, and maintaining power over the masses.

April Year 1:

In the blink of an eye my first year at University is over. Amidst my internal confusion and uncertainty, I reflect upon a year which has brought with it much enjoyment. The indoor squash courts are my favourite place on the whole of campus. They are my sanctuary, my refuge, somewhere where I can single-mindedly use all my physical and mental strength. I enjoy the competition, the comradery.

For the first time in my life, from January onwards it is work which proves a source of stress. The onslaught seems to never cease, with anatomy sheets and lectures and essays and presentations weighing me down. I try to cling on and keep up with everything, but eventually I realise it would be too much. I stop working during the evenings and tell myself that I would have enough revision time during Easter holidays and I would be best served just leaving it all until then. This plan works well. My evenings are freed up for sports and reading and watching videos. My mind becomes focused on exploring religion and theology and philosophy, trying to understand the world and comprehend others' perspectives about it.

James invites me to church with him one evening. It is 'Discover Christianity' week. I oblige happily. I have read much of the Bible and possess a deep interest in the New Testament especially. Being a Muslim I respect and accept all Biblical Prophets, but just don't believe that Jesus is the literal son of God, or that he was resurrected.

The Gospel of Matthew (15:24) for example states that 'I am not sent but unto the lost sheep of the house of Israel.' Jesus described himself as a shepherd, with the goal of bringing together his lost sheep – referring to the ten tribes of Israel who had been deported from Israel following conquest by the Neo-Assyrian Empire several hundreds of years earlier. 'I have other sheep that are not of this fold. I must bring them in as well and they will listen to My voice. Then there will be one flock and one shepherd' (John 10:16). The words of the Bible, Quran and historical documents indicate to me that instead of dying and resurrecting, Jesus in fact survived the crucifixion, as evidenced by the blood and water which gushed out when he was pierced by a Roman soldier just before being taken down from the cross, demonstrating the presence of a beating heart. According to all religions, Prophets cannot fail in their missions. Following crucifixion and recovery, Jesus headed East to preach his Gospel to the Lost Tribes, which could be found as far as Northern India and Afghanistan. Eventually settling in Kashmir, Jesus was buried in Srinagar, having fulfilled his mission of delivering his message to all the Tribes. Historical traditions tell of a man named Yuz Asaf (a name literally translated into Hebrew as 'Jesus the Gatherer'), a Prophet of the People of the Book, who preached to people through parables like those in the New Testament. There is much more that can be said about this theory, however in short it explains a concept that is otherwise described in supernatural and miraculous nature-defying ways. Religion, according to Islam, is not like this, which is one of the foremost reasons that it appeals to me. It is logical, reasonable and can be understood without the need to suspend one's disbelief.

This is what I talk about with those on my table, on a wonderful 'Discover Christianity' evening. Gentle music playing in the background, rain spattering against the stained-glass windows, all of us feeling the thrill of discussing something deep, something meaningful, something close to our hearts. Contrary to my previous perceptions that Christians didn't enjoy discussing faith, I find them to be enthralled by my beliefs and I am intrigued by theirs.

James and I sit on different tables, due to limited seating and both of us having arrived late. He leaves me on a small table of five, but when he returns to find me at the end of the evening there are at least fifteen Christians around the table, asking me questions, trying to respond to my Biblical arguments. As well as discussing Christian theology, I also decide to emphasise the similarities that Muslims and Christians share – our mutual emphasis of love, mercy and tolerance, our common love of Jesus. I try and counter the popular perception of Islam being a faith of harsh and oppressive laws.

"Are you okay?!" James asks me, alarmed at the number of people surrounding me.

We all look round to him, temporarily distracted from our religious thoughts and smile. "Yes, come join!"

6. Islam & Feminism

In August 2018, Boris Johnson, a prominent Conservative Member of Parliament and former UK Foreign Secretary wrote in a *Daily Telegraph* column that women wearing burkas looked like 'letter boxes' or 'bank robbers.[15]' Though many found his comments distasteful and offensive, almost every major poll conducted over the past few years has indicated that more Brits would support a 'Burka ban' than oppose it. The Burka itself – a garment covering the entire body from head to feet – is in no way required to be worn by Islam. However, it is certainly the case that Islam's approach towards gender issues constitutes a stark difference between that of the West's. The question remains, are females inherently considered second-class citizens within the faith? Does their religion liberate them, or oppress them?

To answer this question I took a step back, and compared Western attitudes towards women with the Islamic perspective. Moreover I analysed the benefits and problems that women today face within society, and how Islamic philosophy attempts to negotiate them.

Western feminism has historically been divided into three waves. Martha Lear, writing in the New York Times, coined the terms 'first-wave feminism' and 'second-wave feminism,' and these terms, as well as the current 'third wave' have been used widely as a means of understanding the development of the ideology over time. The first wave occurred between the 1830s to the early 1900, during which the focus was on legal issues, predominantly on gaining the right to vote. In the UK, the early feminists were disparate, unlinked individuals, who had themselves suffered as a result of gender inequality. Caroline Norton, a prominent author and social reformer in the early to mid-19th century, left her husband in 1836. Not long later, her husband blocked her from receiving a divorce and abducted their sons, refusing to tell Norton their whereabouts. English law at the time dictated that children legally belonged to their father and so Norton could do very little to regain custody.

In 1842, Norton's youngest son, William, suffered a fall from his horse and was injured. Her husband, realising that the child was potentially near-death, allowed her to visit. Before Caroline could reach them however, William died. From then on, her husband allowed her to visit their sons with strict supervision and with him retaining full custody.

Norton's own domestic situation prompted her to become deeply involved in politics, campaigning for gender equality and social justice, in particular granting rights to married and divorced women. As a result of her determined campaigning, the British government passed a number of legislative bills including the Custody of Infants Act 1839, the Matrimonial Causes Act 1857 and the Married Women's Property Act 1870. These acts were transformative for women in society. For the first time, they had rights with regards their children, had a separate legal identity from their husband, were able to inherit property and take court action on their own behalf and enabled divorce to become more affordable. Marriage became a contract rather than a tyrannical domination of a husband over his wife.

Then, in the early 20th century, first-wave feminism movements became more co-ordinated and powerful. In 1903, Emmeline Pankhurst founded the Women's Social and Political Union. This was an organisation filled with bloody-minded and often controversial members, who became known for civil disobedience and direct action. Members would often heckle politicians, organise marches and set fire to houses, churches and post-boxes. Even when arrested, women in the group would go on hunger strikes. In 1918, the Government passed the Representation of the People Act, which granted votes to all men over the age of 21 and women over the age of 30. Ten years later, just a few weeks after the death of Pankhurst, the Government's amended Representation of the People Act (1928) granted the right to vote to all women over the age of 21 years. For her struggles for justice, Pankhurst was commemorated with a statue next to the Houses of Parliament, in Victoria Tower Gardens, London.

In the 19th and early 20th century therefore, women in the West were forced to fight for even basic rights, too often simply being treated like property rather than as equals to men. This attitude of women being inferior was ubiquitous in pre-Islamic Arabia. Arabia at the time had a tribal structure and the customs which followed as a result had a strong impact upon women's rights. Each tribe was formed of a group of kindred clans and was led by a single chief (or shaykh), who had complete authority over the rest of the group. Each tribe regarded all other tribes as enemies, unless they had forged alliances with them to protect one another. Warfare was often utilised as a means of resolving conflicts between tribes. In general, the pattern was that the only rules that existed were unwritten ones – that the strong dominated the weak, in a 'survival-of-the-fittest' type society. As a result, a natural by-product was that women were severely oppressed.

The purpose of marriage within pre-Islamic Arabia was simply to increase the number and thus power, of the tribe. As a result, any children that were born were the property of the tribe rather than of the mother and thus the mother had very few rights over her own offspring. Often, especially during times of war, women were captured and sold into marriage. Furthermore, when the husband died, his wife could be inherited by his heir. Such a practice highlighted the way in which women were viewed in the society of the time – as property rather than as equal beings to men. Women in pre-Islamic Arabia were most frequently excluded from inheritance. And most shockingly of all, female infanticide was a common practice of the time. Often this was due to fear of poverty – as girls were regarded as less productive than boys. Girls were viewed as a liability and to feed them was simply a waste of precious resources and money.

The Prophet Muhammad's message of Islam single-handedly orchestrated a first-wave feminist revolution within a matter of years. Islam was the only religion to give women inheritance rights. According to its teachings, daughters were given rights of inheritance from their parents, wives from their husbands, mothers from their children and daughters and sisters from their brothers. Chapter 4 Verse 8 of the Quran states; *"For men is a share of that which parents and near relations leave; and for women is a share of that which parents and near relations leave, whether it be little or much – a determined share."* In the context of the time, considering the heinous gender inequality and barbarism that existed, this was a remarkable step that Islam initiated. Twelve-hundred years before the Western world had caught up, the Prophet Muhammad unequivocally ensured that women could inherit property in a way that no other ideology, belief system, or individual had previously introduced.

Secondly, Islam ensured complete equality between the sexes in a unique manner. Though, as we'll come to later, Islam proposes different roles for men and women based on biological differences between the sexes, the actual status of men and women are completely equal. This is highlighted emphatically by the following Quranic verse, in chapter 33 verse 36:

"Surely, men who submit themselves to God and women who submit themselves to Him and believing men and believing women and obedient men and obedient women and truthful men and truthful women and men steadfast in their faith and steadfast women and men who are humble and women who are humble and men who give alms and women who give alms and men who fast and women who fast and men who guard their chastity and women who guard their chastity and men who remember Allah much and

women who remember Him – Allah has prepared for all of them forgiveness and a great reward."

Due to behaviour and actions of certain Muslims today, many people infer that men are given a higher rank within society than women. From original Islamic sources, this claim would only hold water if it were clear that men were entitled to a greater reward, a greater share of the benefits of the hereafter and a closer relationship with God than women. Just as humans are given a loftier spiritual status than animals due to their higher rank according to Islam, similarly if men were of a higher status than women, they would naturally be granted greater access to God. However, as the verse declares, both sexes in the eyes of God are equally deserving of forgiveness, equally worthy of reward and equally eligible to live a life free from tyranny and oppression. The verse forcefully and categorically highlights this by the fact that it does not just use the collective noun 'men,' or 'mankind,' but specifically mentions men and women by name so as to eliminate all doubt.

Such emphasis on gender equality and women's rights is repeatedly highlighted within Islamic scripture and also in the words of the Prophet Muhammad. Referring to the heinous practice of female infanticide, explicitly forbidden in Islam but prevalent in pre-Islamic Arabia, the Quran (42:50) makes clear that God *"bestows daughters upon whom He pleases and He bestows sons upon whom He pleases,"* highlighting that no Muslim should despair or be unhappy at the gender of their child, but rather appreciate and love them for whoever God has made them to be.

The Prophet Muhammad, in a famous saying, is reported to have said *"The best of you is the one who is best towards his wife and I am the best of you towards my wives."* Domestic violence, particularly ill-treatment of women, has been prevalent throughout history. Even today, 1 in 4 women are estimated to be victims of domestic abuse at some point in their lifetimes. The Prophet affirmed that for men, nearness to God can be attained through their kind treatment of their wives – who, despite being spiritually equal, are often the physically more vulnerable party within the relationship.

The second wave of feminism began in the United States and quickly spread across the Western world. This activity consisted of increasing the debate to issues beyond simply legal matters. Rather proponents focused on issues such as sexuality, family, reproductive rights and workplace rights. In the 1960s and 70s, these issues came to the forefront and feminism became a mass movement. The slogan was *'the personal is political,'* meaning certain issues which, though unjust, were previously hidden from public view. However, the movement sought to generate discussion on these issues, which in their view had been ignored for too long.

The Civil Rights Act of 1964 was a landmark ruling for women. All types of workplace discrimination, including towards women of all races or nationalities, became prohibited. A year earlier, the Equal Pay Act was crafted, with the intention of ending gender inequality in the workplace. This bill, signed by President Kennedy, proved influential in shrinking the gender pay gap and helping to limit discrimination in the workplace.

During this period of history, reproductive rights were also rolled out, such as a woman's right to decide to have an abortion and the right for marital privacy. Over the next decade, this ideology also overtook the rest of the Western world, including the UK, with bills such as the Sex Discrimination Act (1975) passed, as well as the introduction of the contraceptive pill (1961).

Following this era, the third wave of feminism began in the early 1990s. This aimed to continue the progress that previous feminist movements had accomplished, as well as push forward to further enable women to attain equality in various other spheres. However, over recent years feminism has become less coordinated and more fragmented, with different individuals having different outlooks on what the term means and how best to improve society. There are liberal feminists, who believe in individualism, complete free choice and sexual equality through political and legal reform. Then, on the other side there are radical feminists, who view society as a patriarchy and strive to eliminate gender differences completely. They oppose sexual objectification and, unlike liberal feminists, believe that inequality between sexes is due not to legal and political circumstances, but by a societal mindset of patriarchy.

Despite the varying perspectives prevalent in today's society, the term 'feminism' can broadly be summed up by the Oxford Dictionary's definition of the word: *'The advocacy of women's rights on the ground of the equality of sexes.'* Most people within the Western world today would, if asked, support gender equality and women's rights. However, in a poll conducted in 2016 by *The Fawcett Society*, a leading feminist charity, only 7% of people in the UK would describe themselves as feminists. On further investigation, many viewed the word as being confrontational, overly political and controversial. In summary, there is a desire for equality, fairness and justice, but the public in general believes that modern feminism is not a suitable outlet for achieving that goal.

What is certain is that our current society still exploits, degrades and endangers women, in spite of the progress of the past century. Pornography is more popular than ever, partly due to its ease of access and availability. In 2017 alone, Pornhub, one of the most popular porn sites, got 28.5 billion visits. In other words, that's nearly 1000 visits a second. According to their website, enough porn was watched in a single year on the site that all the data would fill 194,000,000 USB sticks. *'If you put the USB sticks end to end, they'd wrap all the way around the moon,'* the site states. Pornography has been shown by extensive research to be as addictive as dangerous drugs. And just like a drug addiction, watchers of porn develop tolerance, meaning that over time they require more and more extreme forms of porn in order to be aroused. For many, their feelings of arousal become combined with feelings of aggression, meaning that they begin to watch graphic scenes of hardcore porn which feature violence against women. Research has also shown that when both males and females view sexual content, they attain a stronger perception of women being sex objects. A 2004 study entitled *"When words are not enough: The search for the Effect of Pornography on Abused Women"* concluded that *"Results of a logistic regression indicate that pornography use significantly increases a battered woman's odds of being sexually abused."* In a 2011 study entitled *"Pornography Viewing among Fraternity Men,"* it was found that 83% of those who used pornography expressed greater intent to commit rape if they knew they wouldn't get caught. An American meta-analysis, which analysed 22 different studies from seven countries agreed with this perspective: *"As with all behaviour, sexual aggression is caused by a confluence of factors and many pornography consumers are not sexually aggressive. However, the accumulated data leave little doubt that, on average, individuals who consume pornography more frequently are more likely to hold attitudes conducive to sexual aggression and engage in actual acts of sexual aggression than individuals who do not consume pornography or who consume pornography less frequently."*

The pornography culture, whilst possessing these long-term dangers, can also lead to habits which are much more immediately toxic to individuals and to society. Revenge porn – the sharing of nude images without consent, has increased significantly over recent years. It can lead to severe psychological harm, especially amongst young people. Prostitution has also become more prevalent over the past decade, especially in Northern England. Doncaster reported a 60% increase in prostitution in 2013, with Sheffield reporting a 166% increase.

The debate of how to tackle issues of pornography and prostitution has raged throughout feminist circles. One prevailing liberal feminist mindset is reclaiming the narrative through changing the vocabulary we use to describe acts like prostitution. For example, the argument goes that by calling it 'sex work' instead, the power from language that men use to maintain dominance will be nullified and women can be empowered and liberated to make their own choices in their own terms. Another example of this is the use of the term *SlutWalk* – a transnational movement of protest marches against rape culture. The first of these marches occurred in 2011 in Toronto. Many young women who participated were scantily clad, objecting against the notion that rape can be in any way excused by referring to a woman's appearance. The theory went that using the term *Slut*, a historically degrading term, in a different, more 'empowering' sense, perhaps could help women to control the narrative and turn the tables on men who use such term to abuse and insult them.

The problem with such a concept is, fundamentally, that whether previously derogatory terms are 'reclaimed' will have no bearing on influencing men's behaviours. Ill-intentioned men will still treat women badly regardless of the terminologies which may be in force at the time. The reality is that the situation can only change once the attitudes of such men change. A kind of feminism which only tries to control the language, or reclaim the narrative, in fact inadvertently moves them closer to the very problems that they are trying to escape from.

We need a new way of dealing with these issues, of combating the shocking statistics that we read. 85,000 women each year are raped in England and Wales alone[16]. One in five women has been sexually assaulted. 31% of young women aged between 18-25 report having been sexually assaulted in their childhoods. The depressing figures are overwhelming and go on and on. Many individuals and groups, well-intentioned, have tried to solve these problems, but somehow over time, as societies and civilisations advance, the threats to women continue to persist.

The Quran is not necessarily the place that you might naturally turn to for advice around such issues, given the negative press Islam receives. However, its teachings, if implemented properly, provide a moral code that would curb the problems we see unfolding today. The Quran addresses men and women separately. It begins with men and emphasises that they control their sexual urges. The primary verse that covers this reads as follows:

"Say to the believing men that they restrain their eyes and guard their private parts. That is purer for them. Surely, Allah is well aware of what they do."

The passage then continues:

"And say to the believing women that they restrain their eyes and guard their private parts and that they disclose not their natural and artificial beauty except that which is apparent thereof and that they draw their head-coverings over their bosoms..." (24:31-32).

The key to understanding these verses lies in the fact that it is men that are first addressed. Anti-Islam proponents like to accuse the religion of teaching that men have a lower standard of responsibility to bear than women. This is not the case. The primary philosophy when it comes to such matters is that men should not get into the habit of gratuitously looking at women. This includes acts like pornography. Though committing such acts may seem harmless in the short term, constantly indulging in objectifying women ultimately subconsciously embeds into their psyche that women are primarily sexual objects. Even on a day-to-day level, Islam teaches that if a man can control his gaze at a time where nothing immediately harmful is at stake, it will help him to regulate himself in more tempting situations, which could potentially lead to more damaging consequences.

The second part of the passage, addressing women, logically gives them the same instruction – to restrain their eyes and guard their private parts. However, it then gives them an extra commandment, to not display their beauty *"except that which is apparent thereof,"* and to *"draw their head coverings over their bosoms" (24:31).* Asking a woman not to actively show off her beauty to the general public is something which has historically been in juxtaposition to Western lifestyle. In 2016, receptionist Nicola Thorp was ordered by her employer to wear high heels to work. When she pointed out that her male colleagues were not required to do so and refused to conform to this policy, she was sent home from work without pay. After media coverage generated a public outcry, the firm was eventually forced to change its policy.

High heels have historically been a powerful sexualised symbol. Magazines and films often display images of women's legs and the wearing of high heels contributes to the sexualisation. Such an incident, however, is only the tip of the iceberg. Women in public office have to endure endless scrutiny for the way they dress, whereas men in similar positions have no such issue. During the 2016 American Presidential Campaign, following a Democratic debate in January, the New York Times reported in detail Hillary Clinton's outfit choices during that and the previous debates. They remarked upon her *'navy collarless suit,'* her *'black pantsuit',* her *'neutral burlap-like coat jacket,'* her *'khaki trousers',* her *'near flat shoes' and* so on. Needless to say, her main Democratic rival Bernie Sanders underwent no such scrutiny.

Former Australian President Julia Gillard was another prominent female leader who lamented in her autobiography that throughout her time in charge, her choice of attire and even her body shape were considered newsworthy unlike in the case of her male counterparts. Needless to say, the constant fixation on a prominent female's dress can severely damage her professional image. For one thing, it shifts the attention away from the things that really matter – the policies and ideas of the individual – and redirects society to instead take notice only on the superficial exterior.

Gillard herself was ultimately forced into a leadership contest within her own party in 2013, which she lost, resulting in her retirement from politics. Many argue that her decline was the inevitable result of a barrage of gendered attacks directed at her from the media and other politicians. Slogans such as *'ditch the witch'* were used by the Leader of the Opposition and repeated over and over. Gillard initially ignored the misogynism directed at her, hoping it would subside, as cameras focused on her bottom and mainstream media focused on her choice of attire. On one occasion, when Gillard was tripped over when on a trip to India, a prominent Australian newspaper reported the incident frame-by-frame in a front-page spread. She later reflected that the continual attacks on her subconsciously formed a judgement in people's minds as to who she was as an individual. Numerous other women in positions of power have faced similar experiences. Sadly, in today's society, gendered attacks constitute a lived experience for successful and prominent women.

When popular media depicts women as leaders, they are often portrayed in stereotypical, negative, over-sexualised ways, often subtly conveying a particular perception of how women in power should think, behave and dress in order to be successful. Other examples of female lead characters in film, such as Katniss Everdeen in *The Hunger Games,* depict women as highly fantastical, providing little opportunity to relate to them as real, human, female leaders.

The two major options that society provides women are either to become over-sexualised or over-masculinised. Neither is adequate. Over-sexualisation as a concept implies the narrative that in order to be noticed, a woman must dress in a revealing way. In other words, while brains, aptitude and hard work may be sufficient for men to attain a successful position, for women there is an extra obstacle – appearing physically attractive. Evidently, as demonstrated in the case of Julia Gillard, such attitudes are both unfair and harmful to their prospects of success. Masculinisation is no better. If the solution to gender equality is simply for women to turn into men in order to attain success, then such a solution feels more like a defeat, a resignation, than a success story.

The point of Islam's teachings with regards to men and women is to try and fulfil the goal that all of us want achieved – to enable both men and women to have equal opportunities for success, with neither gender having to confront extra barriers or hurdles in their way. As a generalisation, men and women, according to Islam, have some different qualities and characteristics and it is by allowing both genders to thrive without trying to turn one into the other, that true gender equality can be accomplished.

The concept is as follows – by not showing off a woman's physical beauty– the focus can shift away from the outer beauty and instead turn towards her character and her talents. Adopting this lifestyle choice, a Muslim woman outwardly asks not to be judged by her looks, but by the same yardstick that a man is generally judged. Moreover, it has the added impact of helping to prevent unwanted forms of sexual approach. Islam does not instruct men to wear head coverings, for example, simply because men do not face the same challenges. They are less sexualised and largely are more judged by their abilities rather than their appearances. However, to re-emphasise, Islam highlights that the primary responsibility is for men to not objectify women, regardless of their dress. Whatever a woman wears, it is never an excuse for a man to treat her with anything other than complete respect.

Viewing Muslim women today, the influence of the media and the heinous acts of some Muslim men means that many of us assume that their headscarf is a symbol of oppression. If women are being forced to wear clothing against their will, whatever the clothing may be, it is against Islam's teachings and the freedom that it affords all people to have choice when it comes to matters of faith. However, the headscarf of Mary, mother of Jesus is ubiquitously recognised as a symbol of virtue and not oppression. Islam's intention is to view and treat every woman in the way that Christians view Mary.

Women wear hijabs for different reasons, be they cultural, political or religious. However, what has been presented here is the Islamic standpoint regarding how men and women should be treated in society and how Islam seeks to solve many of the issues which are plaguing much of the Western world today. Tawakkul Karman, a

Yemeni politician and human rights activist, winner of the 2011 Nobel Peace Prize, was asked whether her hijab was compatible with her level of education. She responded:

"Man in early times was almost naked and as his intellect evolved, he started wearing clothes. What I am today and what I'm wearing represents the highest level of thought and civilisation that man has achieved and is not regressive. It's the removal of clothes again that is a regression back to the ancient times."

As mentioned, men have no right to enforce any kind of dress upon a woman. This discussion is not intended to convey the message that women should all wear headscarves, or that without one a woman cannot be spiritual or close to God. Rather the aim has been to provide a perspective and to clarify the misconception that Islam is misogynistic because it advises women to dress modestly. In fact, Islam provides a compelling solution to a problem that has plagued the Western world for decades.

The recent MeToo movement, which has been established in recent years and grown in prominence and popularity following endorsements from numerous high-profile figures, has aimed to combat the horrific rates of sexual harassments and assault that women in today's society have to face. One American is assaulted every 98 seconds. 1 in 6 women have to deal with rape or attempted rape at some point in their lifetimes. 97% of rapists do not see a day in prison. These are mind-boggling statistics, which highlight the importance of the need for a push-back and a solution. As well as building awareness, the MeToo organisation conducts valuable work in helping survivors of sexual violence, destigmatising rape-victims and attempting to disrupt the forces and power-structures which have historically been culpable in causing misery to women.

The movement's aims and intentions are laudable and the progress they have made to help and empower people has been significant. The benefit of a religion, however, as opposed to worldly movements, is that it can reform people's core behaviours and tackle issues from their very source. One on occasion, a strikingly beautiful woman approached the Prophet Muhammad for some guidance on religious matters and his companion began to gaze at her because of her beauty. Observing this, the Prophet reached his hand to his companion's chin and turned his face to the other side so he would no longer stare at her. Interestingly, the Prophet made no mention of the beautiful woman's attire, demonstrating that the burden of responsibility in these matters rests primarily with men. Nor did the Prophet stand idly by, ignoring the staring of his companion. This emphasises the fact that cutting out needless behaviours or wayward eyes – though seemingly harmless – in fact make a big difference in preventing sexual abuse in the long run. If men dress modestly and take care with every interaction that they have with a woman, then sexual misconducts are eradicated before they even have a chance to develop.

May Year 1:

I sit for the last time by the lake, on a shaded bench underneath a tree one early evening, the sun heavy and low in the sky, looking out over the gliding water. There is near total silence except for the gentle murmurs of nightingales, a thin flow of music from a surrounding flat and the whispers of the wind. Holly and James are sitting beside me, the three of us having a post-exam, pre-summer catch-up, having not seen each other for several weeks. The idyllic scenery which permeates our eyes causes Holly to think deeply for a moment.

"I think there must be more than this," she tells me in a matter-of-fact tone.

"More than what?" I ask.

"More than just this, I mean the world. Like, someone must have made it all, the universe, stars, water. Maybe we'll never know."

"Maybe try praying," I suggest.

"I do, every single night."

"And?"

"Nothing happens."

Well what do you pray for?"

"Just, that I stay healthy and my family stay healthy and well."

"And are they?"

"What?"

"Are your family and healthy and well?"

"Well, yes."

"Well then, your prayers are answered." I smile and she laughs and my light-heartedness dissipates her temporary pensiveness. We sit, relaxed and contented, while the world around us had other plans.

7. War

The murder of Lee Rigby caused shockwaves of horror throughout the nation. It happened in Woolwich, on an otherwise quiet May afternoon in 2013. Rigby was off-duty, walking down an ordinary London street when two men, both Muslims, ran him over before hacking him to death with knives[17]. It was one of the most gruesome and brutal murders, conducted in broad daylight in full view of passers-by. This was more than just another tragic murder. It was two Muslims using their religious beliefs to justify murdering a British soldier. There was almost no act that I could possibly think of that could have been worse for interfaith societal harmony than this one.

In the aftermath of the attack, perhaps predictably, there was a backlash against Muslims across the UK. Mosques were attacked, women's headscarves were pulled off, graffiti was scrawled over Muslim-owned businesses and mosques and Muslims were personally and collectively ferociously criticized on social media[18].

Soon after the attack, former Prime Minister Tony Blair wrote an article entitled *"The Trouble Within Islam*[19].*"* The article began by stating:

"The murder of Lee Rigby on a London street last month does not signify a problem with Islam. But there is a problem within Islam: a strain that has at its heart a view of religion – and about the relationship between religion and politics – that is not compatible with pluralistic, liberal, open-minded societies."

Islam is a fourteen-hundred-year-old religion. It is only natural that over time, adherents to a philosophy or faith lose sight of its original message and teachings and replace it with one that suits their own political or ideological stance. The danger is that clerics or leaders use their own misinterpretations to brainwash scores of individuals including young people, to commit atrocities.

With respect to Islam, the original teachings of the religion have been preserved right from when they were originally produced. In other words, we know exactly what the Quran said fourteen-hundred years ago, since modern research has concluded that its text is identical to today's. Moreover, historical records have preserved in detail the actions and beliefs and teachings of the very earliest Muslims, especially the Prophet Muhammad himself, who founded the religion and serves as the ultimate moral guide.

Tony Blair's summary in 2013 makes an important distinction between the original teachings of Islam and the actions of some Muslims today. Sadly, Islam is being utilised as a means of oppressing those with different viewpoints and killing innocent people to 'avenge' Western foreign wars. In the minds of many Muslims, including young Muslims of a similar age to myself, original teachings have been long forgotten and replaced with a desire for vengeance and cruelty. When even Muslims believe their religion inherently teaches violence, what chance does the rest of society have to understand anything different?

The struggle against radicalisation and societal division which is increasingly worsening today, has an ideological component. Few understand Islam's true teachings relating to violence and war – and if they did then the state of society would be considerably better. An MI5 report published in 2008 concluded that a large number of those involved in terrorism *'lack religious literacy and could actually be regarded as religious novices.'* It continues by saying that *'a well-established religious identity actually protects against violent radicalisation.*[20] *'* The solution to most world problems is education and the solution to preventing radicalisation and extremism is no different.

However, other factors are also pertinent. When we examine some of the recent Islamist attackers in more depth, the MI5 report begins to make sense. Moreover, alongside a lack of education, mental health issues and family difficulties are found to play a major role in their journey towards becoming killers. Michael Adebolajo, Rigby's murderer for example, became a Muslim during his first year at university, at a time when he was dealing with the grief of the death of his nephew, an event which was found to be a major factor which triggered his conversion. Moreover, his conversion coincided with protests against the Iraq war, which was a conflict which profoundly disturbed him. In the years subsequent to his conversion, he became embroiled in a series of criminal offences, such as drug dealing, petty thefts, and assaulting police officers.

His accomplice in the Rigby killing, Michael Adebowale, had a troubled upbringing, brought up without a father, involved in gangs, and had even been stabbed in a fight. During this fight Adebowale saw his friend murdered, an event which caused him to develop numerous mental health problems, including psychotic symptoms and Post-Traumatic Stress Disorder (PTSD). These problems were exacerbated by his regular use of cannabis. His drug-dealing habits caused him to serve an eight-month jail sentence, where he became radicalised.

In March 2017, 52-year-old Khalid Masood drove a car across Westminster bridge, mowing down pedestrians. He injured 50 people and murdered four, before stopping the car to stab PC Keith Palmer, an unarmed parliamentary officer, who died as a result. Masood was then himself shot dead. At the time of the attack, he was already known to police, having been convicted of a range of previous offences, including possession of weapons, knife crime and public order offences. He served a two-year prison sentence between 2000 and 2002 for slashing the face of a café owner with a knife, and converted to Islam during his time in jail. A few years later, he spent time in Luton and was thought to have spent time with Al-Muhajiroun, an extremist organisation led by Anjem Choudary, an ISIS-supporting preacher currently serving a prison sentence.

These three examples demonstrate that Islamic theology is unlikely to have had any impact on their terrorist offences. Other factors, such as poor upbringing, personal crises, perceived stigmatism, mental health issues and a history of criminal activity are much more pertinent risk factors. When analysing all instances of terrorist offences by Muslims, both in the UK and abroad, these same variables repeat time and time again. A 2017 report by the Henry Jackson society, a British foreign-policy think tank, entitled *Converts to Islam and Home Grown Jihadism*[21] highlighted the complex array of issues which contribute to an individual ultimately committing terrorist acts.

"Absence of a father figure, conflicts with parents and a history of abuse in the family very often determine an inclination to further violence in adulthood. In addition to both direct and indirect family influences, a strong link between petty crime, a previous string of convictions in the family and the further appeal of Islamism, as exhibited by the above profiles, is quite alarming. ISIS and other extremist groups based on Islamist ideology can be compared to a gang – one that guarantees belonging, prestige and a sense of purpose. Excessive violence and rejection of socially accepted norms and values becomes viewed as a means of rebellion and defiance. The logic of the attraction of Islamist ideology is similar to the appeal of criminal networks, except that the motivations for participation are not linked to profit but to socio-psychological factors of power, dominance, acceptance and belonging that many of the individuals profiled in this study lacked while growing up."

How does Islamic ideology differ from Islamist ideology however? To help solve the problem of extremism, such a question is pertinent. For example, if Islam itself teaches behaviour which contradicts extremist philosophy and this becomes widely known within society, then Muslims seeking to use religion as a pretext to violence will find it much harder to radicalise young people. As a young British Muslim, I am often asked about Islam's teachings on war and violence, and so understanding it was one of the most important steps during the course of my journey.

In order to understand what Islam teaches about anything, it is important to comprehend how to study it in the first place. Reading into any topic requires an appropriately tuned mindset for its correct understanding. For example, if one tries to read a fantasy novel without employing imagination properly, then much of it will be lost. If a person attempts to study a criminal law case without a proper understanding of different kinds of evidence and analytical techniques, then they will only look like a fool when attempting to analyse it. Similarly, if people do not use a spiritual key to unlock the door of understanding of religious texts, then they will only find themselves confused and most likely mistaken.

Conveniently, the Quran gives extensive guidance on how it should be read. If it is read in the manner that it instructs, then its interpretation becomes far easier.

One of the very first verses of the Quran provides the first secret of understanding it. Chapter 2 verse 3 reads, *"This is a perfect book; there is no doubt in it; it is a guidance for the righteous."* This tells us that to comprehend the Quran it is not sufficient simply to be a scholar, or to be intelligent, or to have studied in an Islamic school for seven years, or to have read it a few times cover to cover. What is truly necessary is to have the quality of righteousness. Without this, however much of a 'good Muslim' a person may consider themselves, their understanding of the Quran will contain elements of perversity. Righteousness is far more important, according to Islam, than being a 'scholar' of the faith, to such a degree that the Quran strongly warns against blindly following scholars simply out of awe of their perceived knowledge of faith. In a metaphorical conversation between man and God on the Day of Judgement, the Quran speaks of certain people realising that over-dependence upon unrighteous religious leaders is what led them away from true, pure faith: *"Our Lord, we obeyed our chiefs and our great ones and they led us away from the way. Our Lord, give them double punishment and curse them with a very great curse (33:67-68)."*

As well as declaring that the Quran is a guidance for the righteous, it meticulously and thoroughly explains what righteousness is. Chapter 2 Verse 178 is often known as the 'verse of righteousness' and provides a summary:

"It is not righteousness that you turn your faces to the East or the West, but truly righteous is he who believes in Allah and the Last Day and the angels and the Book and the Prophets and spends his money for love of Him, on the kindred and the orphans and the needy and the wayfarer and those who ask for charity; and for ransoming the captives; and who observes Prayer and pays the Zakat; and those who fulfil their promise when they have made one and the patient in poverty and afflictions and the steadfast in the time of war; it is these who have proved truthful and it is these who are the God-fearing."

This verse on the topic of righteousness highlights many things. It demonstrates that broadly, Islam requires each individual to perform duties towards God and duties towards mankind. In a sense this is the whole essence of religion – worshipping God and serving mankind. Worshipping God consists of aspects such as prayer and serving humanity consists of spending money on (or in other words looking after and taking care of) one's own family (the kindred) as well as vulnerable people within society, such as orphans and the poverty-stricken. The verse ends by talking about personal morality – telling the truth and fulfilling promises to others and being patient, steadfast and resilient during periods of trial and difficulty rather than sacrificing one's own morals.

To emphasise the point, the 'Islam' of the extremist and the terrorist is evidently a million miles away from the true Islam as taught by the Quran. The Quran says that to truly understand the whole text requires qualities of righteousness and then it explains that righteousness requires one to love and fear God and to serve humanity in such a way that you bear the burdens of others and take care of those in your inner circle as well as wider society. Such a teaching is the antithesis of the philosophy of extremists, who shed the blood of others rather than donate blood and who prefer to kill innocent people rather than to care for them.

Time and time again, the Quran emphasises this point – of righteousness and the qualities of a true righteous believer. It then also discusses complex social and societal issues – such as conducting oneself in a war situation – and asks the reader to always remember and try ones best to follow those qualities of righteousness, even in difficult times.

At the start of Chapter 3, the Quran then gives some very specific guidance on how it should be interpreted. It mentions two types of verses that the book consists of – those which are *"decisive in meaning,"* which form *'the basis of the book'* and those verses which are *"susceptible of different interpretations."* It then goes on to say that *"Those in whose hearts is perversity pursue such thereof as are susceptible of different interpretations, seeking discord and seeking wrong interpretation of it (3:8-9)."* In other words, that righteous people, as defined earlier, will always interpret the interpretable verses with reference to the basis of the book – which is peace and goodness, rather than rancour and discord. This, according to the Quran is the correct way – to look at the Quran as a whole, rather than to be led astray by verses which, if taken out of context, could be misconstrued.

This extract from the Quran also debunks a popular current misconception that Islam can be interpreted in a number of different ways and all of those ways are equally valid. It can be interpreted peacefully or it can be interpreted barbarically and both are intellectually acceptable – but 'good' people would choose peaceful and 'bad' people would choose barbaric. However, as is clear, this is not the case. More than any other book, the Quran gives clear and detailed guidance not just on its major topics but also on how these topics should be analysed and interpreted. If followed correctly, then barbaric or hateful interpretations are completely ruled out.

To illustrate this further, let's look at an extract from the most famous speech by Winston Churchill. In June 1940, he delivered a speech in the House of Commons during the period of the Battle of France, during the heart of the Second World War. During the speech he told the world that *"...we shall fight on the beaches, we shall fight on the landing grounds, we shall fight in the fields and in the streets, we shall fight in the hills; we shall never surrender."* Looking at this extract in isolation it may appear that Churchill was a war-mongering tyrant. However, everyone knows that this was not the case. Why? Because Britain was fighting a defensive and justified war against Nazi expansion and rule. Since any war-related quote out of context can seem unacceptable, it is the context that we must always consider.

When it comes to Islam's teachings on war, the first overriding principle to consider, emphasised over and over again in the Quran, is that of freedom of conscience. In categorical statements, it is written: *"There should be no compulsion in the matter of religion."* In another place, later in the Quran, we read: *"For you your religion and for me my religion."* These two powerful statements highlight the fact that force should never be used to convert another person to Islam, but that others should be entitled to their own viewpoints and belief systems. The Prophet Muhammad was given clear instruction by God as to his remit as a Messenger of God. *"O Messenger,"* Chapter 10 Verse 109 begins, *"Say to the people that now has the truth come to you from your Lord. So whosoever accepts the guidance, follows it only for the good of his own soul and whosoever*

74

treads the wrong path, the consequence thereof would also befall him. And I am not a keeper over you." Again this verse highlights that the mission that was entrusted to the Prophet Muhammad was not to convert as many people as possible to Islam by whatever means necessary, rather it was to guide people towards the truth with powerful arguments and then ultimately let them freely decide whether to accept it. It is evident that if the Prophet Muhammad, the founder and leader of Islam, was forbidden from forcibly spreading Islam then evidently no other Muslim has any right to do so.

The main supporting evidence that anti-Islam proponents give in support of their assertion that the religion is violent comes from the fact that the Prophet Muhammad fought wars. How can a religion which, from its very inception, was involved in military battles, be one of peace? However, reflecting upon this, it becomes obvious that the very fact that wars were fought is in no way proof that Islam itself is barbaric or against peace. Britain's involvement in World War II was not evidence of its barbarism – rather it was evidence of its courage in the face of evil and its determination to liberate Europe from tyranny. In other words, we must consider the reasons why wars were fought before we can make sweeping assumptions about those who participated in them. Were the wars fought by the Prophet Muhammad wars of conquest, or were they defensive battles against tyrannical forces? To answer this question, we must take a brief look at the life of the Prophet himself.

Muhammad, the founder of Islam was born in Mecca, Arabia, in 570AD, amidst a society that was in many ways steeped in barbarism. For example, a culture of deep tribalism meant that the murder of a single camel by an opposing tribe was enough to start a war lasting almost fifty years.

The Prophet's father passed away before his birth and his mother died when he was just 6 years old. He was cared for by his grandfather and then after his demise by his paternal uncle. From a young age, Muhammad was known widely as being extremely truthful, to the extent that he would be sought out to help resolve conflicts between different individuals or tribes.

At various points throughout his life, Muhammad used to go high up in to a mountain to pray in solitude. On one occasion, when he was forty years old, he experienced divine revelation. As the revelations continued, he was instructed by God to guide people to good morals and worship of one God. In other words, he was entrusted with the responsibility of being a Prophet and Messenger of God.

Naturally, when an alternative philosophy or way of life is presented to a society, the initial general reaction is hostility and opposition, with the aim of maintaining the status-quo. This is true in both the spiritual and scientific disciplines. When Galileo, for example, proved that the earth was not in fact the centre of the universe and that it orbited the sun, the foremost power of the time, the Catholic Church, ordered him to stay silent and declared his beliefs as heretical. When a society is steeped in dogma, whether it be scientific or religious, then to turn the tide in another direction requires time, perseverance and resilience. Truly changing the mindset of a people cannot be done by force, but by powerful, irrefutable arguments and an ability to peacefully endure many injustices along the way.

The proof that Muhammad gave in support of his claim of Prophethood came from his logical philosophical arguments, his prophecies, and his own personal purity, to which even his biggest enemies testified. It is interesting how, fourteen-hundred years after Muhammad, people try and raise allegations against him, which even his bitterest enemies of the time did not. The fact that even those who opposed him attested to his excellent morals, truthfulness and peaceful demeanour logically implies that those who accuse Muhammad of barbarism today cannot be correct. For if he was all those things that anti-Islam proponents believe, then his enemies at the time would surely have said so at the time.

At the time of Muhammad the Arabs took great pride in worshipping idols. Therefore, they began persecuting Muhammad and his small band of initial followers, which included his wife, his cousin and his close friend. Islam slowly and steadily began to spread, especially amongst the poorer sections of society, who saw hope in the message of peace, justice and human equality. However, many early followers were tortured and killed in horrific ways. Eventually, the Muslims began a small migration to Abyssinia (modern day Ethiopia) to seek protection there, and then a larger migration to Medina. However even when he had migrated away from them, the oppressors sought to destroy him and his message and attacked the city that had provided him refuge. These Muslims had undergone thirteen years of brutal persecution, such as social and economic boycott, starvation and physical torture. They endured these without retaliating and even after migration were still being hounded by the Meccans. It was at this time that this Quranic verse (22:39) was revealed: *"Permission to fight has been given to those who are being fought, because they were being wronged. And indeed, Allah is competent to give them victory. They are those who have been evicted from their homes without right – only because they say, "Our Lord is Allah." And were it not that Allah checks the people, some by means of others, there would have been demolished monasteries, churches, synagogues and mosques in which the name of Allah is much mentioned. And Allah will surely support those who support Him. Indeed, Allah is Powerful and Exalted in Might."*

The reason that fighting was permitted, therefore, was not to spread Islam or to conquer territories. It was not even solely for self-defence. It was because had they not fought at that time, the very principle of freedom of conscience would have been compromised, leading to Islam and other religious beliefs becoming wiped out, ultimately resulting in widespread tyranny and suffering. It was to protect churches and temples and synagogues and mosques – in other words to protect the religious rights and freedoms of people of all faiths.

Further information regarding Islam's perspective on war can be found from the words of the Prophet Muhammad and his closest companions, such as Abu Bakr, who summed up the Prophet's rules of war as follows:

"O people! I charge you with ten rules; learn them well...for your guidance in the battlefield! Do not commit treachery, or deviate from the right path. You must not mutilate dead bodies. Neither kill a child, nor a woman, nor an aged man. Bring no harm to the trees, nor burn them with fire, especially those which are fruitful. Slay not any of the enemy's flock, save for your food. You are likely to pass by people who have devoted their lives to monastic services; leave them alone. [22] *"*

The Prophet was one of the first major historical figures who unequivocally condemned 'collateral damage,' to the extent that even protecting the environment was of paramount importance during times of war.

Islam is not a bloodthirsty religion and neither was the Prophet Muhammad a bloodthirsty leader. As demonstrated, his own morality, conduct and teachings during war time are unparalleled even to this day. In our modern age, governments are far quicker to take to the battlefield than the early Muslims were and far more readily accepting of civilian casualties than the Prophet Muhammad was. In 1996, the then-United States ambassador to the United Nations Madeleine Albright was asked on CBS's *60 seconds* regarding US involvement in Iraq. *"We have heard that half a million children have died. I mean, that's more children than died in Hiroshima. And, you know, is the price worth it?"* Albright responded: *"I think this is a very hard choice, but the price – we think the price is worth it."* Such an attitude, though not usually acknowledged so explicitly and remarkably, is commonplace in today's world. Killing vast numbers of foreign children for the sake of a hypothetical future peace or fulfilment of a national interest is seen as 'worth it.' This applies both to the Muslim and the non-Muslim world. However, a truly Islamic attitude would mean no civilian deaths and recourse to war only in exceptional circumstances.

According to Islam, war is never desirable. However, if Muslims do become embroiled in a just defensive battle, they should be courageous as far as they can. The Prophet Muhammad used to say to his companions *"O ye Muslims! You should not desire to fight the enemy and remain desirous of the peace and security of God. If however, contrary to your desire, you are compelled to fight an enemy then demonstrate steadfastness."* This attitude of courage and steadfastness is repeated in various Quranic passages, which are often the passages that anti-Islam proponents like to use to try and demonstrate that Islam is violent. Remember Churchill's quote about fighting the Germans on the beaches and shores and never surrendering? Again, this is a perfectly reasonable quote in the context of a war against Nazis and is designed to demonstrate the courage and bravery that British soldiers were prepared to demonstrate for the sake of justice and establishing peace. The same is true of Quranic verses which talk of killing disbelievers. *"And kill them [the disbelievers] wherever you meet them and drive them out from where they have driven you out..."* Sounds bad right? Well, just as bad as Churchill's if we look at it in isolation. Here's the full quote (2:191-194) showing the verses before and after:

"O ye Muslims! And fight in the cause of Allah against those who fight against you, but do not transgress. Surely, Allah loves not the transgressors. And kill them wherever you meet them and drive them out from where they have driven you out; for persecution is worse than killing. And fight them not in, and near, the Sacred mosque until they fight you therein. But if they fight you, then fight them; such is the requital for the disbelievers. But if they desist, then surely Allah is Most Forgiving, Merciful. And fight them until there

79

is no persecution and religion is freely professed for Allah (i.e. there remains no fear of anyone except God in the matter of religion and every individual can profess any faith he so desires with freedom of conscience). But if they desist, then remember that no hostility is allowed except against the aggressors."

This verse is almost completely self-explanatory. Fighting is permitted in very specific defensive circumstances and if the enemy desists, then the Muslims should likewise desist immediately.

The final point to make on this subject is to ascertain why killing disbelievers is mentioned at all. The answer to this is that at the time of the early Muslims, society was divided into 'Muslims' and 'disbelievers,' and thus in the Quran it is referred to as such. As implied previously, the disbelievers were not fought against due to their lack of faith, but because of the fact that they were destroying the very peace of the time, just as the German Nazis were doing during the 1930s and 40s. Just as Churchill's quote was not a standing order to kill Germans applicable for all time, similarly the Quranic injunction to 'kill disbelievers,' was valid only for those very specific circumstances of a defensive war. In fact Islam repeatedly emphasises kindness to Muslims and non-Muslims alike. Chapter 17 verse 35 states:

"Allah forbids you not, respecting those who have not fought against you on account of your religion and who have not driven you forth from your homes, that you be kind to them and act equitably towards them and show benevolence; surely Allah the Exalted loves those who are equitable and benevolent. Allah the Exalted only forbids you from befriending those who have fought against you on account of your religion and have driven you out of your homes and have helped others in driving you out. And whosoever makes friends of them – it is these that are the transgressors."

Few argue against the concept that some wars are just and necessary to maintain peace and protect society against tyrannical forces. This was the situation here. Far from attempting to spread Islam, the

Muslims were fighting courageously, but out of compulsion. Moreover, when considering battles and conflicts one imagines the huge scale confrontations prevalent in the modern world today. However, early Islamic wars, by today's standards, could barely be considered as such. In the Battle of Uhud for example, one of the most famous wars of the time, the Muslim army had only a hundred men and two horses, while their opponents had seven hundred men, two hundred horses and 3,000 camels. In total, significantly less than a thousand men were fighting in a limited conflict without any kind of civilian casualties, collateral damage or environmental impact. With this context in mind, it is almost absurd to suggest that Islam was in any way spread by the sword.

In October 2017, a French family caused an international stir when they chose to call their new-born son 'Jihad.' The authorities of the city of Toulouse took the case to prosecutors and judges ruled that the given name was unlawful and that it must be changed to 'Jahid' instead. The reason given for the name being unlawful was that it would have an adverse effect on the child's life.

The real meaning of the term however is nothing like as controversial as many would think. Jihad, fundamentally refers to one's personal struggle for self-purification. It encompasses resisting evil passions and tendencies and trying to become a moral individual, following Quranic teachings of righteousness and purity.

Fighting in those specific defensive circumstances which have been mentioned is by all definitions also a moral act. Therefore, it is also a kind of Jihad, referred to as 'Jihad by the sword' or 'Holy War.' However, for such a Jihad to take place, those specific circumstances must be met as have been described previously – namely that there should be an aggressor who threatens freedom of conscience, and that other strategies such as migration should have first been attempted as far as possible. Any other call for Jihad is, from an Islamic perspective, illegitimate. Interestingly, the Prophet

Muhammad made quite clear that the primary meaning of Jihad is not related to fighting. On one occasion, after returning from a military expedition he told his followers that *"we are returning from the lesser Jihad (fighting) to the greater Jihad (struggling and striving towards purification)."*

With this in mind, it becomes evident that not a single so-called 'Jihadi' in our modern age is practising anything close to what Jihad actually is. They are using a term wrongly in an attempt to gain religious legitimacy for their heinous deeds. Though many people may not agree with foreign interventions of Western powers in Muslim countries it cannot be said that any world power is directly attacking Islam as a religion, or attacking the concept of freedom of conscience. All wars today are political wars and so 'Jihad of the sword' is not required in this age. This is an important distinction to make. Since the term 'jihad' and 'jihadi' is an Islamic term, the atrocious acts of Muslim extremists today, when referred to as Jihad, contain an implication that they are sanctioned by Islam. In reality Islam out of all religions provides arguably the clearest guidance on warfare, in order to prevent wars as far as possible and ensure that when they must occur, they are carried out within strict guidelines so as to prevent innocent loss of life.

Five years after Lee Rigby was murdered, his killer Michael Adebolajo, apologised for the attack whilst in prison. He added that he had misinterpreted the Quran to justify his horrific act and that he was brainwashed. For Rigby's family, it was an unwelcome apology, and they found his very interaction with them chilling. *"We will never forgive him,"* was their verdict. To me, as someone incapable even of imagining the sorrow and anguish that must have consumed them over the past half-decade, this sounded fair enough. However, his own admission whilst in prison that he had been brainwashed points to a wider issue – that of the responsibility that Muslim Imams and scholars have in training and guiding young people. It also points to the responsibility of the British government in identifying and removing hateful literature and extremist preachers from the country.

As a direct result of the UK-Saudi alliance, there are currently estimated to be well over 100 UK mosques which preach a bigoted Wahhabi ideology. Proponents of the alliance argue that it provides the UK with economic benefits through arms sales, as well as enabling the British government to exert influence over the Gulf state's actions and policies in the Middle East. However, a 2018 report published by the Policy Institute at King's College London[23] contradicted these claims. It found that arms sales brought in just £30 million for the treasury – equal to just 0.004% of its total revenue in 2017. The report also claimed that Saudi Arabia influences the UK's actions more than the UK influences Saudi's. For example, in 2017 the Government withheld the publication of a report into financing of terrorism that would have reflected badly on the Saudis. Moreover, from a reputational standpoint, possessing an alliance with a nation that has bombed large parts of Yemen, leading to up to 85,000 young children dying from starvation, is highly morally questionable.

A Home Office-led report conducted in 2016 found that Britain's Wahhabi mosques have a collective capacity for around a 45,000 membership[24]. For a group of young British men from Cardiff, it was suggested that attendance at the Al-Manar mosque was a significant factor in their radicalisation. The young men travelled to Syria and joined ISIS. The mosque in question laments its negative perception and claims to be a friendly, welcoming environment, but whatever the truth, the reality is that if the British government chooses to allow Wahhabi mosques and potentially extremist preachers in the country, then it would be prudent at least to monitor them closely. Preventing the seeds of radicalisation to sow in the minds of young people like Adebolajo, at a politically-volatile time in history, is essential for the wellbeing of society.

March - Year 2:

The GP practice I am placed at this year is an hour north of the University, and for one day each fortnight I am a passenger in my friend Jonathan's car as we make our way to the surgery. I always enjoy the drive, spending some of the time staring out of the window, watching the changing landscape as we travel away from our city, buildings and traffic giving way to bare expanses of hay fields and sheep. Often by the time we arrive the clouds have layered above us, with a soft breeze and light shower making us wish we had brought umbrellas. On our journeys we tend to avoid discussing medicine or study, instead talking about current affairs, sport, and sometimes religion.

One morning, as we are listening to a radio report on a recent terrorist atrocity in Beirut, Jonathan's expression is pensive. "Do you do Jihad?" he asks me suddenly. I pause before responding. "Yes, absolutely," I tell him. He frowns, perhaps expecting a different answer, and I wait for a moment before elaborating, just to see what his reply will be. A car with loud music blasting from the inside accelerates past us on the motorway. A few drops of rain start to fall on our windscreen. He says nothing, instead waiting expectantly for an explanation. I tell him then, that the word Jihad has been hijacked by extremists, that in reality it has nothing to do with waging an aggressive war, rather it means a personal striving to improve one's character and righteousness. Jonathan's thoughtful frown turns into a smile.

"Perhaps it'd be worth me doing some Jihad too then."

8. Among the Bright Cold Stars

October – Year 3:

Life is more exciting now. My previous life of lectures and seminars has been replaced by hospital placements, starting to learn what being a real doctor actually entails, learning the practical as opposed to just the theory. I wake up at six-thirty every morning, am out the door of my new student house by seven, picked up by Caroline. There are four of us in the car – Caroline and Liz in the front and myself and Akal, an amiable Sikh student sitting beside me at the back. Actually being in hospital, in the real world, I thought was bound to mature me. I would grow up now, I figured and maybe that would mean less laughter, less joy, more responsibility and sense of duty.

I needn't have worried. Caroline, Liz, Akal and I are in the same hospital group, also known as a 'firm,' and thus our rough timetables and ward allocations are the same. We arrive into hospital early most mornings and spend half an hour or so in Costa. I buy a Croissant and a hot chocolate, the others a coffee to get them through the morning. For the rest of the day we amble to teaching sessions, sometimes in the hospital education centre and sometimes on the wards, examining patients under supervision. When we have free time, of which we have much, we spend it in the library or on the wards, hoping for doctors to notice and take us under their wing.

We live relaxed, exciting days, mostly free to roam around and learn as we please, without responsibility, and the four of us become good friends. We laugh together, keep each other's spirits high and enjoy the freedom from the tediousness of lectures that we have had to endure over the previous two years.

There are stressful moments though, and at times our new life in hospitals takes its toll on us. One afternoon I meet Holly by chance whilst on my way back from the supermarket. We take a detour and go for a walk across campus as the sky begins to darken, the clouds swelling like balloons. I ask Holly how her day was and she looks at me with a pained expression. A cold headwind suddenly pushes us backward, lifting her hair away from her neck. "I saw someone die today," she tells me, almost with a whisper, tears filling her eyes as drops of rain, one, two at a time fall on my shoulder. "There was an eighty-year-old lady on the respiratory ward, I had just taken blood from her an hour earlier, she was unwell but just about conscious, she even smiled at me as I entered her bay. I went off for lunch, came back and next thing I know people are shouting, emergency buzzers are going off, nurses and doctors are running to help." The pace of her voice accelerates as the slow trickle of rainfall starts to gather momentum. I walk with her, interested by her story but somewhat distracted by the drenching I know I will have to imminently endure. Her voice starts to break as she recounts the rest of her tale: "So I walked into the bay and people are doing CPR already, it's so brutal you know...them all crowded round her, pounding on her chest and then the nurse doing compressions gets tired and asks me to step up. So in a panic I do, my hands trembling, scared to break this frail old lady's ribs but knowing I've just got to go hard, to save her life." The rain beats down now, pounding the pavement like Holly's compressions, drenching the students who start to laugh at the impossible suddenness of this shower. Holly is lost in her own tale, water starting to flow from her own eyes. "We carried on for twelve, maybe thirteen minutes and then the consultant told us to stop, just as it was my turn to do compressions again. We were standing under a sheltered walkway *now. She paused before vocalising the enduring thought which gripped her mind. "I was the last person to touch her before we officially declared her dead. I cried all the way home."*

December – Year 3:

I love the wintertime. Sheets of mist in the early morning, fresh condensation in the daytime, city lights and decorations in the evening. People singing carols at the front of the hospital to keep spirits high, the clock tower bells chiming above thousands of students buried underneath scarves and anoraks. Winds howling eerily, piercing through the body as students run to their department buildings, where central heating powers at full blast. And then the snowfall. This year it comes with a vengeance, but also with a beauty. I walk back to the accommodation complex where I lived last year and find that the lake which my old flat overlooks had frozen and the grass and the trees surrounding it had become submerged under layers of snow. A day later it is my birthday. I walk with Holly and James and Hassan and four of my other close friends in the evening along the canals, which criss-cross the city like strands of yarn. We find a fancy Italian restaurant to eat in, before heading to the Christmas markets to explore. We walk past an ice rink and a crazy golf course, stalls of handmade crafted gifts, confectionary shaped like animals, toffee apples, pancakes and pies. I buy a hot chocolate as the eight of us explore together, enjoying the city Christmas lights and the rush and bustle of a city very much alive. Wintertime is cold, but at the same time beautifully warming.

I spend a few days before Christmas in Oxford to meet up with school friends. I myself had applied to get into Cambridge, a similar institution, for university and was attracted by the lavish lifestyle. Indeed, when I visit Oxford, I am not disappointed. There are bow ties, fancy events, beautiful sceneries and landscapes and prestigious dining. I see in an evening people living in a way I had imagined I would fall in love with instantly. However, amidst the eloquence and

87

richness and wealth *I* feel a surprising emptiness in my own self, envisaging what it would be like to live such a life. Even the greatest of material treasures cannot truly satisfy an individual. Beneath the desire for wealth, there is something more in each of us. The need for companionship, belonging, purpose. *I* wonder if some of the students there also feel lost in the glorious life they had always dreamed of, like stray wolves wondering vast snow-capped mountains. *I* speculate as to how much of the world's population feel like this, busy and joyful on the exterior but lost and trapped inside their hearts, like prisoners. On the first day there, my friends and *I* end up staying up almost the whole night in the college common room, playing pool, chatting with the students who are also inexplicably awake in those early hours. For some it is a habit, working late into the evenings and staying up much of the night, intermittently socialising before getting back to work. The experience is fun, a laugh, but *I* realise *I* had become glad that *I* hadn't got in to study there myself. The lifestyle doesn't suit me, *I* realise.

This experience gets me thinking about connection again. Islam, *I* believe, is capable of providing benefit to society through its healthy solutions to the world's problems. However, it is on an individual level that *I* now seek to explore the religion. The best way to do this, *I* resolve, is to study the stories of those who had truly lived their faith.

9. Guarded by Those We Lost

It was winter in Iraq. Amidst the bitter temperatures and the biting winds, a snake-catcher decided to venture into the mountains to search for a snake. He wanted to impress people by bringing back and displaying a magnificent creature which they would pay him to see. On top of the highest peak, the catcher discovered a huge snake, lying dead in the deep snow. Fascinated as he was, he dragged the snake back into the city, hoping it would captivate people as much as it captivated him. *"Come see the dragon I killed and hear the adventures!"* the catcher exclaimed and the whole town came running.

As the catcher set up his viewing platform, little did he realise that the snake he had caught was not dead, only dormant. One day, the hot Iraqi sun came and woke the magnificent snake from its hibernation. People started screaming as they realised what was happening. The snake tore loose and started killing people in its hunger. The catcher just stood, stunned by what he was witnessing. His shock turned into fear as the snake came after him, crushing and consuming the poor man. The snake continued on its rampage. Hundreds, perhaps thousands died.

The story of the snake-catcher was written in poetic form by Jalal ad-Din Rumi, a 13th century Persian poet, one of the most famous

Muslim writers and theologians in history. The snake in this tale represents the carnal desires that each human being possesses – those innate, animalistic, egotistical tendencies of greed and lust for power and wealth. Through the imagery that he employs, Rumi conveys the idea that if we leave these desires or control them, aiming for higher, nobler ideals, then we possess the capability to become moral and spiritual beings. However, if we go searching for these passions and allow our egos to roam free, then the destruction that ensues affects not only us, but also those around us. Rumi ends the poem by discussing the necessity of a Moses-like individual, to reform people once they have been overcome by their worldly passions and desires:

> *The snake is your animal-soul. When you bring it*
> *into the hot air of your wanting-energy, warmed*
> *by that and by the prospect of power and wealth,*
> *it does massive damage.*

> *Leave it in the snow mountains.*
> *Don't expect to oppose it with quietness*
> *and sweetness and wishing.*

> *The nafs [ego] don't respond to those,*
> *and they can't be killed. It takes a Moses to deal*
> *with such a beast, to lead it back and make it lie down*
> *in the snow. But there was no Moses then.*
> *Hundreds of thousands died.*[25]

The individual in this tale was not a true snake-catcher, nor an effective one. Rather than catching snakes to save people, he chose to try and simply impress others through his perceived talents. A true snake-catcher would be someone like Moses, an entirely moral, sinless individual who could not only control the snake within himself, but also, by virtue of his principles, tame and catch the inner carnal, serpentine tendencies of those around him.

Moses, according to Abrahamic tradition, was a Prophet of God who was sent by God to the Pharaoh, his people and the Israelites. The people of the time had become arrogant, cruel and inhumane and the task of Moses was to save the Israelites from their bondage, reform the people of Pharaoh and enable them to understand the true nature and reality of God. Of all the Prophets mentioned in the Quran, Moses is mentioned by name most frequently and is considered as the spiritual predecessor to the Prophet Muhammad, the most important Prophet according to Islam.

We inherently know the differences between right and wrong, our conscience acting as a rudder, steering us towards good wherever possible. However, given particular circumstances, our wish to do good may become outweighed by other, stronger desires we want fulfilled. Different people have different thresholds. Some will only be tempted away from goodness by almost inescapable circumstances, while others are prepared to lie and cheat for even the smallest worldly gains. Without specific moral guidance, we are likely to be weaker at curbing our passions and more easily become swayed towards evil. Therefore, for those who question the need for religion, claiming that they already know how to be moral, their claim may well be true. Religion, however, is required to remind them. The Quran describes itself as *'The Reminder,'* emphasising that while people may know already how they can be a good person, without being reminded often, attaining such goodness is a difficult feat.

Islam does more than that, however. It acts as a Reminder for people to do good, but also provides them with a motivation to strive for nobility. It teaches that the purpose of life is to emulate God, the most perfect of all Beings, and inculcates the love of God into a person's heart. It teaches people the techniques and methods to reach Him and through this journey, through growing to love this most perfect Being, we will naturally have the incentive and drive to emulate those attributes in ourselves to our greatest possible capacity.

The Quran provides the theory; however Islam also gives its followers practical examples of those who became the highest moral and spiritual human beings through following this path. It is only individuals like these, such as Moses, who possess the strength and capability to reform the whole society to which they are sent. Among the most famous examples of this is of Jesus, who created a spiritual revolution, transforming a society of materialistic, greedy religious zealots into noble, self-sacrificing, humble people who demonstrated kindness in their words and actions.

One of the greatest beauties of Islamic thought is that it teaches that all peoples throughout history have been sent a Prophet to guide them towards God. The Quran declares that *"There are no people (in the world) to whom We have not sent a Warner" (35:26)*. It mentions 28 Prophets by name, but according to one saying by the Prophet Muhammad, the total number of Prophets sent by God to mankind throughout history has been around 124,000. All the founders of major world religions, such as Confucius, Krishna, Buddha and Jesus, were all Prophets sent according to the needs of the time, to reform and spiritually revive those to whom they were sent.

Some atheists, most notably Richard Dawkins, like to point out that people throughout time have worshipped thousands of different deities. When asked what he would say if his militant atheism was proved wrong and he met God after he died, Dawkins responded accusingly. *"I would say, are you Zeus, are you Thor, are you Baal, are you Mithras, are you Yahweh? Which God are you[26]?"*

I found this reply mildly hilarious and slightly puzzling. Firstly because if Dawkins were to meet the Lord of the Universe, whose existence he had spent his entire career denying and mocking, the first thing to do should be to apologise. Dawkins surely would be in no position to arrogantly interrogate Him.

Dawkins' main point, however, is a fairly common objection that atheists make. The argument is that everyone, even a religious believer, disbelieves in the vast majority of 'gods' that have been worshipped over the millennia – such as Greek gods, Roman deities and Arabian idols. We are all, therefore, atheists in those gods and so odds are that the one we believe in is likely fictional too. *"Some of us just go one god further,"* Dawkins proclaims.

This argument is far from being logically sound. Firstly, because in no other sphere of life does any rational human being take this attitude. Imagine if a scientist was asked about his or her beliefs regarding the Big Bang as the cause of the Origin of the Universe. *"Nonsense,"* the scientist might say. *"None of us believe in the oscillating universe theory for the origin of the universe, nor the steady state theory, nor any of the other ones. Why not just go one theory further?"*

No scientist would ever say this, because life and science and discovery in general is about weighing up evidence and disregarding false beliefs in place of correct ones. Simply arguing that because more than one theory or notion exists, all the others must necessarily be false, is an irrational position.

Secondly, Dawkins' argument is illogical because all of the other so-called gods which he cited – such as Zeus and Thor, are within space and time, so cannot be the overarching creator. Even if those gods were real, there would still be a need for an overall transcendent being, outside the confines of the universe, to initiate the process of creation.

Interestingly, in the combined history of religion, there exist remarkable similarities. As alluded to earlier, Islam's belief is that Prophets have been sent to every people across time, with a message consistent with their intellectual and spiritual states. As their intellects grew, so did the complexity and the nuances of the message. Thus, religion evolved with the passage of time, as humans evolved. The core concepts however, of one God, of prayer and fasting and sacrifice, of following goodness and kindness and a high level of morality, are present throughout time and regardless of location. According to Islam therefore, the presence of various religions and creeds today strengthen the case for the existence of God, rather than weakening it. Islam's core message is that all religions, at their source, were true, as they were all founded by true Prophets of God. It is only later on as time passed that their messages became corrupted, as society grew more materialistic and drifted away from the true message of the faith. In many instances, the Prophets themselves became deified, as was the case with Jesus. It is quite possible therefore, that Roman and Greek gods and other idols, were initially Prophets themselves, whose core messages had been forgotten and whom their followers later deified.

Islam, according to the Quran, is the religion that represents the peak of human spiritual evolution – the perfect faith which was revealed at a time in history where people were sufficiently advanced to be able to follow it. The Quran also makes a prophecy – that even though other religions became corrupted over time and their teachings changed, the same would not occur with Islam. *"Verily We Ourselves have sent down this Exhortation and most surely We will be its Guardian (15:10)."* The promise is that the Quran would be guarded by God himself and indeed in 1400 years, the original text of the Quran still remains, exactly as it was when it was first revealed.

The Prophet Muhammad came 570 years after Jesus and claimed to be the first Universal law-bearing Prophet. He came at the beginning of an era when people were sufficiently connected such that His message could spread far and wide with relative ease. Thus, there was no longer a need for thousands of Prophets to each come to small areas in order to preach. One Prophet's message was enough to resonate across the world. The Prophet Muhammad lived in the deserts of Arabia, amidst morally depraved people, who would bury children alive and had bloodthirsty tribal natures. The Prophet taught them about love and forgiveness and kindness. He taught

94

them about equality – that "*a white person has no superiority over a black, nor does a black have any superiority over a white except by piety and good action.*" Most of all, he taught them how to connect with God and experience the wonders and joys of a relationship with Him. He uplifted the lowest and most oppressed in society and gave them a new life. He taught the richest and most well-off in society how to be kind and act justly towards others. It was decreed that he would have to live a life of often immense suffering, such that he could demonstrate to the world how valuable a connection with God is, how God alone can alleviate all sufferings and sadness and that even in the midst of despair, God can come to one's rescue.

At the time of the Prophet Muhammad's birth, almost the entirety of Arabia was polytheistic, worshipping idols. They lived in a society in which brutality, indiscipline and a lust for war reigned supreme. They were heavy drinkers and gamblers. They afforded women almost no rights and no social status. The Prophet's father died before his birth, and his mother passed away in his early childhood. Therefore, he was predominantly raised by his uncle, Abu Talib. Throughout his early years, he developed a reputation of integrity, trustworthiness and kindness. He often used to be called to sort out matters of disagreement between different tribesmen.

When the Prophet Muhammad was 25, his admirable qualities were noticed by Khadija, a wealthy businesswoman fifteen years his senior. She proposed to him and they remained happily married until they passed away. During these years, the Prophet increased in his love for God. He was completely immune from the idol worship of his fellow citizens and instead possessed a deep faith in a living God, whom he adored. Once, when he was forty years old, he saw a vision from God through an angel, who told him, *"Recite thou in the name of thy Lord Who created, created man from a clot of blood. Recite! And thy Lord is the Most Beneficent, who taught man by the pen, taught man what he knew not."* These were the first revealed verses of the Quran, Islam's holy scripture. Throughout the remainder of his life, the Prophet continued to receive revelations, all of which compiled together ultimately became the full Quran. Throughout every difficult stage in his life, throughout his challenges, trials, tribulations and dilemmas, the Prophet received guidance which was compiled in its exact wording. The entirety of this guidance – the Quran – remains unchanged to this day and the principles contained within it are timeless. They are timeless because though societies and civilisations change, the human psyche has not. Thus, the Quran's advice and teachings appeal directly to human nature and it is through following these teachings in their entirety, that individuals can attain true love for God, true inner peace and true morality and spirituality such that they can help others and bear their sufferings and burdens. Thus, the Quran is not simply a book inspired by God, rather Muslims believe that its words are His literal words, as revealed to his most loved Prophet.

The responsibility that the Prophet was given, therefore, was immense. His task was to lead the world into a spiritual revolution. It was to reform a world that had become corrupt and distant from God. It was to demonstrate through his own practical example how to live the best possible life. After the incident in the cave, he asked his wife, *"Weak man that I am, how can I carry the responsibility which God proposes to put on my shoulders?"* His wife replied that God would help him and never let him fail. *"You are kind and considerate to you relations, help the poor and the forlorn and bear their burdens,"* she told him. *"You are restoring the virtues which had disappeared from our country. You treat guests with honour and help those who are in distress. Can you be subjected by God to any trial?"*

Indeed, one of the greatest beauties of Islam is the way in which it began. After his wife, his friend Abu Bakr was the next to accept the Prophet's claim. Abu Bakr was out of town when the Prophet's experience in the cave occurred. On his return, he began to hear rumours that his friend had gone mad and was receiving messages from angels. He knocked on the Prophet's door and asked him what had happened. The Prophet began a lengthy explanation, but

Abu Bakr stopped him. He asked simply whether an angel had come to him and given him a message. The Prophet started to explain again, fearing that his friend would misunderstand, but Abu Bakr stopped him again and asked him the same question. *"Yes,"* the Prophet said finally. At once Abu Bakr declared *"I bear witness that you are a messenger of God."*

This conversation is arguably among the most beautiful in human history. Why? Because it was between two friends, one of whom having made an extraordinary claim and the other accepting that claim, not because of lengthy evidence or logical proofs, but simply because of trust. It was a trust so strong that it reverberated through Arabia and indeed across the world. Abu Bakr did not require an argument for the truth of the Prophet, for he already had the most compelling one of all – that being the unshakeable moral integrity of his friend, a man who would never lie about another person, let alone about God. Abu Bakr was humble enough to recognise that his own knowledge was not all-encompassing and people more moral and spiritual than himself could have a wider experience of God's attributes. Just as a medical student trusts his more knowledgeable lecturer to provide him with accurate information and does not insist to see everything before believing it, so did Abu Bakr believe the Prophet. It was from this foundation that he himself scaled the spiritual heights to become one of the godliest of Muslims. As with all worldly disciplines, the first step in faith is to trust those more knowledgeable and powerful and qualified than yourself, and from there work up and develop certainty through personal experience.

A few others accepted Islam soon after. As well as the Prophet, his wife, and closest friend Abu Bakr, his young cousin Ali also accepted him, as did a black freed slave by the name of Bilal. It was a powerless group, who claimed that God was with them and would help them to spread the message of peace throughout the world.

Soon, a trickle became a steady stream and numerous people, young and old, men and women, began to join Islam. The faith became so prominent that the Meccan chiefs feared that their own power and prestige may weaken or diminish as a result of the Prophet's message. To destroy it, they decided to draw the sword. Women were mercilessly butchered, men were killed, slaves who had accepted Islam were dragged over boiling hot sands, even the Prophet himself was verbally and physically assaulted. Alongside this persecution, the Meccans also decided to economically boycott all the Muslims. As a result they became poor, hungry and homeless. For thirteen years the Muslims suffered in this way, yet remained steadfast. The Prophet's wife Khadija passed away as a result of the boycott, as did his uncle Abu Talib.

Eventually, the Muslims began to migrate away from Mecca under the instruction of God. Some went to Abyssinia and later, others, including the Prophet himself, migrated to Medina. By that time, the message of Islam had reached Medina and so they greeted the Prophet with songs of love and tears in their eyes. In the city there were three groups – Jews, Arab pagans and Muslims. The Prophet, who was invited by mutual agreement to become the political leader of Medina, initiated a covenant between the groups based on principles of justice and secularism, ensuring that each faith could be practised freely and every individual could live peacefully. He established a welfare state, promoting literacy and education, establishing rights for women and slaves, protecting workers from exploitation. He introduced a judicial system and put measures in place to maintain tracks and lanes. The Arabs, who had been previously living lives of barbarity, were for the first time introduced to a civilised existence.

For a few months the Muslims lived without threat, however the Meccans were simply planning their next assault. They forged a series of alliances and raised a large army, marching towards Medina. For the next several years, the Prophet and his followers were forced to engage in a large number of battles, fighting against heavy odds, their fighters far outnumbered by enemy troops. During the difficult periods of war, the spread of Islam was hindered enormously and the Muslims of the time were fighting simply for their own survival, the survival of the religion and the survival of their values of freedom of conscience.

The Muslims craved an end to the military assaults which were consuming them, but still remained steadfast and courageous. Eventually, six long years after they had emigrated from Mecca to Medina, the Prophet saw a dream in which he was entering Mecca with the key to the city in his hand. With hopeful hearts, he and 1500 companions left for Mecca with the intention of performing the holy pilgrimage. The Chiefs of Mecca stopped them. Fearing another conflict, the Prophet attempted to come to an agreement with the Chiefs. Eventually they drew up a treaty, known as the Treaty of Hudaibiya. It was incredibly one-sided against the Muslims, but at least guaranteed them peace for a period of ten years, during which fighting was prohibited. According to the Treaty, however, the Muslims were forced to return to Medina without entering Mecca.

As a result of the peace treaty, Islam's spread accelerated, far more than it had done during all the years of battles. At the time of the treaty there were 1,500 men with the Prophet, but just two years later, that number had grown to ten thousand. One of the Arab tribes, known as the Khuza'a, entered into an alliance with the Muslims and knowing their perceived security, another Arab tribe, the Banu Bakr, decided to attack them as a result of some past differences. They ambushed them at night and killed many of their men. This was in direct contravention of the Treaty of Hudaibiya and the Prophet was obliged to help their allies.

He prepared the Muslims of Medina to march towards Mecca. In less than a decade, a group persecuted and oppressed, dragged through the streets under the scorching sun and burning sand, had become an army the size of which no Arab had ever seen before. Tribes which had previously been fiercely in opposition to Muslims had all converted and were marching proudly singing songs praising God and raising slogans of peace. The Bible refers to this remarkable incident in a prophecy – *"The Lord came from Sinai and dawned on them from Seir; He shone forth from Mount Paran and he came from the midst of ten thousand holy ones; at His right hand there was flashing lightning for them"* (Deuteronomy 33:2). As they marched into Mecca, the Prophet declared that everyone would have peace and that those who had previously been the bitterest and cruellest enemies of the Muslims would be forgiven.

Stanley Lane Poole, a prominent British orientalist, writer and archaeologist, described the Prophet's victory in the following words:

"The day of Mohammed's greatest triumph over his enemies was also the day of his grandest victory over himself. He freely forgave the Quraish all the years of sorrow and cruel scorn they had inflicted on him; he gave an amnesty to the whole population of Mecca... The army followed his example and entered quietly and peacefully; no house was robbed, no women insulted... It was thus Mohammad entered again his native city. Through the annals of conquest there is no triumphant entry comparable to this one.[27] "

In 632AD, the Prophet felt as though his life was nearing its end. He made a pilgrimage and addressed his people from the top of the Mount of Arafat. His words on that day serve as a testament to the true teachings of Islam and his own character. Their purpose was to reach not just the Muslims present on that day, but followers of Islam for all times to come. He reminded the men to always treat their wives with kindness, he reminded people to treat everyone with justice, to observe the central components of Islam – prayer, fasting, charity, pilgrimage and obeying one's leaders. He reminded them that no one has any superiority for being of a certain race or colour.

Throughout the Prophet's life, God revealed to him different verses of the Quran, whenever the necessary situation arose. For example, in Mecca, when Muslims were facing severe tests and trials, he was revealed verses regarding the beauty of Islam, the wonders of nature and the importance and rewards of peaceful steadfastness. When the Prophet became the ruler of Medina, he was then revealed verses regarding how to maintain societal peace and the rules necessary to best maintain law and order within a community or a nation - and how to balance individual rights with the welfare of a society. During times of conflict, the Prophet was revealed verses about war etiquette and throughout his life, God revealed portions of the Quran regarding aspects such as family life, how to treat relatives as well as strangers and general Islamic theological points. As such, the Quran was revealed piecemeal, a small number of verses at the time and the Prophet and his followers were therefore able to memorise and compile it once completed. It is a book for all times and its exact words remain today exactly as they did fourteen hundred years ago - untarnished and unchanged. It is poetry and prose and music, all in one book. It needs no amendments, even in modern times, because its teachings account for differing societal structures. It is based on human nature and the human psyche, which even in over a millennium have not changed.

What the Quran does require, however, is individuals who are capable of reading it and properly understanding its message. Sadly, with so long having passed since the religion was founded, many now fail to comprehend its true teachings, or lack spirituality and desire to find God. Thus, they wilfully pervert the message of Islam. The Prophet Muhammad repeatedly warned of a time in the future when the earth would be filled with Muslims, but the Imams and so-called scholars and clerics would be completely bereft of proper knowledge. The Prophet predicted: *"In the End Times men will come forth who will fraudulently use religion for worldly ends and wear sheepskins in public to display meekness. Their tongues will be sweeter than sugar but their hearts will be the hearts of wolves.*[28] Even more strikingly, he predicted a situation which appears to completely epitomise the state of the Muslim world today:

"There will come a time upon the people when nothing will remain of Islam except its name only and nothing will remain of the Quran except its inscription. Their mosques will be splendidly furnished

101

but destitute of guidance. Their divines will be the worst people under the heaven and strife will issue from and avert to them.[29] *"*

In other words, the Prophet predicted that though the outward form of Islam would appear to be present, the inner state of its followers would be completely corrupt. Labelling the Muslim leaders of the age as the very worst of people provides an insight into the depths of dishonesty and degradation of which the Prophet warned.

There is no need to delve into the atrocities committed by so-called Muslims today, including those in high positions of power. Terrorist attacks, internal conflicts, persecution of minority groups and financial corruption abound throughout the Muslim world.

This prediction further highlights that this state of Muslims is not representative of the Prophet's Islam. Rather it is the complete antithesis of the teachings which he espoused. The degradation of a pure religious message is, it could be argued, a natural process which has occurred to all faiths and belief systems. For example, just a cursory glance over Europe during the medieval period and late antiquity leads us to find all kinds of examples of human sacrifice and mass murder, all committed in the name of someone's understanding or political moulding of Christianity. It is illogical, however, to assert that such acts were committed as a result of Biblical teachings simply because its perpetrators claimed to be Christian.

What is the solution to this degradation? Knowing that the true nature and essence of spirituality and religion would eventually crumble from people's hearts in this era, Islam claims that God provided a remedy. It is a remedy which echoes in Islamic scripture, but also in all holy texts spanning thousands of years.

The Bhagavada Gita, an important Hindu scripture, talks of a time in which *"there will be a gradual decay in righteousness and faith, civilization and culture, piety and purity, age and strength...The unlearned and the ignorant will pose as wise holy men and will deliver sermons from the high pulpits...places of worship will be deserted and desolate and wine shops and taverns will be much frequented..."* It continues, with numerous other signs indicative of today's age. It then predicts the coming of Krishna at this period of history and describes the fact that *"he will be raised from a place which will not be in accordance with the expectations of the Hindus and the superficial observer therefore, will not be able to recognise him.*[30] *"*

Guru Baba Nanak, known today as the Founder of Sikhism, also predicted that *"a time shall come in the latter age when people shall cease to act upon their scriptures and observe no fasts or prayers...then a perfect teacher shall crush them all.*[31] *"* 'Crushing' in this context means destroying a philosophy, rather than any individuals.

Similarly, Jesus talks of his own second coming. *"For as lightning cometh from the east and shineth unto the west, so shall the coming of the son of man be."* According to Christ, in Matthew 24, the return of the Son of Man would not be one of physical pomp or grandeur. Explaining why, Jesus used a metaphor of an owner of a house and a thief: *"But understand this: If the owner of the house had known at what time of night the thief was coming, he would have kept watch and would not have let his house be broken into. So you also must be ready, because the Son of Man will come at an hour when you do not expect him"* (Luke 12:39). If the Messiah of the Latter days were to come in immediate full view of the entire world, at a time of great religious corruption, then the powers that be would have killed him immediately. Jesus therefore warns that he would come like a thief in the night, to steal away the authority and rule of crooked clerics.

And what of Islamic scriptures themselves? They speak extensively of the nature of the coming Messiah and like the Hindu scriptures, provide extensive description of the time period in which he would come. Like Jesus, the Prophet Muhammad conveyed that the Messiah would come from the Eastern world and that he would be of Persian origin. In a famous incident, the Prophet put his hand on

103

the shoulder of his Persian companion and announced that, *"even if faith ascended to the Pleiades [completely disappeared from the earth] there would be a man from his people who would restore faith back to earth.*[32] *"*

The concept of Prophethood is important. Historically speaking, those throughout history who have lived around the times of a prophet have enjoyed immense inner contentment, even in the midst of trials and tribulations. Today, many people's young stories, including mine, are about attempting to find true inner peace, in a world devoured by depression and other mental health problems. There are many components which contribute to causing such disorders – many provoking and precipitating factors. There are also several factors which protect against their onset. These include aspects such as gender, personality-type, good family support and financial stability, as well as spirituality of some kind. The dearth of dependable religious leaders capable of providing people with hope and meaning certainly has an adverse effect on society's mental wellbeing. The reality also, is that two people living similar lives side-by-side can have vastly differing inner states. Such a concept reminded me of an answer to a question posed to the Prophet Muhammad, in which he discussed the nature of paradise and hell in the afterlife:

"Oh Muhammad, if you consider the fact that Paradise's width is as that of the heavens and the earth, then where would hell be?"
The Prophet replied: *"Just tell me, when the night covers everything with its darkness, where is the day?*[33] *"*

Heaven and hell begins in this very life and is not necessarily a physical space but an internal experience. My understanding of this deepened through an interaction with an old friend.

January – Year 3:

I had known Toby since I was a young child. We were neighbours and friends and then from the age of eleven, we both ended up at the same secondary school together. Toby was never my closest friend, but we were comfortable around each other, having spent so much of our lives in close proximity. Throughout our years as friends, we felt as though we were similar to each other. Both of us came middle-class families. Both of us had lived similar lives, with similar friendship groups and similar interests. We went hiking together, played for the same football team, walking in each other's footsteps for much of our teenage years.

It was only in our mid-to-late teenage years that I truly noticed any discrete, substantial difference between the two of us. When we had time to ourselves, I used to spend my hours very differently to him. I was content whether I was in company – such as playing sports or going to the cinema or to a meal with friends- or whether I was alone, for even during times of solitude I found meaning and hope and a vague connection with a Higher Power. From later conversations, however, I realised that Toby was not so content with time alone. He knew not what to do with himself and often found himself out late at night, drinking with friends, or even strangers. He formed several relationships, which started off as exciting and intriguing for him, but always eventually either fizzled out or came to a sudden and unhappy end.

Toby's life seemed exciting to me at first and a small part of me wondered what it would be like to have the highs that he experienced – living teenage life, as many would say, to the full. Was my faith a positive force for good in my life, or would it turn out to be an inconvenience - a hindrance to the excitement I could otherwise have? Though he never directly said it, I could tell that Toby, whilst respecting my principles, pitied me for not engaging in all of the teenage activities like everyone else. He looked up to those people who had more attractive girlfriends, or went clubbing more frequently than him and looked down on people like me, who had few of the things that he most aspired to have.

We went to separate universities and lost contact somewhat, but one evening, two years later, I meet Toby again. Sitting on a friend's sofa, we catch up on lost time and discuss the events of the time we had spent apart. Toby was always a boy who seemed to love life, whose eyes lit up with every new experience or encounter, who was the life and soul of every meal out or get-together. However on this occasion, when I speak to him, something has changed. There is a mysterious resignation in his demeanour, a noticeable sadness beneath his ever-present smile, a heart and soul that seems broken by the ceaseless motion of time and by the bitterness and deception of the world. Few else would have noticed it, but having known Toby since early childhood, I can sense this shift.

Toby had been suffering from mental health problems for the past two years, on and off and severe depression had severely impacted upon his studies. The years of university, with all their apparent charms and excitements, had apparently broken him. An individual whose life I had once wondered what it would be like to live, had responded to me with a single, unspoken, sad smile on that sofa.

I reflect upon heaven and hell. States beginning in this very life, perhaps continuing to the next, until eternity. Strange, I think, how two people, living the same material lives, could get to our early twenties with such radically different internal states. Strange how our outer appearances never reflect our inner experiences, how beneath every smile there is a different story. Today, for all too many, that story is one of sadness and despair.

According to mental health support charity *Mind*, in 2018, approximately one in four people in the UK experience a mental health problem each year, with one in six reporting a mental health issue in any given week. Around a fifth of all individuals in the UK have reported having suicidal thoughts, with around 7% having attempted suicide at some point in their lives. Across the world, depression has seen an 18% spike in recent years and has become the leading cause of disability and poor health around the world according to the World Health Organisation (WHO). Depression and anxiety disorders are easy to hide, relative to many physical disorders but their impact is just as debilitating, if not more.

Our society, though apparently prosperous and healthy, is less content than we might notice at first glance. Reasons for this are multifaceted. Economic inequality, loneliness and chronic disease have an impact, as well as the fact that sections of our populations have become sedentary, overfed, sunlight-deficient and socially isolated.

According to research conducted in the United States, depressive symptoms sharply increased in prevalence from the period of 2010-2015. For example, according to results from the National Survey on Drug Use and Health, 50% more teens had clinically diagnosable depressive symptoms in 2015 compared with 2011. Other indicators of mental health, such as self-reported feelings of loneliness and suicide rates also followed a similar trend over these years.

Though it is incorrect to attribute this trend to a single factor, the emergence of smartphones and of social media occurred over this exact time period. In late 2012 in the United States, the percentage of the population owning a smartphone crossed the 50% mark. Moreover, several studies conducted in recent years have clearly shown that young people who spend more time on screens report higher rates of depression and lower rates of happiness, even when adjusted to account for potential confounding factors such as race, gender and socioeconomic status. Even alcohol use is declining among young people – a recent study demonstrating that nearly 30% of 16-24-year olds abstain from drinking entirely[34]. There was a danger, I thought of becoming too enticed by worldly pleasures, when the world itself could be so bitter and deceptive. As well as my encounter with Toby, my experience with Callum back in first year also reinforced this perspective. I had only known him a few weeks, but he seemed so self-assured, so content within himself, so connected to others. Little did I know that, in his own words, he felt like a swan, battling his own insecurities, trying to make his way in a world and find some sense of belonging. He had made many friends in his early days of university and had many more from back home but I realised that he still felt alone, even amidst the furore and excitement of life.

There is perhaps no single way to overcome or prevent depression or anxiety, but as I thought back over my experiences and those of my early friends, I realised that there do exist protective factors, things that we can do as individuals to try to reduce our risk of suffering some types of mental illness. It also made me realise that heaven and hell in this life depend not on the material comforts we possess, but upon our outlook on human existence and on how we as individuals are able to deal with the everyday challenges of the world.

One man who recognises the emptiness that so many feel is Jordan Peterson. A Canadian clinical psychologist, he rose to prominence initially due to his opposition to Canadian hate speech laws in 2016 and then following a series of fiery but fascinating television appearances, including a standout performance in a Cathy Newman interview on Channel 4 News[35]. His book, *12 Rules for Life* has sold over 2 million copies and become a worldwide bestseller. His appeal for many is his attitude to life – one based on fulfilling responsibilities before demanding rights. The concepts which he espouses – such as setting your house in order before criticising others, telling the truth, pursuing what is meaningful rather than simply what is expedient, rejecting immediate gratification in favour of deeper values such as self-sacrifice and kindness – are all fundamentally religious principles. People respond to Peterson's words due to the fact that they transcend the lower desires of human nature and encourage a deeper way of thinking and behaving. His words are steeped in psychology, and many of them possess similarities to the teachings of figures such as Jesus and Muhammad.

Peterson's success perhaps serves to highlight the need for a real Prophet today – one who preaches the most beautiful, unifying teachings and also acts them out in reality, serving as a practical model for others to follow. The world needs not just a political leader but a spiritual and moral guide in a tumultuous age. Religious people wait and wait for this Prophet to appear, not realising that, just maybe, he may already have come.

10. Cries of the Liars and the Righteous

John Alexander Dowie was born in 1847 in Edinburgh. When he was 29 years old, having established himself as a spiritual man and a religious leader, he was summoned to the house of a small girl dying of diphtheria. He prayed for her and after a long and deep sleep, the girl awoke, completely recovered.

A year later, Dowie launched a healing ministry. Over the subsequent twelve years, he claimed that he had cured dozens of serious illnesses, from cancer to blindness to arthritic pains. Dowie was not the first to promote and engage with the concept of 'faith healing.' In 1843, a Lutheran pastor Johann Blumhardt established a 'faith home' in Mottlinger, Germany, where he cured the sick. Around the same time in America lived Ethan O. Allen, who taught that true belief in Jesus Christ could result in individuals attaining extraordinary abilities in physical healing. He was inspired by Dorothea Trudel, who opened a healing ministry in a small Swiss village, Mannedorf, situated on Lake Zurich. The 1880s also saw a flurry of books published by Christian authors on the topic of divine healing. Titles such as *'More Faith Cures,' 'The Lord That Healeth Thee,' 'The Ministry of Healing,'* and *'The Prayer of Faith,'* became widely distributed across the Western world.

Dowie was the first to make money from faith healing projects. He attained a substantial following and in 1901 he established the city of

Zion, USA, his own utopian land filled with his followers. He announced to the Church worldwide that he should be obeyed, since he was *'the Messenger of God's covenant.'* Dowie claimed to be the Second Coming of Elijah, sent by God to prepare humanity for the second coming of Christ. By 1902 he had amassed 150,000 followers worldwide and had a fortune of over $10 million. He lived a life of luxury and planned his world domination, sending missionaries as far as Africa to preach his word.

Dowie seemed invincible. He had it all – devoted followers, material wealth, even a whole city to his name. However, as his popularity grew, people began to take notice. With regards his faith healing, he was widely condemned by both mainstream Protestant ministers and medical specialists as being a fraud and a charlatan. Many of the illnesses he claimed to be curing were found to be psychosomatic and other healings were simply staged. Investigators and reporters attended his healing displays. One reporter wrote that *'those who go to Dowie for healing and are not healed are simply accused of being short of faith and Dowie lets it go at that.'* Other reporters were far less polite. New York newspapers branded him as a *'shame-bereft, money-greedy adventurer.'* Infuriated, Dowie responded, denouncing his critics as *'dogs,' 'maggots,' 'lice,'* and *'pigs.'* Investigations also found that Dowie, who had demanded ten percent of the income of every resident of Zion, had been using the money *'as his personal piggy bank.'* Suddenly, this figure, previously seen as Christ-like by over a hundred thousand people, was exposed as a con-artist. Soon after, a coup was orchestrated against him from within. He was deposed as leader of the church and replaced by one of his lieutenants, Wilbur Voliva. Two years later, in 1907, Dowie died at the age of 60, thoroughly disgraced. His city, Zion, quickly transformed from a religious 'utopia' to an ordinary, secularised suburb of Chicago.

Though his name has died, long forgotten in the annals of history, some of John Alexander Dowie's practices still live on. Faith healing is still practised worldwide and it was undoubtedly his influence which paved the way for others to continue. Suffice it to say that many of these 'healers' have been thoroughly exposed as frauds. The practice itself has resulted in numerous child fatalities due to parents rejecting medical treatment in favour of spiritual healing. Between 1975 and 1995, around 300 children are thought have died, almost half of whom having an overwhelming likelihood of surviving had they accepted medical intervention. In Southern Africa, around 15 million people belong to Zion Christian churches, who, influenced by Dowie, continue to adhere to the practice of faith healing.

Dowie was a false Prophet, whose concocted doctrines and philosophies, whilst initially proving attractive, caused significant suffering to many people. Over a century after he died, the fraudulent practices from which he profited continue to wreak havoc to this day.

Rashad Khalifa, born in 1935, was a Muslim and a claimant to Messengership. He wrote several books, with his most well-known work involving using computers to analyse the frequency of different numbers and letters in the Quran. He claimed that he had discovered a mathematical code in its text, a claim which garnered little attention in the West. However his work did attract the attention of a small group, who initially were based in Tucson, Arizona. The latter stages of Rashad's life were marred with controversy, after being accused of sexual assault and sexual contact with a minor. He was murdered in 1990, following which his movement somewhat lost momentum. Though still existing in many countries, the organisation possesses few members and are decreasing in strength and popularity.

Cyrus Teed was an American physician and alchemist, who claimed to be a 'Messiah' in 1869. He was visited by a spirit who told him that he was the Chosen One. Teed changed his name to 'Koresh,' and proposed a new philosophy, 'Koreshanity,' based on the authority he claimed to have been given. Teed believed that the earth did not revolve around the sun, instead asserting that the sun was simply a battery-operated contraption and the stars refractions of its light. He also taught alchemy, communism and reincarnation and believed in practising celibacy. Teed accrued a few hundred followers and peaked between 1903 and 1908, when he was beaten up outside a grocery store. His followers expected his resurrection, which never came. His group eventually died out.

Apollo Quiboloy still lives today. He is the founder of the 'Kingdom of Jesus Christ, The Name Above Every Name, Inc.' who has made claims that he is the Appointed Son of God. He lives a lavish lifestyle, owning a private jet and a helicopter. In August 2018, however, he was accused of attempting to smuggle hundreds of thousands of dollars out of the United States aboard his jet. His character can perhaps best be summarised by one of his famous sayings: *"You cannot fight the devil if you are a saint. You can only fight the devil if you are more of a devil than the devil himself."*

Over the past few centuries, numerous claimants to Prophethood, Messiahship, or Second Coming of Christ have emerged. Most of the philosophies they bring quickly peter out, leaving little legacy behind. Some claimants, like Dowie and Quiboloy, are disgraced and exposed within their lifetimes. Some, like Teed, preach beliefs so absurd it is difficult for any sane person to take them seriously. A few have ends which prove tragically comical. Arnold Potter, born in New York claimed that during a trip to Australia, he had transformed into 'Potter Christ, Son of the living God.' He wrote a book which he declared was dictated to him by angels. He engaged in enthusiastic prayer sessions with his followers, who were said to have been "few but devout." In 1872, Potter announced that it was time for his ascent into paradise. Accompanied by his followers, he rode to the edge of some cliffs and leapt off the edge, intending to ascend into the heavenly skies. Unsurprisingly, Potter instead fell to his death.

❖❖❖

Lo! How manifest is the Light of God,

Who is the ultimate Source of all light;

The whole universe is turning into

A reflective mirror;

For the eyes to perceive Him.

Last night while watching the moon,

I became so agitated.

In the beauty of the moon

Were the traces of the beauty

of my Beloved.

Mirza Ghulam Ahmad was born in 1835, son of a chieftain of the Punjab and landowner of the village of Qadian, India. Due to a lack of schools in his area, Ahmad was home-tutored throughout his early life, but sought most enjoyment from his own private reading. In contrast to his later years, he spent much of his time in solitude, intently studying Islamic, Christian and Hindu scriptures. Though his father had ambitious worldly plans for him, Ahmad felt a strong pull towards spirituality and decided his life ambition lay in the cause of faith, rather than in material pursuits. He silently and openly lamented the fact that the true essence of Islam lay dormant beneath layers of corrupt clerics and materialistic scholars and that the real beauty of the religion, which Ahmad believed he had identified, was a hidden treasure which needed to be revealed.

After years of study, Ahmad published a monumental work detailing proofs of the truths of the Quran and of the Prophethood of Muhammad. Much of the prose in this work expresses the idea of a living God, one with not only the capacity to listen to the prayers of His servants, but also with the ability to respond. The true purpose of life, he argued, was to journey towards God, entailing three stages

– fana (passing away), meaning the total annihilation of one's ego for the sake of God, baqa (subsistence) – the attaining of a new spiritual life through prayer and good deeds and liqa (meeting) – the state of achieving union with God. Ahmad's poetry conveyed his love towards his Creator and his yearning for others to achieve a similar state:

"When all of His attributes are manifested,

How can it remain hidden that He speaks!

Yet what eyes and sight you have,

That you cannot even see the sun!

Disgrace for His sake is better than any honour;

Poverty for His sake is better than riches."

Whilst Ahmad's writings were initially widely praised by Muslim leaders across the subcontinent, when he declared that God had revealed to him that he was the spiritual reformer, or Mujaddid, of the era and then later that his status was that of the *'Promised Messiah,'* and spiritual second coming of Jesus, opposition against him began to take shape. His claim was he fulfilled all the ancient prophecies relating to the latter-day reformer. He was the metaphorical embodiment of Krishna, of Buddha and of Jesus. Through complete submission to God and to the teachings of His chief Prophet, Muhammad, Ahmad claimed that God had raised him to the status of a non-law-bearing Prophet, with the purpose of guiding mankind back to a Creator whom they had forgotten. Muhammad, the spiritual sun for mankind, had lived and died and Mirza Ghulam Ahmad had come as the spiritual moon, to reflect the light of Muhammad such that his teachings and truth could continue to shine in this modern age, as they had done almost a millennia and a half before. *"To walk in my footsteps now is a source of blessings, while to go in opposition is a source of disappointment and despair."* Such a bold claim did not sit well with Sunni or Shia clerics at the time and as Ahmad's movement grew, their dismay and opposition grew in equal measure as they found their own power and influence beginning to wane.

Ahmad's lyrical prose, depth of theological insight, peaceful teachings and renowned high moral values has made him one of the most talked-about Muslim figures in the modern world. From Qadian to the remotest corners of the globe, the Ahmadiyya Community has grown and flourished, with its numbers exceeding tens of millions and its rate of current converts unmatched by any other Muslim sect. Today the Community spans over 206 countries and whilst many adherents live in peace, some face a growing barrage of opposition and persecution. In Algeria, Indonesia, Bangladesh, Egypt and many other countries across the world Ahmadis struggle to freely practice their faith under threat of violence and discrimination. Even in the UK, years of underhand hate speech against Ahmadis ultimately culminated in the murder of Glasgow shopkeeper Asad Shah in 2016.

It is in Pakistan however in which the persecution is at its most vociferous. Under the national law, Ahmadis are declared non-Muslim, unable to practise their faith publicly, build mosques, make the call for Muslim prayers, or undertake any kind of activity that may constitute 'posing as a Muslim.' Ahmadis are routinely beaten, imprisoned and even killed, with May 2010 the most recent massacre, in which 94 Ahmadis were murdered during Friday prayers.

A century after he died, the teachings and claims of Mirza Ghulam Ahmad continue to create controversy, discord and widespread denouncement across all sects of the Muslim world. However, through all the opposition his devoted peaceful following has not only remained, but vastly increased over the decades. His movement, far from being a passing fad, represents a revival of the religion of Islam, which has resonated across all parts of the globe at an accelerating pace.

◆◆◆

In the early 1900s, Mirza Ghulam Ahmad, this Indian claimant to Prophethood and John Alexander Dowie, Scottish-born American 'Messiah,' engaged in a spiritual duel which was widely reported across the world. Dowie spent much of his life criticising Islam vigorously. When he became aware of Ahmad, Dowie referred to him as a 'silly messiah of India,' and would mock Islam by using the derogatory term 'Muhammadanism,' to describe it.

Ahmad then made a startling prophecy. He challenged Dowie to a prayer duel to determine who the true Messiah was and predicted that if Dowie accepted the challenge, he would die before him and would die amidst adversity, thoroughly disgraced. It is worth noting that Dowie was eleven years younger than Ahmad and during the early 1900s when the prophecy was made, it was Ahmad himself that was suffering from health problems. One publication, The Munsey's magazine in 1902 reported that *"Alexander Dowie ranks with the outstanding personalities who founded a new city capable of housing a million people. A city, which its founder proposes to convert into a spiritual headquarters of the whole world."* Dowie appeared invincible, with thousands of people joining his movement. In fact, he even claimed as much, asserting that he was free from all diseases and capable of healing the illnesses of others. Referring to Mirza Ghulam Ahmad and his prayer challenge, Dowie wrote in December 1902 in *The Leaves of Healings: "Do you think that I shall reply to these gnats and flies? If I put my foot on them, I would crush out their lives."* He further stated that his movement would lead to Islam being *"swept away."*

Ahmad replied back, stating that *"I am an old man of 66 years and Dr. Dowie is eleven years younger, therefore on grounds of age he need not have any apprehension. Moreover, I am suffering from various diseases and my life does not depend on health but upon the Will of God. If the self-made deity of Dr. Dowie has any power, he shall certainly allow him to appear against me and procure my*

117

destruction in his lifetime and he will have in his hand a clear manifestation of his mission."

Over thirty American newspapers published this challenge and covered the back-and-forth between Ahmad and Dowie extensively. A few months later, Ahmad again warned Dowie that the false Messiah in this contest would be disgraced. *"Though he may try hard as he can to fly away from the death which awaits him,"* Ahmad wrote, *"yet his flight from such a contest will be nothing less than a death to him and the calamity will certainly overtake him in Zion..."*

Almost two months after this announcement by Ahmad, Dowie held a rally in Madison Square Gardens, New York. Tens of thousands of people were in attendance, such that the venue was overflowing. They waited in eager anticipation to hear Dowie speak. To them, his voice was magical and his words entrancing. However, inexplicably, on this – the largest of platforms – Dowie was unable to deliver a powerful speech of his usual quality. In fact, it went so poorly that the crowd were furious. They stormed out of the rally so ferociously that a stampede was formed. The following day, The New York times published the headline *'Massive Gathering Deserts Elijah.'*

This rally was the beginning of the end for Dowie. He decided to go on a world tour to reignite his support, however wherever he went he was disrespected and ignored. In Australia he was deserted by his main follower and he was not provided accommodation by any hotels. In Honolulu, he was embroiled in a scandal involving inappropriate sexual behaviour. In Germany, the US Ambassador refused to give him a meeting with important dignitaries. And in England, he was so widely ignored that he left the country humiliated.

The disgrace continued. Zion was dying out, Dowie became embroiled in yet more scandals, to the extent that his wife and son decided to disown him and he was found with closets full of wine despite publically condemning alcohol. Most shockingly, Dowie became completely paralysed after a series of collapses, the first of

118

which occurring during a public meeting in front of the few followers he had left.

In February 1907, Ahmad wrote that he had received a revelation from God that very soon, a clear sign would be shown to the world indicating his truth. Within a fortnight, Dowie passed away.

Given the media attention that this duel provoked, Dowie's disgraced death was a remarkable fulfilment of an unlikely prophecy, made by an Indian man in 1902. Following Dowie's demise, The Boston Herald published a double-page spread featuring a photo of Ahmad, with the headline *'Great is Mirza Ghulam Ahmad The Messiah.'* Just underneath this, the subheading read: *'Foretold Pathetic End of Dowie And Now He Predicts Plague, Flood and Earthquake.'*

When I first read about Ahmad's encounter with Dowie, I was impressed, but not astounded. Impressed, because the decisive and public nature of Ahmad's prediction was evident and that he knew that if he were to die before Dowie – as reason suggested should happen – then Ahmad would be exposed as a false Prophet by his own definition. I was not astounded because I thought that such an occurrence could feasibly have happened by chance. Maybe Ahmad, despite living thousands of miles away in India in an age without reasonable communication facilities - somehow had some inside knowledge that Dowie would crumble. Or maybe he just guessed, or used his intuition and put all his eggs in one basket to seem impressive, when really he was just taking a calculated risk. The main reason I was not blown away was because it was one event, that occurred over a hundred years ago and to truly become convinced that Ahmad was truly as he claimed – a Prophet and Messenger sent by God to bring peace to the world – I would need more evidence. I started by re-reading the Boston Herald's subheading and figured that maybe the Plague, the Flood and the Earthquake would help me.

119

February Year 3:

Faith is a powerful thing, even when it is blind.

I am in the basement room of the student union, sitting opposite a young man with thick black hair and large spectacles. I have been watching him ponder for the past four minutes, staring at the chessboard in front of him that has captivated our attention for the past half hour. I am in a winning position and starting to get mildly impatient by the way he has slowed the game dramatically since falling behind. Distraction gets the better of me. I line up the pieces I have taken so all their heads face the same direction. I look out of the window to my right and can see only darkness, the night having already enveloped the city. We are the only two people left in the room, with chess club having officially ended ten minutes ago. This is my first time here. I stopped playing chess during the latter years of my schooldays, though the game was a prominent part of my childhood. I was a regular county player and participated in numerous national tournaments. I was a strong competitor. My mentality on advice from my parents was to never give up, nor to ever accept or offer a draw in any match. "Whoever's there in front of you, you can beat them." It wasn't true. But it felt true to me at the time. The faith I had in myself that I could win no matter who I was playing served me well for tournament after tournament, each victory reinforcing the belief into my ten-year-old brain that I was almost unbeatable.

This attitude displayed itself most powerfully during my first year of secondary school. I was taking part in an internal tournament open to everyone in the school. There were seven rounds of matches played over lunchtimes, with one or two matches played each week. To everyone's surprise I was the overall winner, despite being one of the youngest students who took part. I was eleven and defeated sixteen and seventeen-year olds. As a result of my triumph, I was rewarded with a place in the school first team. As I wandered into

120

the school canteen for my first match, nervous but excited, I suddenly noticed who my team-mates were. I had beaten three of them over the course of the tournament, having no idea that they were some of the school's top players. My entire attitude changed. I realised that they were not easy opponents, rather they were the school's best, older than me, more knowledgeable than me. Who was I to compete with them, surely I must have just fluked my victories? My faith in their abilities grew stronger than the faith I had in my own.

For the next six years, I never beat any of them again.

Faith is a powerful thing. Even when irrational, the things we have faith in and the strengths of those beliefs can impact upon our state of mind, our thought processes, and ultimately even the trajectories of our lives. This perhaps is how faith healers still manage to maintain credibility in people's eyes. The 'healing' which they enact is nothing miraculous, rather it comes from within the mind of the individual being healed – their own faith in the healer, the confidence they have in themselves to become healed, the community atmosphere and their belief in God, among other factors.

Islam's aim is to get a believer past the stage of just 'faith,' emphasising the combined use of intellect, rationality, logic, objective evidence and spiritual searching. Faith then, in theory, can become certainty.

"Dude, I moved, you know it's your turn now right?"

11. The Great Sign

I once saw a card trick that astonished me. During one of his shows, the late Ricky Jay, a world-renowned magician, put each of the four queens face-up in different places on the table, spread out from one another. He then took out twelve different cards from his deck and put three cards on top of each queen. He picked up one of the piles, with the queen still visible and with a few hand motions made it disappear. He did the same with the next pile and the next, before revealing that, somehow, all four queens were in the fourth pile, despite them being visibly apart only a few seconds earlier.

I have long been a casual admirer of magic and having attempted to learn some myself, I am only too aware of both the incredible skill that it requires and the seemingly impossible feats that a magician can perform. Acts which appear incredible are miraculously accomplished and to the untrained eye there seems no possible way in which they could be done. When the solution is finally revealed however, it is often laden with disappointment, for the incredible effect has not a supernatural solution, but relies simply on some basic deception and simple trickery. In the popular children's novel, The Wizard of Oz projected himself as a fearsome and awe-striking creature, whereas in fact he turned out to be an ordinary man. This is the illusion that magicians in our world beautifully seek to create – performing magic that appears beyond the realms of what is possible, whilst behind it all is a normal, hard-working entertainer, who enthrals us with his tricks. His secrets lie not his powers, but in his grafting, his work-ethic and his showmanship.

It is perhaps these thoughts which echo in the mind of Richard Dawkins, when asked what it would take for him to believe in God. In an interview[36] he says:

"I used to say it would be very simple. It would be the Second Coming of Jesus or a great, big, deep, booming, bass voice saying "I am God." But I was persuaded...that even if there was this booming voice in the Second Coming with clouds of glory, the probable explanation is that it is a hallucination or a conjuring trick by David Copperfield."

Dawkins concludes that no phenomenon could persuade him of God's existence, since any extraordinary event, such as the stars aligning to form the word 'God,' could be explained through other means. Though through this interview, Dawkins' closed-mindedness is extraordinarily apparent, in many ways he makes an almost valid point. If a booming voice appeared, or a man walked on water, or levitated into the sky, a simple magic trick could potentially explain it. However, what Dawkins fails to realise is that no true religion, at its source, expected an individual to believe in God as a result of observing magic tricks.

Fundamentally, all holy texts claim that prophecies provide complete and irrefutable evidence of the existence of the divine. A Prophet of God is bestowed knowledge which an ordinary human being could not concoct. It is a kind of knowledge that is different from political predictions or other educated guesses. It is a certain knowledge of an otherwise unlikely set of circumstances coming to pass. The theory is, that since the Prophet makes these prophecies repeatedly with complete certainty and complete accuracy, claiming divine communication as the source, there is no other way of explaining it except through the existence of God. Prophecies are more beautiful than beguiling acts of deception, or cheap magic tricks and are immune from being reproduced by conjurers or illusionists. If one wishes to truly ask the question as to whether God exists, it is this evidence, rather than Dawkins's hypothetical concocted evidence, that must be scrutinised.

The Quran sums up this concept in the following words: *"He is the Knower of the unseen and He reveals not His secrets to anyone, except to him whom he chooses, namely a Messenger of His (72:27-28)."* Mirza Ghulam Ahmad, referring to this verse, writes: *"Those people who partake in the excellences of prophethood are informed by God, Most High, about future events before their occurrence. This is a magnificent sign of [the truthfulness of] God's appointees and messengers. Indeed, no other miracle is greater than it."*

Ahmad's claim to prophethood was continually supported by his uncanny success at predicting unlikely events before they took place. Some, like the death of Dowie, were signs for the whole world, whereas others related to smaller aspects of life. His greatest prediction, which in his own words, the truth of his entire claim depended upon, was fulfilled in the form of an unexpected war, which turned out to be the greatest to ever have struck mankind.

Wilfred Owen spent 1913 as a language tutor in Bordeaux. He spent a lonely Christmas in South-Western France, complaining he had received no Christmas cards from his former English pupils. Owen was only 20 years old at the time and had hopes and dreams for the future, unaware that only 5 short years later he would be killed while in the front-lines of battle. Though times were politically turbulent in 1913, the unprecedented scale of tragedy and disaster that was to come was impossible for anyone to have predicted.

On April 8th 1905, Mirza Ghulam Ahmad stated that he had received the following revelation from God: *'A calamity resembling Doomsday. Save your lives. Indeed, Allah is with the pious. My Grace has drawn close to you. Truth has come and falsehood has vanished.'* Commenting on this prophecy, Ahmad wrote that God would soon show a fresh sign, which would be a shock for the people. It would be awful in its intensity and more terrible than previous calamities. He even likened it to Judgment day. In other similar prophecies he received around that time, the calamity was described as an 'earthquake,' though Ahmad clarified that this was not necessarily a literal description, rather a depiction of a tumultuous event that would shake the earth. Given the fact that Ahmad anticipated that the revelation related to a global calamity, he instructed his community to publicise it throughout the world. Thereafter, these words were spread to Eastern and Western Europe, to America and Canada, to Australia and Africa and East Asia. Many newspapers wrote articles relating to Ahmad's bold prediction. The New Zealand Herald, on 21st April 1906, published an article entitled: *'Predictions of Earthquakes: An Indian Prophet.'*

Seven days after his first revelation, Ahmad received several more pertaining to the specifics of this calamity. From these revelations, Ahmad composed a lengthy poem regarding particular events relating to this prophecy, that he predicted would occur. The full poem, composed of twelve couplets, is presented below:

"A Sign will appear some time from now (today is April 15, 1905) which shall overwhelm villages, towns and meadows.

The wrath of God will bring a revolution in the world; the naked one will have no time to fasten his trousers.

Suddenly a calamity will severely shake them all – whether they be humans, trees, rocks or oceans.

In the twinkling of an eye the land will be turned upside down and streams of blood will flow like the water of a rivulet.

Those whose night garments were white as Jasmine will be in the morning [as if clad in red] like the Sycamore tree.

Men shall lose their senses and birds their consciousness and nightingales and pigeons will forget their songs.

That hour will bear heavily upon every traveller and wayfarers will lose their way in confusion and deliriousness.

With the blood of the dead, the running waters of highland streams will turn red like Bistort syrup.

The terror of it will exhaust everyone, great and small and even the Tsar at that hour, will be in a pitiable state.

That divine Sign will be a specimen of terror. The sky will attack with a drawn sword.

Hasten not to repudiate this, thou undiscerning fool, for my truthfulness depends entirely on the fulfilment of this Sign.

This is a prophecy based on divine revelation and will surely be fulfilled; wait then awhile in righteousness and steadfastness."

This poem, based on divine revelation, predicted that the event would be unexpected, global and unprecedented in its ferocity. It predicted that there would be significant human casualties, immense blood loss and also affect the natural world. It would be fought in various terrains and landscapes – in cities, towns, rocky terrain, as well as in the sky and sea. Particularly markedly, the poem spoke of the Tsar of Russia and how he would suffer during the course of this calamity. The event, according to the poem, would cause a global revolution and transformation.

This prophecy, when read as a whole, can refer to no other event except World War I. In June 1914, a Bosnian Serb nationalist assassinated Franz Ferdinand, heir to the Austro-Hungarian throne and his wife Sophie, during a visit to Sarajevo. Following this, a month later, the Austro-Hungarian Empire declared war on Serbia. Seven days later, Germany, Russia, France and Britain had entered into the war. *"Suddenly a calamity will severely shake them all,"* – from a single assassination to a global conflict, this war was almost unprecedented in its speed of escalation.

Further emphasising the speed of escalation, another line of the poem reads, *"The naked one will have no time to fasten his trousers."* Though, on the surface, this can appear to simply be a

126

poetic figurative comment rather than a literal one, in reality during some battles people literally had no time to dress. One report, issued by a correspondent of *The Sphere* on 28th November 1914, relating to the Belgian town of Contich, read: *"The German guns had been brought up to the bank of a river nearby and from the position they threw shrapnel into the doomed town. There were many who had to flee naked as they were down the streets in panic, when the enemy opened fire on them. The place presented a picture of utter desolation."*

Each line of the poem, in fact, provides specific details relating to the nature of the global calamity, all of which were extraordinarily fulfilled. An Ottoman Turkish officer, Major Mahmut, wrote that during and after the battles he had experienced, *"The fire changed the colour of the sea with the blood from the bodies of the enemy – a sea whose colour had remained the same for years."* This vivid scene, of running water with blood was painted exactly by Ahmad in his couplets.

"In the twinkling of an eye the land will be turned upside down." As mentioned in the prophecy, the war had devastating effects not just on human life, but also on villages, towns and fields, which had been reduced to barren wildernesses. The specific mention of devastation of trees in the prophecy is also noteworthy. According to the French Forestry service, 350,000 hectares of forest were destroyed during the war.

At the beginning of the war, not even the most knowledgeable and advanced political and military thinkers predicted that World War I would end up being the largest and bloodiest conflict the planet had ever seen. "You will be home before the leaves fall from the trees," was the common saying, as troops from around the world left their houses and their nations, to fight in this Great War. The total casualty figure from World War I was estimated to be around 37 million and the terror certainly encapsulated everyone, great and small.

"And even the Tsar at that hour, will be in a pitiable state." Tsar Nicholas II, Emperor and Autocrat of all Russia, succeeded his father to the Russian throne on 20th October 1894. By the eve of war in 1914, Nicholas II had such great wealth that in today's terms, he would be worth around $300 billion. He was not only the richest man of the time, but also estimated to be the fifth richest man in history. The outbreak of war initially strengthened his power. On 2nd August 1914, around a quarter of a million people crammed the Palace square, where the Tsar and his wife proclaimed war on the German Empire. The cries from the crowd were of love and adulation for their leader. The national anthem, *"God save the Tsar,"* echoed around the iconic Palace streets.

This had soon changed, however. In September 1915, Tsar Nicholas decided to assume direct control of the Russian armies, travelling to the frontline. During the course of the war, Russians suffered heavily. They endured devastating defeats and huge losses. Their nation was economically damaged. Widespread poverty increased, there were major food and fuel shortages, with crippling levels of inflation. The Russian population, in their discontent, organised mass demonstrations. Civil unrest and anarchy followed. Tsar Nicholas was forced to abdicate. Fearing for his life, he attempted to seek asylum in Europe, but was refused. He eventually was forced to remain at his Palace, albeit under house arrest, but still maintained a comfortable lifestyle. However, he was constantly harassed by guards, who would humiliate him. Crowds used to gather at the Palace gates, hurling insults at their former leader. In August 1917, the Tsar and his family were relocated, before being exiled by the Bolsheviks in April 1918. They ended up in the town of Yekaterinburg, imprisoned in Ipatiev house, treated awfully by the guards, officers and residents of the town, who held staunch anti-Tsarist sentiments. On the night of 17th July 1918, the Tsar, his wife and his children, were mercilessly shot to death by a group of radical Bolsheviks.

From complete power and dominion, the Tsar had truly been left in a pitiable state, dying a death of humiliation and disgrace. Not only was the Tsar destroyed, rather Nicholas was the last Tsar of Russia, after his brother Mikhail declined the crown, thus forever ending the Tsarist autocracy. The Tsar, indeed as prophesied, was in such a pitiable state that no Tsar would ever again appear in the future.

The end of Ahmad's poem stated that: *"My truthfulness depends entirely on the fulfilment of this Sign. This is a prophecy based on divine revelation and will surely be fulfilled..."* At the time that Ahmad made that prediction he had already amassed tens, if not hundreds of thousands of followers. Without a true certainty of the fulfilment of this incredibly unlikely prophecy, it stands to reason that he would never have risked his reputation and made it.

This prophecy, of World War I, not only predicted its coming, nine years ahead of time, but also provided specific details related to the event, many of which have not even been mentioned thus far, including the timeframe that this calamity would occur – within a few years of Ahmad's death. Each and every detail was fulfilled literally during the course of the war, to such a degree of accuracy and precision that it appears almost impossible that a man in an isolated village in India could have made it of his own accord.

There is a book called *'Tadhkirah – English rendering of the divine revelations, dreams and visions vouchsafed to Hadhrat Mirza Ghulam Ahmad of Qadian.'* The book is a diary of every such encounter with God that Ahmad claimed to have had and the date on which the encounter occurred. Many of the dreams or revelations prophecy specific future events, which were later fulfilled, witnessed by hundreds or even thousands of people. The book is over a thousand pages in size. Predicting the War in itself is a remarkable feat. However, as demonstrated by this book, Ahmad's prophecies numbered well into the thousands. Some were of small scale, affecting just one individual, but still remarkable in accuracy. From 1868, one such prediction refers to Lalah Bhim Sein, a lawyer from the district of Sialkot: *"When he appeared in the law*

129

examination from the district, I told him based on a dream that: 'It has been decreed that all candidates who have appeared in the law or attorneyship examination from that district would fail, but you alone will succeed in the law examination.' I also communicated this to about thirty other people. So it came to pass that with the exception of Lalah Bhim Sein all candidates who sat for the law or attorneyship examinations were declared unsuccessful...This sign is mentioned in Barahin-e-Ahmadiyya published twenty years earlier."

To predict the exam results of multiple people, having no personal knowledge of the candidates or the examination, is a kind of miracle. The book is full of similar such examples. As well as the War, Ahmad also foretold the occurrence of other great world events, such as the Great Plague of India, which killed over 12 million people from 1896 to 1926. The prediction was in the form of both poetry and prose and like the war, was fulfilled in each aspect, including the revelation from God: "*Do not threaten us with fire, for fire is our servant and indeed, the servant of our servants.*" Regarding this, Ahmad wrote a short analysis, one which was proved correct by future events: "*The truth,*" he wrote, "*is that a true servant of God will not be afflicted with the plague.*"

Two of the primary attributes of God according to Islam are *Rahman*, commonly translated as 'Gracious,' and *Rahim,* meaning 'Merciful'. In reality *Rahman* refers to the fact that God created faculties, abilities and resources for all human beings without any effort or striving on their part. These include the natural world, the sun and moon, the clouds and air and means for leisure, health and security. *Rahim* on the other hand relates to the capacity of God to reward the efforts of human beings, answer their prayers and grant appropriate successes and protections based on their strivings. The balance between these two attributes provides ultimate fairness. Even on a human level, on an economic sphere, justice dictates the government should provide each citizen with at least a basic standard of living, with food, water, shelter and education. However, beyond that individuals should also be rewarded for their personal efforts, hard work and achievements. With regard to the plague prophecy, God's attribute of *Rahim* came into operation. Ahmad and his followers were saved from death in remarkable numbers, far greater than would be expected statistically in comparison to the rest of the population.

In April 2015, I attended a dialogue in Whitehall, London, chaired by BBC news reporter Catrin Nye entitled *'Atheism or Belief: Which is Evidence Based?'* The speakers at this event were prominent atheist Arif Ahmed, a senior lecturer of Philosophy at Cambridge University and Ayyaz Mahmood Khan, a scholar from the Ahmadiyya Muslim Community. By chance, at this event I bumped into an old acquaintance from school, who was now the chair of the Atheist Society at his University. He told me what he was expecting from the evening – a back and forth dialogue on the oft-repeated philosophical arguments for and against the existence of God. The Design argument, the Cosmological argument, the Ontological argument, and so on. After the event, he looked at me, with a smile and told me that the actual discussion points were not what he had expected.

Arif began proceedings with a twenty-minute talk arguing that belief in God was illogical and contrary to reasonable evidence. Ending the talk, he stated: *"I can give you a list of fairly clear and testable and precise things that would convince me that religion was true. Suppose, for instance that earthquakes had been predicted all over the world on a specific date in the Quran and that they did occur and there was no explanation of this. That would very strongly raise my confidence in religion."*

Khan then delivered his talk. Far from being a run-of-the-mill abstract philosophical speech, he spent almost the entirety of his time discussing two prophecies. One, from the Prophet Muhammad related to today's modern technology and the other, Ahmad's World War One prediction. Arif had provided a criterion for what

131

he considered sufficient evidence for the truth of religion and Khan immediately provided it, almost to the letter. The conditions that Arif had demanded were, coincidentally and extraordinarily, completely met in the very next talk.

The event then became a question and answer discussion, much of which discussed the concept of both prayer and prophecy as a means of proving God's existence. It was an engaging and engrossing event, a wonderful demonstration of how people with vastly differing perspectives on life can come together in a respectful and good-humoured manner to discuss big topics. Freely available on YouTube[37], the event is well worth a watch.

In reality, it is fairly absurd for anyone to demand specific, particular signs before they are prepared to contemplate or believe in the existence of God. It is also contrary to the way in which all of us acquire knowledge in day-to-day life. In every other circumstance, we gain knowledge from whichever means it is provided to us. None of us disbelieve in the sun because we cannot taste it. None of us disbelieve in black holes because we cannot personally perceive them. None of us disbelieve in the existence of love because we cannot physically see it. Rather, we believe in the sun because when our eyes are open, we can see it. We believe in black holes because other, reputable individuals have told us they exist. We believe in love, not because we can see it, but because we can see its effects.

If the God that is described in all major religious texts exists, then He is an Omnipotent, Omnipresent, Omniscient being, infinitely greater than human beings. It stands to reason, therefore, that we have no right to demand particular signs from him, like kings ordering their jesters to dance. Rather we are the lesser beings, who perhaps cannot fully detect God through our own weaknesses and deficiencies rather than His. We can only get so close to the sun. Anything nearer than 93 million miles away and our bodies cannot survive the heat. Maybe our distance from God is for a similar

132

reason – that we are not strong enough spiritually to be able to palpably and unequivocally perceive Him. Maybe, like our belief in black holes, we must first accept, or at least strongly consider, those more knowledgeable than us. Those truthful people who have claimed to be Prophets and Messengers of God, who demonstrate such signs as Ahmad did, are our spiritual scientists. Perhaps we cannot become astronauts ourselves until we have accepted the testimonies of those before us and adapted their methods of discovery. Perhaps like love, we will never be able to see God, but at some stage of our discovery, we will believe in Him because we perceive His beauty and the effects that He has on us as individuals and the world at large and He becomes part of our life like he did Ahmad's. As the poem goes: *"They said that the most beautiful things cannot be seen with the eyes, but with the heart. I believe that must be the reason why God is invisible for us in this worldly life."*

We are not like Kings, demanding God to provide signs for us, rather we are like young children who, dependent on their mother, ask her for things to sustain us, to nourish us. When a child, seeing the brightness of the flame, desires to put his hand in it, the mother will refuse to let him. Sometimes even sincere prayers to God are not accepted for this very reason, that God knows better than us as to what is most beneficial. What we pray for may not be in our best interests. However, in this age, God's signs still reverberate across the globe and his existence remains perfectly possible to detect. In a poem, written by Mirza Ghulam Ahmad, he conveys his own perception of God and his love for Him: *"O mine of beauty, I know from where you have come: You are the Light of the Lord who created this world and all. I love not anyone else, Thou alone art my love; It is through this love that Thy Light has come to me."*

12. Just Talk To Me, My Friend

Various chapters of the Bible describe in detail the conversation between God and man. In today's age, such dialogues seem mythological, fictional, even crazy. I once discussed the concept of two-way conversation with a Muslim friend of mine. When I mentioned to him that I believed God could speak, he let out a chuckle. *"You know what they say,"* he told me. *"You talk to God, you're religious. God talks to you, you're psychotic."* I later discovered this quote was taken from the TV show House, delivered by Hugh Lawrie's character. Variations of it, however, had persisted throughout recent times. According to modern society, it's fine to worship and pray to an All-Powerful, All-Knowing deity – perhaps it gives you comfort, or hope in times of trouble, or meaning in a confusing world. However, suggest that that deity responds, or talks back, then suddenly you become a bit strange. Hallucination and delusion are the words which immediately spring to mind.

I always found this bizarre. If we accept the existence of a conscious Being, who exists beyond time and space, possessing the intelligence to create the universe and everything in it, then surely, for that Being, talking shouldn't be too much of a stretch. 'He hasn't got a mouth,' some might argue. Well neither has he physical hands and yet still He was able to fashion out an entire cosmos. It always seemed to me that logically, if God couldn't speak, then He probably didn't exist. I spent much time in my early University months investigating this concept through the methods and means that all major religious figures endorsed – prayer.

There is a famous Islamic saying, which is said to have been revealed to the Prophet Muhammad by God. Addressing humanity, God says, *"I am as My servant thinks I am...If he draws near to Me an arm's length, I draw near to him a cubit and if he draws near to Me a cubit, I draw near to him a fathom. And if he comes to me walking, I go to him running."*

It was through direct interaction with God that I knew I could become totally convinced of His existence. And as I talked to others within my Community, I realised that almost everyone had a story. The main reason, I concluded, that people generally find the concept of revelation so bewildering and difficult to believe, is because they personally have not been spoken to by God. But if you ask the right people, those who have prioritised their faith over the world, who pray numerous times each day whilst still living like everyone else, still having normal jobs and families and existences, then suddenly a whole new world opens before you. Those who seek God truly and persistently, never fail to find Him.

"I'll just start reading a bit, I'll just start praying. Let me just take that first step, let me get to know God." Hamza Ilyas is a compelling speaker. An American convert to Islam, Hamza often speaks openly about his own transition from being a desperate, lost soul, a drinker, a smoker, no hope, no prospects, to discovering God and finding liberation and inner contentment. He describes a time in his life, in the early years of the new millennium, in which he had just accepted Islam, but felt unsure of his decision:

"Love the ladies, love the drinking, love having fun, this whole Islam thing, quite foreign to me, you know what I mean? You've just become a Muslim, is this really where you want to go? What if this is just one of the many isms that people get themselves into because of boredom?"

Hamza describes how that night, as he walked home, he looked to the stars and prayed. He wanted to understand the truth, if God really did exist, but craved certainty. There was nothing worse, Hamza thought, than being a hypocrite.

"I lay out and before I know it, I hear the sound, like the sound of plane when it flies too low, combined with a train, it's like a roaring sound, but it was a voice. And the voice said: 'Number one, preach, there is none worthy of worship save Allah. Number two, preach, there is none worthy of worship save Allah. And it just kept repeating like vibrations in a tuning fork – it was like I became a tuning fork as someone knocked me on the edge of a table and I just sat there vibrating. I was so emotionally shaken. I was thinking, what's just happened to me?"

Astounded by his experience, Hamza decided to call a friend. Perhaps expecting him to be amazed, Hamza was shocked at his reaction.

"He's like, don't worry. This happens to people all the time."

If true, then perhaps this is the greatest secret that exists today - that millions of people, living normal lives, have regular, consistent experiences which originate from beyond the confines of the physical world. Though a compelling story, it is true that Hamza's is just that – a single testimony. And though he is as sane as they come, a subjective experience is nonetheless unverifiable. But when these stories are multiplied over and over, not limited by time or by geography, suddenly we are forced to take them more seriously.

Some stories are verifiable. In 2003, following the passing of Mirza Tahir Ahmad, a new Caliph (Khalifa) of the Ahmadiyya Community needed to be elected. Ahmadi Muslims believe that just as Prophets are chosen by God, similarly their successors – Caliphs, are too. Through an election process, Ahmadis believe that God guides the electorate, so the appointment is a divine one. There is no canvassing during or before the election. No individual is permitted to put his own name forward for the role. The election process works by individuals in the electorate, composed of around two hundred senior members of the Community, nominating someone for the role. Once there are no more nominations, there is an open vote – a show of hands to determine who the Caliph will be.

Prior to the election, hundreds of people from the Community were shown clear dreams regarding its outcome. Accounts of these dreams are viewable freely online in a document entitled *'Dreams Foretelling the Fifth Khilafat*[38].*' A couple of these accounts are related below. The first is by Mrs Rizwana Shafiq, a lady residing in Austria, who wrote the following letter to the Imam of the London Mosque:

"On the day of Huzoor's [the previous Khalifa's] *death my husband departed for London. I was alone and remained constantly glued to the television...Every eye was fixed on the closed doors of the London Mosque. I was very tired and momentarily went into a state that can be described neither as sleep nor wakefulness. In that state I saw a light descend from the heavens and enter the election site. It occurred to me that the Khalifa's name will begin with the letter 'M'...Thereafter, that light entered a man whose name is 'Masroor'. The following words echo in my heart and also come to my lips: 'Allah has already made His choice and has filled the heart of that person with light.' At that moment the vision broke and I returned back to full consciousness. I was trembling all over, but internally I was convinced that Allah had made His choice and now it was only a matter of time before that decision would be revealed. I called my husband who was outside the London Mosque and narrated to him what I had experienced. He then told me that an announcement was being made and asked me to hang up...the very next moment I heard you announce that Hadhrat Mirza Masroor Ahmad had been elected the Khalifa...*

In another letter dated Nov 2nd, 2005 she further explained: "Before his election I had never even heard of Huzoor [the new Khalifa]. *The same was the case with my husband, neither of us knew him in any way. Only after he was elected to his office did we first see him and hear his name."*

Those involved in the electoral process themselves received divine indications as to who they should vote for. Muhammad Ameen Johar was the Head of the Ahmadiyya Community in Mauritius. Following the death of Mirza Tahir Ahmad, Johar flew to London for the election and funeral. On the plane journey to London, he prayed for guidance as to who he should vote for:

"Thereafter, I was resting, when the word 'Masroor' came to my lips. At that time I was convinced that this was a guidance from Allah. I was not much familiar with Huzoor at that time...When departing from Mauritius, I had someone else in mind [to vote for] *though I had not shared it with anyone else. When I reached London I noted 'Masroor' on a scrap of paper and the time and circumstance when it had occurred to me. I sealed it inside an envelope and handed it to Sadr Khuddam-ul-Ahmadiyya* [Head of the UK Ahmadiyya Muslim Youth Association] *for safe keeping until after the election. This letter was in his possession at the time of election at the London Mosque and had not been opened. In fact, he had no idea to its contents. After the election and the bai'at* [pledge of allegiance to the new Khalifa], *when we were given permission to disperse I went to him and asked him to open the envelope and see its contents. He was much delighted and surprised to see the name 'Masroor' on the paper inside. It is still in his possession and he can bear witness to this matter."*

For Ahmadis across the world, stories like these are so numerous that they become a normal part of life. Incidents such as the remarkable acceptance of prayer in unlikely circumstances, spiritual dreams and other forms of revelation are perfectly achievable with patience, resilience and a striving to perform one's duties towards God and towards fellow man.

Experiences with the Khalifa also provide a faith-affirming boost to Ahmadi Muslims. As mentioned, according to Islam, a Khalifa, or

Caliph, is God's representative on earth at that particular time, elected under the direct guidance of God and helped by God at every step. Most Muslims in the world yearn for a Khalifa in the world today to guide them across these dangerous times. They believe that the time is near when this will happen, due to indications from the prophecies of the Prophet Muhammad. However, for Ahmadi Muslims, due to their acceptance of Mirza Ghulam Ahmad as the Promised Messiah, they have subsequently accepted the system of Khilafat which succeeded him.

The presence of a Khalifa (affectionately known by his followers as 'Huzoor') provides Ahmadis with countless benefits. Firstly, they have a role model, a guide to follow during confusing times. Secondly, they receive direct moral and spiritual guidance from him on a regular basis, steering them clear from aberrant behaviour or beliefs. *"You will never find any case of radicalisation in our community,"* Mirza Masroor Ahmad affirms confidently. Thirdly, through the Caliph, Ahmadis experience remarkable 'miracles,' which provide them with direct signs of the existence of a Living God.

The current Khalifa, Mirza Masroor Ahmad, elected in 2003 following the demise of Mirza Tahir Ahmad, lived in Pakistan in his early life. He studied Agricultural Economics at University, before deciding to give up a personal career for the sake of serving his faith. Under the instruction of the then-Khalifa, he was sent to Ghana to engage with development projects. *"I was a free man, fond of sowing seeds and harvesting crops – a simple farmer."* His agricultural work left a lasting impact upon the West African nation, as he became the first person to ever successfully grow wheat on Ghanaian soil. In 1985 he returned to Pakistan in various administrative roles for the Ahmadiyya Muslim Community, before his election to the position of Worldwide Head, or Khalifa, in 2003. Speaking of the election itself, Mirza Masroor Ahmad relates, *"The aura of the gathering was such that I did not have the courage to peer up and glance around...thus I sat with my gaze down. When my name was presented, I felt instant fear, so I lowered my head. When the votes were counted and the announcement made, I was confident that there must have been a mistake in the count. What happened after this made me tremble; there was no choice but to accept the decree of God."* He continued, *"How I felt in that moment, the whole world saw on MTA* (the official television channel of the Community). *It was as if the weight of a mountain had been placed on my shoulders. It was midnight or even past midnight when I got to my residence. There, in my room was I, the darkness of the night and the blessings of my God.*[39] *"*

Ibrahim Ikhlaf is the UK head of the Ahmadiyya Community outreach department. Having encountered him on several occasions, I have found him to be a passionate and lively individual, with a zeal for discussing religion. He has a permanent smile, a welcoming face and a body language which conveys a deep respect for others. I have also met his young son, a playful child with boundless energy. During a gathering of young Ahmadi Muslims, Ikhlaf told the story of his wife's pregnancy five years earlier. She was diagnosed with amniotic band syndrome, a disorder in which the foetus becomes entangled in amniotic bands in the womb. Sometimes, these bands can wrap around a limb, resulting in the baby being born missing an arm or leg. In some cases, the bands can wrap around the baby's face, causing cleft lip and palate. In a large proportion, the baby can also be born with clubfoot. The disorder can also cause miscarriages, when the band wraps around the umbilical cord. It is an entirely random disease, with no risk factors identified and no known genetic link. Ikhlaf relates his story:

"When we went to the doctor, they analysed the scan and they said that the chances are 99.9% that he will lose one of his hands. My wife went to the Khalifa, crying and Huzoor said, 'don't worry, nothing will happen to him. I assure you.' She said, 'But the doctors said this!' Huzoor said again, don't worry, nothing will happen to him'. Every time my wife went for scanning the doctors said the

140

same. On the 32-week scan, the doctors said, 'the risk is very high now, there is nothing we can do.' She saw Huzoor straight away after and he said again, don't worry, I assure you. Two days later her waters broke. The ambulance came and took her into hospital. She had a caesarean section and my son was born, completely fine. On our next meeting with Huzoor, he told us – 'His name is Talha, his hand should protect Islam Ahmadiyya. His hand was not destined to be cut off in the womb.'

The purpose of Caliphate is to spiritually guide people and strengthen their faiths. Caliphate has no political aims or aspirations and no hidden motives. Thus, however deeply a person delves, they will not find even a trace of dishonesty, corruption or self-interest. The Khalifa of the time lives a relatively simple existence, residing in a flat attached to a mosque and leading prayers five times every day. Despite leading tens of millions of people, he has an exceptionally close relationship with all his followers. Thousands of letters are written to him and without fail a personal response is received. Not only this, but the Khalifa meets with dozens of ordinary families almost every day. Many Ahmadis have stories similar to that of Ibrahim Ikhlaf – of remarkable personal incidents with the Khalifa.

For a period at University, I was a committee member of the Psychiatry Society, having a deep interest in this field. One talk which we organised was by a researcher at Imperial College London. He and his team were testing the effect of psychedelics in treating depression and addictive disorders. Psilocybin is the psychoactive compound that occurs naturally in magic mushrooms. Over the past few years, the research team have tested the efficacy of this substance in patients suffering from mood disorders. Results thus far have shown improvements in mood and stress relief in previously depressed patients. Psychedelics provide transcendent, mystical, hallucinatory experiences which can prove extremely emotionally powerful. As one of the Imperial College researchers, Professor David Nutt described it: *"When you see that you are more than*

141

your current self and you have experiences as our patients do, feeling you are taken outside of your body and floating off into space and into other worlds, then you see the bigger picture. You realise you don't ever die. No one ever dies. You stop breathing. You stop thinking. But the atoms are still there."

Such an experience can essentially described as a drug-induced 'spiritual' experience. It highlights the fact that reality is a strange concept. The world is not just what we see in day-to-day life, rather there are many layers that we know exist and many layers that others have compellingly claimed to have found. There is the normal world, identifiable by our five senses, which everyone with those senses intact can perceive. Then there is the dream-world, identifiable to everyone but to different degrees and intensities. There is the powerful psychedelic experience. And then there are those deeper aspects of reality that, throughout history, including today, perfectly healthy individuals have claimed to perceive, who perceive them not through their physical senses but through their spiritual ones. After all, the neurological faculties already present in the brain can be activated any time by the Being who created them. One of the benefits of establishing a relationship with a Living God, according to Islam, is similar to that described by Professor Nutt when referring to psychedelics. Through our own experiences, or by hearing the experiences of others, a relationship with God enables us to transcend our material bodies and allows powerful new perspectives to emerge. We develop a deeper sense of connection, towards God and towards those around us.

13. Outcast

In my heart I knew that Mirza Ghulam Ahmad's awareness of God was exceptional, partly through reading about him, partly through his prophecies and miracles and partly through his poems, which permeated through my heart like a cool breeze.

I wanted to love God as much as this man, the man whom I believed knew Him best in this age.

> *O the Powerful, the Creator of heaven and earth*
> *O the Merciful, the Benevolent, the Guide;*
>
> *O the One Who knows what is in the hearts;*
> *O the One, from Whom nothing is hidden;*

Eighteen years old, searching for friends to connect with, to spend time with. Early on at medical school I came across a group of Muslims in my year. They were friendly and funny and seemed to be kind, but their devoutness scared me somewhat. Often they would turn up for lectures or small group sessions late because they had been praying. They would stick to their beliefs and principles and stick together in a clique, as people, as Muslims, whilst still spreading kindness to others. I admired them somewhat, but was anxious given that most of them were of Pakistani origin and had dedicated religious natures. If they were so committed to their faith, perhaps they had also inherited the anti-Ahmadi prejudice that their forefathers would likely have possessed. I got texts from them sometimes, asking if I wanted to join them in praying together. I didn't tell them that I was a part of the most controversial movement within Islam and that I couldn't engage in certain activities with them. I ignored, or avoided the issue.

As a Muslim, praying together in congregation with others is encouraged – indeed it is an essential part of religious practice. The format is that one person is the designated Imam and leads the prayer, while the others follow behind. As an Ahmadi Muslim, I am not allowed to pray behind Muslims of other sects. This can be a tricky concept to explain and people sometimes get the wrong impression – for example that it is an intentionally divisive act. In reality this is not the case. At the time of the Founder of the Ahmadiyya Community, Mirza Ghulam Ahmad, when opposition was growing, other Muslim leaders used to claim that their mosques had to be cleaned dozens of times over if an Ahmadi entered them, such was their hatred for the community. As such, for the purposes of preserving relative peace, Ahmad told his followers to keep away from other Muslims' mosques so as not to antagonise them. There is another, theological reason though too. Ahmadis believe that Mirza Ghulam Ahmad was the Imam of this Age, chosen by God to guide people. If a Muslim therefore rejects the Imam chosen by God and labels him a heretic and a liar, then how can such a person legitimately and logically be an Imam himself? Obviously, Muslims are free to accept or reject Ahmad, but Ahmadis are also free to choose who to say their prayers behind. The Imam of a congregation, after all, is like the representative of the whole group in front of God. Each of us is free to choose who they want and don't want, to represent them.

If You see that I am but the embodiment of disobedience and mischief;
If You have witnessed that I am of an evil nature;

Then, smash into pieces this evil one;
And thus make happy my enemies;

Having a misconception about another person is a dangerous thing. It has the potential to destroy a relationship before it has even begun. Each of us, after all, are humans with unique thoughts,

144

feelings, backgrounds and beliefs. We are individuals and if the world judged everyone as such, before looking at the colour of our skin, or tribe or ethnicity or religion, then the world would surely be a better place. I was concerned that if my Muslim friends knew I was an Ahmadi immediately after I met them, then they would view me negatively, as the result of the misconceptions that many Muslims have about Ahmadi Muslims. *"They're agents planted by the British in order to divide and destroy Islam,"* is a common one. *"They don't believe in the Prophet Muhammad as the best and highest of all Prophets,"* is another false assertion. *"They have a different Kalima (declaration of faith),"* is another. *"They believe the birthplace of their founder to be more holy than Mecca." "They face a different direction while praying." "They are Jewish agents." "They are secretly lizards."* The list of misconceptions goes on and on (well, except for the lizard one perhaps). My faith had always taught me to be broad-minded and open-minded, to let others believe what they wanted and respect them whatever their faith. Growing older, I became dismayed to learn about the persecution and opposition that Ahmadi Muslims endure and the enemies constantly on their tail. As an eighteen-year-old simply searching for friends at university. I wanted my Muslim friends to judge me for who I really was, rather than who they might wrongly perceive me to be. So I initially didn't tell them I was an Ahmadi. I was a Muslim just like them and though I did not pray behind them, I went into the Medical School prayer room at a time they weren't there. We became friends.

And make the cloud of Your Mercy shower on their hearts the rain of Your Mercy;
Grant them every wish of theirs, Through the Grace of Yours;

And let my dwelling be gutted in a blazing fire;
Be my enemy and let my works go to waste.

In 1974, under Prime Minister Bhutto, the Pakistani constitution was amended, declaring Ahmadi Muslims as a non-Muslim minority for the purposes of law. This amendment created significant difficulties for Ahmadis living there. As well as feeling like second class citizens, unable to legally identify as how they wished, they were also the target of numerous attacks and harassments by extremist groups, who were emboldened by the legislation.

Then, ten years later, under General Zia-ul-Haq, Ordinance XX was introduced, making it a criminal offence for an Ahmadi to *'directly or indirectly, pose himself as a Muslim, or refers to his faith as Islam, or preaches or propagates his faith, or invites others to accept his faith, by words, either spoken or written, or by visible representations, or in any manner whatsoever outrages the religious feelings of Muslims...'* The punishment prescribed for breaking this law was defined as being either imprisonment for up to three years and a fine.

Putting this in to context, from 1984, Ahmadis, who regard themselves entirely as Muslims, have no longer been allowed to call their places of worship mosques, they have been unable to discuss their faith openly and even offering the Muslim greeting of peace – *Salaam* – is enough to be regarding as posing as a Muslim – thus becoming liable to imprisonment. Ahmadis have been attacked mercilessly since the introduction of these laws, but their persecutors and tormentors are rarely punished. Astoundingly, it is usually the Ahmadi victims who are blamed when they are attacked. Just by being Ahmadis, they have *'outraged the religious feelings of Muslims,'* and thus are worthy to be killed. Since 1984, over 250 Ahmadis have been killed, hundreds have been assaulted for their faith and dozens of Ahmadi mosques have been demolished, burned or forcibly occupied. Ahmadi bodies are even known to have been exhumed after burial. Children at Pakistani schools are taught that Ahmadis are enemies of the state. Anti-Ahmadi rallies attract many thousands of people, during which they are denounced as 'infidels.' The government requires that elected officials in Pakistan must declare that they do not belong to the Ahmadiyya Community before they begin their terms in office. When applying for a passport, all Muslims must sign a form agreeing to the declaration that *'I consider Mirza Ghulam Ahmad Qadiani to be an imposter nabi [Prophet] and also consider his followers...to be non-Muslim.'*

146

For most reasonable people, such behaviour must seem like insanity. However, the depth of hatred for Ahmadis means that huge numbers of people who have been brought up in Pakistan have been brainwashed into regarding Ahmadis as treacherous imposters. The lies and deceptions that are continuously repeated by elected officials, religious clerics and the mainstream media mean that few think positively of Ahmadis.

The nature of the persecution of Ahmadis is unique – perhaps unlike that of any other group today. Most persecutions throughout history have been based on differences in faith. Catholics and Protestants are divided as a result of their respective views on Luther's reformations. Sunni and Shia Muslims argue because of their open differences with regards to the nature of successorship after the Prophet Muhammad. Hindus and Muslims have vastly diverse and varying opinions on the nature of God and have clashed over the course of specific periods in history. *"Convert to our way of thinking, or we will oppress you,"* religious tyrants have stated vociferously. In the case of the persecution of Ahmadis however, bizarrely the opposite is true. Ahmadi Muslims vocally and strongly affirm that they believe in the fundamental creeds of Islam, in the five pillars and the six articles of faith. They affirm that they believe in the Quran in its entirety and believe in the Prophet Muhammad as the Seal of the Prophets, or *Khatamun-Nabiyeen.* Ahmadis affirm that their belief is exactly identical to that of Islam when it was founded. In other words, Ahmadis claim to represent a true, pure, uncorrupted form of Islam. Despite this, the persecutors and oppressors of Ahmadiyya Islam, who exist in numerous countries throughout the world as well as Pakistan, simply demand that Ahmadis declare themselves non-Muslim.

Look beneath the surface and the reason for this becomes obvious. It is not that Ahmadiyya Islam is shaming or defaming the religion – rather it is the opposite. Ahmadis are arguably the most highly respected single Muslim group in many parts of the Western world, including Britain. Whenever a terrorist atrocity occurs, it is Ahmadis in great number who commemorate and mourn with the victims, holding placards with the words *Love for All Hatred for None* and *Muslims For Peace.* It is Ahmadis who set up blood drives and charity events and homeless feeding campaigns, as well as regularly holding large peace conventions, attended by many high-profile MPs and dignitaries. The annual Peace Symposium, held at Baitul-Futuh – the largest mosque in Western Europe, brings together politicians, civil servants, military personnel, members of the emergency services and a vast array of other individuals and groups, who attend to join hands with a group around which they feel safe.

The real and only logical reason that Muslim clerics demand that Ahmadis call themselves non-Muslims is because they feel threatened by their very existence. Knowing that they would lose their own power and influence if the masses understood and accepted the true teachings of Ahmadiyya Islam, they instead spread fears, lies and misconceptions about the Community. Despite the negative propaganda, the Community remains the fastest growing sect in Islam. It is established in over 200 nations worldwide and has formed over a thousand free secular schools, dozens of free hospitals, over 17,000 mosques and also established *Humanity First* in 1994, an international world-leading NGO which helps the impoverished all across the world. From the oldest member of the Community to the youngest, Ahmadiyya Islam follows the simple, yet beautiful creed of true Islam, as articulated by Mirza Ghulam Ahmad: *"There are only two complete parts of faith. One is to love God and the other is to love mankind to such a degree that you consider the suffering and the trials and tribulations of others as your own and that you pray for them."*

Ahmad, the founder of the Community, claimed that God had appointed him as a non-law bearing Prophet, sent not to change Islam, but to revive its original teachings, which had been forgotten and misinterpreted over time.

Yet, if You count me among Your servants;
If You consider Your threshold to be my Qiblah [direction of
Mecca]—
—the pivot of my being;

148

If You witness my heart to be replete with such love for You
as the secret of which
Is unknown to the world, except You;

Then, treat me with love, O You
And manifest a little these mysteries;

May – Year 4:

I am a minority within a minority. The West portrays Islam negatively. Mainstream Muslims portray the Ahmadiyya Muslim Community negatively. Some might describe me as being part of an oppressed group within an oppressed group. Maybe that makes me an outcast, an outsider. But I have never felt this way. I have always felt free, to befriend whomever I choose without being suffocated by a single crowd of people.

I am on my way to a post-exam meal with my non-Ahmadi Muslim friends, the silence of my taxi journey allowing me to reflect upon one of the first times I had socialised with this group, all the way back in first year.

It started with a kickabout in the park. As we were walking back after an enjoyable session, they agreed to all go back to one of their houses to pray together. I was caught in a situation from which there was no escape and so I told them I was an Ahmadi. They responded politely, slightly surprised but inquisitive, realising that many of them had little knowledge of my belief system. We discussed it for a while and when we arrived at the house they let me lead the prayer, to my surprise. When I told my mother about this that weekend, she smiled and predicted that my Muslim friends would discuss Ahmadiyya Islam with their families and after that they would never let me lead them in prayer again. Indeed, they never did. However, the fact that all of them were kind-hearted, genuinely good people and that I had established a pre-existing friendship with them meant that they never treated me with anything other than respect and kindness.

The taxi drops me off and I spill out untidily. It is a warm Thursday night, and I make my way to the half-Indian, half-Italian restaurant *that we plan to eat at. A bizarre combination, I remember thinking, though the food turns out to be tasty. Fast forward an hour and two of us are discussing religion. Engrossed in intriguing dialogue, the nature of which we have never engaged in before, our minds were locked in thought and our attentions undivided. Suddenly, Hassan interrupts and I jolt back into the room, remembering the presence of the others. I have some news, he tells me hesitantly, as his mouth breaking into a tentative smile. "I'm getting...married," he says, almost in a joking way and as I stare blankly the others around us look at me inquisitively. 'Go on then, aren't you going to congratulate him?' someone says and it is only then that I know he is being serious.*

**O You, Who comes towards every seeker of Yours
And are aware of the burning passion**

Of the one who is afire with love for You.

**For the sake of that love of Yours,
Which I have sowed in my heart,
Manifest Yourself to exonerate me.**

**It is indeed You Who are my Refuge;
It is indeed You Who are my Protector;
It is indeed You Who are my Shelter.**

The Ahmadiyya Muslim Community describes itself as one body. And the beating heart of that body is the Khalifa. In 1984, following the draconian laws of Ordinance XX, Ahmadis were no longer able to publicly preach or even disclose their faith. Therefore the Khalifa, at that time Mirza Tahir Ahmad, was forced to migrate away from Pakistan. London became the new central headquarters of the Community. Mirza Tahir Ahmad passed away in April 2003, but to this day, the central headquarters have remained London. Up until April 2019, the current Khalifa, Mirza Masroor Ahmad, lived within the complex of Fazl Mosque in Southfields, Wandsworth. Inaugurated in 1926, this was the first ever purpose-built mosque in London. It was also used as a bomb shelter for locals during the Second World War and has recently been listed as a Grade II building by the Department for Culture, Media and Sport, thus marking it as an important site and affording it greater protection. In April 2019, the Headquarters were transferred to another site, *Islamabad*, located in the Surrey countryside. Every Friday lunchtime, the Khalifa delivers his weekly hour-long Friday sermon, as per Islamic tradition, either from Islamabad or from *Baitul Futuh* in Morden, the largest mosque in Western Europe. Each sermon is simultaneously translated into numerous languages and televised live online and on MTA (Muslim Television Ahmadiyya), where it is viewed across the world. The sermon enables the Khalifa to directly address his followers, offering them moral and spiritual guidance and sometimes commenting on recent world events.

Through the flames of that fire,
Which You have kindled in my heart,
You have burnt all that is other than You;

With the same fire my countenance light up You;
My dark night, into a bright day, convert You.

For years, as anti-Ahmadi attacks increase in intensity in Pakistan, but also in other nations such as Indonesia, Bangladesh and Algeria, the Khalifa has responded through his sermons. First, he pays tribute to those victims injured or killed through the barbaric attacks of extremist Muslims. Then he sends a warning to those individuals, groups and nations perpetrating such brutalities. God would not be with the oppressors. Though Ahmadis would not lay a finger upon those who persecute them, that does not mean they should feel themselves secure. "*If governments stand against us, they will be disintegrated. If organisations stand against us, they will be shattered.*" Each time an attack occurs, the same message is given. Ahmadis are taught to respond to barbarism in the same way that the Prophet Muhammad and his followers did – with peace and prayers, without retaliation or revenge. Ahmadis seek the help of God and believe firmly that the final victory will be theirs. The early Jews, at the time around Moses were heavily persecuted by the Pharaoh of the time, such that all their new-born sons were ordered to be thrown into the river and drowned. The Egyptians would

151

enslave the Israelite Jews and treat them worse than animals. The early Christians, having believed in Jesus, were persecuted for 300 years. Some were thrown to wild animals, some were trampled or stoned to death. Some fled underground and lived in caves and labyrinths to escape the merciless brutalities which they would otherwise have faced. The early Muslims were dragged through the desert streets, burning stones were placed on their chests, some were stabbed to death with swords and cut into pieces. All of the Prophets who were oppressed eventually became victorious, against all odds. In time, teachings and commandments may have changed and become distorted, however the ultimate principle throughout history has been that persecution cannot prevent the spread of a true religion. Not only this, but persecution is necessary and essential to test the resolve and courage of the early believers, such that the strength and depth of their faith may be visible for all to see. The current Caliph, Mirza Masroor Ahmad, was himself imprisoned for his Ahmadi beliefs in Pakistan for eleven days in 1999, four years before his appointment as Caliph.

To be able to endure the suffering that oppressors inflict upon a religious group, those in that group must have a faith that is unshakeably strong. Faith, to a believer in God, is not simply a hunch, or a blind hope that a Creator exists, rather it is a certainty that is borne from personal evidence and experience. Not long after Mirza Tahir Ahmad was forced to move to London from his home in Pakistan such that he could conduct his duties as Caliph, he addressed the persecutors of the Community he led. *"I say that do as you may please, try as hard as you can; I swear by God that we shall not be moved, we shall not be moved from the paths of Muhammad... Human history bears witness that the paths that you walk are the paths of failure and exasperation...But I swear by God that the paths that we walk are the paths of prophets and of their true slaves. These are the paths that turn into galaxies and shine across the heavens.... So try with as much power as you can muster. O enemies of Ahmadiyyat, martyr as many Ahmadis as you wish to martyr...You will most surely die of complete failure and complete mortification."*

The psychology of Ahmadi Muslim persecution and response is thus an intriguing one. Numerous politicians, through their own initiatives, have attempted to take up the fight, urging the Pakistani government to abolish its infamous blasphemy laws, which target not only Ahmadis but also Shias, Hindus, Christians and Atheists. In May 2018, MPs held a debate in the House of Commons on a motion on the persecution of the Community, opened by Siobhain McDonagh, MP for Mitcham and Morden, a passionate advocate for Ahmadi rights in Pakistan.

Then, in August 2018, a glimmer of hope came. Prominent Pakistani politician and ex-cricketer Imran Khan was elected as Prime Minister of the nation. In his opening address, he put forward a compelling vision of the Pakistan of the future. He declared that it was to become a humanitarian state based on justice and peace. He said that the impoverished would rise under his rule and their living and working standards would improve. He promised that under Pakistani law, all people would be equal. He even declared that he would not live in the traditional government house, instead preferring to live in a more simple residence, with the Prime Minister's house to become an educational institution.

In a further move of apparent progress, Prime Minister Imran Khan appointed a prominent Ahmadi Professor of Economics Atif Mian onto his Economic Advisory Council. His decision was widely lauded by Pakistanis and non-Pakistanis as a move towards tolerance, equality and justice. Other members of the government, such as Information Minister Fawad Chaudhry praised Khan's decision. *"Pakistan belongs as much to minorities as it does to the majority."* This mentality of an inclusive Pakistan constituted one of its most important principles during the time of its creation in the 1940s. Pakistan's founding father, Muhammad Ali Jinnah formed the country with the dream of making it a haven of peace for all. *"You are free,"* he exclaimed. *"Free to go to your temples, you are free to go to your mosques or to any other places of worship in this*

State of Pakistan. You may belong to any religion...that has nothing to do with the business of the state."

Sadly, this mentality didn't last long. Despite Imran Khan's apparent attempts to revive that initial founding spirit, within a few days he had backtracked astonishingly. Just three days after Mian's appointment, there was internal dissent within Khan's cabinet and apparent reports of protests backed by religious hardliners. Mian was asked to step down from his role and the dream of a fair, free Pakistan was once again in tatters. Fawad Chaudhry, who just a few days earlier had praised Mian's appointment, also quickly backtracked, describing it as *'not appropriate.'* In fact, far from helping the Ahmadi cause, since Khan's appointment, anti-Ahmadi hate crimes have risen. An Ahmadi mosque was set on fire, 6 Ahmadis were shot and in Faisalabad, extremist mobs harassed Ahmadis outside their homes.

Make this blind world open its eyes;
O God, Whose assault is vehement, manifest
The Might of Yours;

From heaven manifest the Sign of the Light of Yours;
Exhibit a Flower of the Garden of Yours;

The situation for Ahmadi Muslims and indeed all minorities in Pakistan is bleak. The irony, however, is that the crippling anti-Ahmadi laws caused a mass migration, enabling Ahmadis to not only settle but thrive in other parts of the world. Persecution was supposed to end the Community once and for all, but in reality it only enabled it to progress and spread its message globally. Wherever Ahmadi Muslims live, whatever their material states, they live with a sense freedom from the shackles of the world, true connection caused by hard effort and sacrifice, and most of all, hope in their hearts. A dawn will come, they believe, the new day will arrive.

I see this world to be full of impiety, sinfulness;
I see that the unmindful remember not the time of death;

I see that they are ignorant of facts;
I see that they are stranger to facts;

I see that they, like kids, are fond of stories alone;
I see that the love of God exists not in their hearts;

I see that their hearts have, as it were,
Turned away from God;

I see the severity of the flood; I see the pitch darkness of the night;
BE KIND and MAKE THE SUN RISE, MY LOVE.

14. To See Our Souls Before Us

July – Year 4:

Even the children are captivated. I look sideways, across the grand marquee in which I find myself situated and see only people, one in front of another, in neat lines, with each one resting his hand on the shoulder of the person in front. They wait in silence, sitting in this position for a number of minutes. As he arrives the atmosphere changes. They watch as he walks into the front of the marquee, in an elegant long brown coat that had been passed down across generations. They are enchanted, transfixed, ready. He sits down on the floor a few metres in front of the main stage and as he sits his entourage follows suit. 'Ashhadu,' are the first words which flow from his lips. 'I bear witness,' and as the congregation hears them they repeat them back loudly, with conviction and emotion. After a few Arabic phrases there is a couple of seconds silence and then the translators simultaneously give their translations loudly through their microphones. His Arabic then changes to English, stopping after a few words for the congregation to repeat. Each repetition feels like the blowing of a wind from heaven. It is harmonious, emotive, passionate. At times the emotion grows too strong.

'O my Lord, my Allah. I wronged my soul and confess all my sins. Pray, forgive me, my sins, for there is none else except thee to forgive.'

As these words echo from the marquee, tears flow from the eyes of the young and the old. All, together, expressing their own weaknesses whilst in the security of a human chain 40,000 in size. The crowds overflow. Outside the main marquee, the Hampshire countryside is filled with people, all part of this chain leading back to the Khalifa, who's every word is repeated with fervour, from the very depths of the hearts. 'I will obey you, as the Messiah's Khalifa, in everything good that you may require of me.'

This ceremony, the International Bai'at, or 'initiation,' constitutes one of the highlights of the Jalsa Salana UK – the annual three-day convention of the Ahmadiyya Muslim Community. Guests from all around the world attend this convention, as well as dignitaries, religious leaders, MPs, mayors and other important public figures, who are given opportunity to address the crowd over the course of the weekend. I have attended this event every year since I was born. It is an event of beauty, filled with individuals from all different races and ethnicities and cultures. In Islam, everyone is equal. Regardless of status or colour, everyone prays side by side, feeling the spirituality of the occasion. For the past few years, my duty for the event has been showing around members of the UK and International Press and conducting and coordinating interviews with various journalists. Given its status as the largest annual Islamic gathering in the UK, the event garners significant media attention every year. 'This reminds me of Glastonbury,' some journalists tell me, remarking on the countryside setting, with marquees and tents transforming the farm into a temporary city. 'But then where's the music?' I smile. 'Being here our hearts can sing without music.' Even those journalists who do not believe in God can feel the spirituality and remark upon it. There are exhibitions, poems sung melodiously, plentiful food, addresses by dignitaries, speeches by the Khalifa, and the initiation ceremony on the Sunday afternoon. There is the opportunity to catch up with long-lost friends and relatives and pray alongside tens of thousands of others, in unity and peace.

These annual Jalsa gatherings occur across the world, as per-tradition of the Community. The last to be held in Pakistan, in 1983, attracted an attendance of around 250,000. This was the last glimpse that many Pakistani Ahmadis would get of their Khalifa, before his migration to the UK as a result of the bitter persecution the Community faced.

There is an almost magical connection here, between each and every attendee. There are no conflicts, confrontations or petty squabbles. This is a time for prayer, for kindness, for excitement. It is a time to realise the grandeur of God and for a young person, to feel linked to something of splendour and magnificence. When at Jalsa, surrounded by flags of every country, with the Ahmadiyya Islam flag in the centre adjacent to the Union Jack and surrounded by friends and smiling faces, it is impossible to feel alone.

Ummad Farooq is a friend of mine. In his late 20s, he appears initially as a reserved, shy individual. However, give him time and opportunity to speak and he converses with an eloquence that few others can muster, despite English being only his second language. I have three things in common with Ummad. Firstly, we are both Ahmadi Muslims and of Pakistani ethnicity. Second, we both enjoy sports, particularly football. And thirdly, we have both been to the Queen Elizabeth Hospital in Birmingham. Our similarities end there. The QE hospital is a magnificent building. From the outside it resembles a spaceship, its curved structure appearing almost celestial and its radiant white shining across the city. From the top floor of the hospital one can see across almost the entire city, with a particularly scenic view of the University campus, in the centre of which lies 'Big Joe,' the largest free-standing clock-tower in the world. I have spent many a morning at the hospital as a medical student, roaming the wards for interesting patients, or sitting in outpatient clinics with friendly consultants. I have spent many a lunchtime eating at the hospital's impressive canteen and many an afternoon at the cosy, comfortable library, pouring through

158

textbooks and revision notes, trying to second-guess the exam questions I will face.

Ummad's experience at the QE hospital, however, was less idyllic. In October 2012, Ummad flies back to Karachi, Pakistan from the UK for his brother's wedding. It is a joyful event. Everything has gone to plan and Ummad is enjoying spending precious time with his family. Four days after the wedding, as the family are travelling for Friday prayers, everything changes. Ummad and his father are in a car, with his brother following behind on his motorbike. Suddenly they hear a gunshot. As they stop the car, Ummad looks out of his back-seat window to find two armed men on motorbikes, who stop beside them and begin to open fire. Ummad's father is shot six times and Ummad is himself shot on his forehead. As they look back, they see Ummad's newly wed brother, in a critical state, having been shot multiple times. Ummad and his brother find a way to find each other amidst the panic and the pain. Ummad cannot see, the gunshot to his forehead has rendered him temporarily blind. "Bhai!" Ummad shouts desperately, waiting for a response from his older brother, his closest friend. There is none.

"Imagine spending every day with someone, knowing them completely, sitting and having dinner with them every single evening and then one day, two days after their wedding, having them die in your arms."

We are at Jalsa and I am with Ummad and a journalist, who had requested to speak to a victim of anti-Ahmadi persecution. Both of us are listening intently to his every word. Ummad's voice begins to break a little, as the emotions of that fateful day resurface to the forefront of his mind. Not that they were ever really anywhere else.

Ummad's own bullet wound was treated by a private surgeon in Birmingham, in a unique operation. The bullet was removed through Ummad's nose, using a new piece of equipment which had rarely, if ever, been used in this way before.

I find a video from November 2012, only a month after the horrific incident had occurred. Ummad is being interviewed about the event *from another member of the Ahmadiyya Community. His father is still in the Intensive Care Unit at the time, his life hanging by a thread. Many would be consumed by bitterness and hatred. But when asked what his response will be, Ummad replies calmly. "The only weapon we have is our prayers," he tells his interviewer.*

Each of us is weak, our hearts fragile, our minds susceptible. But perhaps it is only when our souls acknowledge this vulnerability, such as during the Bai'at ceremony, or when we suffer losses, such as that which Ummad faced, that we can truly appreciate our helplessness. Maybe that relieves some pressure; maybe it strengthens our connections to those around us. Whether we believe in a Higher Power or not, it is clear that we are not the Highest Powers. For we have no real control over anything. I was moved by the relationship Ummad had with his brother and the sadness and suddenness of his death, as well as his response – patient, rational, courageous. As my University journey progressed, I began to learn more and more about the horrors and sufferings that all too many face today.

15. Forget Their Faces And They Will Haunt Us

March – Year 5:

They never had faces before.

It is in a quiet corner of Camden, a bustling London suburb, that I first encounter Linh. She is a Vietnamese girl, of similar age to myself and her nature and temperament – reserved, mild-mannered, slightly apprehensive– makes her instantly relatable. I am sitting in a run-down office block, owned by the Helen Bamber Foundation, a charity which supports refugees and asylum seekers who have experienced hardships and cruelties. I am there as part of a project for my University intercalated degree, having taken a year out from medicine to do a BSc in Public Health. As we sit and gently discuss her life story, I let my mind wander for a few seconds here and there and reflect upon how my female relatives and friends would react, being thrust into the dark desperate world that she has become devoured in through no fault of her own.

Linh describes her childhood – living in an idyllic, tranquil Vietnamese village by the sea, with the best parents in the world. She describes the fateful day that she received the news that her father and uncle had drowned at sea during a fishing trip. There was no goodbye, no last moments, she tells me, her eyes filled with emotion. She describes how she and her mother coped, with difficulty, for the next two years before she too died, leaving Linh a

161

teenage orphan. I used to stand at the edge of the sea and think of drowning myself, she relates. Other villagers would help her, with food and shelter and moral support. One even offered her employment with a friend in Hanoi. The man turned out to be horrifically cruel. Linh was made to work in brothels throughout Vietnam, China, Russia – being sold like property from one person to another. She describes how she was abused, aged only 15, and as she stares out of the window into the London afternoon city scene I notice the lines on her forehead betraying her past sufferings. I notice the weight of history in her eyes, her constant hyper-alertness, but also her determined resilience, forged by her desire to take care of her 9-month old daughter. I sat for a while, just listening to her and then to others like her - stories of torture, slavery and abandonment by a world that seemingly views every individual as a commodity, a product, rather than as a beautiful beating heart, a living person with thoughts and dreams and desires. Linh will carry the mark of a prisoner for the rest of her life now, I am sure of that. It is late in the day and after having seen the psychiatrist after me next door, Linh walks past the room in which I sit alone, emotionally drained from the harrowing tales I have heard. This time it is her that looks at me with pity. Go home now, she tells me, smiling.

According to the UN Refugee Agency, 44,440 people every day are forced to flee their homes due to persecution or conflict. By the end of 2017, there were 68.5 million individuals globally who were forcibly displaced due to conflict, violence, persecution or human rights abuses. The levels of displacement worldwide are now the highest they have ever been.

The policy of the West to attempt to *'solve the problem'* has been continual interventions in the Middle East, to try and bring *'peace and stability.'* After the UK and France had bombed Libya, it had turned from Africa's wealthiest nation, with the highest life expectancy and GDP per capita on the continent, into a failed state. Indeed, Libya, Iraq and Syria were the most modern and secular nations in their respective regions, with among the highest standards of living and the most successful women's rights records. Women in Gadaffi's Libya had the right to hold jobs, have equal education and have equal income to men. Gadaffi was in fact praised by the UN Human Rights Council for his promotion of women's rights. Conversely, today Libya has become a breeding ground for extremist Islamist forces to impose their own perverse interpretations of religion, including clamping down heavily on gender equality. It has been reported that according to the Tunisian President, two million Libyans, out of a total population of six million, left the country to take refuge in Tunisia.

Libya is still in crisis. And yet the issue has struggled to break through media spaces in the same way as it did over previous years. Over five hundred fleeing refugees lost their lives in the Mediterranean Sea over the first three months of 2018. Battles between armed factions in the country are ongoing. In August 2018, dozens of people were killed in Tripoli as a result of intense militia fighting. As a consequence, thousands of people became stranded without food or water.

Libya possesses the largest oil reserves in Africa and the tenth largest in the world. While corruption existed at the time of Gadaffi, since the vacuum left by his death, it now envelops the entire fabric of the country. Corrupt elements within the society exploit the fact that the dollar buys four times as many dinars at the black-market rate compared with the official one. Therefore, businessmen buy foreign goods and cash them at the illegal rate, meaning little is left for vital imports. Oil traders can also exploit this discrepancy, meaning the country obtains far less than it is due for its oil. As oil money vanishes into foreign bank accounts, Libya's economy shrinks further and further. After the initial intervention in 2011, France declared that it was *'fair and logical,'* for its corporations to benefit from the turmoil. Whilst ordinary people were thrown into devastation as a result of the harrowing civil war and Western intervention, companies and corporations such as BP, Total and Shell, rubbed their hands with glee.

We live today in a materialistic, profit-centred world, in which money, rather than human kindness, is the driving force for too many governments and leaders throughout the world. In order to protect national interest, parliamentarians over recent years have often used dehumanisation as a tactic to prevent the general public from identifying with the displaced and desperate. Dehumanisation subconsciously allows us to view the millions of refugees and asylum seekers not as equal human beings, with hopes and dreams and families, who deserve shelter and warmth and food, but simply as statistics. If our eyes are not consciously open to the reality that these people deserve the same as us, then we can continue to largely ignore their existence. We would not like our own families to be sacrificed as *'collateral damage,'* in bombing campaigns and wars conducted as a result of evidence that is scanty, at best. And yet we all allow and, in some cases, actively vote for our governments to engage in military campaigns abroad, despite the undeniable fact that most, if not all, of the campaigns conducted over the past two decades have resulted in nothing but failure, suffering and deepening global instability.

Dehumanisation comes in many forms. It comes in the form of David Cameron describing migrants in Calais as *'a swarm of people*[40].*'* Such a metaphor evokes in the imagination images of irritating pests circling around us, while we are desperately trying to swat them away. Why would we let such creatures enter our country willingly? It comes in the form of prominent journalists, such as Jennifer Hewett writing in *Financial Review* describing refugees as a *'horde*[41].*'* It comes in the form of Nigel Farage and UKIP's infamous billboard, as part of their Brexit campaign, depicting huge numbers of migrants, with the caption *"Breaking Point."* The implication was that our own quality of life would be diminished if we helped them, that far from having an obligation to help refugees, we should instead feel threatened by them, for they might steal away our jobs and our houses, along with our happiness.

Dehumanisation comes in other forms too. In September 2015, Ahmed Mohamed, a 14-year-old Texan schoolboy was arrested on suspicion of bringing a hoax bomb into his school. He had in fact reassembled the parts of a digital clock in a pencil container and had brought it in with the intention of impressing his teachers. Instead of seeing an intelligent, nerdy teenager wearing a NASA T-shirt, they wrongly chose, either consciously or subconsciously, to see a potential terrorist. Even after all the facts had been brought to light, certain prominent personalities, such as Richard Dawkins, decided to believe that Ahmed had deliberately concocted this hoax in order to get arrested and claim compensation. In one tweet, Dawkins likened Ahmed to a child soldier of ISIS, who was preparing to behead a Syrian soldier.

Due to the disproportionate barrage of anti-Muslim media coverage, the narrative that Muslims and in fact all people from the Muslim world have extremist tendencies, or are a threat to the West, has become pervasive. Subconsciously, the assumption, in a nutshell, is that all white people are innocent until proven guilty, or that as a group, white people are generally good, except for the few rotten apples within it. Conversely, when it comes to Muslims, or people of South Asian or Middle Eastern origin, the assumption is the opposite – that all are extremists, apart from the exceptions – the 'good Muslims.' This mentality has far-reaching implications. If as a collective we accept this narrative, then it becomes easier for us to also accept Western bombing campaigns or invasions. It becomes easier for us to forget about the half million children who died as a result of the Iraq war, or of the hundreds, or even thousands of Syrians killed as a result of Allied airstrikes.

Dehumanisation enables us as a society to deprive others of their human status and thus the rights that they are due. And yet all sections of society, even those in positions of relative privilege, demand their own rights and obsess over these rather than thinking

165

about fulfilling their obligations towards others. Thinking about our rights rather than our responsibilities causes great problems on a community, national and global level. It means that relatively few people are truly willing to sacrifice any of their own comforts for the sake of those needier, thus perpetuating the injustices and inequalities that our world currently faces.

Islam provides a solution to this. During the annual UK Peace Symposium hosted by the Ahmadiyya Muslim Community, the Khalifa suggested that *"people of the world should not only be concerned for their own rights, but should also look at their own obligations and be concerned for the welfare of others. This principle should apply at an individual level, a national level and an international level...without this any effort that takes place will only have a temporary effect and will not guarantee permanent peace."*

What the Khalifa is suggesting, in essence, is a shift in perspective. Instead of being content once our own rights have been provided, we should instead remember that our primary goal should be to discharge our own duties towards others. Their status in society or the colour of their skin is not important, rather our responsibility as humans, simply is to help other humans.

This concept constitutes the very core principles of Islam. People associate the religion with harshness, but this is only because it provides such comprehensive teachings regarding war conduct. In wartime Islam teaches courage, but total justice and no unnecessary loss of life. In peacetime, Islam teaches equity and kindness.

This can be illustrated beautifully from the sayings of the Prophet Muhammad, which constantly urge goodness, gentleness and compassion:

'Do you know what is better than charity and fasting and prayer? It is keeping peace and good relations between people, as quarrels and bad feelings destroy mankind.'

'Who is the most favoured of God? He, from whom the greatest good comes to His creatures.'

'The perfect Muslim is not a perfect Muslim, who eats till he is full and leaves his neighbours hungry.'

'The merciful are shown mercy by the All-Merciful. Show mercy to those on earth and God will show mercy to you.'

'Kindness is a mark of faith and whoever is not kind has no faith.'

'Son, if you are able, keep your heart from morning till night and from night till morning free from malice towards anyone. O my son! This is one of my laws and he who loves my laws verily loves me.'

Even from its very foundations, Islam humanised those who had been dehumanised by the society of the time. This can be demonstrated by its teachings on slavery, a practice which was commonplace and rife in 7th century Arabia. Some are unaware of the giant leaps Islam took to eradicate slavery and allegations are often raised as to why Islam did not simply free all slaves immediately. However, when analysed more deeply, the process by which the Prophet Muhammad liberated slaves was filled with deep wisdom and kindness.

The liberation that the Prophet desired for slaves was not simply a sudden declaration of freedom. Rather, he craved for them a genuine freedom – that they may possess the ability to stand on their own two feet after their release and attain the economic strength and respect from society to build a life for themselves. Such a process was only achievable in stages.

The first stage was to change the mindset of society. Instead of looking down to slaves, the Prophet encouraged slave-owners to view them with respect, dignity and even as equals. For a start, he abolished the sexual mistreatment of female slaves, which was ubiquitous in Arabia at the time. The Quran makes clear that using

167

female slaves for non-consensual sexual gratification is totally forbidden – *'...and force not your maids into unchaste life by keeping them unmarried if they desire to keep chaste, in order that you may seek the gain of the present life.'* Not only did the Prophet speak out against cruelty, he taught that slaves should be treated as though one would treat a close relative. It is narrated in a tradition that the Prophet would state *"Your slaves are your brethren. Hence, if an individual has a slave under his control, then he should feed him what he eats himself and he should clothe him with what he wears himself. Do not burden your slaves with a task that is beyond their capacity and if you do, then assist them in this task yourselves."* This teaching was implemented to the letter by the Prophet's followers. For instance, when shopping, Hadhrat Ali, one of the Prophet's closest companions, would buy two sets of the same clothing. When asked why, he replied that one set was for his slave and one for himself. The Prophet himself treated his slaves with such love that his own freed slave, Zaid bin Harithah, preferred to stay with him than return to live with his parents. Referring to the Prophet Muhammad, Zaid told his family, *"I am not the kind of person who would ever choose anyone in preference to him."*

With just this single teaching therefore, of treating slaves with decency, the Prophet enabled them to attain a kind of liberation even more prized than physical freedom. He endowed them with a genuine value and gave them a respect in the eyes of their owners.

The second stage was to physically free the slaves. As mentioned, the Prophet knew that freeing all the slaves immediately would create economic and social problems within the society, such that it would be difficult for these slaves to prosper and thrive in their communities. Therefore, he gave teachings such that they would be freed steadily, but not all at once. He taught that the freeing of a slave was a virtuous act, which would lead a person near to God. The Quran states: *'And what should make thee know what the ascent [of goodness] is? It is the freeing of a slave...'* Freeing a slave, according to Islam, would increase God's love for that person and

168

also constituted an action which could atone for past sins. According to the Quran: *'He who kills a believer by mistake shall free a believing slave and pay blood money to be handed over to his heirs...but whoso finds not one, then he shall fast for two consecutive months.'* Interestingly, despite slavery being widely prevalent in the society of the time, the verse provides provisions for those unable to find a slave. This indicates that Islam, from the very beginning, aimed to end the practice of slavery completely, eventually creating a time when there were no slaves left to free.

Moreover, in certain circumstances, the Prophet ordered that slaves must be released. For example, if a Muslim maltreated a slave in any small way, then the Prophet ordered that the slave be set free. If a slave turned out to be a relative, then freeing that slave became compulsory. During a solar eclipse, a slave had to be set free. Moreover, Islam initiated a system known as Muktabat, in which a master was obliged to free his slave if that slave was willing to work to buy his own freedom. This was a compulsory system, meaning essentially that whenever a slave desired freedom, the Prophet had provided a means for that freedom to be attained. On top of all of this, Islam forbade the taking of slaves under any circumstances, except as temporary prisoners during wars.

In 1861, Abraham Lincoln became the 16th President of a deeply fractured United States. The country was suffering during turbulent times and soon became embroiled in a civil war which threatened to tear it apart completely. The issue of slavery was largely the driving controversy which sparked the conflict between the loyalists of the Union in the North and the Confederates in the South, who advocated for the rights of individual states to uphold slavery. On January 1st 1863, Lincoln issued his famous Emancipation Proclamation and in doing so liberated several million enslaved individuals immediately. Following the war, the 13th amendment was passed into law, which abolished slavery entirely. To this day, the courage and nobility of Lincoln stands tall in the hearts of the world.

169

Hailed as a hero for the oppressed, he ensured that discrimination and prejudice were replaced by a new birth of freedom.

Fast forward a century and a half, however and the echoes of slavery in America still remain. Black people in America are still downtrodden, still the victims of large numbers of hate crimes. An average African-American household possesses just 6% of the wealth of a typical white household. Black people have far lower rates of home ownership than white people, graduate college at lower rates and have significantly higher rates of mortality. For much of the 20th century, many white people believed, perhaps accurately, that having a black family in a white neighbourhood would lower property prices in that area.

What Lincoln achieved was both commendable and heroic. However, even 150 years later, black individuals in America are still not treated equally in America. Why? Because even though black slaves had been legally freed, they were still bound by cultural chains of oppression. The hearts and minds of their slave-owners had not shifted and no legislation could wipe away their prejudices, which had been passed on through generations.

In contrast, the story of Bilal bears testament to the success of the Prophet Muhammad in liberating slaves, both physically and culturally. From a persecuted black slave, Bilal rose to a position of such heights that left many a tribal chief envious – all within the lifetime of the Prophet. The Prophet Muhammad granted him the honour of becoming the first Muezzin of Islam – the caller to prayer. For the past fourteen hundred years this call has been recited continuously in the world, five times each day from hundreds of thousands of mosques and homes across the globe.

Once, after the death of the Prophet Muhammad, during the spiritual leadership of Caliph Umar, a couple of high-ranking Arab chiefs came to see the Caliph. At the same time, Bilal and another ex-slave, Sohaib, had also arrived to see him. When the Caliph had been made aware of his visitors, he immediately called in Bilal and

Sohaib and left the Arab Chiefs outside, even though they had come slightly earlier. *"The slaves are admitted to audience while we, the nobles of Arabia, stay at the door,"* one of the Chiefs remarked. Another chief retorted, *"But who is to be blamed for this? The Messenger of God invited us all with one voice but we refused his call and offered severe resistance to him. On the other hand, these slaves came forward and made a positive response. It is their right now to get preference over us in this world and the next, we have no cause for complaint."*

Such an incident highlights the fact that Islam does not care for race or ethnicity or worldly status. Equality between all human beings is one of the hallmarks of the faith. In a famous saying, the Prophet Muhammad stated, *'God does not look at your forms and possessions but He looks at your hearts and your deeds.'*

Such a picture of Islam is rarely painted in the mainstream media, which often prefers to view Islam as a barbaric, merciless religion. When practised in its true, uncorrupted form, the faith is one which preaches equality and liberation of the oppressed and vulnerable. It humanises those who have become dehumanised and today there exist far too many whose voices the world has forgotten.

Britain has historically been a nation that has helped the vulnerable and protected the weak. However, some would argue that today it has lost its heart somewhat. In the past two years, the UK has only admitted 20 unaccompanied child refugees, despite the vast numbers of vulnerable children in conflict zones in North Africa and the Middle East. Sometimes it requires personal experiences to truly wake us up, to help us understand the true nature of the suffering that people today are consumed by, to help us see the faces amidst the facts and figures. Though most major philosophies and belief systems today, whether religious or secular, preach kindness and good treatment of others, what is required now, in these desperate times, is individuals and governments sacrificing their own comforts for the sake of justice and peace. In our globalised world, though patriotism – love for one's nation – is important, nationalism

171

– care for one's nation at the direct expense of others – is toxic to world peace. What is needed is for each of us to value our responsibilities over our rights and not let our inner prejudices lead us to discriminate or fail to help those in need around the world.

I occasionally take some time to look back at my life so far, at the progress and adventure and tests that I have faced, amidst a world in turmoil. As many across the world struggle with poverty, destitution, war and famine, I see myself lucky enough to be on a boat, relatively far away from the chaos of reality. However, from a distance I see the flood approaching. During this period of history, it approaches us all, no matter our wealth or fame or social status. Sometimes the flood of suffering and despair takes us in our childhoods, sometimes it leaves us for our later years. The flood comes in different forms. For Linh it was losing her family and being betrayed and trafficked. For hundreds of thousands of Syrians and Libyans and Iraqis, it comes in the form of losing one's home to the devastation of war. For Ahmadi Muslims in Pakistan, it comes in the form of religious persecution. For the Western world, it comes in the form of crippling mental health problems, which affect one in four people, or persistent poverty, which affects around 4 million of the UK population. Even more worryingly, the threat of war looms large, given the complex and persistent deterioration of the West's relationship with Russia. Since 2011, the Khalifa of the Ahmadiyya Community has been warning of the potential grave consequences of political and socio-economic injustices occurring across the world. In September 2013, the Khalifa delivered a Sermon in which he spoke of the Syrian crisis highlighting that the Syrian Crisis, which at that time was in its early stages, could be the flashpoint to the Third World War. A year earlier, the Khalifa wrote numerous open letters to the most powerful world leaders, expressing his concern that the world was falling headlong into a major catastrophe. To President Obama, for example, the Khalifa talked of *"using diplomacy, dialogue and wisdom,"* when negotiating with other nations, rather than using force to suppress them. *"A Third World War looms almost certainly before us,'* he continued. *'Such a war would surely involve atomic warfare; and therefore, we are witnessing the world head towards a terrifying destruction."*

At the time, many politicians and influential world figures dismissed the Khalifa's perspective as overly pessimistic. However, six years on and tensions between nations continue to augment. Fears of nuclear war have become mainstream, yet solutions still seem few and far between.

From an Ahmadi Muslim perspective, the solutions are simpler than one might expect. The Quranic concept of *"let not a people's enmity incite you to act otherwise than with justice,"*– a verse oft-repeated by the Khalifa, creates the perfect antidote to chaos. Without justice there can be no peace and even where others are acting with rancour and hatred, one most always remain committed to adhering to the principles of justice. Such a philosophy, as the Khalifa reminds his Community, applies to everyone – on an individual level, at the level of local society, and in the national and international spheres. Such an approach, the Khalifa argues, can be most reliably implemented through a sincere belief in a benevolent God and a relationship with Him, for it is only via such a mentality that people can feel truly accountable for their moral actions and choices.

When the world tumbles into the precipice and the flood engulfs it, only one thing can save us - a boat strong enough to withstand the onslaught. Part of the boat we build ourselves, with our own hands, our own efforts. We prepare for the flood, we ensure we have the resources and supplies to survive it, we anticipate its coming and learn skills to help us deal with the challenges we might face during and after it. We migrate to other parts of the world, if necessary.

However even the boat created through our own physical efforts can only get us so far. The reason that the Prophets of God were immune from the sufferings around them was because of their

173

spiritual status, their friendship with an All-Powerful Being who had revealed Himself to them as a result of their prayers, high moral strivings and pure natures. There are no atheists in foxholes, so to speak and so the Khalifa affirms that developing a relationship with God before the time of desperation is vital.

The analogy of the boat and the flood is not my own. In 1902, Mirza Ghulam Ahmad penned a book entitled *'Noah's Ark,'* in which he affirmed that sufferings and tribulations would occur aplenty in the subsequent two centuries and the key to personally avoiding them lay in boarding the 'ark,' and finding comfort and solace in God, the Ultimate Protector.

"Board this Noah's Ark," he urged. *"In the name of Allah is its course and its mooring. On this day, none can be saved from the decree of God, except by Him. It is only He who can show mercy."*

16. Hearts, Connected

Putney, UK. It was a cold December evening. Through the vicious darkness I walked towards a haven, a place of light amidst the bitterness of physical reality. As I walked towards the oldest mosque in London, I heard distant voices from the other direction of young people, shouting and screaming in their drunken delights. I thought then of who I had become, how not so long ago I was fighting the inner urge to try a life like theirs, of merriment and girls and freedom. Maybe I was missing something, I used to think. Maybe how they behave is necessary to get through the trials and sufferings of life. Perhaps escaping, just for a few hours, transcending one's problems and forgetting the deception of life, is what we must all do to survive. Now this kind of living appeared distant to me. I had come over the bridge of thorns and hurdles and could see a glimmer of light, which was enough to immerse me, making me forget about what I had left behind. When I had arrived at the gates of the mosque, my thoughts had scattered, leaving my mind completely focused on what I was about to do, on the promise which that evening had made me. I was taken into a waiting room, with crimson red carpets and historic photos displayed across the walls. I sat for the next hour, composing myself, waiting for my turn to meet the Khalifa.

I had wanted to wait until I felt totally pure before meeting him, to be spiritually ready to face him. But it had been twelve years since his appointment to the post of Worldwide Head of the Ahmadiyya Muslim Community and still I had never organised a meeting with him, even though it was easy to do so. The longer I waited the more embarrassed I felt to do it, since I figured he would wonder why I

175

hadn't met him earlier. Maybe he would question my commitment to my faith. Maybe my lack of presence at his door would mean he felt I was weak, disinterested. Anyhow, how would he know I hadn't met him before? After all, this was a man who meets dozens of families every single day. For all he knew, I could just have been someone he had forgotten.

My name was called and with my heart pounding I made my way to the front of the waiting room. I was ushered left, where a guard stood next to a door. He opened the door for me and I was in another room, the room of the Khalifa's staff. I was told to wait and I sat again. Around me was the noise of typists typing and printers whirring, but at that moment I noticed none of it. Racing past my soul I saw flashes of my life. Images of my past carved through me and I sought to compose myself once more. I would count to ten, I told myself and by then it would be time to enter the Khalifa's office.

One...

3am on a chilly November night. Standing outside my flat, shivering, wondering when the screeching fire alarm will stop, when the fire services will arrive. My flatmates bring our sofa outside and they sit, yawning, weary. I am fully alert, euphoric, after having been praying for the past half hour, the flames of my soul erupting from inside me. I am generally happiest in the dead of night, just me and my Creator, the silence stirring up a spiritual atmosphere which penetrated through me. I need to pray, anyhow. My new independent university existence has thrown me hundreds of questions. How am I to live in circumstances in which the morality of my faith contradicts the expectations of university life? Could religion and spirituality, provide me with the key to lasting contentment? I feel good when I pray, but is a euphoric feeling the same as proof of His existence? The questions scream out in my mind, with the same shrillness and intensity as the fire alarm deafening me at that moment.

Two...

176

The Khalifa is the ultimate snake-catcher, I sometimes think. Imploring us to do good, to act kindly, to serve humanity and to rid ourselves of the devilish snakes which can otherwise sit inside, consume us, become us. I spend my evenings listening to dozens of hours of his question and answer sessions and speeches, attempting to get to the bottom of the true nature of faith.

Three...

I meet Zeeshan for the first time at the end of my first year in a coffee shop on a corner of campus. He is a reserved, tall Pakistani-born boy, slightly older than me. I catch his eye and he stands and comes towards me. We sit for hours and we make progress, discussing how this society will be set up, how we will manage the finances and manage resources and how we can entice people to join our group, people who will discuss and debate with us, people whose minds we can open and who can open ours. Over the next few weeks and months the two of us get to work and by Christmas the Ahmadiyya Muslim Students Association (AMSA) is officially established.

Four...

I reflect one evening about the thing that most appeals to me about Islam - the that there exists no monopoly on salvation. People of all faiths and none can become loved-ones of God and attain paradise. Reaching heaven depends not upon the faith that a person claims to profess, but rather upon one's environment, upbringing, personal circumstances, actions and deeds and the extent to which they followed their conscience. Only God knows a person's heart and so no-one has the right to condemn another. The Prophet Muhammad once reported a story which conveyed that even those perceived by society as the least moral individuals can, in an instant, become immensely loved by God. *"There was a dog moving around a well whom thirst would have killed. Suddenly a prostitute happened to see it and drew water in her shoe and made it drink, and all her sins were pardoned because of this."*

Five...

One night I dream that I am in my grandparents' house. We are all there, my parents, brothers, aunts, uncles, cousins, gathered together from different parts of South England. All are present except my grandmother, a noticeable absentee from her own home. It is a Sunday and I know in my dream that this is the second consecutive day that we were all congregating. I see my grandfather outside, by the front gates of the house and I walk outside to join him. Suddenly I feel a flurry of excitement. *The Messiah himself, Mirza Ghulam Ahmad, is approaching our house.* I see him then, on foot with a companion on each side, walking swiftly and gracefully into the broad, open, front driveway. He looks glowing, evoking a sense of awe in my heart, his spiritual luminance brighter than the afternoon sun. I am too shy to approach him, but seeing my grandfather confidently stride and shake his hand encourages me to take a step closer. There is commotion behind me, people's hands outstretched, desperate for this man to come nearer to them. The last hand he shakes is mine, just as I start to think that my lack of boldness would cost me. As he shakes my hand he holds it, for one second, two seconds, three. My heart dances then, with a colour and a light and an electricity that I have never experienced before. He moves on then, going inside the house as I desperately rush to keep up with him.

As I enter the front hall I realise I have lost him. It is a large house and I rush around every downstairs room to try and find him, but to no avail. In my temporary foolishness and panic I start to wonder whether he has just disappeared, or teleported. Finally I hear voices from the one room I had forgotten – the lounge only reserved for important guests or for major gatherings. With my ear to the door, I hear my grandfather talk about some of his past memories and recollections and I ascertain that he is showing Ahmad some old photographs, displayed on the shelf of the lounge. I realise why Ahmad is here. It is to express his condolences following the passing away of my grandmother.

178

Six...

She has had dementia for years, slowly but steadily declining, but despite no physical signs of it at present, I take this dream to be a sign that her remaining days may be few in number. I pray for her then, ardently and intensely, but after a couple of weeks, as the effects of the dream begin to reduce in my mind, the prayers become less frequent. One night, around four weeks later, I awaken to the voice of my mother in my mind. In this dream she is frantically telling me, *pray for your grandmother, she is dying.*

Less than a month later, my grandmother passes away, in her own home on a chilly February Sunday. All our extended family are there, as they were the day before. Every detail matches my dream two months earlier. She had deteriorated rapidly and suddenly, with little prior clinical indication. We feel not despair, only the sensation of wounded hearts and aching souls. This is the first time I have seen Death, but I am fortunate for I see it not in its brutality or its power or its madness, as Ummad was forced to witness. Today I see the beauty of Death. Its ability to end suffering after a long illness. Its relief. Its hope. We ride these waves of consolation amidst our sadness.

Seven...

I help organise the AMSA Student Retreat, an event held for Ahmadi Muslim university-age individuals in a picturesque lodge in the middle of the countryside. We discuss sports and politics and religion and life. We discuss the bridge between faith and earth. The final session is held outdoors, underneath the fiery summer sun. The grass is freshly cut, with a gentle sprinkling of brown leaves resting on the verdant paths. I get elected then, as the new National President of the Students Association. For years I have tried to avoid being the snake. Now I must attempt to become a snake-catcher.

Eight...

October Year 6:

179

Catherine is my inter-faith buddy. A Catholic Geography student with a passion for finding unity in a divided world, we team up seamlessly. We know each other only for one year – the final one of our University lives. Our greatest success is organising Speedfaithing events, open to any and all students on campus. A concept which became popular in America, I try to promote it on Facebook by giving it an enticing and mysterious description:

"Ever wanted to explore the beliefs and worldviews of others? To discuss and share your own perspectives on the big questions? To understand and unite with those of differing faiths, amidst a world consumed by conflict?

You've heard of Speed Dating, now try...Speedfaithing! A unique event in which participants have a series of one-to-one discussions to explain and answer questions about their faith, or lack of faith and delve into the belief systems of their opposite number.

With a time limit on each round of conversations, this event enables each individual to encounter numerous different thoughts, perspectives and ideas. Misconceptions, stereotypes and stigmas can be clarified and bridges built, such that each participant can leave with an expanded mind and new friends.

What will you discover?"

A pale full moon hangs vastly in the evening sky, travelling with me as I walk to the first speedfaithing event, wondering how successful it will be. Whether anyone else will even turn up.

People come. Of all faiths and none, conveying powerful snapshots of their spiritual experiences, providing islands of hope and optimism amidst the oceans of divisiveness and fear that circulate in our world. I hear stories about people's identities, their insecurities, their doubts. Some feel connected through their faith and spirituality, others feel anxious and alone, trying to juggle their *various disparate cultural influences, living under the bustling city lights, belonging everywhere and yet nowhere.*

In order to understand the deeper elements of life, I have travelled to Cathedrals and Gurdwaras, to the ruins of old religious sites, to holy sites through barren deserts, watching wild camels traipsing across the distant wilderness. In this single evening, however, our numerous profound, meaningful conversations teach me more about the impact of faith on real people. I learn that in our own individual ways, we all crave peaceful, pluralistic societies free from intolerance or prejudice. I learn that one of the keys to this is empathy and it is only through dialogue that we can emerge from the wreckage and live harmoniously.

Nine...

It all starts to slip away. Soon memories begin to fade from my mind, but the imprint of all those moments are still left upon my heart; a mark upon my soul. Like in my dream, I try and reflect further, but the more I am pressed to, the less I can remember. Only the most recent events remain in my mind, everything else goes. This, I realise, is why being kind to others is the most important thing. It is because everything else eventually disappears, becoming a blur, a haziness. It is only our actions and our morals which stay with us, in our hearts and souls, as sparkles or as blights. Each action we perform influences the next and the next and so on. All of us have both, I realise. We are capable of the greatest goodness and the most horrific evils. Who are we, as human beings, except consumed by paradoxes? We are the light and we are the darkness. We are the morning breeze and we are the violent storm. We are the snake-catchers and we are the snakes.

Ten. I returned to the room with a silent gasp as I heard my name called from just in front of me. The man guarding the next door, the door to the Khalifa's office was beckoning me towards him and as I approached he opened it. With eyes that danced and twinkled in wonder, I saw a sight I would never forget. Sat down a few metres

181

away from me was a man glowing with spiritual radiance. It was he. Walking towards his outstretched hand, I was unable to say a word. His elegant, black kameez contrasted with his wonderous white beard and sparkling turban.

I shook his hand and he held it for a while, his gaze directed at me. He spoke to me in Urdu then, confirming my name. *"This is your first time here,"* he said immediately thereafter. It was not a question, it was a statement of confidence and my mind was left awestruck, if not slightly disappointed by the fact he knew. He told me to sit then, opposite him and for the next ten minutes time stood still as we spoke to each other. It felt like home. I had arrived at a point on my spiritual journey which felt like the promised land, shaded and protected from the darkness of inner turmoil. The Khalifa's office felt like a fortress, a Noah's ark, which was immune from deception or immorality or betrayal. It was just myself and him and I felt myself acutely aware that I was sitting in a place that many in faraway lands were yearning that they could one day sit. I was talking to a man that people dream of, a man who offers a sanctuary through his words and his prayers.

Two main things struck me about my meeting with the Khalifa. The first was his memory. Within three minutes of my meeting, he established various members of my extended family, reeling off the names of various of my cousins and uncles and grandparents. The second thing that struck me was his love. It consumed me from the moment I entered to long after I had left. It was unlike any love I had ever felt. I was a stranger to him and yet within a second I felt as though I was his favourite, as though he was thinking of no-one except me. It was a strange feeling, for most often love is displayed through actions or words. His love however reverberated through the air, a powerful magnetic force that drew us together and bound our souls.

July – Year 6:

182

All three of them, James, Holly and Hassan are staying here to work as doctors, in this university city we have called home for the past half-dozen years, while I move on to pastures new. There will be new people, new challenges, however my time here has given me tools to deal with much more than I could when I arrived. The sun shines high, lighting up the windows of the University Great Hall as four hundred new doctors become qualified. We recite the Hippocratic Oath in unison – our pledge to protect patients, to do no harm, to care for others in the best way we can. We step outside then, greeted by the sight of marquees with refreshments, photographers taking snaps, lecturers beaming as they catch sight of us, parents searching for their sons or daughters and the gleaming blue sky etched above us with a permanence, a beauty. The world slows down in front of us, like a haze. This day has a kind of permanence about it too. And like the cloudless summer sky our minds are clear, carefree, untroubled, at this time neither knowing nor worrying about what the next chapters of our lives will bring.

As I look back at the clock tower for the last time, walking away from the city at the end of the day, the scenery of the university etched in front of me like a picture book, I reflect on the main challenges we have faced over the past six years. Holly's involved witnessing the journey of life and death, from a shaking student to a confident doctor. Her transformation is complete – she has a cool head, a sharp mind, an ability to find solutions when all around her is chaotic and a newfound love for acute medicine, the speciality she hopes to ultimately work in. James's major challenge was negotiating the world of relationships, with girls and with God, not knowing what he would find, constantly learning, discovering. His search still goes on. Hassan had to grow up earlier than us, bearing the responsibility of a family, leaving medical school not just with a degree, but also with a wife and one-year old daughter. He, like me, navigated the world of university living as a Muslim and came out the other side a more confident, assured person.

Indeed, what binds us all as human beings is the fact that we all have our own demons, our own struggles, goals, problems. Like clouds drifting across the sky, each of our own lives is about a slow, steady journey, to find ourselves, who we really are, and to find and connect with one another.

What began for me as a personal identity crisis turned into a deep quest to try and discover the true meaning of life, the nature of reality. Over the course of this journey I discovered different ways of thinking, different temptations, different worlds.

The culmination of that quest led me to the conclusion that Islam is not a burden, but rather acts as a source to bear one's burdens and provide the respite, escape and fulfilment required in life.

Attacks on religion today come in numerous different forms, many self-inflicted by so-called religious people themselves. Religion must be rational, it must be reasonable and it must be in accord with the human conscience.

Following a religion, particularly in today's age, is no easy business. This is the reality, the uncomfortable truth. Almost anyone can follow a belief system in a way that suits them – skipping over the difficult parts and ignoring the aspects that require hard work or sacrifice. We are all guilty of this to some degree or another. Over my journey throughout University I have discovered that one of the keys to inner contentment is to understand who you truly are, to move away from that bridge of uncertainty and find a side to dwell, preferably one that also entails benefiting the world at large. I am a young British person, and I made the choice to be a young British Muslim. I did this because Islam provides a complete code on how to live, claiming to come from a Divine source. I tested this concept of a Deity, both subjectively and objectively, through both reason and through spirituality and found myself convinced. I discovered a large group of other young British Muslims, from the Ahmadiyya

Community who, inspired by their faith, live life altruistically. I established that the ills and misfortunes of society were addressed by this belief system and that despite the terror that the mention of 'Islam' evokes in the hearts of many today, its reality is vastly different, vastly more peaceful, vastly more beneficial. I realised that one of the keys to world peace today is for people to just understand Islam a little – so that when they see ordinary Muslims they can feel empathy and not mistrust, so that when terrorists commit atrocities, society's default position does not become one of hatred and division towards innocent members of the community or nation.

I am of a similar age to Salman Abedi, Michael Adebolajo and to other Muslim extremists who have committed the most horrific atrocities on British soil this century. As their faces and their heinous words are plastered across television screens and newspapers, it is easy to know what is in their minds. Hatred, confusion, animosity. It is more difficult to understand what is in the minds of ordinary Muslims who walk the UK streets day to day. Perhaps this is why society views them with suspicion.

This book is my mind. Each chapter is like different groups of neurones at different stages of my early adult life, firing, processing, connecting. Passing through the window of my consciousness I have seen the strong, the humble, the helpless and lost. Each experience builds the overall picture and before long the mist from the glass begins to clear and through this window I start to see the kind of life worth living, the kinds of personal values worth protecting. At times the road is isolated, for, in the words of Rumi, *"whoever is parted from one who speaks his language becomes dumb, though he have a hundred songs. When the rose is gone and the garden faded, you will hear no more the nightingale's story."* The road has only the concrete greyness, the watching trees and the encompassing silence of the starlit darkness.

After all, finding a contented heart is like searching for a perfect view. You can imagine it in your mind, so vivid, clear. You know how it must look, how it must feel, but you know that you must

185

struggle to get there, starting from the darkest of roads. Climbing to the top of snow-capped mountains, crawling across glaciers of ice, plunging into seas of coral - at times the view seems as close as your fingertips, at others as far away as the moon. The best views, like the most contented of hearts, are found after the greatest of strivings. And when you finally reach them, there are no nasty surprises, no bitterness or deceptions. The search is always worthwhile, because the end result stays with you for a lifetime.

And then, one day, you meet someone who has seen a view even more spectacular than you have. He has beaten perfection with a greater perfection and then you start striving again, your journey continuing. Except this time there is less pain, only joy, excitement, the longing to see and feel a beauty of transcendence, a part of infinity. This is life, this is all it is. And perhaps even after life, we enter a greater reality, with hearts and souls of even greater capacity for love, for contentment, for peace. And our striving continues even then. Each of us has our own strivings, our own songs.

The Khalifa reminds his young followers during a UK Ahmadiyya Youth event in the Surrey countryside of the need to create a view of beauty, not simply for themselves but for the world at large. His speech highlights the fact that his Community live as integrated citizens, but also in a world very different from much of society:

"You should be the ones who work day and night to refute those who defame Islam's name. You should be the ones who are at the forefront of spreading the enlightened teachings of Islam far and wide so that we come to see that blessed day where the world unites under the banner of the Holy Prophet, Muhammad peace be upon him. You should be the ones who fulfill your pledge of being ever ready to sacrifice everything for the sake of your faith. Only then will you be playing your role in bringing about a spiritual revolution in the world...only then will we see the dark clouds of today begin to part, replaced by an emergent blue sky. For this great task you must be ever ready and ever willing, until your last breath. This task shall

186

remain with you every day that you walk upon this earth. It is the single greatest purpose of your lives."

A few dozen pages ago this concept, of striving, or Jihad, for the cause of Islam, may have seemed like a call to war, whereas the reality is immeasurably different. Islam is peace, it is love. It is common human experience that love towards another enables a person to make sacrifices and do good actions for the sake of that which one loves. The Khalifa tells his young followers to worship God, the ultimate beneficent Being, so that they can be truly able to love human beings, who were created by that same God.

The aim of this book has been to provide a perspective – an insight into the mind of an individual. By doing so, it has aimed to bring to light important facets of today's world and highlight that each of us has an identity, a story, a soul. Numerous individuals have committed atrocities in the name of religion over recent years. Subsequently media stories have continually woven the narrative of Muslim men typically being dangerous extremists, of Muslim women typically being backward and oppressed and Islam itself as being a threat to a progressive, advancing, pluralistic society that most of us aspire to live in. This book has attempted to demonstrate that even though certain Muslims commit heinous crimes, the religion of Islam is neither dangerous, nor oppressive, nor at odds with positive Western values.

I have spent my whole life in Britain and most of my friends have been white, liberal-minded atheists or agnostics. This country has afforded me with the opportunity to live the dream, in a sense, and now I have just started work as a junior doctor in the National Health Service. I have faced little to no obvious discrimination, nor been harassed or abused because of my faith or ethnicity. In fact, my beliefs, opinions and ideas about the world and the purpose of life, have intrigued and interested my friends and university colleagues and through mutual discussion, we have opened each other's minds

187

and enriched each other's lives through articulation of our differences. This has been the beauty of Britain, yet today we stand at a crossroads. To ensure that this beauty continues to manifest itself for generations to come, we must keep listening to each other, keep respecting each other and not let deranged 'Islamic' terrorists or the tabloid media drive us all apart.

Today, it is not just fear of Islam that is on the rise, but also xenophobia, misogyny and antisemitism. What we must remember is that regardless of our ethnicities or belief systems, we all have our own identities, forged by our genes, our parents and our societies. Beneath our masks or our accents or our veils we are all people – living, breathing, feeling. Every which way we act towards one another determines whether our society turns into one of peace and pluralism, or one of hatred and bitterness.

The world is like a snowy mountain. Beautiful from a distance, but often cold and bitter in reality. If we be kind to one another, make each other that little bit warmer, insulate each other from the frosty ice of division, maybe the mountain can become lusher, more life-giving, more hospitable. Like a shout from a mountain, each of our actions creates an echo, which travels across space and across time, through cultures and languages and races. If we know a thousand people in our lifetimes and each of them know a thousand, that makes all of us one person away from a million and two away from a billion. We are truly a global village and the echoes of love or of hatred which we decide to create ultimately reverberate back to us.

This book has also aimed to demonstrate that to be a peaceful, law-abiding, pluralistic Muslim does not mean that certain Quranic teachings have to be ignored or discarded. Rather there are tens, perhaps hundreds of millions of Muslims around the world who love their faith with all their hearts, but also love their fellow human beings of all faiths and none. They love their communities and cities and nations. Their love for others is embedded deep inside their hearts and comes from a deep-rooted connection with a Creator on whom they rely on for sustenance, for guidance, for help in the

188

darkest moments. They possess a love for their Creator so profound that they are willing to make personal sacrifices for His sake. They are willing to control their desires, passions and harmful emotions such that others may not be harmed by their actions. Everyone has a breaking point, but these people try to become capable of maintaining their morality even in the midst of extensive hardships and personal suffering. Through the Quran they see the wisdom and kindness of God. Through the Prophet Muhammad and all the other Prophets, they see God's beauty and mercy. Through the sun and the moon and the stars and the galaxies, which dance and twinkle light-years above us, they see His majesty, His omnipotence, His power. Through their own hearts and their own experiences and the personal miracles that unfold before their eyes, they hear His whisper, amidst the storm of the world. He speaks softly, at first. But before long that whisper becomes a voice and the voice becomes a friend and that friend, all-Powerful, envelops their souls and delights them, over and over. This is Islam, not a religion of hate or injustice, but one that aims to bind human beings together in love and connect man to God.

In times of political upheaval, the threat of nuclear war, global warming and huge levels of mental health problems, many lie lost, wondering how to fill the individual and societal void that devours them. Even if not lost, we all seek greater meaning in our lives, a transcendence that can enable us to escape from the bitterness and deception of materialism and of consumerism. We live in a world in which each of us are, throughout our lives, treated like mere brains, like information-guzzling machines, defined only by our material productivity. Ultimately, while beneficial to the society in some respects, this attitude is not compatible with a genuine and lasting contentment and happiness. Alcohol provides temporary escapism, but in recent years, shunning it has become mainstream among young people, a third of whom, according to a study of 10,000 16 to 24-year olds, are now teetotal. [34] Other methods of achieving satisfaction and contentment have grown and flourished over the past decade in Britain, most notably mindfulness, an ancient Eastern

189

concept which now forms part of psychological therapies, prison-programs and educational institutions. It aims to provide tools to people such that they can better cope with the difficult emotions they might face on a day-to-day basis and allow them to find peace in a hectic world. On a similar line, numerous Westerners describe themselves as 'spiritual but not religious.' After all, many crave for the comforts, contentment, hope and divinity which faith can bring them, but are disillusioned by organised religion, viewing it as burdensome or corrupt.

It is ingrained in human nature to seek something to 'worship.' Islam reminds us, however, that ultimately, the worship of anything except God will only lead to disappointment. Islam conveys the message, present from the beginnings of human history, to put all trust and love in God. Everything in this world is transitory and everything will perish but He. Moreover, only in completely loving God, the ultimate beneficent being, can we learn to be completely moral ourselves in imitation of Him. Through morality and striving for kindness, the urge for personal fulfilment and inner peace can be found.

As media furore continues to circulate around Islam and Muslims, ultimately people will start to see through the false narrative that terrorists and extremists truly represent Islam. Rather many will start to see the benefits that the faith can provide on an individual and a societal level. As materialistic objects, cultural fads and political revolutions come and go, ultimately it may be the return of organised religion, but this time in its purest, most rational form that can fill the void of society.

Whatever the future may hold, and whatever people's beliefs or perspectives, in a world where universal sympathy grows, souls will be able to sing songs once more, and emerge anew with light and with life.

Acknowledgements

Foremost, I am grateful to God Almighty for His mercy and beneficence, and granting me the opportunity to write this book. I thank the Holy Prophet Muhammad (peace be upon him) and his servant in this age, the Messiah Mirza Ghulam Ahmad. My gratitude to His holiness Mirza Masroor Ahmad, the current Khalifa of the Ahmadiyya Muslim Community, for his guidance, prayers and compassion.

I thank my parents for their unending support, and my brothers Humza and Zayn for being among my very first readers.

My thanks also go to those who kindly agreed to provide their insight and guidance to this work. These include: Jamal Akbar, Athar Warraich, Umar Bhatti and Hashim Nasser, Taha Nasser and Tahir Nasser. And a special mention to my cousin Umar Nasser for his guidance during this endeavour.

My special appreciation is also to those mentioned in this book – those such as Ummad Farooq, who have given me permission to tell their stories, and my university friends and colleagues with whom I have shared some wonderful years.

My final thanks are to you, the reader, for your time, and I hope you found this a worthwhile read.

About the Author

Damir Musa Rafi was born in Newcastle-Upon-Tyne, UK in 1993. He completed his grammar school in London and his undergraduate studies in the West Midlands - graduating as a medical doctor from the University of Birmingham in 2018. He now works as a junior doctor in East Kent, and hopes to ultimately become a psychiatrist.

Damir is a member of the Ahmadiyya Muslim Community, and during his University years was an active member - and for two years the National President - of the Ahmadiyya Muslim Students Association, organising a wide range of interfaith dialogues and discussions. He has been a contributor to media outlets including the Huffington Post and the Independent. He is currently the blog editor of Rational Religion, a website which aims to make sense of spirituality, tackling the big questions with a light touch. Damir enjoys sports, and is an avid squash and tennis player.

References:

1. Rafi, D. (2017). *I'm a British Muslim the same age as the London terrorists - I know why we turned out so differently*. [online] The Independent. Available at: https://www.independent.co.uk/voices/london-bridge-terrorist-attackers-british-muslim-man-islam-saudi-mosques-wahhabi-different-a7775116.html [Accessed 18 Feb. 2019].

2. Farron, T. (n.d.). *Liberalism has eaten itself - it isn't very liberal any more | Tim Farron*. [online] the Guardian. Available at: https://www.theguardian.com/commentisfree/2017/nov/28/liberalism-eaten-itself-british-religious-liberty-christianity-tim-farron [Accessed 18 Feb. 2019].

3. Khazan, O. (2012). *Charlie Hebdo cartoons spark debate over free speech and Islamophobia.* [online] https://www.washingtonpost.com/blogs/blogpost/post/charlie-hebdo-cartoons-spark-debate-over-free-speech-and-islamophobia/2012/09/19/4b3ba988-026b-11e2-9b24-ff730c7f6312_blog.html?utm_term=.febfc6a36f46. Available at: https://www.washingtonpost.com/blogs/blogpost/post/charlie-hebdo-cartoons-spark-debate-over-free-speech-and-islamophobia/2012/09/19/4b3ba988-026b-11e2-9b24-ff730c7f6312_blog.html?utm_term=.febfc6a36f46 [Accessed 5 Feb. 2019].

4. Jyllands-posten.dk. (2008). *The Cartoon Crisis - how it unfolded.* [online] Available at: https://jyllands-posten.dk/international/ECE3931398/The-Cartoon-Crisis-%E2%80%93-how-it-unfolded/ [Accessed 18 Feb. 2019].

5. The Independent. (2006). *Leading article: A right that comes with a moral responsibility.* [online] Available at: https://www.independent.co.uk/voices/editorials/leading-article-a-right-that-comes-with-a-moral-responsibility-6109588.html [Accessed 18 Feb. 2019].

6. Edition.cnn.com. (2010). *French Senate approves burqa ban - CNN.com.* [online] Available at: http://edition.cnn.com/2010/WORLD/europe/09/14/france.burqa.ban/index.html [Accessed 18 Feb. 2019].

7. Nardelli, A. (2015). *From margins to mainstream: the rapid shift in French public opinion.* [online] the Guardian. Available at: https://www.theguardian.com/world/datablog/2015/jan/08/french-public-opinion-charlie-hebdo-attacks [Accessed 18 Feb. 2019].

8. BBC News. (2015). *Charlie Hebdo attack: Three days of terror.* [online] Available at: https://www.bbc.co.uk/news/world-europe-30708237 [Accessed 18 Feb. 2019].

9. Ahmad, M. (1989). *The Philosophy of the Teachings of Islam.* Tilford: Islam International, p.141.

10. Pengelly, M. (2015). *Ben Carson says no Muslim should ever become US president.* [online] the Guardian. Available at: https://www.theguardian.com/us-news/2015/sep/20/ben-carson-no-muslim-us-president-trump-obama [Accessed 18 Feb. 2019].

11. The Independent. (2018). *Third of British people believe there are Muslim 'no-go areas' in UK governed by sharia law.* [online] Available at: https://www.independent.co.uk/news/uk/home-news/uk-no-go-zones-

muslim-sharia-law-third-poll-hope-not-hate-far-right-economic-inequality-a8588226.html [Accessed 18 Feb. 2019].

12. Express.co.uk. (2016). *SHOCK POLL: Four in ten British Muslims want some aspect of Sharia Law enforced in UK.* [online] Available at: https://www.express.co.uk/news/uk/738852/British-Muslims-Sharia-Law-enforced-UK-Islam-poll [Accessed 18 Feb. 2019].

13. Muslims for Peace. (n.d.). *The Covenant.* [online] Available at: http://www.muslimsforpeace.org/holy_prophet/the-covenant/ [Accessed 18 Feb. 2019].

14. Ahmad, M. (1992). [online] Alislam.org. Available at: https://www.alislam.org/library/books/Religion-Politics-in-Islam.pdf [Accessed 18 Feb. 2019].

15. Sky News. (2018). *Boris Johnson mocks women in burkas who 'look like bank robbers'.* [online] Available at: https://news.sky.com/story/boris-johnson-mocks-women-in-burkas-who-look-like-bank-robbers-11463209 [Accessed 18 Feb. 2019].

16. Rapecrisis.org.uk. (n.d.). *Statistics - Sexual Violence / Rape Crisis England & Wales.* [online] Available at: https://rapecrisis.org.uk/get-informed/about-sexual-violence/statistics-sexual-violence/ [Accessed 18 Feb. 2019].

17. Halliday, J. and Dodd, V. (2013). *Lee Rigby killing: two British Muslim converts convicted of murder.* [online] the Guardian. Available at: https://www.theguardian.com/uk-news/2013/dec/19/lee-rigby-killing-woolwich-verdict-convicted-murder [Accessed 18 Feb. 2019].

18. BBC News. (2013). *Murder sparks anti-Muslim backlash.* [online] Available at: https://www.bbc.co.uk/news/uk-22664835 [Accessed 18 Feb. 2019].

19. Blair, T. (2013). *The Trouble Within Islam / by Tony Blair.* [online] Project Syndicate. Available at: https://www.project-syndicate.org/commentary/lee-rigby-and-the-struggle-to-contain-violent-islamists-by-tony-blair [Accessed 18 Feb. 2019].

20. Travis, A. (2008). *MI5 report challenges views on terrorism in Britain.* [online] the Guardian. Available at: https://www.theguardian.com/uk/2008/aug/20/uksecurity.terrorism1 [Accessed 18 Feb. 2019].

21. Rushchenko, J. (2017). *Converts to Islam and Home Grown Jihadism.* [online] Henryjacksonsociety.org. Available at: http://henryjacksonsociety.org/wp-content/uploads/2017/10/HJS-Converts-to-Islam-Report-web.pdf [Accessed 18 Feb. 2019].

22. Gulam, H. (2019). *Islam, Law and War.* [online] Classic.austlii.edu.au. Available at: http://classic.austlii.edu.au/au/journals/UNELawJl/2006/12.pdf [Accessed 18 Feb. 2019].

23. van Rij, A. and Wilkinson, B. (2018). *Security Cooperation with Saudi Arabia: Is it Worth it for the UK?.* [online] Kcl.ac.uk. Available at: https://www.kcl.ac.uk/sspp/policy-institute/publications/uk-saudi-arabia-security.pdf [Accessed 18 Feb. 2019].

24. The Irish Times. (2017). *Saudi Arabia largest funder of extremism in UK, report finds.* [online] Available at:

https://www.irishtimes.com/news/world/uk/saudi-arabia-largest-funder-of-extremism-in-uk-report-finds-1.3144020 [Accessed 18 Feb. 2019]. The Irish Times. (2017). *Saudi Arabia largest funder of extremism in UK, report finds.* [online] Available at: https://www.irishtimes.com/news/world/uk/saudi-arabia-largest-funder-of-extremism-in-uk-report-finds-1.3144020 [Accessed 18 Feb. 2019].

25. Rūmī, J. (1265). *Masnavi-ye Manavi, bk iii.*

26. YouTube. (n.d.). *If I Met God After Death.* [online] Available at: https://www.youtube.com/watch?v=TLL8o01SXZQ [Accessed 18 Feb. 2019].

27. Higgins, G. (1829). *Apology for Mohamed.* London, p.ixxi.

28 Tirmidhi, Zuhd. (n.d.), 60.

29. Mishkat, Kitab al-'Ilm; Kanz al-'Ummal, 6:43. (n.d.). pp.6:43.

30. Shah, Z. (2014). *Prophecies related to the coming of The Promised Messiah in all world religions.* [online] The Muslim Times. Available at: https://themuslimtimes.info/2014/07/26/prophecies-related-to-the-coming-of-the-promised-messiah-in-all-world-religions-part-2/ [Accessed 18 Feb. 2019].

31. Janam Sakhi. (n.d.). p.527.

32. Sahih Bukhari, Kitab-al Tafseer. (n.d.). .

33. Salafī, '. (2010). *Description of Paradise in the Glorious Qur'an.* Riyadh: Darussalam.

34. the Guardian. (2018). *Nearly 30% of young people in England do not drink, study finds.* [online] Available at: https://www.theguardian.com/society/2018/oct/10/young-people-drinking-alcohol-study-england [Accessed 18 Feb. 2019].

35. YouTube. (2018). *Jordan Peterson debate on the gender pay gap, campus protests and postmodernism.* [online] Available at: https://www.youtube.com/watch?v=aMcjxSThD54 [Accessed 18 Feb. 2019].

36. YouTube. (n.d.). *Richard Dawkins in conversation with Peter Boghossian.* [online] Available at: https://www.youtube.com/watch?v=qNcC866sm7s [Accessed 18 Feb. 2019].

37. YouTube. (2015). *"Atheism or Belief: Which is Evidence Based?" A Dialogue with Dr Arif Ahmed and Ayyaz Mahmood Khan.* [online] Available at: https://www.youtube.com/watch?v=cn9YnVS0vqs&t=2623s [Accessed 18 Feb. 2019].

38. Alislam.org. (n.d.). [online] Available at: https://www.alislam.org/topics/khilafat/dreams.pdf [Accessed 18 Feb. 2019].

39. Basit, A. (2018). *Huzoor's Recollections of April 2003 (English translation).* [online] Weekly English Newspaper | alhakam. Available at: http://www.alhakam.org/huzoors-recollections-april-2003-english-translation [Accessed 19 Feb. 2019].

40. Elgot, J. and Taylor, M. (2015). *Calais crisis: Cameron condemned for 'dehumanising' description of migrants*. [online] the Guardian. Available at: https://www.theguardian.com/uk-news/2015/jul/30/david-cameron-migrant-swarm-language-condemned [Accessed 18 Feb. 2019].

41. Hewett, J. (2019). *Refugee crisis: horde will test European Union*. [online] Australian Financial Review. Available at: https://www.afr.com/opinion/refugee-crisis-horde-will-test-european-union-20150913-gjlgeq [Accessed 18 Feb. 2

Printed by Amazon Italia Logistica S.r.l.
Torrazza Piemonte (TO), Italy

12996784R00116

YESTERDA
AND TOM(

By

David Griffiths

Yesterday, Today and Tomorrow is one common name for the shrub *Brunfelsia pauciflora*. It blooms purple, then turns lavender and then white. It has all three flower colours at once as more bloom.

To Sue who was there at the beginning and Jenny who was there at the end both of whom offered support and encouragement in this endeavour.

My thanks to Pat Barrow whose final proofreading prevented some embarrassing gaffes.
Any errors that remain are mine.

PROLOGUE

One wheel moves rhythmically under the action of the pedal, the other almost still, moving only through the forces pulsing through the frame of the upturned bicycle. The frame is bright black, the trim gleaming in the midday sunshine; there are no other colours to spoil the chrome save the bright red maker's name on the cross bar. Turning the pedal is a boy, just thirteen, now over the hurdle into teenage years, hence the bike. He, slight framed, mousy haired, sits half-squatting, half-lying on his hip alongside his two-month-old birthday present, its original sparkle maintained with meticulous cleaning. One slender arm props up his body whilst the other operates the wheel. His summer shorts reveal legs slightly too long for his body, lightly bronzed in the summer sun. His scuffed shoes and scratched legs pay testimony to the active life of any normal young teenager. His outward appearance then, earns no special comment.

But beneath the conventional image things are far from normal. There is no emotion in his face, no pleasure, no inquisitiveness, nothing. It is a face that, even this young, has learnt to distrust outward displays of feeling. His last birthday, the one that yielded the bicycle, coincided with the coronation of Elizabeth II and was swamped by the euphoria of that day. Yet he had felt, not resentment but relief, relief that instead of being the centre of attention his presence in the world was pushed into the shadows, for it was here that he had come to belong, where he could be separate, detached, distant. Given the date of his birth, his conception must have coincided with the outbreak of the second world war when world history conspired to overshadow him. But even if that were biologically true, it was only later that his need to withdraw from life took root. Only in early childhood did barriers arise, attitudes set, emotions become stunted, joy give way to bleakness.

1

He puts his hand up his trouser leg and pull his underpants away from his body, only subconsciously aware of the hormonal changes deep within him.

The puncture repaired, he now fiddles aimlessly with the machine, his mind detached from the world around. He turns the pedal robotically. As the bearings engage, the sound ricochets off the brick wall of the house and the paved patio beneath. Click, click, click. In the opposite direction it fans out across the small lawn with its sharp edges and tailored weed-free grass to finally lose its strength in the vegetable garden beyond the flower beds.

The sun, which today reflects off the leaves of the recently mown grass to show the alternate paths of the mower, picks out the bright inside of the rotating rim of the wheel, casting patterns of light which flicker across the brickwork before disappearing off the edge of the back wall of the small detached house. Flick, flick, flick.

The comforting, hypnotising even, pattern of sensation drowns out the world around. The movement of the wheel seems as relentless as passing time, its speed varying with the effort on the pedal of the upturned machine, just as time seems to endure or enjoy its own speed depending on the emotion of the moment. He sits, meandering in the doldrums of pre-pubescent lethargy, anaesthetised by the rhythms his hand creates. Click, click, click. One, two, three. Flick, flick, flick. Then, now, when.

Now another sound; a gurgle, a strangled shout, wheels rattling in their bearings. But different wheels, those on a wheelchair. And in it a girl, younger than the boy but heavier than him, her pale face framed by almost-black hair pulled into two strands by tartan ribbons on either side of her head, the ribbons matching her kilt. Her feet are held in heavy iron-supported boots stretching to her knees. Her face is distorted. With what? Pleasure? Anger? Fear? It is a strong reaction, stronger than she normally offers. Usually, she sits placidly, her head twisting as if to catch a distant voice, her face angled, as though squinting at some vague image beyond her focus, her mouth hanging slackly open, saliva dribbling onto her cardigan, her hands intertwining in shapes quite unconnected with the other movements. But now all this activity is heightened and intense. Her head is jerking from side to side as if seeking communion with the rhythms around her. Her face is distorted as her jaw pulls away to one side; her voice is raised in incoherent song; her body is straining at the harness that is meant to ensure her safety.

The boy breaks off from his past-time to watch his sister's performance and is at first alarmed, though by habit does not show it. The bicycle wheel, now unpropelled, slows down and the movements in the wheelchair slow in concert. Click - click - click. The girl settles into a gentle contented humming, rocking slowly back and forth. Is that a smile on her face? The boy sees the connection and reaching for the pedal, speeds up the spinning wheel and watches with crude satisfaction - a long way from pleasure - the responses of his secured sister. He sees he can control her; he has found the power to do it, but still shows no emotion. Does this offer revenge since for all her active life it is she with her misshapen appearance, with her capricious and clumsy movement, with her raucous shouts who has held power over him? Her behaviour and appearance attract the eyes of the world to him and from that attention there seems no escape. Nowhere to hide from this repeated, persistent, intense humiliation so vivid to the growing boy and so profound in its effect on him. No anonymity within which to develop and explore. To him it seemed he was always in the spotlight and for self-protection he turned inward on himself to avoid its brightness. Like a snail who when touched recoils into its shell where it is safe, so he too contracts to his private place. But for him, it is not a place of comfort but coldness. He withdraws into this place for, like for the snail, it seems the safest option; but unlike the snail it is not an instinctive response, it is one that has been learned and developed through unremitting experience.

Now he sees he can get his own back and he pedals faster. Click, click, click. Flick, flick, flick. The frenzy returns and she begins to shout. He is fuelled with the capricious cruelty that sometimes infects boyhood. He relishes his power but is alarmed by the responses from the source of his unhappiness. He can taunt her; perhaps he could torment her. But he doesn't; some embryonic sympathy restrains his actions. Although he knows she exerts an unintended damaging power over him, he has no wish to cause her hurt despite the malign effect she has had - still has - over his developing being. Though he hates what she had done to him he cannot bring himself to hate her. He understands that just as he is trapped within the gauche shell he has created so there lies within the cruel straight-jacket of her physical frame, a real her. So, in a perverse and tragic symmetry although she, in her helplessness, cannot avoid harming him, he, even with his healthy strength, cannot bring himself to hurt her. He presses on the brake and the clicking stops abruptly. The girl becomes alarmed by this sudden discontinuity and lets out a single piercing scream.

Their mother's face appears at the window. A face sharpened by the constant drain on her emotions as she raises her handicapped daughter. Gone the softness that had once caught her future husband's eye, gone the joyousness that greeted the news she had given birth to a daughter, gone the expectation of a normal family life. Now just a brittle shell, enough to survive the daily chores but not strong enough for more. She sees her son's guilty face staring back up at her, but before she can confront it directly, he is gone, out of the side gate along the narrow path and away up the main road. Behind him he leaves his weary mother patting her daughter's hands, stroking her hair and wiping away her tears as she tries to hold back her own.

Now his bicycle is his means of escape. Not to anywhere to begin with, but away from. Away from her. Away from them. Away from the family that should have been his source of comfort and stimulation but which has become the cause of his condition. He speeds down the road, the passers-by anonymous as he looks straight ahead. Then down a narrow lane with high hedges into a small copse.

He hides his bike in the undergrowth of his secret den, climbs up a solid sycamore and views the world, hidden by the full summer foliage. In the world but not part of it, he sits astride a branch his arms circling the main trunk and feels the strong neutrality of the wood.

Here introspection weaves its insecurities. He is bright enough to detect his condition but, robust though his intelligence is, he cannot override the tight control something holds over his emotions. He envies the feelings other children seem to have, their laughter, their inhibition, their physical contact, their rage, their impertinence, their confidence, their freedom, their daring, their raw insensitivity. They are not only in the world but help make it what it is, whereas he is only at its mercy. He is not like them. Why? He knows, but he doesn't understand. It's her; she causes it. He cannot get beyond that simplicity. What would it be like without her? What would he be now, if she had never lived? How would it be, if he killed her?

So here hangs this sad boy, damaged by the past decade of his life, suspended above the world in which he finds no comfort but for which he has no alternative. He has ground rules, undeclared but dominating. Don't speak unless spoken to. Don't show emotion lest you bring attention on yourself. Don't step forward, step back. Don't share in case all is taken from you. Don't attempt lest you earn ridicule. Yet he is still only half way through the pre-adult experiences that will form his life. There is still puberty to endure. What more damage will be done? How does this human being, sensitive, thoughtful, clever, kind, conventional, hopeful, but sadly numbed, make his way through life? He survives, of course, as most of us do. But what sort of life will it be? Is there no salvation?

ONE

The airport bus jerked to a standstill outside the departures building, its brakes hissing. Malcolm stepped off the bus and waited for his luggage to be unloaded from the hold. Two large suitcases highlighted the substance of his journey; this no holiday jaunt. He nodded to the driver but said nothing and offered no tip. He had not spoken to anyone since the bus left Birmingham not even the passenger next to him, his window seat giving a justification for ignoring all others. The journey through a mid-January England, its green landscapes dulled by the remains of polluted winter snow, seemed to validate his decision to leave.

He struggled to get the cases onto a trolley and with some uncertainty he joined his queue at the check-in desk. The situation was new to him and he felt a little overdressed in his jacket and tie, a rain coat folded over his angled arm. Several times he checked the destination flagged over the desk, fearing an administrative change would wreck his organization. It confirmed he is en-route to Nairobi. He scanned the members of his queue to see if they seemed plausible fellow travellers but tried to avoid eye contact. They were mainly white but with more black and Asian faces than he had expected; a turban stood above the heads near the front. Parents subdued the excited activity of their young, variously promising reward for good behaviour or punishment for bad. A family a few places in front caught his interest. The adults were peering over the heads of the queue for signs of movement. The young girl clung to a fluffy toy; her fair hair bunched into two strands sticking outwards from the back of her head. The mother tucked a washing label inside the back of her son's shirt. The label tickled his neck and he put his hand inside his shirt to scratch his back, re-exposing the label as he withdrew his hand. He guided their luggage trolley, edging it on as the queue advances, and crunched the heels of a saried lady in front. His mother scolded him hoping the firmness of her voice would convey apology. In fact, its shrillness only revealed annoyance. The Asian lady turned and said something rendered unclear by her accent, but her body language suggested sympathy. Heads in the queue turned to the incident, glad of something to relieve their boredom, sorry there was no greater incident to engage their interest.

He came to the front of the queue with a window seat still available. Beyond the desk his cases joined the main carousel skipping with a joyful inhibition he would have found hard to imitate. As he turned round to leave the desk, he came face to face with the couple behind him. The man was the smaller of the two. He wore a type of safari jacket and a straw hat which seemed to suggest a greater significance to where the wearer was going to, than where he had come from. The woman was wearing a floral dress buttoned down the front. Her skin was browner than the winter pale of others in the queue and her steel grey hair was pulled tight against her head and secured in a bun. She was smiling at him, leaving him little option but to smile back. Before she could speak, he walked away to the departure lounge escaping human contact, seeking anonymity.

In the crowded departure lounge he sought a seat as far away from other people as he could but they were difficult to avoid. Around him groups, families, pairs as well as singletons like himself sat waiting, some excitedly, some moodily, most impatiently. They might notice a twenty something man with no distinguishing features and no apparent emotion sitting among them but he didn't want their attention. He felt separate, detached from their lives. But this feeling was not new to him, he had lived it all his life He was not alone - the situation would not allow it - but he was lonely in a way that only he knew. It did not sadden him since, paradoxically, this loneliness was his protection. Loneliness was comforting. Loneliness meant safety.

Anxiously he opened his passport, as he had done several times even though it had got him through check-in. But if was not his, then whose? there was no one else's it could be. He turned to his personal details. Malcolm Chisholm Bryant, born 02/06/1940 were all familiar to him, the other details less so it being his first passport. He found it difficult to look at his own face. He knew it was odd but he was odd. Not odd in a frightening way but odd in a frightened way certainly. Anxious eyes stared back. He closed the booklet, putting it in an inside jacket pocket.

But these other people were going to somewhere and, as far as he could tell, looking forward to it. He too was going somewhere as his boarding pass reminded him when he last checked it; a night flight to Nairobi, 12 hours with stops at Rome and Entebbe. Most people would be excited, full of anticipation but not he. For him it was just the next step on a path he had chosen blindly. He was to have a new life as a researcher in an agricultural development centre somewhere near the capital. He'd looked in an atlas but couldn't find the name given on the government documents offering him the post and the centre had only a Nairobi post box number. However, he would be met at the airport by the station chief so the exact location was unimportant. Later, when he knew the country and lived among its people, he would convince himself there had been some altruistic motive in coming to help a post-independence nation emerging from colonial rule but at this moment his motives, flimsy as they might be, were purely personal. Even if he was going to something, it was what he is leaving behind that occupied his mind more, but equally what he was carrying with him. All those positive things which constitute a childhood and define the adult had been squeezed out of his life. If he wasn't scarred, he was at least numbed.

His degree course in Biology delivered a 2.1 which allowed him to begin a three-year postgraduate research programme into cereal production, but it came to a premature end without the doctorate he had aimed for. This failure meant many jobs in the UK were closed to him, although a two-year contract at a college of FE gave him a period in which to earn some money.

A chance viewing of an advertisement in a Sunday newspaper by a government aid agency came to his rescue. The contract offered was at a plant research station in Kenya. Writing for an application form, remembering personal details, finding references, going for an interview became a conveyor belt of process where each stage was easier to take than not.

Filling in the application form caused an unwelcome review of his early life. The details of his school education inevitably brought back his childhood. He felt that lurking within every response was some stark and embarrassing evidence of his miserable childhood. Even his handwriting seemed to betray him. His CV was convincing enough but his personal activities seemed a bit thin. Fell walking seemed to reflect some interest in physical activity and allowed him hours of self-containment. Playing Bridge seemed both cerebral and sociable and the need to remain physically unresponsive at the core of the game limited the need to be convivial and this made it tolerable; even here his public involvement was negligible preferring to play the games presented in the newspapers to actual competition with humans.

He thought of stamp collecting to fill it out a bit but rejected the idea. It was not strictly true anyway. As a schoolboy, stamp collecting had been a private and non-threatening activity but he had long since stopped, although the albums were still around, lying dormant in one of those boxes or cases that contain the residues of human lives, impossible to discard when the owner is alive but guiltily unwanted after the owner's death. If his childhood involvement with overseas lands and the grandeur and excitement implicit in their stamps inspired this career move now, then the effect was subliminal. Nevertheless, he was prompted to get out his old album. There inside the front cover his name and address ending in *The World, The Universe*, in handwriting which seemed both familiar and alien, written by someone he knew but not him. From nowhere, the names of unfamiliar shades listed in the catalogue came flooding back - carmine, myrtle-green, lake, cobalt, bistre - and this flow of colour brought an unexpected warmth to his being, something more than the cloying comfort of nostalgia. He turned to Kenya and found animals, birds, mountains, lakes all in bright clean authoritarian colours framed with strong imperial designs. He could not know that these scenes would soon be an accepted part of his life. Now, they only magnified the greyness of his present existence. He closed the album symbolically shutting out the past but also convincing himself, on those flimsy grounds that can be used to support capricious decisions, that it was a glimpse into the future too.

Still, he felt that only two pastimes seemed a bit limiting. He wished he could have put something akin to amateur dramatics or ice skating, accepting he would never have had the confidence to perform in public even if he had had the talent. Walking and cards would have to do.

Next of kin was a problem. He had no parents, no siblings, no cousins; only an elderly relative in Edinburgh. He wasn't quite sure who she was and how he was connected to her, only that, unfailingly on his birthday and Christmas, a postal order would appear in the post. The amount of the order had remained unchanged and Malcolm wondered if the old lady realized he was now an adult. It seemed that the genealogy of his family had compounded his isolation. Yet it didn't bother him one bit, indeed it was almost a relief that he had no family commitments. His need to complete the form correctly and unambiguously made him declare his aunt and he dutifully wrote to her so that the death of a distant relative in the middle of Africa would not come as a complete shock.

The application drew an invitation to on interview; this, in London, passed easily enough. Two of the interviewers were formal, bureaucratic and practical. They dealt with his origins, his education, his salary, his health, all the things that had been on his application form anyway. A picture of the Queen hung on the wall behind them staring down disinterestedly. When asked a question his eyes reached out to his monochrome monarch feeling her less likely to judge him than his inquisitors. The questions seemed more designed to find out not so much what he was, but what he wasn't. His responses were suitably oblique with those about family background being truthful within limits. He invested his hobbies with more vigour than they deserved.

The third man would prove to be his new boss, Arthur Rogers. He must have once been above average height but now his body was foreshortened as he slumped in his chair. He seemed out of sympathy with the formal environment. As his colleagues probed, he watched Malcolm's reactions, occasionally pulling out a pipe from his pocket as if by habit, then returning it unlit.

When it came to his turn he sat upright in his chair. He dealt with some routine aspects of agriculture in tropical climates before asking about leisure interests. Rogers' tie was a well-worn regimental one quite unlike the university one, Malcolm was wearing for the first time since graduation day. Malcolm noticed the slim end of the tie hung below the fatter end on which Malcolm could see a stain which might have been egg. Whatever its origins the stain provided a secure focus for his eyes rather than Rogers'. Malcolm was able to reply with rare confidence as the questions seemed to centre on his area of expertise. Rogers, judging that Malcolm was a man he could work with (a quality which raised him above some better qualified candidates) had selected these areas on purpose so that his UK based colleagues would not find reasons to reject him. His research station, whilst not out in the bush, was some way from major towns and colleagues would be working cheek-by-jowl. He needed someone who would fit in and in Malcolm he detected no sharp edges.

A letter offering Malcolm the post arrived a week later. He was not to know two other candidates had withdrawn from the interview and a third was discovered to be offering bogus qualifications. He was however preferred to two others. He read it several times; for him the neutral print was a satisfying private acclamation of his worth. He didn't take long to accept; his life was going nowhere as it stood. His immediate family were all dead and he had no close friends and cared little for his colleagues and acquaintances. If his current job had been merely routine, he might have been content to stay with it, but it had become boring to a degree even Malcolm felt unsatisfying. So, although his decision to leave was not altogether a positive one, he was hoping to leave something rather than find something when he arrived.

The call to the gate came on time but he waited for others to stand up before him so that he would not be conspicuous, but there was no one near him for his flight. Looking neither left nor right, he walked cautiously to the invitingly open gate.

Walking through this portal and along the passenger ways to the aircraft he felt an easing of the tensions that had so be-devilled his life. Surely, he was free now? There was no going back now, but why would he want to go? The physical remnants of his life were stored away in a warehouse. However much he wished he could have left them behind, his insecurities were coming with him. Would they swamp his new life as they had engulfed the old one?

TWO

The long uncomfortable flight was broken by two scheduled stops. In Rome, an unexpected delay caused several hours of looking through a transit lounge window onto an illuminated runway. He chose a seat as far from his fellow travellers as he could get and tried to get his tongue round the phrases in his Swahili vocabulary book. The words were alien in their structure, lots of Ks and too many Ns in places that hindered pronunciation. He had spent many hours in his lodgings with this book and the edges of its bright yellow wrapping were torn revealing the dark cover underneath. He had mastered several phrases and constructed quite ambitious sentences but had little idea of their required sound or tempo. Despite this success, he doubted if he could summon the courage to speak them out loud; even now the embarrassment of long-past French lessons at school still haunted him. His solitude was broken by the couple who had been behind him in the check-in queue. They came to sit in seats facing him glowing with conviviality.

'Hello.' Malcolm felt an aggressive cheeriness in the woman's greeting.

'This is a nuisance, isn't it? We can't have a snooze. Not knowing how long we'll be, I mean. Not in these seats any way.' She bounced her bottom on the plastic seat to emphasise her point. Her action sent a shiver down the row of seats and another passenger further down the row glared disapprovingly at being woken up.

'My name's Fay. Fay Hammond. And this is Dennis.'

Her husband smiled. It had to be her husband, thought Malcolm. They didn't look or behave like lovers off on some erotic voyage; not that he knew what lovers should look like. He had a brief picture of Fay Hammond in a sarong and wondered whether the name Fay was at all flamboyant. He hadn't come across a real person with that name so perhaps it was. Fay paused and Malcolm felt unable to avoid response.

'I'm Malcolm. Malcolm Bryant.' He had no interest in them and he certainly didn't want them to know anything about him.

'We're going home, you know. To Gulu. That's in Uganda. So, we're getting off at Kampala. The next stop. Assuming we get going at all,' she said, pleased with her own wryness. 'We run a mission, don't we, Dennis.'

Definitely husband and wife; lovers don't run missions. But still the name Fay worried him; it was more lounge bar that leper colony, though Dennis was fair enough.

Dennis smiled agreement.

'Have you been in Africa before?' he said, judging he knew the answer.

'No. It's my first time.' First time! Would there be others?

'We've been to lots of places in Africa. We were in Lagos for a while and then went over to Nyasaland. That's got a new name now hasn't it. We've been in Uganda for ten years now. It hasn't changed its name.' Fay, fielding the response, made it sound an admirable stance. 'We're with the CMS.'

'Church Missionary Society,' said Dennis helpfully sensitive to Malcolm's mystification.

'Did you notice that little boy in the queue playing with the trolley? Took us back didn't it, Dennis? It's such a trial for little ones - queuing. He's called Simon - same as our eldest. He's in Mexico now.'

'He really ought to have been a solicitor by now but gave up his law studies in Leeds to join a cruise ship - liked Mexico so much he stayed,' Dennis made it a duet as Fay plunged into her handbag.

'Our eldest daughter, Naomi, is married. She lives in Australia. Look here's a photo of them. No children yet - so we're not grandparents.

'Her husband's a mining engineer. They met when he was on a course in England. Do you know Worksop? No? Nor us.

'And then there's Mary. Little Mary. They've all got biblical names.'

Malcolm wondered whether there was a Fay in the Bible. Or Dennis.

'We had a lot of fun going through the Bible didn't we Dennis? Some aren't very suitable these days. Can you imagine what Simon would have said if we'd called him Shadrack? No, the Bible's got some nice names but they're not all appropriate now, are they? Mind you a lot of the Africans take biblical names - Obadiah, Moab, things like that. Anyway, where was I? Oh yes. Mary. Well, she's at teacher training college in Surrey. She's very good at games. Wants to teach deaf children. She writes home a lot to tell us what she's doing - not like Simon - he doesn't write at all. I wonder is the post bad in Mexico.

'They were all brought up in the African bush.'

'Well, they went to boarding schools in England when they were old enough,' chimed in Dennis.

'We like living in the bush. Well, we do - not the children so much.'

Malcolm could never have been as forthcoming about his own family. He was born just after the outbreak of the Second World War and his sister Marion was born after one of her father's leaves from service in the Far East. After the war, his father became a clerk in a warehouse and his mother stayed at home to look after her daughter who was mentally and physically impaired. Her condition became conspicuous as her brother was emerging from infancy into the greater awareness of childhood. Whenever they were out as a family, his father would tend his daughter's wheelchair, manoeuvring it in and out of the traffic, up and down pavements and around cafe tables.

When they went on a bus his father would lift Marion out of her wheelchair and carry her onto the bus whilst his mother folded the chair and put it in the luggage space with varying degrees of help from the conductor. All of this activity was in the full view of the other passengers and Malcolm found himself in the middle of the commotion, yet side-lined by the needs of his sister. It was impossible to go into any public place with Marion, without attracting attention. Her uncontrolled body movements and her high-pitched shrieks drew her to the attention of anyone close. Any remarks made were friendly and sympathetic but most people managed to look at this family without making eye contact, their body language indicating a slight distaste for this public display. Cafes were quick in providing the service that would see this family on its way.

Malcolm became inured to being in the public gaze, not because of achievement, or acclaim but by association with a spectacle. He developed strategies to cope with his intense embarrassment. In the street he would hold himself close to his mother on the side away from Marion pulling his head close to his mother's body. In cafes he sat trance-like ignoring the performance around him. With his head down he ate his food slowly so that eating would occupy the whole time they were seated. He concentrated on the food, its taste, its smell, its texture and tried to see nothing and feel nothing beyond the plate in front of him. But although the aim was physical detachment, alongside it, emotional detachment became a way of life. And his parents' preoccupation with Marion did little to help him. His quiet disposition made few demands on his parents' energies and these became denied him.

Mrs. Bryant had been a striking woman, slim, clear featured, lively auburn hair. There was a Scottish element in her family background and Malcolm owed his name to this heritage. Occasionally words and phrases would infiltrate her speech to reclaim this ancestry. She was prone to wear tartan in her clothes and this gave an air of strength and resolution to what would otherwise have been a faltering demeanour. At first her daughter's condition was a disappointment but not a tragedy. She gave her maternal energy knowing she would not see Marion reach full womanhood. Her days became full of a devoted routine of feeding, cleaning, washing with little time for herself. She had a fund of songs which she sang to Marion in an attempt to get beyond the limitations of her physical being. But in time disappointment gave way to resignation and then despair as her daughter took over her whole body when once she had occupied only her womb. Marion's relentless calls on her time and her spirit took their toll. She lost her bloom; her eyes came quick to tears and her manner became timid. She was encouraged to get out of the house to evening classes, bingo, cinema but no activity lasted very long and she was drawn back to the cloying drudgery of family responsibilities. Later the physical changes became more pronounced. Her skin tightened over her bones as her weight decreased, her hair greyed, her house work became more obsessive.

Mr. Bryant was raised to value duty, modesty and truth although none of these derived from conventional religion. He had no doubts about his parental responsibility for Marion, but found it easier to meet her bodily needs than to contemplate the nature of her being. His attitude was more stoical than his wife's and his war experience had tempered his mind to disillusion. His jokes were rather laboured, but were attempts at humour rather than products of any bitterness. His energy in meeting his daughter's physical needs seemed at first unlimited but just as Marion drained her mother's spirit so she sapped her father's strength. He spent much of his leisure time in the family garden. Here he placed Marion in her wheel chair, in the hope that the smells and sounds of outdoor life would stimulate some part of her being beyond the reach of her family. Malcolm, too, was encouraged to work in the garden. There, his father taught him much about gardening. Mr. Bryant preferred flowers but Malcolm, perhaps as a way of creating separation, grew vegetables in his own plot at the far end of the garden, well away from Marion. There, he grew his own world, a high bank of runner beans creating a protective screen from the rest of the family. He learnt to take cuttings, gather seeds, make compost. In time Malcolm's patch came to provide the family dinner table with most of its vegetables and for a while he basked in the parental acclaim this brought him. But this soon faded into the family routine, overtaken by more demanding events and its contribution to family life was increasingly unacknowledged.

In the winter months Mr. Bryant tried another tack. He bought Malcolm a stamp album and a packet of stamps and for a while they became his son's main hobby. He brought home stamps from the warehouse office and in the quiet of Malcolm's bedroom showed his son how to remove them from the paper and to identify and mount them. In these rare moments father and son were together, but neither felt quite at ease with the closeness. In time, this joint activity, too, would wither. As Malcolm became more expert so his father became less useful and left his son to an activity, he had hoped would bring them close, but in the end eased them apart. Both in their separate ways found the distance between them easier to cope with than the closeness. Malcolm explored the whole world through these stamps meeting people, using languages, scripts and currencies, seeing monuments and mountains without leaving the security of his own bedroom. The role of global spectator suited his temperament but the seclusion reinforced his isolation.

To say that he was neglected would be a harsh judgment on his parents but Marion's demands were so relentless and so time consuming that they failed by omission. He, on the other hand, demanded so little, made so few claims on parental energies, that he was denied the rich and varied interactions of family life that make for a well-balanced human being. Thus, his own meekness contributed to his own exclusion and he inherited little.

As Malcolm progressed towards adolescence, he felt his father become colder and more withdrawn; until then he had thought him merely stern. Whether this change was real or just a signal of his own growing sensitivity, he did not know. On one occasion, his father pulled Malcolm to him and held him in a firm enveloping embrace. The youngster did not respond but held his arms rigidly to his side. He felt his father's breath touching the top of his head as he exhaled open-mouthed in one long sigh. He smelled the slightly sweaty odour from his father's working clothes as his face rested near the shoulder. Nothing was said and it did not happen again. No reason was given, although its significance always puzzled Malcolm. As a youngster it embarrassed and confused him. If it was a clumsy attempt to make the boy feel wanted and included, it failed because Malcolm could not deal with the uncertain message it gave. But the gesture was not intended to comfort the son; it was the father who needed it.

Despite the demands of Marion his parents ensured he was well clothed and well fed and they made special efforts to encourage his school work. Marion was never brought near school, but those of Malcolm's school mates who knew of her condition, were not averse to using it to embarrass him which in turn sustained his need to remain outside their circle of adolescent insensitivity. The school library was a useful refuge and although he was ridiculed for his isolation, he was not physically bullied. In class Malcolm kept out of the limelight. He never put his hand up to answer a question and he replied briefly, and usually correctly, when asked one. His handwriting was legible but functional. His test marks were high enough to avoid censure but low enough to avoid praise - both would have been an unwelcome signal of his public existence. He was absent for only the most severe illnesses. He was never late for school nor broke any school rule. This low profile was a necessary camouflage of daily life. His school life was tolerable and he did not need more than that.

His bicycle was a source of help. In mid-teens it provided the short term escape he needed and changed the routine if not the mood of his life. Little sorties into the countryside brought some sense of adventure and freedom, quiet country lanes led to hidden tracks. Here he could build secret dens, their crude camouflage allowing a voyeuristic engagement with the world. Once, he saw a woman relieve herself in the nearby grass and found his mind filled, not with some minor erotic thought, but with the shame and embarrassment, he assumed, she would have had if discovered. The bare buttocks beneath the hoisted skirt, the long legs as she pulled up her knickers, all exposed to another and she did not know it. Her vulnerability disturbed him not her sex.

As he got older, he went further afield, biking and hiking into the sparsely populated countryside. These sorties not only legitimised his absence from home, but put him into an environment free of the proximity of other human beings. There being no requirement for social skills, his need for detachment was satisfied, but his inability to connect reinforced.

But Malcolm' behaviour in childhood not only served his immediate needs, it set a template on his developing personality which would constrain him for life. He learned that if you wanted to be free from ridicule, immune to hurt, saved from disappointment you should never display, never commit, never aspire. His life would be spent within these narrow emotional and behavioural limits. He would be denied the exhilaration, the joy and the comfort of more normal freedoms because he would not, and in time could not, run the risks of achieving them. Like most children he could not imagine an upbringing other than his own and only intermittently reflected on its abnormally corrupting effect on him.

School life had given way to university where he read Biology. He had reached adulthood incomplete. He was intelligent in a pedestrian way, had a good working knowledge of the world about him, was not unpleasant to look at but was only at ease when left to himself; the rest of the world was a threat, waiting to sit in judgment, poised to ridicule. He lived alone in digs; he joined no clique and certainly no society; for his fellow undergraduates, his would be the face in the photograph whose name no-one could remember. Here the normal student life was eschewed in favour of diligent study. The separation from family was welcome respite, but he did not have the skills to exploit it and although he was freed from the presence of Marion her lingering influence remained. His countryside sorties as a schoolboy gave encouragement to hiking and hill walking. He found great comfort in reaching some vantage point and sitting quite alone, untroubled by the rest of humanity he could see infiltrating the landscape. As long as he did not make a visible, public commitment to this world and its inhabitants he was safe. To others his life might have been seen as unbearably lonely yet for him it was a comforting solitude.

Sexual activity was an anathema to him. In the first instant he found it impossible to look at any female with any degree of intent, quite unable to flash those subtle messages of sexual interest that spark a relationship and, so, most women concluded that he was gay or so dull that they could not contemplate spending the rest of the night with him still less the rest of their lives. Thankfully, in his own eyes, his responses were never put to the test. But had that barrier been overcome he could not have coped with the physical side of sex, its physical absurdity, its uncontrolled action, and its personal inhibition.

In a cerebral way, he recognized his condition; he suspected he was not like other men but that did not distress him, distress itself being too strong an emotion. He could have blamed his parents since he needed there to be blame for his condition. Instead, he found the cause in the seemingly inescapable figure of his sister. Whenever he felt incomplete, unable to respond, incapable of emotion, he saw as a symbol of that inadequacy the figure of Marion, herself damaged, unresponsive, unemotional, drawing him to her, swamping his being.

Marion's life expectancy was known to be short so her death caused no surprise. His father, having left a message at Malcolm's

21

student digs for him to ring home, told him the news without emotion and without regret. The funeral was a pathetic affair. Malcolm was aware of how there were no family friends; the relative in Scotland sent her apologies. Such had been the commitment of time to Marion, the family had never really looked outward. The family was outnumbered by the vicar, the organist, the undertakers, Marion's social worker and an elderly lady who gave out hymn books at the functional entrance to the crematorium. His parents had agreed to a conventional service and acquiesced with the suggested hymns but the family involvement in the actuality was minimal. Their baleful attempts to follow the tunes was disguised by the over-hearty contribution from the vicar and piercing support from the women at the back. The minister made an awkward address, full of platitudes to explain Marion's place in the world and once referred to her as Mary. He concluded she would rest in a peace. As the coffin disappeared behind the curtains, Malcolm felt nothing, neither sadness nor relief, for he had no reservoir of feeling on which to draw.

In life Marion had denied her parents a peace of mind that could not be reclaimed after her death. Malcolm did not know whether they showed selfless dedication chosen in face of other possibilities, or whether they fell into a bewildered habit of caring, as much impaired as their daughter. Whatever the case, her death left a gap in their lives or confirmed the emptiness of them. She had become the reason for living and although having no conventional personality to speak of, her presence had dominated family life. Yet, her absence revealed an abyss in theirs; neither would live much longer. Mr. Bryant died of a stroke amongst his precious flowers; his wife died ten months later, her will to live exhausted. With neither funeral were there tears, the telling of personal reminiscences, the clammy clutching of mumbling relatives. Both lives slipped away to leave a silence. For them the crowded quiet of eternity; for their son the lonely silence of continued life. Yet it did not trouble him; in a crude way it was an escape. But where it would take him, he could not contemplate.

'Do you have a family?' Fay had in mind a wife and children.

'No. They're all dead now.'

'Oh. I'm so sorry.' Fay imagined an awful tragedy and couldn't decide how to continue.

Malcolm didn't have the ability to respond; he couldn't possibly tell the whole saga. He turned away abruptly but he felt the slight touch of a hand on his elbow.

'May they rest in peace. God bless you.'

'Amen.'

He wasn't sure which of them said what. He couldn't recall a moment where anyone had expressed a comforting emotion for him. Caught off balance, he felt his eyes prickle with the salt of tears he had not felt before. He walked off; it was all he was able to do. He knew they were watching him and memories of childhood surveillance shuddered through him.

A voice at the exit brought the passengers to their feet. Most, unsure of the announcement, followed the rest in resigned hope of continuing. There was much stretching; groups of people, mute strangers in the departure queue, now comrades against the common foe of institutional failure, chatted like old friends. The young girl with the bunched hair woke up and yawned. Her face was creased and had a red blotch where it had rested against her father's arm. He tickled her leg and she smiled; not once in fifteen years had Malcolm's father had a recognisable smile from his daughter. As they shuffled to the exit the young boy held his mother's hand. Malcolm watched this conventional family make their way, statistically just as his own but a world apart in experience.

The second leg into Africa itself was all in darkness and even though it was clearly cloudless, little could be seen below. There were little points of light on the ground – camp fires perhaps but they would be too small. Whatever they were they indicated human habitation. Africa was not just a dark mass; there were people there. Surely, they would not all want to stare at him. He drifted away into intermittent slumber to be awoken by changes in engine noise or the movement of passengers down the aisle to the toilets. Finally, he woke to the noise of footsteps down the aisle and voices stretching from sleep. Lifting his window blind, he saw his first African dawn. Removed from outside temperature, he experienced only the pale red sky strafed by whiskery clouds. As the sun rose, it lit more and more of the scattered clouds turning grey into silver and silver into dazzling white. As he looked out Malcolm was filled with apprehension for this step in his life. This was not routine, might not even be safe; this was a risk. But he couldn't change it now, couldn't ignore it. He was at the mercy of the plane and where it took him. A mild exhilarating panic swelled in him; it sent warmth around his mind like strong spirit reviving a cold body.

The plane cruised downwards through a bank of thin cloud and, when it emerged, Malcolm was surprised to see the water so close below. A solitary boat was making its way towards the reed-covered banks of an inlet, its lone occupant pulling on a single paddle. Even from this height, the nets in the boat were visible. In them fish glinted in the strengthening sun. Beyond, the water stretched to the horizon. A generation before Malcolm might have been landing on the lake as his flying boat lake-hopped its way down the Rift Valley. Today he landed on solid ground. The bounce of the aeroplane on the runway introduced Malcolm to the unpredictable land of Africa.

As he left the aircraft the warmth and humidity of lakeside Uganda reminded him of the hothouses which protected the tropical plants in England; it seemed a daunting precursor of climate to come.

'Good bye. Malcolm. Good luck,' it was Fay shouting against the noise of the engines as she and Dennis made their way to the customs shed. The words brought him into a public focus he did not want, but the other passengers had more on their minds than him.

In the terminal building the food was imitation English. Was the manager trying to reach some perceived standard international business cuisine or was this just a residue of a colonial past designed to bring familiarity to those in a strange land? On both counts it failed. Crude cornflakes derived from local maize and heavily treated milk failed a familiarity test; the eggs and bacon exuded a foreign oil. Malcolm, already discomforted by the humidity, now felt nausea. He left his food and went outside to the small garden in front of the airport building. Between the building and the runway was a large parking area; on it stood a motley collection of aircraft including a single-engine light aircraft towards which he saw the two missionaries struggle with their luggage. Fay waved. She had looked for him despite her preoccupation with her luggage. It drew an unusual response from him. Without thinking he raised an arm and waved back.

The morning air was losing its clamminess and he felt the warmth of his first African dawn. He returned to the lounge to join the group returning to the plane for the final leg to Nairobi. The young girl was now in tears, unhappy with little sleep and strange food. The noise of her crying filled the room. Malcolm looked at her brother, clearly embarrassed, and he thought of himself trying to avoid association with Marion. He knew he didn't have to hide physically now but his shortcomings still lurked inside him, concealed from the outside world.

THREE

Malcolm queued impatiently for immigration control, his anticipation of the world beyond the cubicles overcoming the fatigue of the long flight. He held his passport and the visitor's entry form. None of the details revealed his deeper self so he was indifferent to giving them. When he got to the desk the official behind it paused and wiped his heavily sweating forehead and neck with a large handkerchief. He was too big for his uniform which cut into his neck and stretched tight across his chest pulling on the buttons down the front. He said something to the official next to him and put his hand out for Malcolm's documents, revealing a patch of sweat in his arm pit. He took the form robotically. Barely looking at the information on the form he stamped it and added it to a growing pile on his desk behind the partition. After a cursory look at the passport, he stamped it, returned it and waved Malcolm through.

As the baggage carousel began to move, passengers flocked to its rim. The young boy, Simon, wheedled his way between adult bodies and began straightening those cases that had fallen askew the conveyor belt. He examined the label on each blue suitcase almost being dragged along as his reading speed fell behind that of the belt. Eventually recognising the one he needed, he attempted to lift it off. It was too heavy for him and he was dragged along with the carousel bumping into other passengers until his father took the bag to the family trolley. Here the boy waited, leaving his father to recover the remaining luggage. The crowd thinned as bags were recognised and reclaimed. Eventually Malcolm recovered his own. Being one of the last through immigration, he found all the trolleys had been claimed and he had to carry his suitcases and hand-luggage, as he made through customs to the exterior.

Out in the public area faces of all colours jostled to seek recognition. Further back, uniformed drivers held hand written placards with the names of various hotels and tour companies. Those nearer the windowed walls were mere silhouettes against the bright sunshine beyond, their notices unreadable outlines. He cast around for his new boss who had promised to collect him. Malcolm didn't recognise him immediately. At the interview in London, Arthur Rogers had been wearing a formal suit and a regimental tie which made him blend in with the austere furniture of a government office. Now, he was wearing a light khaki shirt and shorts. His bare knees topped long stockings and some safari boots. His arms were rather scrawny but the tan made them seem healthy. In London his hair was short and brushed flat adding to his military appearance. Now it was longer and windblown making his face gentler.

'Hello. You've made it. Welcome.' Rogers took one of the suitcases from his sweating protégé. 'Come. Follow me. Let me take a bag.'

Malcolm would get used to this staccato style and learn it was a protective gruffness against familiarity with those who might be only transient acquaintances. Leaving the airport building, Malcolm was dazzled by the sunlight. The air was hot but without the oppressive humidity of Uganda. His jacket and raincoat were slung over his case like saddles as he struggled to manage his baggage. A young African boy came racing up from the shade of an outbuilding, zigzagging a luggage trolley through the flow of dispersing arrivals. Rogers said something to him in a language Malcolm later knew to be Kikuyu. With some effort the boy picked up Malcolm's cases and placed them flat on the trolley. The boy was not so much introduced as declared as being, what sounded like Googie. This seemed unlikely to Malcolm who only knew the name as one belonging to a film star his mother used to like.

'Please give me that, sah,' Ngugi said precisely, pointing to Malcolm's hand luggage. Taking it, he placed it with some exaggerated care on top of the suitcases. As the two men set off for the car park, Malcolm trailing Rogers, the youngster struggled to keep up. His slim body was nearly horizontal as he tried to get purchase on the tarmac surface with his bare feet. It didn't seem quite right that this urchin should manage a heavy load whilst two grown men carried practically nothing. But no-one, not even the boy, seemed to consider anything strange.

The large Peugeot estate car was covered in a brown dust, so that its white paint was not immediately obvious. Rogers opened the door at the back of the car and the boy heaved the cases up into it and, pausing only to abandon the trolley against a mesh fence, jumped in after them. Rogers spoke abruptly to the boy in Kikuyu. The boy scrambled out and following Rogers' pointing finger, returned the trolley to a bay before sliding into the back seat, his head just above window level. Malcolm got in the passenger side and was met by a wave of hot air from the interior.

'OK, when we're moving. Open the window.' Rogers was removing an old towel, which had been shading the steering wheel from the sun. Malcolm pulled the door shut. It failed to engage the catch. 'Give it a slam. This jalopy gets a lot of rough treatment.' Rogers was looking in his mirror.

As Malcolm slammed the car door, little jets of dust blew out of the gaps between the door's upholstery and the metal frame. He leant back and the heat from the seat back forged through his thin shirt searing his back. He eased slightly forward peeling the shirt off the back rest. He wound down the window and then rested his arm on the frame. The metal was very hot and burnt the tender underside of his arm. Quickly he pulled back his arm from the sharp heat and rubbed his smarting skin. Then he placed his hands between his knees beneath his jacket and rain coat well away from any part of the car's bodywork. He hoped Rogers would not see his plight but his boss was looking out of the driver's window seeking a gap in the cross traffic. If Rogers noticed the incident, he didn't show it. He'd seen such often enough though. Another rookie. The same set of lessons to be learnt and another set to be unlearnt.

The airport was out of town, so the first part of the journey was through the scrub that Malcolm had seen as the plane approached the runway. He had hoped to see some game but all he had seen were signs of human habitation - roads, petrol stations and, grotesquely, a large open air cinema screen. The car journey yielded little better. Some large birds circled over to one side. Malcolm hoped they might be vultures.

'Storks,' came the stabbed comment from Rogers who had seen his passenger looking.

The central reservation of the road into the city was rich in bougainvillea bushes, their magenta flowers immediately grabbing visitors' attention. Passing several tight roundabouts and turning off one of them, down a rundown street strewn with handcarts, they finally arrived at the hotel where he would spend the night. Rogers drove round the back and parked in its car park.

'Leave the window. It'll be OK. Askaris. '

He nodded towards an African in a dark brown uniform standing in the shade against the wall. The man carried a large stick and stiffened as Rogers looked his way. Rogers opened the rear door and Ngugi ran round to haul the suitcases from the boot. Before he could get far, a porter arrived with a luggage trolley. He wore a red fez and a flowing white robe. He took the cases from the boy who seemed annoyed at his role being usurped. Before the porter could move, Ngugi grabbed the hand luggage and ostentatiously handed it to Malcolm.

Rogers gave the boy some money and said something in Kikuyu. Cheering up, the boy walked off, his bare feet untroubled by the rough floor of the car park. His shirt and trousers were part of the same light brown uniform. The trousers had been patched at the bottom with a material which didn't quite match the rest of the garment. Below his trousers, yo-yoed two slim legs darker brown than the uniform. They made him bounce and jig with the inhibition of youth. Before Ngugi turned the corner of the building towards the main road, he turned and waved at the two Europeans, his dark face emphasizing the whiteness of his smile. Malcolm envied the simple confidence of the gesture and felt his arm move in response. Before he could raise it, the boy had disappeared. Malcolm thought him to be about ten years old.

'Will he be alright?'

'Yes, he'll be fine. There's a stall down there. He'll get some roasted maize and a drink. Then he'll sit in the shade and watch the world go by. The big city is an adventure for him. Didn't you find big cities exciting at his age?'

Malcolm remembered once when the family went to Birmingham for the day. The dense traffic and rushing pedestrians might have been exhilarating to some but provided only a hazard to Marion in her wheelchair. The big city, with its pavements and steps, made the family's progress slow and conspicuous. Malcolm's memory was not of having watched the world go by, but of the world having watched him.

At reception Rogers explained who Malcolm was and hovered close as his charge completed the formalities.

'You pop upstairs. Get a wash. Change perhaps. We'll have some lunch. I'm just popping to the bank. See you outside the main door.' He pointed. 'Forty minutes. OK?'

The porter led the way up to the room, effortlessly carrying Malcolm's bag, his flowing robe dissipating the heat which for Malcolm clung between his skin and his clothes. Eventually they arrived at his first-floor room. As he was leaving the room the porter hesitated as though obeying some international protocol. At the thought of a tip, Malcolm froze. He wasn't used to tipping. He had no local money and felt sure the man wouldn't want sixpences. He stood still, powerless to do or say anything, a flood of English inhibitions supporting his personal reserve and holding him fast.

The porter smiled and before leaving the room said, 'I hope you enjoy your stay in our country.' Did he stress the *our* Malcolm had wondered that night? It was *theirs* now. In the past a European might have thought the country *ours*. Some still did.

The room was cool. The window was shaded from the sun and looked out over a courtyard with a large wire mesh bird cage in the middle. Growing in the centre of the bird cage was a mature tree, its branches spreading well beyond the boundaries of the cage. Beneath the tree, shaded by its foliage, were tables at which people sat in groups while waiters ferried drinks and snacks to them.

In the room the washstand and bath were slightly old fashioned but the rest of the furniture was standard hotel style. A mosquito net hung coiled above the bed. He turned on the taps in the washbasin. Nothing came out. He turned them to the full and looked underneath to see if there was some stop tap. There wasn't. He went into the bathroom and used the toilet. It flushed but didn't refill. He opened his case and found some lightweight clothes. They looked rather more English seaside than tropical Africa and before he went down, he glanced self-consciously in the mirror.

He found his way to reception and out to the front terrace where he had arranged to meet Rogers. He paused on the hotel steps looking at the road beyond the terrace and the park land beyond that. For the first time he was in Africa, part of it, both an observer and an inhabitant. In time it would be routine but today the most ordinary of views and trivial of incidents held interest. The sun shone off the tarmacked road and the leaves on the bushes and trees beyond seemed bowed down by the heat. Several groups of African men sat in the shade of the larger trees. Further down the street, a group of people clustered around a brazier from which exuded little puffs of smoke. The stall holder wafted a piece of cardboard beside the coals to create a draught and for a moment, flames engulfed the maize cobs lying on its grid. He looked for Ngugi but, if he was there, Malcolm did not recognise him.

A taxi drew up at the front its wheels raising the roadside dust. From it came a tall young African woman, her hair coiffured straight, gold jewellery complementing her dark brown skin. She came up the steps her high heels stabbing the stone, her sunglasses providing inscrutability. She wore a white silky blouse which highlighted her colour and a close-fitting skirt which emphasized her shape. Through her blouse could be seen her white brassiere clearly outlined against her dark skin. She came towards Malcolm and as she passed him, he smelt her perfume. She passed by without a glance and disappeared into the shadows of the hotel foyer. Her elegant figure was so at variance with the images of African women his upbringing had provided that he was momentarily confused. The African stewardesses on the plane had been homely he thought, sisters almost, though the comparison was not apt for him. But this figure looked as though she had stepped out of the cinema screen and a man more experienced than Malcolm would not have been thinking of his sister. His thoughts were refocused as he heard his surname being called. Looking along the terrace he saw Rogers and joined him at a table, pleased to find himself shaded by a large umbrella.

'Beer?' The enquiry seemed to suggest no other liquid was available or, if it was, it would not be appropriate to offer it.

'Yes. Fine. Thank you.'

'Lete mbili Tusker baridi, tafhadali,' he said to the waiter who was alert to the custom.

Malcolm tried to link the words to his phrase book but the speed of delivery left him confused.

'Sort of lager. Local brew. Quite acceptable.' Rogers' word parcels crossed the table. 'Room, OK?'

'There was no water in the taps.'

'No. Middle of the day. Bore hole problems I expect. Or the pumps. Hotel tanks aren't big enough now.' He seemed unsurprised that a major hotel should have no water.

The waiter returned with two bottles of beer. He poured them into the refrigerated glasses already showing condensation from the warm air. After the waiter had placed the glasses before the two men, Rogers put a note on the tray and then took some of the change leaving a handful of coins on the tray.

'Assante sana, bwana,' said the waiter. Rogers nodded imperiously.

'Thank you,' said Malcolm to Rogers, echoing the waiter, although he didn't know it.

The cold beer was very good and Malcolm realised how dehydrated he had become. He felt the beer, colder than he was used to, passing through his body to his stomach which contracted slightly at the coldness.

'Is it always this hot?'

'No. Hot season. No wind in town. Gets cooler later in the year. It's better at Kimura'

Kimura. It was the place Malcolm had searched for in the atlas.

'Is it a big place?'

'No. Four houses and an office. There's a coffee plantation nearby and the village next door has about twenty huts. Other than that, we're on our own.'

Malcolm found Rogers' terseness irritating. If he had to be in company, he needed to be with people who could converse as he could not. Here neither man seemed capable of a sustained conversation. There was a danger of dialogue stopping altogether.

'Lunch is laid out inside. They do a good curry. We can bring it out here.' Again, the possibility of an alternative seemed to be denied.

Inside was cool and large ceiling fans moved the air silently. Along one side was laid a long row of tables. On them were dishes of cold meats, fish, vegetables, sauces, and at the far end trays of rice, a large sufuria of chicken curry and smaller containers of chopped bananas, nuts and chutneys. Malcolm was sucked behind Rogers to the curry and took a similarly laden plate back to the table outside. He ate tentatively at first but then with enthusiasm. Any connection between what he was eating now and what he had eaten in the UK was purely one of vocabulary. Seeing their empty glasses, the waiter who had served them earlier approached the table.

'Would you like another beer?' Malcolm wanted to reciprocate although over full with the food.

'Yes. Why not? Thanks,' Rogers replied leaving Malcolm to face the waiter.

For a moment Malcolm struggled to remember the Swahili words but gave up and pointing to the glasses said, 'Beer.' He held up two fingers with as little vulgarity as he could.

'Two beers for you sir. Tuskers?' the waiter said in clear but accented English.

'Yes. Thank you,' came the relieved reply.

In the event a full glass of beer proved too much. Rogers came to his rescue.

'You need some shut eye. Siesta. What. Pick you up tomorrow.' He nodded towards the bottom of the steps leading from the terrace to the street below. Seeing Ngugi waiting on the pavement he barked an instruction and the youngster sped off around the outside of the building. 'I'll pull up there at ten o'clock. Save me going round the back. If you could be ready.' Then he was off, back through the hotel leaving Malcolm to contemplate a restful afternoon.

He woke feeling cold. He had gone to sleep naked on the bed and it was now late afternoon and the sun was on the other side of the building. He could hear the toilet cistern filling. Hot water was available so he had a bath then took an age to dry out.

At about six there was a knock on his door. He was just about to call out although hadn't quite decided what to say, when the door was opened by a man, small and very black, with the same uniform of robe and fez which was the hotel's stamp.

'Excuse me, Sah. I've come to kill the dudus.' He chuckled.

The man lifted his insect spray and pumped some chemical throughout the room. He folded back the bed cover, put down the mosquito net and before he tucked it in gave one more burst of insecticide.

When he had gone Malcolm looked out of the window. There were several unoccupied tables in the courtyard. He took his vocabulary book and made his way down to one.

Once seated he constructed a sentence from the phrases in his book and he saw it as a rough approximation to what Rogers had said. He repeated it several times before summoning a waiter. As the waiter approached, he rehearsed his sentence. The waiter smiled at his attempt and interpreted correctly, 'Good. Mzuri.' He returned with the beer. Malcolm, pleased with his own boldness, sipped it slowly and looked for other phrases.

The sun went down quickly, more so because of the hotel buildings, but he was surprised to find it so comfortable to sit outside in the quickly gathering darkness, so unlike the damp gloom of England. Bored with his book he took a greater interest in his fellow drinkers. One or two faces emerged from the darkness when caught by the light from the table lamps, appearing and disappearing as their owners leant forward and back in the flow of conversation. Insects flew in and out of the light from his own lamp occasionally bouncing off its frame. Snatches of conversation came by, none English that he could detect although from behind him he thought he heard familiar words. A glance over his shoulder showed them to come from a group of African men two tables away. They were speaking English but the accents and speech rhythms meant he could not get the gist of their conversation. A loud sentence in German followed by a shriek of laughter drew him to another table. He hadn't been amongst so many foreigners since his student days. It occurred to him he was not in his own country; he was a foreigner now.

He was the only one alone at a table. Although for many, solitude would have been a denial, Malcolm was in his element. He watched. He listened. He didn't have to speak. His history was unexplored, his feelings not tested, his values not judged. The warmth and the darkness brought him a peace of mind he had rarely experienced. Marion was a long way away.

Later untroubled by a different bed, exhausted after a tiring day, unaccustomed heat, too much food and several beers he slept well that night.

FOUR

Throughout his life Malcolm had dreamed copiously. His dreams had varied in their impression on him and only a few made more than the usual claims of childhood. For him, it might well have been that, feelings, held tight in check in daytime, broke free to disturb his sleep at night. That first night in Africa was no exception, but when he awoke, he could remember none of his dreams. Nor could he remember where he was. The net above him veiled the contents of his room creating a cocoon, hiding him from the outside world. He often sought such anonymity, but the shroud-like form frightened him now it seemed to have materialised. After the first moments of anxiety had eased, he lay for a few minutes taking in his new surroundings as they took shape through the gauze. Inside his room the furniture connected his memory back to reality. He raised himself on one elbow and saw his suitcases on the low unit by the dressing table. Outside, the sun was on his side of the building and the caged birds were greeting it, giving Malcolm a novel morning call. He lay back again in his bed aware of where he was and pleased to be there. Realising the time, he rose and showered. The warm water was a mistake and when he emerged his body felt unrefreshed. He showered again, this time in cold water.

As he went down to breakfast, he could see the bright sunlight warming the white walls of the courtyard outside. With the rising sun, shadows were growing shorter and shafts of light knifed through the branches of the courtyard tree stirring the birds to greater volume. An unusual emotional reflex made him want to sing with them but his best attempt was to hum a muted fanfare.

Breakfast was another lavish spread with very much an English preference. Flowing gowns and red fezzes dealt with his every wish, the eggs and bacon more appetising than yesterday's airport fare. He assumed the coffee, richer and tastier than he was used to, had come from the plantations that surrounded Nairobi.

He returned to his room to pack. As he re-packed one of his cases, he saw the travel label, his name and old address turned up to face him. He wanted to reject and forget the past life and pulled at the label sharply. The string, which attached it to his case, failed to snap but the soft cardboard label broke away and he threw it in the bin. He wanted to think he had been reborn and that all labels linking him to his past could be destroyed as simply. But the labels that described him were etched deep inside him; they could not so easily be discarded. The best he could expect was that they remained obscure.

At reception he settled his bill with some of his travellers' cheques and studied the change he was given. The notes and coins had an unfamiliar look and feel and he had no sense of their value. He went outside to wait for Rogers on the steps of the terrace leaving his suitcases just inside the shaded foyer.

There was much activity. Hotel staff were watering the flower beds and hanging baskets. He wondered why they didn't preserve the water for the bathrooms. Not for the last time he saw a colonial routine Africa found hard to break. On the pavement a youth with a large bag slung round his shoulders was trying to sell souvenirs to the tourists queuing to get into a zebra-striped minibus. Their interests were elsewhere and no sales were made. As the bus drove off, the youth decamped to the shade of a tree opposite and lit a cigarette. The road was tarmacked but the roadside opposite was a dirt track and its dry dust blew into the road only to be scooped into the air by passing traffic and settle capriciously on anything close. Further down the street two African men were unloading a tall fridge from a van into a small shop. Their cries of advice, as to where to hold and when to lift, carried to the hotel. An Asian man in a suit watched the progress. On the terrace, two cleaners stacked the chairs and tables to one side as they swept the floor, first damping the dust by splashing water from a bucket.

A car horn brought Malcolm's attention back to the road in front. Acknowledging Rogers' arrival, he went back to the shade to collect his belongings and put them in the back of the car.

'Jambo,' said Rogers. 'You'd better learn some Swahili. Jambo's easy enough. It means hello.'

'Jambo,' replied Malcolm quietly, not wanting his voice to sound beyond the car.

'Sleep well? You look better today.'

'Yes. Thanks. Like a top,' in replying he unwittingly parodied Rogers' speaking style. 'You've no helper today,' referring to the youngster who'd carried his bag.

'School.'

Rogers, dressed as the day before, said little as they drove across the city. That suited Malcolm who was soon absorbed into the city life. Modern buildings and modest shop fronts stood side-by-side; a mosque claimed the sky. People scurried from place to place crossing the road without much regard for safety. It registered in him that only a minority where white. Knots of people stood on street corners, some hassling passing tourists to buy their carvings, others were having their hair cut; none was white. On the tree-lined roadway handcarts held their own with large modern cars, not many British made. People crossed the road with some risk and drivers established their status with blasts on the horn. Malcolm's feelings were a jumble of apprehension and anticipation. The colour, the informality, the inhibition, the disorganization drew him in. Deep within him, nerves, veins, synapses released a trickle of feeling which was new to him. Through the windscreen was a stage, the actors no more than stereotypes for the moment, acting out disparate crowd scenes with no principals in sight. Much against his instincts, he began to anticipate a walk-on part at least.

He was dragged back from this reverie as Rogers pulled into a parking bay outside a bank. Once again Rogers would make Malcolm's choices for him.

Rogers knew who to speak to and he left Malcolm with an Asian woman who took him to a small office where he was absorbed painlessly into the system. The woman was small and delicate. Malcolm would have described her as a girl rather than the mid-thirties woman she was. Her brisk handling of his affairs was a welcome contrast with the anarchy outside. He paid in his travellers' cheques retaining some money for himself. The numbers on the notes were larger than sterling and he felt a false sense of wealth. The creation of a bank account and the issuing of a cheque book gave Malcolm a small foothold on his new world.

Outside he found Rogers standing in the shade of one of the bank's classic pillars. He was smoking his pipe, the elbow of one arm supported by the palm of the other. He was gazing at the ground in front of him lost in thought. As Malcolm approached, he looked up.

'Sorted?'

'Yes, thanks.'

'Let's go.'

Back in the car and through some traffic lights they arrived in the forecourt of a car showroom. Again, there was little alternative but to accept Rogers' guidance. As they wandered amongst the models, many of which Malcolm had not heard of, they were approached by a short-sleeved Asian salesman. He obviously knew Rogers, who introduced Malcolm to him. Most of the models he was shown had prices which made Malcolm hesitate. He knew what his salary would be but he had no idea what it would buy him. He had to convert from Kenyan shillings to English pounds before he realised what he might be letting himself in for. He had only had one car before and hadn't got the technical knowledge to ask the right questions or test the important features. He was wary of paying out a large sum of money for a dud.

Rogers persuaded him he needed a reasonably big car with some power as the thin air at this altitude reduced performance. He suggested a particular car, whether through experience or impatience was not clear. Malcolm liked the look of the car which was much bigger than he had imagined buying and at a much higher price he would have wanted to have paid. He dared not refuse when offered a test drive and, under the salesman's directions, he drove tentatively around the broad avenues and tight roundabouts. Malcolm felt he was taking his test again. Only reluctantly did he get into top gear and even then, his foot hovered over the brake; dangers might have come from any direction and he was prepared for all of them.

'Suit you?' asked Rogers when they returned to the parking lot.

Malcolm couldn't contemplate *no* as that would entail another test drive so he was resigned to this one by default. 'Yes, but the price seems beyond me.'

'The ministry will grant you a loan which you pay back out of salary. You won't notice after a while. In the long run it's worth buying something decent. Reliability's important here. Garages are a long way apart. We can talk price.'

Rogers spoke to the Asian, 'Usual discount?'

'I can knock off seven hundred shillings. OK?'

'Come off it. You can do better than that. Make it a thousand.'

The salesman dropped his lower jaw in mock horror. 'OK.' He smiled.

Rogers looked at Malcolm and nodded his head slightly.

'OK,' said Malcolm with resignation, hoping he'd got the currency straight and wanting only to get out of a situation in which he was ill-equipped to engage.

'Good. We'll pick it up on tomorrow. Make sure the tank's full. I'll ask PK to bring Mr. Bryant down. He'll do the paper work then.' Rogers had taken over again. The Asian shook Malcolm's hand, whether for courtesy or contract was not clear, and the two Europeans drove away. On the brief journey to the centre of the town Malcolm asked how they could be sure there was nothing wrong with the car.

'His brother, PK, works with us at Kimura.' Malcolm thought it a reassuring explanation.

They parked in a slanted parking slot outside an open fronted restaurant. Rogers covered the steering wheel with the towel and nodded towards the restaurant.

'We'll eat there later. We'll just get you sorted out by the ministry first. Strictly speaking you're working for them don't forget. And they're going to lend you the money to buy that car.'

The ministry was just round the corner. The doorman let them through judging their white skin as evidence of soundness. Lifetime assumptions were not to be undermined by political independence. They reached an open plan office up two flights of stairs. Rogers went straight to one desk and stood in front of it, opposite an African man.

'Good morning, Mr. Njoroge. This is Mr. Bryant, my new assistant. We've come to sort out the paperwork,' said Rogers showing more deference than he had to other Africans.

'Good morning,' the reply was more bored than dismissive. He gestured to them to sit down. He got from his chair and took several forms from various files in a filing cabinet. There were a lot of filing cabinets.

'Please fill in these.' Without sitting down again he walked off out of the office.

Rogers looked sheepishly at Malcolm. 'He and I don't get on. The chap before him, Peter Watkins, and I got on famously. Still, times change. Times change,' Rogers spoke quietly.

The forms required the normal personal details although he was surprised that he had to sign the Official Secrets Act. Next of kin had to be his aunt in Edinburgh. Having finished form filling they waited for Njoroge to return. After a while one of the other staff in the office came over.

'Finished?' she asked smiling, her teeth showing a brown stain.

'Yes,' said Malcolm meekly, influenced by Rogers's quietness.

'I'll see Mr. Njoroge gets these.'

'Good,' from Rogers.

'Thank you. I hope they're alright,' said Malcolm referring to the forms and responding to her friendliness with a grace that had escaped Rogers.

'Well, we'll sort it out if they're not.' She nodded goodbye.

As they passed another office on the way out, they saw Njoroge, cup of tea in hand, joking with another African man seated at his desk and leaning back in his chair. He glanced at them as they passed, but made no gesture of recognition. As the two Europeans started down the stairs, they heard Njoroge and his friend burst out laughing. Both experienced their separate and different feelings of paranoia.

'Time for lunch I think,' said Rogers when they reached ground level.

They sat at a table on the pavement and with Rogers' car at the kerb. Before taking his seat, Rogers wound down the window to keep the car cool.

'Beer?' This time the question came from Malcolm. Nothing that Rogers had said or done was unacceptable. Indeed, he had achieved in a couple of hours what Malcolm would have taken days over. His invitation had the dual function of staking some kind of independence and repaying a debt of gratitude. Rogers nodded avoiding the need for words. Malcolm was puzzled by how he could be so helpful without being friendly.

From nowhere Rogers, jerking his head towards the street, said, 'I hate this place. Town life is awful. It's not the real Africa. There's a loss of innocence here. The people have lost their gentleness.' From Rogers it was more like a speech than a comment. Malcolm looked around; there seemed no reason for his boss's remarks.

The beers arrived and Malcolm handed over a note and collected most of the change leaving a rather bigger tip than he realised.

As they sat, several street sellers walked by, stopping to offer their wares - carved wooden animals, elephant hair bracelets, drums –

with a stoicism which invited rejection. Rogers was expertly dismissive. They ordered lunch and another beer. Malcolm paid again.

As they ate, a street beggar approached. He was an adult male but his torso was shrivelled and twisted, its features covered by a tattered rain coat. He wasn't walking but was seated in a little wooden trolley built into the chassis of a child's pram. He propelled himself by moving the wheels with one hand and sought alms in the tin mug he held in the other. There was no doubt that he was approaching them. The few coins in the mug rattled accusingly as it was thrust towards the two diners. Malcolm took the change from the beers which was lying on the table and put it in the mug.

The man looked at Malcolm, his gaze steady and lively. He said something that Malcolm didn't understand but took to be gratitude. As the man pulled away Malcolm thought of Marion in her wheelchair. Like this man Marion had had no use in her legs but unlike him was mentally impaired as well and didn't understand her predicament. This man knew full well what he was and what he might have been. Unlike Marion, he had to share the knowledge of his impairment with the world around. He could not hide if he wanted to live; to eat he needed to swallow his pride every day of his life.

Malcolm didn't like to look at Rogers because he knew his eyes were moist, so he kept on looking up the street as the man paddled away. It was not for Marion that he cried, but for himself. The misshapen figure meandering down the road had reawakened feelings he had begun to believe were in the past. His new world was still vulnerable to echoes from the old.

'Small amounts are best. Many beggars about. City attracts them. Where else?' Rogers commented.

'Why so many?' Malcolm had noticed several around the bank.

'Birth defects, illness, accidents,...... retribution.'

Malcolm looked blank.

'The Emergency, the insurrection, the rebellion, the fight for independence; call it what you will. The Mau Mau. A couple of hundred Europeans died, some children of course, awful but hardly a massacre. Its main effect was to set African against African. Freedom came at a heavy price for some. It was nasty. Very nasty.'

His understatement eluded Malcolm and the older man assumed a greater knowledge on Malcolm's part than was justified. He paused, pulling on his pipe, not for effect, but to allow himself time to decide which of his memories should be described.

'I arrived at the start of it. They didn't say much in London. Hoping it would soon be over I suppose. Found out soon enough when I arrived. Kimura was largely spared although we would find bodies some mornings. Not a pretty sight. Mutilation. That sort of thing. It took its toll on all of us. I'd seen some sights in the war but this was different. Awful.'

He stopped; his eyes moist now. He cleared his throat and drank some beer. He was thinking and saying more than usual on these occasions. This newcomer's sympathetic interest in the beggar had an old-fashioned ring to it which prized open a gap in Rogers' truculent shield. Once the warm air of compassion filtered through, rough edges softened. Perhaps alcohol played a part. He could not fail to continue.

'The missions had a hell of a time. Forgiveness had a rough ride. There's a priest in the village near the station. He was there the whole time. Flynn. Irishman. Catholic, of course. The Catholics do quite well amongst the Africans. Something about the ritual and the costume I expect. You'll meet him. He had to tend the damaged and bury the dead. He had to tell them the killing was wrong. And he did, fair play to him. He was taking a risk. I just kept my mouth shut. Tribalism played its part though we want to down play it now. There's a bigger prize at stake.'

In those few moments Malcolm saw Rogers anew. Here was a man, like himself, who was what he was because of what had happened to him. An innocent bystander to life's harshness. He'd had the same experience with his father who would briefly talk about his war service, but usually retreated into silence. Later, after Marion died, he tried to say things about her. But the things were too big for his vocabulary.

Tribalism meant nothing to Malcolm but clearly the country, like him, had a past which it wanted to forget. But he knew from his own experience that some things dwell in the shadows waiting to spill out when least expected.

'Better get back. Work to be done,' said Rogers. He strode out of the restaurant, knocking out his pipe on the kerbside before getting in his car. He was back to normal.

FIVE

The road to Kimura passed through the richer suburbs of the capital. Bungalows with bougainvillea spilling over their surrounding walls bordered avenues lined with jacaranda and flame trees. Beyond the city limits, these were replaced by patches of maize and bananas and later bigger areas of coffee. The purple and red of town ornament gave way to the blue, green and brown of unsophisticated country. Here the trees and shrubs so abundant in the city were now isolated features in a broad semi-cultivated panorama allowing Malcolm to see over some considerable distance. The surrounding land was gently hilly and tiered into cultivated terraces delineated by the brown soil and the green crops. Dwellings sprouted from the slopes, some lone, some in groups, some thatched looking like pointed mushrooms on the hillside, others with sheeted iron rooves looking like garden sheds. Here and there clumps of trees rose to rob the countryside of its smoothness. At each side of the road was a narrow dirt strip which served as a pathway for pedestrians. Here, toddlers trailed behind mothers with babies shawled to their backs. Young girls balanced packs of sticks or water cans on their heads. Older women strained forward, the thongs of a heavy bags of maize meal bearing on their foreheads. Young boys drove goats and men forged ahead with traditional detachment from the industry behind them. Most wore the drab over-used clothes of the chronically poor, though here and there splashes of bright, even garish, garments challenged their wearers' deprivation. Others, mainly young adults it seemed, wore fresh clean modern clothes - suits, ties, tight skirts, neat blouses - as though they had stepped from an urban office on to a city street. Yet for these aspirants to a modern world their appearance, incongruous in the open countryside, seemed only to emphasise their helplessness. Movement was slow and capricious and the brutally fast flow of traffic seemed an insult to the rural calmness. Country buses pulled up at informal stopping points, part on the road, part on the pathway, their heavily laden rooves and tilted chassis seeming to defy physics. Bunches of bananas, crates of chickens, tins of oil were deposited carelessly on the pathway by enthusiastic acolytes of the driver. One bus moved off too quickly in a frantic race to secure passengers before a rival, leaving the helpers to climb down the side of the bus to the safety of the interior whilst the vehicle stormed along the road. Their shouts of joking abuse for the driver were left hanging in the air along with the dust churned up by the bus's wheels. It was a snap shot of rural Africa which didn't pretend to compete with the post card life of wild animals and big mountains but was more authentic.

Malcolm took this in as he sat with the warm air blowing in through the open window pulling at the strands of his short hair. The warmth, the light, the colour seemed to enliven his body. He felt different. England was in his past but he was not thinking about it. All his thoughts were on today.

The road narrowed as they crossed a bridge and the pedestrians ran a greater risk of being run over as they jostled their way across. The bridge went over a deep ravine and through the flimsy handrails Malcolm could see the boulders below. There was little water in the river at the bottom of the chasm and what there was, was part hidden beneath the rocks.

'That's the Changa river. Rises up in the Aberdares and goes into the Rift somewhere, I expect,' was Rogers' minimalist contribution to topography. 'Good fishing further upstream if you're interested. Trout.' Malcolm nodded but had no interest.

After some miles they turned off the main road onto a road with two narrow tarmac strips just far enough apart to take the wheel base of a vehicle. The roadway which contained these strips sometimes narrowed as it passed through a canyon of maize plants or banana trees, but was generally wide enough to allow two vehicles to pass if each moved to one side.

Before long the tarmac strips petered out and the road was just dirt. Almost immediately a lorry passed them at some speed in the opposite direction. It threw up clouds of dust which Rogers avoided by winding his window up. A back draught sucked some dusty air through the passenger window onto Malcolm. The state of Rogers' car seemed excusable. The road had stretches which had become corrugated with the passage of vehicles and Rogers managed to hit the right speed to ameliorate their effect. Malcolm would take some months to acquire this much prized skill. Once or twice, Rogers had to slow into second gear to negotiate ducts caused by heavy rain which had run across the road, the springs of the vehicle groaning as it dipped into the depressions.

Just when the trip was losing its novelty the country opened up. On the left and far ahead, beyond a stretch of barren ground, was an area of coffee stretching as far as some wooded hills in the distance.

'That's Larsen's estate,' said Rogers indicating the coffee bushes. 'His house is further up the road. Our next-door neighbours you might say.' Malcolm studied the bushes. He had a theoretical knowledge of coffee production but was intrigued to see the source of the brown granules that had played such a part in his common room life; the link was not obvious. To the right the land sloped down towards the bottom of a shallow valley. On it some goats grazed. Then just ahead was a settlement of houses with terracotta coloured tiled rooves like a regimented Cotswold hamlet.

'Here we are. Home.'

Rogers pulled off to the right into an open square in the centre of which was a sparsely grassed area beneath a big tree, its overhanging branches offering a wide shade. On the right-hand side of the square were two identical bungalows fronted by small open plan patches of dry grass which elsewhere might have been gardens. Between them was a flat-topped concrete building. On the outside edge of each pair was a car port its roof sloping away from the house to carry the rain water. The bungalows on the left-hand side were mirror images of those opposite except that the car port of the furthest building was covered with bougainvillea. Rogers stopped in the shade of the tree opposite the first bungalow on the right.

'This one's yours. We're over there,' he said, nodding towards the bougainvillea. He got out of the car. 'Come on'.

As Malcolm got out of the car, he realised that even though he had been in the continent for over 24 hours he was stepping on real African soil for the first time. He looked down at it and disturbed the dust with a movement of his foot. It was dry and soft and as Malcolm raised his foot, he saw the imprint of his shoe, sharp at first but its edges eroding as the light dust was caught by the slightest of breezes.

Rogers set off diagonally across the square with Malcolm following. It was mid-afternoon and the sun was hot on their faces but the breeze gave some relief. On the side of the square furthest from the road was a business-like building with a sign outside which read *Kimura Agricultural Research Station* and beneath in smaller letters *Director A R Rogers*.

'Come in and meet the wife,' Rogers threw the invitation over his shoulder.

This was the first time there had been any mention of a Mrs. Rogers since his arrival and Malcolm's lack of small talk had not discovered her. She appeared at the front door having seen their approach from the kitchen. She, like her husband, was approaching what Malcolm considered middle age, but unlike him was slightly plump. She had on a flowered skirt and simple white blouse which showed off her bare arms. Her skin was sunburnt rather than tanned. On her feet she wore green flip-flops the single thongs separating her big toes from the rest. Her head was haloed by fair hair going grey. There was simplicity about her smile of welcome.

'Hello dear. This is Mr Bryant.' Rogers paused as if forgetting his new colleague's name.

'Malcolm,' he was reminded.

'Malcolm. This is my wife.' He paused again as though forgetting his wife's name.

'Alice. We're all on first name terms here. Arthur usually forgets to say so. Takes it for granted I suppose. You take lots of things for granted don't you Arthur.' She laughed and squeezed his arm. And then to Malcolm, she said, 'Anyway it's very nice to meet you. You're very welcome here. Have you had a good trip?'

'Yes. Thank you.'

'Come on in and we'll have a nice cup of tea. You must be very tired. It's awfully sticky in Nairobi at this time of the year. Was your hotel alright? We like it. It's a little old fashioned but it suits us. I suppose we're old fashioned,' she finished with a little self-conscious giggle. Alice Rogers was clearly more outgoing than her husband.

She led him through the bungalow to a veranda stretching the full length of the rear of the house. Two large black dogs nosed him as he stepped out.

'Shoo,' said Mrs. Rogers. This was enough to send them galloping across the greenish-yellow lawn to the shade of some shrubs.

The tea and cake were brought in by an elderly African man in white shirt and brown shorts with flip-flops on his feet. His sparse bare legs made him seem like a grandfather paddling at the seaside with rolled up trousers.

'Thank you, Simeon. Mr Bryant here is coming to live here. He's just arrived from England.'

'Jambo, Sah.'

'Jambo,' Malcolm felt self-conscious about his mumbled reply.

Alice Rogers poured the tea and continued, 'He'll be living at... ,' she hesitated, '.. number four'. This was not to inform Simeon who already knew but to set up the next bit of the conversation. 'The bungalows were numbered when we came but I thought it would be nice to give them names. To make it homely, you know. But people come and go and the idea petered out. We've kept our name. We call it *Kahawa.* That's Swahili for coffee you know. I like the sound. Ka-ha-wa. Arthur doesn't bother. Did you notice the sign outside? It's in nice poker work. I got a man on River Road to do it. What were the other names now? Next door, where the Harringtons live, you'll be meeting them later. That was *Boma* - that's a sort of stockade, a little hamlet in the middle of the bush. I've forgotten what yours was called. Do you remember that funny Welshman, Arthur? He took the original name down and put one up in Welsh. At least I think it was Welsh. I couldn't pronounce it, anyway. Didn't he go to Saudi Arabia in the end? We don't hear from him. Don't really mind in his case, do we Arthur?'

Rogers said nothing but gestured some kind of assent.

'Oh. I know. It was *Nyumbani.* That means Home. And we do think of them as homes. You may find that strange. You've got a home in England.'

Malcolm wanted to disagree but said nothing, savouring the name and wanting to claim it. But it is my home; at least there is no other, he wanted to say despite the sad sentimentality of the thought. 'But this is where we belong at the moment. We've got a little cottage near Weymouth for when we retire, but it's not home. Not yet. House names say a lot about the inhabitants don't you think. Although I suppose most of us don't choose the names, we just inherit them with the property.'

The Bryant family home had no name.

'The one in Weymouth is called *Periwincle.* I don't like that. Do you? I'm going to call it *Kahawa* too. I'll make the locals think won't it. I'm going to take the sign from here. It's not government property, not the sign, so that's all right. Anyway, we hope you'll find yourself at home here, don't we Arthur. Now what was number three called Arthur? Oh, my memories getting awful. I must be getting old.'

She smiled expansively while her husband sucked on the pipe he had lit up during her monologue.

Throughout the snack Alice Rogers chatted away saying so much about so little. Malcolm was required to part with the barest details of his life which Mrs. Rogers absorbed and converted to anecdotes of her own. She liked to talk but Arthur wasn't very chatty. She often went over to Connie Larsen's or down to the club. And sometimes Flynn would drop by. He liked to talk. And she had the clinic.

'*Chai*. It was called *Chai*. Number three,' Arthur intervened.

'Oh yes of course. *Chai*. Tea. Tea and coffee opposite one another. Bernie lives there now. Tea and coffee? More chalk and cheese,' she said enigmatically.

'Let's get you moved in. Come on,' said Rogers.

The three of them set off back to the car parked outside Malcolm's new home. Rogers climbed the two steps and unlocked the front door. He held the keys by their fob so they jangled beneath and handed them to Malcolm. Alice Rogers took Malcolm round the house while her husband recovered the luggage from the car. The front door opened on to a hallway which ran through to the back of the building and had doors leading off it. To the left was a kitchen; to the right a bathroom and toilet. On the left beyond the kitchen, was a lounge with a dining area at one end and a large window overlooking the back garden beyond a veranda at the other. On the right beyond the bathroom was a bedroom with a small window set high up the wall on the side of the house overlooking the car port and the roadway beyond. Beyond it a second, bigger bedroom with its window facing the garden. The bed in there was made up. A large double door from the main hallway led to the veranda which spread the whole length of the house. From this he could see the road along which they had come earlier. Directly ahead and beyond some substantial bushes at the bottom of his garden he saw into and across the low valley with the goats. Immediately in front of the veranda was a lawn spreading to the flower beds around the boundary of the garden. This garden was separated from its twin by a chain link fence about a metre high.

Malcolm thought it rather better than he had been used to. The literature he had received left him to interpret the phrase *government standard accommodation* and while he had not expected a mud hut, he was not expecting this either. The floors were a plasticised tile and were brightly polished. Indeed, everywhere looked clean. Mrs Rogers had made sure he would feel welcome. And there was more.

'I've got a few things in for you, just to start you off. And you must come to dinner. At seven o'clock?'

'Yes. Thank you.' Malcolm wondered how often he had used those words today.

He knew his accommodation had basic linen provided but he hadn't given any thought to food. It was obvious there wasn't a corner shop to pop out to. Mrs. Rogers, with more enthusiasm for a newcomer than her husband had seen his arrival as an opportunity for home building. In the kitchen the fridge, buzzing busily, held cartons of milk and orange juice and several bottles of beer. The freezer compartment contained a tray of ice. A wall-cupboard contained corn flakes, bread in a plastic box, tea, instant coffee, sugar and several tins of meats and vegetables. He looked at Mrs Rogers and burbled his thanks. She beamed at his satisfaction. She must have done this as often as Mr Rogers had collected people from the airport yet she showed no sign of boredom.

'It's fairly quiet here,' she said. 'People coming are quite a highlight,' she continued by way of justification.

'People going, as well,' said Rogers from the hallway where he had put Malcolm's suitcase. It was a clumsy attempt at humour as an embarrassed antidote to his wife's generosity.

'We'll leave you to settle in now. See you at seven. We don't dress for dinner. Come as you are.' She took her husband's hand and led him gently through the door and across the square. Malcolm watched them go, savouring the simple kindness she had shown. Alice Rogers was too young to be his mother but she had insinuated a protective wing around him. It felt strange to have someone give him so much attention, something his own mother had been unable to do.

He wandered around opening drawers and cupboards. Everything he needed was there - crockery, cutlery, a tin opener. Off the kitchen to the side of the house was another door and it was this from which came a gentle knocking. Opening the door Malcolm saw a slightly built African man. He was wearing slacks and a white open necked shirt. His hair was flecked with grey and his face bore a number of tribal scars. The scars suggested a ferocity with which Malcolm felt uneasy, but his position at the top of two steps gave him some confidence.

'Greetings, sah. I am looking for work in the house. I can cook and iron.' He gave the 'r' in 'iron' a distinct roll creating two syllables. His voice was soft and suited the enforced humility of his quest. 'I used to work in this house for Bwana Shelley. He has given me a reference.'

The man took a very worn envelope from his back trouser pocket. With deliberate care he extracted from it a piece of paper folded twice and offered it to Malcolm. As Malcolm unfolded it a small stream of brown dust ran along the crease of the paper.

It read: *To whom it may concern. Joseph Karui worked as my cook and cleaner for two years. His cooking is adequate (but don't encourage him to make cakes); his cleaning excellent; his ironing not as good as he thinks (but better than mine). For me he was honest and reliable. He has no family with him. Signed Thomas J. Shelley, Kimura Station.* The vertical stroke of each d was faded and the down tails of some letters were tinged with red. It was dated seven months previously.

Handing back the paper Malcolm asked the man what he had done in the last seven months.

'Ah, nothing, sah. There is no work here.'

He had known from the grapevine that Shelley would be replaced eventually. The seven-month delay was just one of life's taunts, no worse than failed rains or a bout of malaria.

Malcolm was nonplussed. He hadn't contemplated staff although he'd read it was usual to employ help in the house. He wouldn't know what to pay him or what to ask him to do. Seeing Mrs Rogers as his saviour, he told the man to come back the following morning.

'Thank you, sah. I will come then.' He seemed relieved even at this noncommittal response.

As the man turned to go through the garden gate. Malcolm saw he had no socks and his shoes, slightly too large, were flopping from his feet reveal the scaly white of his heels. The prospective employer stepped down from the back door and watched the man walk slowly down the road and out of sight.

Turning to go back inside he became intrigued by the small building between his bungalow and the next. The entry to it was offset from the kitchen door and he walked down the path the short way to the opening. From there he could not see directly in because of the design, but there was obviously a small yard with rooms off it. He went through and turned left to see a crude room with a door and window both closed. It was much like the garden shed his father had had, although that had been wooden and stood alone. This was twinned with another which belonged to the neighbouring bungalow. Between the two was a smaller room which would prove to be a simple shower-room and toilet. He found it difficult to accept he was looking at two lots of living accommodation.

In the small courtyard was a low charcoal stove with a cooking pot boiling on it. Venturing further in so that he could see the whole of the minute courtyard, he saw a young woman, he guessed no more than twenty, sitting in the opposite corner breast-feeding a baby. Her hair was covered with a scarf drawn to the top edge of her forehead. Her patterned dress, buttoned down the front had the top three buttons undone. He had not expected to find anybody there and he certainly hadn't expected a female breast but he was held fast by confusion not fascination. As the baby suckled, the surface of the breast moved up and down displaying a golden sheen which contrasted with the dark colour of the baby's hair. She knew he was there but she held her eyes downwards and kept them so until Malcolm withdrew in disarray.

Back in the kitchen, he realised he'd never seen a live female breast before; he'd not seen Marion without clothes since she was very young and breasts an irrelevance. The image stayed with him for a long time. It had been so beautiful and so full of life to his eye; so soft, so warm and so gentle to his imagination.

That evening there were many things to ask of Mrs Rogers but women's breasts were not among them. As he walked across the square his way was lit from the windows of the four bungalows. He found it difficult to reconcile the warmth of the air with the blackness of the sky above. For him darkness had meant gloom and cold. Not so here, where it seemed to be invigorating. Even the stars, normally harbingers of frost, seemed to add to his feeling of well-being. He knocked on the door exactly at seven-o-clock. It was opened by the African man who had served tea earlier but this time he was dressed more formally. He wore black trousers and a white shirt over which he had a black waistcoat. On his head he had a red fez and Malcolm wondered if this item had any tribal significance.

'Jambo,' he said then stopped forgetting the man's name in his struggle to remember the greeting.

The man stepped back and with a little bow beckoned Malcolm through.

'Jambo, sah. Karibu.' Malcolm tried to memorise the word hoping to look it up in his phrase book but the meaning was obvious and he went in.

'Hello, Malcolm. Nice to see you. Do come through.' Alice Rogers appeared in the hall way and took him through to the veranda. Her husband was sitting in one of several cane chairs smoking a pipe.

'I hope you don't mind,' he said indicating the pipe.

'Not at all,' said Malcolm. 'It'll frighten off the dudus.' It was an easy word which he learnt not from his phrase book but by hearing it from another human being.

Rogers looked at him quizzically then shooed a large Labrador off one of the chairs. 'Take a pew.'

The valley on Rogers' side of the compound widened beyond the station and the view from the veranda looked down towards the hills where the valley curved left into the darkness. The hills were mere vague outlines against the starry sky. Simeon appeared at the veranda door.

'Would you like a drink, Malcolm?' asked Mrs Rogers, unlike her husband inviting some choice.

He accepted, asking thankfully for beer and then remembered his own potential employee.

'After you left a man came to the door looking for a job as a ....'' He didn't know how to describe Karui's position.

'Do you know we used to call them house boys but that's frowned on now - since Independence. So, we don't do it. At least we try not to. Old habits die hard. You don't think about these things unless you're challenged. I was in Nairobi last week - getting some things for you - and I heard someone call one of the waiters, boy. Nobody said anything but it sounded awful to me and yet a few years ago, I'd not have thought about it. I suppose we must have said some awful things over the years.' Alice had side-tracked herself.

'But he's older than my father.'

'Exactly,' Arthur interjected.

'What should I do?'

'Most people have help in the house. Some big houses in town might have three or four servants - more perhaps.'

'Servants?' queried Malcolm.

'I suppose that's not much better than boy, is it? Better than slave. They say some of the foreign embassies and the multinationals - treat people no better than slaves.'

'But we don't know that do we, Alice. People like to say these things to make us seem better than others.'

'It's not what I think, Arthur. You know that,' Alice bridled.

'No, I know you don't,' said Arthur gently. 'Anyway staff, if you want. It's all in the mind.'

'So, I should take him on?' Malcolm was more concerned about practicalities than the social ethics.

'It's up to you,' said Rogers.

'Yes. I think you should. Apart from anything else the money you pay him will support his family in his village,' said Alice. Her husband drew on his pipe.

'And he's probably a better cook than you,' Rogers blew a stream of tobacco smoke into the night air.

Will he be satisfactory? Will I be safe? is what Malcolm meant.

'Well, Karui's all right as far as I know. He's been around here as long as we have. I've never heard any criticism. I think he'll be all right. But you mustn't be too generous to start with. Have a period of probation if you know what I mean. I suggest you take him on for a month at a hundred shillings.'

'A hundred shillings!' Even Malcolm knew how little that was.

'You can be a lot more generous later when you're more confident. Make sure he's punctual. Eight o'clock should mean eight o'clock, not twenty-past. I think you should make it clear he is not to share his accommodation with anybody. It's only meant for one person. And no alcohol in his room. If he wants to drink, he must go to the village but don't encourage it. Remember he's leading a bachelor life and there are always temptations. His family live in his home village, quite a way away, so they won't come down. He'll want to get up to see them. You'll need to make it clear when he can go.'

59

To Malcolm it all seemed a bit draconian. He was surprised how easily he could afford it and surprised the man would find it agreeable.

Just after the beer arrived a young couple arrived to join them. John and Teresa Harrington were about the same age as Malcolm. They were both below average height and a little overweight. In the UK they might have looked unhealthy but here their bronzed skin suggested fitness. She wore a brightly coloured top over a short white skirt and pale tan sandals. Her blonde hair whitened by strong sunshine was tied back in a ponytail. His top was clearly the same fabric as his wife's but the pattern was more subdued. He wore light coloured slacks and a pair of sandals on his bare feet. His face was ringed by dark ragged hair and a beard which struggled to hide his skin beneath.

With Mrs. Rogers inside the house organising the meal, the conversation was slow to start but gradually facts and opinions began to emerge from the formality.

'How long have you been here?' asked Malcolm.

'Nearly eighteen months now. Six months more and then somewhere else I expect?'

'Don't you want to stay longer?'

'Yes and no. It's fine here but there's a lot of the world to see. They say Singapore's great. What do you think Arthur?'

'Yes. So I hear. But will they be offering jobs? They're much more developed than here.'

'I suppose so. But there may not be a job here much longer either. The expats are being squeezed out. And Teresa can only get temporary jobs. Anyway, there's lots more to see here yet. That Zanzibar business is a bit of a nuisance. I quite fancy going there. We went to Malindi earlier this year and got up to Lamu. That was great.'

Malcolm envied their self-assurance. He tried to remember the places they had mentioned. When he was researching his posting his map reading didn't go far beyond Nairobi.

From the house a gong rang. Mrs Rogers ushered her guests into the dining room. The table was very formally laid with lighted candles. Each place setting had a hand-written card with their names on.

'You sit here Malcolm, between Teresa and me. I've made a beef dish. I hope you eat meat. I read that a lot of people are vegetarians now. Not us though. I suppose it was the war. Having gone without things for so long we saw good food as a sort of reward.' She put her hands together and said a simple grace catching Malcolm unawares. He managed to put his hands together just as she finished. The phrase *for what we are about to receive* lingered in his mind not so much as a promise of food to come but of a life he had begun to anticipate.

After each course the cook was summoned to clear the table by Mrs Rogers ringing a small handbell. Malcolm smiled inwardly at the incongruity between this contrived formality and the casual friendliness he had met earlier.

Following coffee and brandy, which Malcolm did not like but could not bring himself to refuse lest he should seem unappreciative, he returned to his bungalow. The effect of the daytime sun on his skin together with the alcohol in his blood made his body glow as he crossed the square and his mind lacked the focus he'd come to expect. He tried to remember the Swahili name for his house. Number. No. *Nimbuni.* No. Dam. He would find out tomorrow. No, he could look it up in his vocabulary book. Home. That was it. Home.

As he approached his house he reached in his pocket for his keys and in doing so dropped them on the ground. Falling to his knees he ran his hands over the ground to locate them. The soil was still warm to his touch. He scooped some up in his hands and let it filter through his fingers. Its fineness had a silky quality against his skin. He scooped up another handful and let it run from his clenched fist held like an egg timer.

Straightening his back, he gazed upward to the sky which was filled with more stars than he thought possible. After years of little rooms, small talk and limited ambitions he was suddenly in a bigger world. He felt exceedingly small but instead of feeling fear at its enormity, he rejoiced in his own insignificance. He wanted to shout out loud, I am here, and to have his words reach outward and upwards forever. Not to draw attention to himself but because he felt the vastness of the surroundings would swallow up his words leaving him unobserved, honouring him with the anonymity he sought. He drew breath to call out, but some trigger within him stopped his action. He would be heard. Within that big world was a smaller one. Someone must be close. Perhaps Mrs Rogers was in her kitchen supervising the cook. He couldn't let her see him being so uninhibited. In fact, only Simeon was in the kitchen. He saw Malcolm, back towards him, down on his knees and was surprised by the public display. The Europeans were usually more private about their religion. He had seen the Muslims get down on their knees like that but not a European. Perhaps he was a Muslim too.

The opportunity for expression had gone but it didn't remove Malcolm's sense of well-being. Inside his house he located his vocabulary book. After failing to find Home in the Swahili list he finally discovered the English list and there the word he was looking for. He sounded out the syllables *Ny-um-ba-ni* and convinced himself it was just right. *Nyumbani*. Home. I've come home. And in the way alcohol has of imbuing crude sentimentality with deep significance, he felt it was true. Already layers of apprehension were falling off him and it would not be long before the sober Malcolm considered himself to be at home and sheltered from his past.

Whilst getting undressed before his open bedroom window he heard the baby crying in the cabin next door. As he lay in bed, he found himself thinking of a golden undulating breast. He imagined it warm and silky like the fine sand outside and he fell into a comfortable sleep, his second in succession - a novelty for him.

SIX

Malcolm woke earlier than his alarm demanded. No one sound had woken him but many unfamiliar noises brought him to consciousness. Had it been a crying child, or the bleat of a goat or the cry of some exotic bird stretching its wings against the warmth of morning? That it was just a passing car would have undermined his hope he had escaped from urban life. Bright sunlight becoming familiar, got him up. He shaved, giving no thought to how the water came to be hot. Images of the previous day flitted into his mind only to be banished as he concentrated on each stroke of the razor. When he had finished, he doused his face in cold water and as the towel moved from his face he gazed at his own image, looking himself squarely in the eye. When young he could not have done that. At the barber's he would sit in the chair taking in the racks of combs, the bottles of lotions, the discreet signs for contraceptives. Anything to avoid looking at himself, needing to avoid acknowledging his own self. But shaving and adulthood had changed that. Now looking at his own face he felt a thrill about the move he had made and a slight apprehension about the consequences of it.

The kitchen was bright and airy compared with that in his UK flat and from its window he could see across the square to the bungalows opposite. There an orange robed figure moved in the light behind the frosted glass of the Harrington's bathroom. A small lizard popped its head over the rim of his kitchen sill but quickly disappeared when Malcolm moved forward to get a closer view. Peering to the left across the road towards the distant coffee estate he could see the labourers already well into their day's work. A thin column of ants made its way to and fro between a hole in the edge of the window frame and the sink. He swatted them away with a tea-towel but they kept on coming. They could wait until later; he was hungry and had to start work.

He flicked through drawers to find what was there and selected a spoon and bowl for the corn flakes. From the fridge he took a carton of milk and, opening it, inexpertly poured some of the contents over the cereal. Blobs of milk spurted over the working surface. As he turned from putting the carton back in the fridge, there was a knock on the door. It was Karui, dressed as before, looking rather apprehensive. Malcolm didn't wait for the question.

'Yes, that'll be OK. You can work here. When can you start?'

'Now, sah,' said from a delighted face.

Malcolm told him what he would pay but drew back on declaring the other conditions. These could wait. He did not ask if Karui found the pay acceptable fearing the man would say no. He didn't think it enough but wouldn't have known how to proceed if Karui had disagreed. He was not to know Karui would have worked for less. He would consider the food he could spirit out of Malcolm's kitchen and the free electricity and water in his quarters to be significant benefits alongside the cash he would take away.

Malcolm let him in but didn't know what to do then. Karui, familiar with this kitchen, seemed clearer and, reaching under the sink, took a dishcloth and wiped the working surface clean of milk. Then he flicked the trail of ants away and chewing a piece of card from the corn flakes packet he squeezed the pulp into the hole in the window frame.

'We will need some spray,' he said. Malcolm made a mental addition to his shopping list and then wondered about the *we*. Were they partners then?

He had intended to eat his cereal in the kitchen standing at the working surface but since he was no longer alone, convention took over and he went to the dining area in the next room. He listened to the noises from the kitchen, a tap running, crockery knocked together, the fridge door opening and closing with a slight squeak. Karui appeared with a tray, on it a pot of coffee, a cup and saucer, milk in a jug and sugar in a bowl. He put them down.

'Would you like toast, sah?'

Ill at ease with the encounter Malcolm declined. He did not want to be called *sir* but let it ride.

He sat alone in his dining room facing the window which opened onto the garden. He heard a man's voice - he assumed it to be Karui's - speaking at the entrance to the quarters. A woman's voice replied, part speech, part laughter. He wondered if the baby was breakfasting too. Karui came back into the kitchen and ran some water into the sink.

But the young European and the older African began their day separated by more than the wall between them. A gulf of culture, experience and expectation distanced these two people physically so close together. If they were partners, they were like the balls on a dumbbell, separated by a rigid bar keeping them apart. But it was not a partnership; the master/servant relationship was dominant and each had to retain his dignity within it.

On leaving for the station Malcolm gave Karui a key for the back door he'd found in a kitchen drawer - he didn't know Karui had one already. He was a little reluctant to leave the house and its possessions in the charge of a virtual stranger though the contents were no more his than Karui's. He did not know, either, that Karui's code would not have countenanced theft. Taking food perhaps, but this was sharing with a stranger and quite normal, but to remove an object, a watch, a book, some clothes - never. His children, with different expectations, might not be so punctilious.

As Malcolm set out from his door the young woman, he had seen breast-feeding yesterday appeared from the servant's quarters on the side of the block away from his house. She wore the same simple patterned dress and her baby was kept in place on her back by a shawl tied in a knot in front. Her head was covered by a scarf wound so as to conceal her hair. He couldn't stop himself looking to her breasts. The shawl passed diagonally across her chest covering and subduing one breast, but the other filled out her thin dress. She was young and slender and moved with an easy style and although he found her mildly attractive his strongest emotion was embarrassment. In a mild panic he forgot the only Swahili greeting he knew. Both his greeting and her reply were in English. He was saddened that he could not speak her language and had required her to speak one not her own. He remembered the phrase book on his bedside table, but did not know Swahili was not her first language either.

Although she looked at him her eyes displayed no emotion. As she walked away the top of a baby's head could be seen hidden away in the folds of the shawl. Below it her hips eased from side to side with a gently swaying motion, the movement soothing the baby as much as it excited Malcolm. He watched her go, now more conscious of her womanhood than her motherhood.

'Morning. Sleep well?' The greeting as abbreviated as possible. Rogers was shouting across the square from the steps to the office.

'Yes, thank you,' the same words again and then 'Very well.'

'Come on in I'll show you around. Meet the gang.'

Together they went up two steps into the hallway. On the left was Rogers's office from which he had seen Malcolm's approach. They stepped inside for a moment. The spartan room was equipped with standard government furniture. Apart from the front wall which had a window in it, each wall had a notice board with a variety of notices and charts. Parts of the pin board had outlines of previous notices surrounded by the discoloured area exposed to the sun and air leaving pale rectangles against a darker brown background. On one board was pinned a calendar showing an English cathedral set in rolling English countryside. It was eight years out of date.

Rogers led the way through the door to the right which was a general office occupied by two men One sat at a desk the other was leaning against a filing cabinet. The first was introduced as Phillip, the clerk. He was wearing a lounge suit and his tie was fastened to his shirt with a thin golden clip. His hair was short and parted conspicuously. The second man was Boniface who was the general handyman. He wore a grey tunic with yellow flip-flops on otherwise bare feet. He was altogether darker than Phillip and hadn't shaved for some days. The room was a mirror image of the first but with fewer notices. On the wall beyond Phillip's desk was a portrait of President Kenyatta. He would soon learn this picture was obligatory in public offices much as the Queen's had been at the interview room in London

Malcolm was introduced as Mr Bryant, Mr Shelley's replacement and they by their first names. Each nodded and shook hands in response. Malcolm was conscious of having touched African skin for the first time in his life. It felt different, cold when he had expected it to be warm. He felt uncomfortable about his reaction and wondered what he felt like to them. But he was not an expert in physical contact. He had never held anyone in his arms, never stroked a cheek, never kissed a lip. The only human physical contact he could recall was hand to hand. As Phillip sat down behind his large old-fashioned typewriter Malcolm noticed that beneath his shining black shoes, he wore no socks.

As the two Europeans went down the corridor to the back the two Africans spoke in their own tongue and laughed. Malcolm felt annoyance that his lack of knowledge of the language made the simplest conversations seem sinister.

Towards the back of the building behind the general office was a kitchen and rest room. It was sparsely equipped, badly decorated and neglected in a male way. Along the length of the outside rear wall ran a working surface containing a sink unit and ending with a calour-gas stove. On the stove sat a large kettle its exterior grimy and stained, its whistle on the working surface beside. A hot water geyser was fixed to the wall near the door and below was a sink. A cockroach was on the floor by the cooker. It wasn't moving and Malcolm took it to be dead. The far wall was occupied by the back seat from a passenger bus its springs tearing through the fabric of its sides. Against the back wall opposite the window was a table and four chairs. The formica top to the table was scored and its metal trim was coming adrift from the frame. From hooks on the edge of a wall shelf above the table hung a row of mugs, no two the same.

'Must do something about this pigsty. Standards are slipping,' Rogers mocked. 'It's all too easy to come out of the shamba all hot and dirty and slump here I'm afraid. Good job the womenfolk don't come this far, eh. I've seen worse though. When I was in India ....,' he stopped and looked at Malcolm self-consciously shrugging. 'That was a long time ago. Come on.' Later Malcolm looked it up in his vocabulary book. Shamba: allotment, small-holding, garden.

Across the corridor from the kitchen and behind Rogers' office was another office which housed the records of the experiments taking place on the station together with research data from elsewhere. In here they found an Asian who Malcolm placed in his early thirties. It was his car, passing at the bottom of Malcolm's garden, that had woken the newcomer up.

'This is PK. We've given up on his full name.'

The Asian welcomed him smiling slightly stiffly. They shook hands the formality rather more on the Asian's side.

'Welcome. It's nice to see someone new. I hope you will be happy here. If I can help in any way please don't hesitate to ask,' the English was impeccable; the Asian accent obvious but unobtrusive.

'It was PK's brother you bought the car from yesterday. PK will take you down to Nairobi after lunch. You can collect your car and pick up some stuff from the supermarket. Come and see what we get up to.'

At the rear was a yard fed by a road which passed behind Malcolm's house and hidden from it by the bushes at the bottom of the garden. To the right-hand side were some outbuildings and beyond the yard a large cultivated compound surrounded by a high chain link fence. Inside it were small plots containing a variety of plants. He instantly recognised maize, bananas, and coffee but not some of the other plants too small to be identified from afar. The plots were separated by pathways along some of which threaded hose pipes. In one of the plots, he could see John Harrington and an African man in khaki shirt and shorts talking together. The African was indicating a patch of the allotment where three other African men were breaking up the soil with large hoes.

'A fresh face I see.'

The words, in a rather mannered voice, came from behind them so the fresh face could not be seen by the speaker. Turning, Malcolm was confronted by a medium sized man with brown eyes and short dark curly hair brushed flat to his scalp, his skin pastier white than European pink. He was thick at the waist and his shorts were slightly too small for him. He was introduced as Bernie. It came from his surname, Bernard, and Malcolm didn't find out his first name for some time although his initials, AB, appeared on the rota sheet.

He lived in the bungalow next to Malcolm's, the one nearest the allotments. *Chai*. He had been at the station for five years now. He, like PK, was employed on local terms, unlike Malcolm and Harrington who were subsidised by the UK government. He had come from South Africa via Mozambique. He had no permanent residency and every year had to apply for a work permit. In the past this had been a formality but Africanisation was bound to ease him out soon. Where to, he did not know. Although he shook hands and uttered the usual cliched greetings there was no warmth behind the words. Perhaps he knew that in the pecking order Malcolm was in front of him even though a newcomer. He was the least friendly person Malcolm had encountered over the last two days. Njoroge, at the ministry, had at worst been surly; Bernie had a sharper edge and his manner suggested resentment.

'I'm off up country now. On safari, so to speak. I'll see you again, I expect. We're neighbours after all.' This sounded like the statement of the inevitable rather than some expected pleasure. He got in his car and drove away. 'Bit of a character,' said Rogers, without any warmth.

The two men wandered into the compound and Rogers explained the purpose of the various plots. Malcolm's inexperience of tropical plants would not be a handicap as most of the work was routine planting, measuring, counting, recording.

They greeted Harrington. 'This is Gitau,' said Rogers turning to the African. 'He's been here as long as I have and much longer than the rest of them.' Rogers seemed to be declaring his personal pecking order.

The African seemed pleased at this introduction. He wiped his hand, wet from the hose pipe he was holding, on the piece of rag he had tucked in the belt of his shorts, and offered it to Malcolm. He wasn't sure whether to use his one word of Swahili when Gitau greeted him in English and so he replied in kind. So many of the Africans he had met so far seemed to have been in a subservient capacity - waiters, house servants, office runners. He didn't know whether this man was similarly cast or whether he might be a research officer like himself. He didn't know whether Gitau was his first name, which seemed a way of designating inferior status, or it was his surname as used by a master in a public school.

Malcolm would find Gitau's status would derive from his reputation and record not from his job title. Gitau was the foreman for the workers who tended the crops. He ensured that the various plots were watered and fertilised according to schedule, that pruning and planting were done in the prescribed manner and that all was recorded in the ledgers. He insured, too, that none of the workers took any of the produce away at the end of the day, it not being obvious to them that good food carefully grown should not be eaten. One of Rogers, Harrington, PK, Bernie and now Malcolm had to be on duty at any one time. Often some would be away visiting other stations, farms and estates to gain information on developments in the real countryside rather than the artificial one they had created. This was where Bernie had just gone and this activity would take Malcolm throughout Kenya and beyond. Gitau was the only permanent feature on the staff. He lived with his family in the village up the road beyond Larsen's house. There he lived in his community, thankful for its strengths and contemptuous of its weaknesses. His strong independent character gave him a status amongst his fellow Africans which rivalled their chief.

Although Malcolm had not long arrived for work the others had been there since the early hours while the air was cool. It was time for their break and the non-Africans settled in the rest room.

Harrington took some mugs down from their hooks. 'We each have our own,' he explained, 'and we're each responsible for washing our own mugs. That way we've only got ourselves to blame if we get the squitters.' The word was new to Malcolm but he correctly interpreted its meaning. It was not in his vocabulary book.

'You'd better have this one for now. It was Taffy's. Shelley - he had your house. So, it hasn't been used for months.' Harrington said dousing the mug with hot water from the kettle and drying it on a tea towel. Malcolm looked at the cloth sceptically.

The mug was inscribed *A present from Pwllheli* on one side and something in Welsh, which Malcolm took to be the same message, on the other. The glaze was cracked and the interior stained. Malcolm vowed to purchase his own as soon as possible. Another item entered his shopping list.

'We didn't call him Taffy, not to his face. He demanded Thomas. Not Tom. Not Tommy. Thomas. He was a difficult bugger. Mean minded as well as stingy. It's a wonder he didn't take this mug with him when he went. He's never written. I wouldn't reply if he did. Even Alice didn't like him and she's usually very generous. He went off to Saudi, I think. Teresa and I thought of that. Well paid, but it's a bit draconian. No alcohol and so on. Wouldn't have bothered Taffy though. He never bought any one a drink anyway.' Even the teetotal PK smiled.

After the break Malcolm's job was to prune some coffee bushes. This was a new experience for him. Gitau kept a solicitous eye on his performance and brought him an old straw hat when it became obvious Malcolm began to suffer with the sun. After an hour Rogers sent him back to the kitchen to cool down a bit and he dozed off on the bus seat.

That day it was Harrington's turn to provide lunch and his cook had provided some meat pies and salad. There was an unwritten rule that alcohol would not be drunk in the research area so soft drinks arrived too. Spouses, too, were barred, it being argued that the area was a work area and it was desirable to separate it from the family activities on the same site.

Afterwards PK drove him into town. Before they set off PK handed him a card with his full name, address and telephone number. 'I don't mind the abbreviation. We do it in my own community. But I wouldn't want you to think I am just a set of initials.'

The journey, the reverse of the previous day's, was clearly downhill as they could see a long way in front of them and ultimately Nairobi itself. The road had its full share of foot passengers, mainly women carrying things, some alive and some dead. PK was more forthcoming on the journey down and certainly a more interesting companion than Rogers. He lived in a family house part way to Nairobi. He pointed to the rough road which led to it as they passed. The house itself was hidden amongst some mature trees. His family had been in Kenya for generations having come over when the railway was being built at the turn of the century. He had considerable knowledge of the UK but was unfamiliar with Malcolm's home town. In addition to the car salesman, he had two other brothers, one of whom lived in England, and two sisters. His father ran a restaurant and some hotels in a Nairobi suburb. His grandmother lived with them but was a widow. PK was unmarried but had declined an arranged marriage some years ago. His grandmother was distressed at this but his parents, bowing to the changes life away from India had pressed on them, acquiesced to his rebellion. PK did not provide all this background without prompting. Unusually, it was Malcolm taking the initiative, intrigued by a man whose family history was so different from his own. He felt at ease with a man who could judge him as he was, having no knowledge of his past. But PK detected, as he had done so often before, the unstated assumptions in the mind of this new but unoriginal Englishman.

In Nairobi, they stopped at a supermarket in a back street not far from the hotel where Malcolm had spent his first African night. Unlike Rogers, PK remained in the car, leaving Malcolm to make his own decisions. Between the parked car and the door was a beggar. His legs were chopped off above the knee and the stumps were hidden by a pair of shorts with the bottoms sown up. The rest of his body was well proportioned. He was not deformed but truncated. Unlike Marion whose whole body was distorted, his was a near perfect body whose legs had been removed. And whereas Marion was unaware of her deformity he seemed only too conscious of his indignity. With his full body he would have been powerful, attractive, vigorous; truncated he was none of these things. He was propped against the shop wall seemingly marooned there although later Malcolm would see him propelling himself by swinging on two small crutches held under each armpit which raised his stumps above the level of the ground. He was hauling himself with well-muscled arms along the dusty pavement his impressive head the level of the waists of passers-by, the hems of his shorts leaving trails in the dust behind him like those of twin snakes shimmying through the sand. Now he was stationary his hand holding a lidless chocolate tin. As he approached, the beggar, he said something which Malcolm could not understand and pretended not to hear. Whether it was *Please* or *Yes* or *Sir* he didn't catch but the sibilant hung in the air as he passed. Malcolm could not find the courage to stand in public view, search for appropriate coins and put them in the tin so chose to hurry past and enter the shop. He vowed to give some money on the way out.

Inside Malcolm filled his trolley with familiar names in unfamiliar packages; sugar in heavy duty plastic bags, jam in tins. The meat counter had an impressive display of flies but they did not inhibit him from buying some steak. He was surprised to see fish which was fresh water from the Rift Valley lakes. He bought several types of beer placed in a wooden crate. He remembered to get a mug, this one unadorned, some insect spray and a straw hat to protect his head from the sun. The total cost barely dented his settlement grant and he began to see how far his money, previously measured in Europeans terms, would go. It would certainly go as far as giving the beggar something and he sorted out some coins before leaving the pay desk.

The beggar had gone from outside the supermarket a tell-tale trail in the dusty foot-way tracking him to a cafe fifty years down the road. Two youngsters carried his goods back to the car. Malcolm felt the coins seeming to glow in his hand. At the car he gave the money to the youngsters as they clearly expected. Malcolm was aware he had given two able-bodied youngsters some money and the disabled man nothing. He thought of Marion again. He remembered the stigma of being part of a family with a deformed child reminding the world of its imperfections. He remembered, too, absorbing the embarrassed stares of strangers as though directed at him. He knew he should have gone after the man and put some money in his tin box. He wanted to do it now but he couldn't. To do that, to be seen doing that, would have once again put him in the goldfish bowl with Marion. As he drove off with PK, Malcolm knew he had turned his back on one of life's victims. He felt deep unease at his lack of courage; his compassion was no more than self-indulgence. Thereafter he always gave money to the beggars and later in life he took some consolation that on the occasion he had not, he had at least felt shame.

At the garage he took ownership of his car and whilst PK and his brother had an animated conversation in their own language Malcolm transferred his shopping to his new car. He quickly got used to traffic as he followed PK out towards the Kimura road. It had been arranged that he would follow PK until the Indian struck off to his own home and Malcolm would find his way back to Kimura. He spent the journey rather tentatively, giving wide berth to cyclists and animals. He did have to overtake one heavily loaded van labouring upwards from the city but he was overtaken far more often by Peugeot estate car taxis - the matatus - overflowing with passengers, their roof racks piled high with suitcases and, on one, a crate of chickens. As they passed, arms, hanging outside to make more room for the many passengers inside, waved in mild triumph at their overtaking. He took particular care in negotiating the Changa bridge slowing to let through a bus coming in the opposite direction its driver exhibiting few inhibitions about two vehicles passing on the middle of the bridge.

On the way down with PK, Malcolm had taken mental notes of the various landmarks but on the way back he found clumps of banana trees and fields of maize remarkably similar so he found his mental notes largely useless. In the event, he recognised the dual-strip road and from then everything was clear. The corrugations on the dirt road defied him, his cautious speed insufficient to enable the car to glide from ridge to ridge. The journey was slow, bumpy and dusty. When he arrived back at the compound his car, clean when he left Nairobi, had an appreciable covering of dust.

As he pulled into the shade of the car port alongside his house Karui came out and insisted on unloading the boxes whilst Malcolm went through to the veranda. There a smell of polish in the hallway and the sunshine outlined in the doorway reflected back off the tiled floor. As he passed his bedroom, he saw his bed made up and the top sheet folded back.

On the veranda were two chairs like those he had seen at Rogers' and between them a bent wood table. Malcolm sat in one of the chairs, quite tired with the day's activities. The first day's work, the nerve-wracking journey and the fatigue of living at over 6,000 feet above sea level had taken their toll.

Karui appeared and asked did he want a beer. He had no doubt he did. He realised how dry he was and how uncomfortable he was in his slacks and summer shirt. He opened the buttons on his shirt. He looked down at his untanned skin and felt it looked unattractive and unhealthy. As Karui put down his beer he looked from Karui's short sleeved brown arm to his own skin and made the contrast. Karui was now dressed in shorts and Malcolm would soon follow suit.

As Malcolm sat with his beer, he saw the clothes he had used since setting out from England hanging on the line at the side of the garden. He began to realise he would not have to make his bed, wash dishes, clean the windows, iron his clothes - all the chores that had been integral to his home life and which to an extent had underpinned it. He had a servant; another human being who would be at his beck and call. He savoured it for a moment but then wondered how far he could go, how far he should go, how far he would go with his new found power. The beer finally relaxed his body into slumber.

He awoke to the smell of steak from the kitchen and realised he had not asked for steak; Karui had decided. Who was the servant and who the master? Malcolm might have most of the power but Karui seemed to have most of the control. He considered going through to the kitchen to make clear he would decide what to have for meals. But he was ill-equipped for such a confrontation and rationalised his reluctance by deciding it was not an important issue anyway.

The steak and chips seemed to reflect his new status although the oil used for cooking wasn't quite to his liking. This was followed by a fruit salad - mango, paw-paw, banana, pineapple. Coffee on the veranda sealed the feast. It mattered not to him he'd dined alone. With Karui in attention there was more company than he was used to. The sun had gone and the warm darkness had settled. Moths and beetles gathered around the light in the veranda ceiling colliding with the bulb with such force it was a wonder they came to no harm. Karui switched on a second light at the other end of the veranda before switching off the first. The insects transferred their attentions to the new beacon leaving Malcolm unmolested.

Having ascertained Malcolm had no further needs Karui bade goodnight. It had been fourteen hours since Karui had first reported for duty. Malcolm wondered about overtime. He was not then to realise it was not necessary. Karui was more than pleased to work for a single European male. Such creatures normally didn't spend much time in the house and were not very demanding. Rather him than a married lady with time on her hands and standards on her mind. He paused as he looked round the kitchen before leaving for his cabin alongside. He was employed again, perhaps for two years. For today, at least, his lot was a happy one and, in his world, it did not pay to look too far ahead.

Both men settled to rest in their separate homes content that, for that day at least, life had exceeded their expectations. Malcolm sat for only a short time deciding if he was going to sleep it might as well be in bed. After a cool bath he climbed into bed setting his alarm for the morning.

SEVEN

A car door banged somewhere close. The sound woke Malcolm abruptly and after looking at his alarm clock he turned onto his back to wake up more gently. His right arm was numb where he had slept heavily on it. The car started up and drove off along the road to Nairobi. It went from earshot leaving a soothing silence soon broken by a bleating goat. Then, from the far distance, the sound of a hand bell revived primary school memories. Both sounds carried clear and sharp through the morning air. Otherwise, it seemed the world had stopped.

It was Malcolm's second Sunday. The previous weekend he had been minded by the Rogers and the Harringtons. On the Saturday the former had taken him up to the top of the escarpment overlooking the Rift Valley, its size and magnificence drawing only the most routine of clichés. They descended on the escarpment road and lunched at a lakeside country club. The Harringtons had more modern tastes; with them he had spent the day at the pool side of a luxury hotel ignoring the *Residents only* sign. That day lunch was also al fresco, but here within a walled compound under canvas umbrellas.

But now, one week later, waking to another day of leisure, he took stock. His first full week had gone well. He found out what he was expected to do and discovered he could do it better than he thought. He'd had increasingly relaxed conversations with his colleagues who enquired less and less about his background as it became clear he had little to say about it. Gitau taught him some words of Swahili and, through them, he eased his way into the African life. Although the effect on Malcolm was subliminal, the foreman had transformed from being an African called Gitau to being Gitau who was African.

The previous day Malcolm had gone to Nairobi to look around, to buy some food and other odds and ends. Already he felt superior to the tourists who clambered from tourist buses and taxis although he too had to refer to a guidebook to find his way around. He had found the cinema, the post office, the vegetable market and the Indian bazaar. He had stood looking at the street-sellers' carved wooden animals but declined to buy. He didn't have anybody to buy for and the idea of ornaments in his own house was foreign to him. Besides he didn't want to face the expected bargaining that was entailed in all such purchases. He had bought a couple of books, one of them on the peoples of East Africa and had skipped through them as he lunched at a pavement restaurant. With the map in his tourist book, he had driven in a loop around the town taking in its suburbs before branching out along the road which was now becoming familiar to him.

Evening was spent with his books after a schoolboy raid on his fridge when he remembered Karui was not on duty. He and Karui had decided what routine was best for both of them. That Malcolm would need to do very little became clear; that Karui welcomed the commitment and responsibility of a household was not so obvious. Yet the African took a curious pride in running the house according to customs and conventions that had no place or meaning in his own family world. He would spend his days in a microcosm of England sustaining an alien bubble within his own land. They agreed Karui would have every other weekend off unless Malcolm was having a special occasion, an event so unlikely in his mind that he gave it no thought. Karui would travel back to his village to visit his wife and children, to pay his dues and tend his shamba. He would be returning home from being abroad in his own country and this side of Karui Malcolm would not see.

But now, lying in bed, Malcolm had to decide how to spend Sunday. A perfectly logical consequence of his lifestyle, but completely unanticipated, was the leisure time he had at his disposal. He decided to explore the neighbourhood and after breakfast set off along the dirt road away from the compound. He had smothered himself with sun cream and wondered whether he was in danger from another source. The presence of so many human beings suggested attack by wild animals to be unlikely; the danger could only come from human beings themselves. Yet, despite the image of savage Africa depicted in novel and newsreel, he had not once felt threatened and indeed had discovered a gentleness he had not expected.

With a few things in his day bag, he set off much as he would have done on his country walks at home and with as much determination to steer clear of people. After a few hundred yards, the coffee on his left gave way to a small group of buildings. The nearer ones were farm buildings of some sort. A small tractor stood in an open lean-to. A roadway ran to one side of the buildings to what were obviously dwellings beyond. One large bungalow was separated from two smaller ones by a large well stocked flower garden. One of the farm buildings was an accommodation block larger than the one next to his bungalow but similar in severity. The sign outside the main gate confirmed it to be Larsen's estate. On top of the sign was secured the skull of a large animal which Malcolm could not identify. Larsen's name had frequently been mentioned in conversation at the station - not always reverently. He and Rogers co-operated on some coffee research and the station did have a small plot on Larsen's estate. Apart from a barking dog there was little sign of life and he moved on.

Beyond the estate, the land became a bit wilder with small trees eventually giving way to some taller ones. Further still was the village he'd been told about. It was about fifty yards from the road so he could continue his walk without intruding. There were thirty or so huts visible from the road. The land around them had long since lost its grass and in the residual dust roamed hens and children in equal numbers. A tethered goat's bleats seemed to be cries for help. The huts were mud walled with thatched rooves. Between these dwellings and beyond the village, were little areas of cultivated land, mainly maize and ground level crops; occasional banana trees gave a more substantial presence.

Two buildings stood out because they were brick or stone. The one near the road was clearly the local bar which even at this early hour was open for business. Most of the front of it was open and revealed a simple wooden counter against which lounged several men. From within came the sound of tinny music on a radio. The sign above this opening said, in crude blue paint, *Tavren*, the misspelling irrelevant; the locals were oblivious or indifferent and passing trade was unlikely.

Beyond the village stood another building, solid and rectangular with a simple cross showing its religious role. In England, Malcolm might have included a church in his itinerary, entering to see its stained-glass windows, its decorated altar, its age-worn pews and flagstones, an architectural rather than a religious interest. Had he entered here he would have found nothing of aesthetic value except its simplicity.

A child came running towards him dragging others in his wake. It was, Ngugi, the boy who had come with Rogers to the airport.

'Hello. How are you?' he said in exaggerated style but with great confidence.

'I'm fine thank you. And you?' Too late Malcolm remembered the Swahili greeting he had learnt from Rogers.

'OK'

A jumble of OKAYs came from the rest of his gang. The children were of all ages and both sexes providing an inclusivity that contrasted with Western inclinations. Malcolm's mind sought something - anything - where their lives might touch.

'Do you go to Nairobi much?'

'Yes. I am Bwana Rogers' assistant.' He grinned. The R in Rogers didn't sound quite right.

The smallest child put his hand around one of Malcolm's fingers. Malcolm stifled his reaction to withdraw. It was the gentle familiarity he found strange. The hand was soft and warm. The boy examined Malcolm's skin intently. He brushed away a fly that had settled on the corner of his eye. The liquid from his runny nose had hardened on his upper lip leaving a snail-like trail. As he looked up at Malcolm's face, he saw the European looking at him and backed away.

'Do you go to school?' asked Malcolm in desperation.

'Yes. It's over there,' Ngugi inclined his head backwards and to one side at the same time in the direction from which Malcolm had come. 'On the main road'

'And what do you learn?'

'Reading, spelling and sums,' said Ngugi.

'And scripture,' said another voice referring to the village school not Ngugi's.

'And singing,' from another.

'And what do you want to be when you leave?' Malcolm struggled - and failed - to be original.

'I want to work in a hotel. In Nairobi.'

'Are these your brothers and sisters?'

'Yes, they are.'

'All of them?'

'Sure.' The relationship was not one Malcolm would recognise.

Beyond the group a woman was tilling a small plot of land with a large hoe. She had been bent from the waist her legs ramrod straight but she stood upright to speak. In response the children ran off towards her, some chickens scattering in front of them.

'Kwaheri. Goodbye. I hope we meet again soon,' came the mannered comment from Ngugi as he ran off. And from his little band came disparate echoes of his farewell.

As Malcolm continued on his way, he thought of his own school days. He could cope with lessons themselves. All he had to do was to keep his head down, give minimal replies to questions and ask none himself. This way he drew as little attention to himself as possible.

Teachers, grateful for a lack of a robust challenge, gave him high marks for 'diligence.' 'concentration' 'application' and he moved seamlessly towards qualification. Breaktimes were another matter. His fellow pupils knew about Marion and he was ridiculed because of her. 'Spaz'. 'retard'. 'moron' populated the banter. Her existence blighted his. He coped by withdrawing to secluded parts of the playground, avoiding conflict and making no friends. A pattern of withdrawal from social life was established and entrenched. So, he survived secondary school and elected to go to a college for his A Levels. Students more interested in themselves than him caused little distress and he became to be seen as an oddity who attracted neither enmity nor affection, a welcome position as far as Malcolm was concerned.

After a while the road wound tightly round so as to leave the village in its bend, whilst the incline down into the valley to the right became a lot steeper and the road took a downward path. Ahead the land degenerated into rock and scrub which extended towards the hills in the near distance. A small group of trees on the right-hand side of the road provided shade from the sun high overhead and from it he got a view taking in the whole valley. In England such a spot would have had a park bench for elderly citizens to while away their time. Here there was no such thing. He looked to rest on some large boulders but they were uncomfortably hot to touch so he stood taking in the scene. A hundred yards away he saw some ant hills, tall and thin and dark orange in colour, their presence adding extra insight to his background reading. Although intrigued he lacked to confidence to venture off the road.

After a while during which no great sound or incident impinged on him, he continued up the road. Soon, it began to get narrower barely big enough to allow a vehicle and rough enough to make driving tedious. On either side, the countryside became more open and, because of its inhospitality, not cultivated at all. There were a few birds in the air but he saw no wildlife on the ground. It was clear the road held little scenic interest and was heading towards a break in the hillside. Judging the hills too far away for today's journey he decided to retrace his steps.

By the time he reached the bend below the village it was mid-afternoon. The rocky outcrop he'd seen before was now in shade of the trees as the sun had moved round. He flapped at the rocks in case of danger lurking and sat on a low rock his back against a taller one. The hot sun on his day bag had made the cheese in his sandwiches run and the beer, so thirst-quenching when cold, was now flat and bitter. Even the banana, in its own land, was unappetising. Nevertheless, he consumed them all, as habit dictated, he should. His journey at higher altitude and temperature than he was used to had made him tired. He lay back and watched the vapour trail of some passenger jet high above the continent. He soon dozed off.

He awoke to the sound of thunder from a storm brushing the hills at the far end of the long valley. With an unimpeded view, he saw such lightning as he had never seen on his walking trips in England. Forks broke from clouds which plunged columns of rain onto the ground below. He looked above him fearing a soaking but the sky was clear. The storm was in another land and he was like a god above a subject world, viewing it with detachment, immune to its elements. The storm lasted about twenty minutes before the clouds drifted further north and settled into a thick blanket on the far hills.

A noise behind him startled him. He got off his seat turning to meet its source. He half expected the hungry lion or ferocious warrior of celluloid. Instead stood a medium sized European wearing a floppy white hat, and light-grey dog-collared short-sleeved shirt and slacks.

'Hello. Hello. I'm sorry if I startled you. I'm Flynn. Father Flynn. Joseph Flynn. Joseph. Please call me Joseph. You're Mr Bryant, aren't you? Having a breather, eh. Don't blame you. That storm will clear the air. We could do with the rain here though. Can you smell the rain even at this distance?' He paused to sniff ostentatiously. 'It's not the rain of course but the effect of the rain on the dry soil. I think it's a beautiful smell, better than perfume. And it gives us hope the rains are on their way. They don't always come of course and then times are hard. It's no wonder we pray for rain. Some people have rain gods, don't they? It's a nice spot, isn't it?' He didn't wait for a reply. 'I often come here when I need a bit of peace. Do you think we're nearer to God here?' Malcolm felt the priest ought to know that better than he did. 'Ngugi said you'd come up this way. He's a bright lad. Not that you have to be all that bright to know where someone's going. When there's only one road I mean. What do you think?'

When Malcolm realised he was referring to the view he said 'Well, it's rather different from what I'm used to. It's not exactly pretty, is it? But you can find lots of places in England that aren't pretty - rocks and moorland and so on. Yet they still have something. I quite like remoteness. I've never seen anthills before.' He was pointing to the orange columns he'd seen earlier.

'Remarkable aren't they. All that industry. There's a queen down below and all the workers build a castle around her. Human beings don't show such patience. Some say we need impatience or we'd die out. He's not just clever you know. Ngugi. He's smart. Shrewd.' The priest leapt from one topic to another.

'He said he went to school on the main road but the others said they went to school at the church. Your church I presume.'

'Oh yes, my church, my church. There's hardly room for another. And hard enough to fill mine. The village children come to me for some very basic instruction. Ngugi's far too quick for us. I arranged for him to go to the government school on the main road. It's only four miles. His father was quite willing. Encouraged it in fact. He works with you, you know. The father I mean not the boy. You'll know Gitau of course. Although the boy does some errands for Arthur. They're a good family. Not in our sense perhaps but father doesn't drink and he's only got one wife. Several kids of course. Four,

I think. Yes, four. Father's lived here all his life. His father divided up some land between three sons and Gitau's still got his share. One of his brothers died recently - he drank a lot I'm afraid - and Gitau looks after his family, another five children, would you believe. All part of the extended family culture. Very civilised I think - although a bit difficult to untangle the strands sometimes. There's a third brother who works in Nairobi and comes back to look after his land and family when he can.' Malcolm was quite pleased for the priest to ramble on. It took away his responsibility in the conversation. 'Won't come to church though. Gitau, I mean, not his brother. Says he won't trust a God who forgives everything. He says some things are unforgivable. And who can blame him, eh, who can blame him? He's seen some bad times. We all have in our way. But I couldn't manage without Him? And we all need some kind of God. Do you pray Mr Bryant?'

'No,' his reply was immediate They was a hint of dismissiveness in his tone and he quickly regretted it. He'd gone to church with his mother for a while Nothing they heard there gave any satisfactory reason for Marion nor any practical help to cope, so they just stopped going. He couldn't remember when. He just leapt in with, 'Please call me Malcolm', before the priest went on.

'Well never mind we all have our own ways of talking to God. Malcolm, you say. Ah yes. A king of Scotland, I think. Are you Scottish? You don't sound it. But that's what education does. Takes away our birth right.'

'No. I'm not Scottish. My grandparents, my mother's parents, they were Scottish but I never knew them. I think Malcolm's a family name. When I was at school, we did Macbeth and the teacher made me play someone called Malcolm. I did it so badly she got someone else to do it.'

'So, you're not a very good actor then?'

'No.' He was a poor performer, no doubt, but much of his life had been an act. Perhaps he was an anti-actor, suppressing emotion not displaying it.

Flynn moved on, 'I'm Irish of course. You can still tell from my voice, can't you? I hope so. I don't want to lose that. I'm not sure why. I haven't been back for a long time but I still remember it. There is a part of me that is forever Ireland. Ha. Ha. Silly me. But you can't give up the past, I think. It won't let you. And perhaps that's for the good. Perhaps we need to be secured to the past to be secure in the present. What do you think?' The priest was pleased with the alliteration. Malcolm felt he should debate the point but unhappy with his own past decided not to declare an opinion. It didn't matter. Flynn was off in another direction.

'When I first came here - I was quite young then - I thought they would all convert in the end. I only needed to explain the beautiful simplicity of it all and they would see the light. It's not been that way I'm afraid. Perhaps I didn't try hard enough or put things in the right way. Perhaps I've failed. I think God would have told me though. Given me my cards so to speak. I'm not so ambitious now. But I shouldn't go on like this. It's this place that does it. This is peaceful spot. I feel nearer to God and I'm sure He understands.' Malcolm was tiring of a conversation which he could only join with a jaundiced view. 'I feel refreshed already. It must be your company as well.'

God and me, in partnership. My, my, thought Malcolm.

The priest pointed towards the end of the valley. 'There she is. Isn't she wonderful!' he exclaimed.

Malcolm followed his finger to see that the distant cloud and mist had gone and there was Mount Kenya, a jagged snow-capped double cone, rising out of the surrounding countryside back-dropped by a sharp blue sky. It was beautiful but its stark outline and gleaming glaciers gave it a severe aspect - a precondition for any icon

'She's there all the time but only shows herself at dawn and dusk and not always then. That's were all the gods are. Up there. I can't compete with that. Gitau looks to Ngai not to me and my God.' His tone now more mischievous than melancholic. 'You must excuse me. I have to go now. It is Sunday and we have a service soon. You can come if you like.'

'I'm not a believer.'

'Our congregations would be very small if we depended on believers. You'll always be welcome. I'm not looking for commitment anymore. Brotherly bewilderment will suffice. Do come again. As you can see, I enjoy talking and you seem a good listener. Not many people come this way. The main attraction is towards Nairobi and its bright lights. It's Sodom and Gomorrah again, isn't it? Perhaps they'll be changed into pillars of salt. Or ant hills here. Yes, yes, that's it. Ha ha. Those ant hills are sinners cast into pillars because of their behaviour. I wonder if I gave them confession would they turn back into human beings. And who would they be, eh, eh? I like that idea. But then we talk about a pillar of the church. How confusing. Anyway, you're not a pillar. Perhaps you were sent to me. A gift from God. Have you got a message for me?'

'I'm afraid not. But I'll come again, if I may. I've enjoyed our chat. And you must look in on me. I hope you will.' He was surprised and pleased at the vigour of his own invitation. He could not remember any occasion in his life in which he had had such a simple friendly conversation with another human being. And it had been so easy, so unthreatening. There was an emptiness in his life which he had tolerated but not enjoyed and Flynn's friendly voice had echoed gently in this void. Here was another human being whose company he could look forward to, unlike those of the past whose company he was conditioned to avoid.

'I'd love to. Goodbye for now. God by with you.' Flynn too had enjoyed the encounter. He detected in Malcolm's manner a man who responded to company and although he did not expect to convert him to religion, he did at least hope he could reconcile him to life. Even such a success would be a welcome justification of his own vocation.

As Malcolm passed the village the simple bell was tolling and a few figures made their way towards the church past the still-open *Tavren*. One man lay alongside the bar fast asleep, despite the attention of some hens.

The dusk brought a stillness on everything. In his ten days here, he had met many new people, none of whom knew about his past. To them he was what he seemed on the surface. This country knew nothing of his history; it had few expectations of him; if it had preconceptions, they were almost certainly wrong. His sense of rebirth was stronger. Marion was dead; surely her ghost could not find him in this big land. He saw his house from the turn of the bend and felt a little glow of relief. This was his refuge, but not one in which he had to hide. He put his key in the lock and felt the tumblers click in recognition. As he opened his front door, he had a greater sense of going home than he had ever done. *Nyumbani*.

EIGHT

The following weeks reinforced Malcolm's sense of belonging. His work provided the sort of routine which made few demands on his communication skills or his personality, but the new group of human beings whose life he had entered began to invite more scrutiny. In his former life he had found strangers mildly threatening but now in this more intimate environment he had become unavoidably close to a motley collection of newcomers. Although he managed to maintain the engineered obscurity of his own past, he became more interested in the diversity of his companions, probed their history and assessed their personalities. Those who he had met in a blur of novelty began to acquire sharper outlines.

PK was the one with whom he worked closest and a quirk in the rota system often had them on duty together. Their professional interest coincided over maize and Malcolm soon became acquainted with the research issues as well as local problems. He was pleased how his academic knowledge became enriched by a specific and practical research programme. PK was assiduously helpful, polite and, as far as Malcolm could tell, friendly. He found the last characteristic difficulty to assess. He had to overcome a thoughtless collection of expectations about an Asian and this made their relationship initially very formal.

'My father was in India. During the war. Well only for two days on the way back home.'

'It's not everyone's cup of tea. Not mine in fact.'

'But you are Indian?'

'Well, I'm a Hindu.'

'But you were born there?'

'Oh no. I was born here. I've been to India of course. I studied there. Four years. Not a good place to live if you know of elsewhere. I've been on holiday. It's quite cheap. You should go and have as look while you're here. But all my close family are here.'

'So, you're Kenyan?'

'I'm not a citizen. I hope to get a British passport.'

'But you haven't been there.'

'Not yet.'

'So, you won't stay here.'

PK shrugged. 'Who knows what the future may bring.'

'Would you go back to India?'

'I can't go *back* to India as I don't come from there in the first place,' he responded rather tartly.

'Well, how do you see yourself then? Are you Indian, Kenyan, English?'

'Do I have to be any of them? Can't I be all of them?'

'Don't we all belong somewhere?'

'Where do you belong?' And to that Malcolm hadn't an answer. His past claimed him and by any measure he belonged there. But he wanted to escape it, to belong somewhere else. But where and with who?

Bernie was an enigma. His confidence elicited a grudging admiration, his brashness distaste. His hedonistic lifestyle brought a prurient curiosity from the inexperienced but disapproval from more mature adults. His humour was at times witty, at other times crude. He could be sincere or deceitful and neither he nor his companions knew for sure which he was being at any moment. Although his nearest neighbour, Malcolm saw little of him. His work took him away a lot and when at home he spent most of his leisure time in Nairobi from where he would often return drunk and presumably having driven all the way. Malcolm saw more of the young woman who he saw breast feeding and turned out to be Bernie's house keeper, Hannah. Her job description needed to be elastic, although not time-consuming, since Bernie was rarely at Kimura, awake and sober at the same time.

Late into one night Malcolm was woken by the sound of shouting. From his veranda he could see Bernie dancing on his lawn illuminated by the light from his house. He was whirling around like a disorientated discus thrower. He let go of the bottle in his hand in an attempt to project it over the end of his garden into the bush beyond.

'And it's a new world record for Kenya. Hip, hip, hurrah.' The whiskey bottle landed on Malcolm's lawn. Bernie looked around until his swaying gaze caught Malcolm.

'Sorry, old chap. A slight mis-judgement.' Bernie was no stranger to mis-judgement. 'Just high spirits. High spirits. Haaaaaaaa. Whiskey. Spirits. Get it.' He fell over on his back. Malcolm went to his help and as he reached the prostrate figure Hannah came from the accommodation block and the two of them helped him into his bed.

'I will lock up. He will be all right.'

'Are you sure?'

Bernie was snoring. 'Yes. It is OK. I will be safe,' said Hannah.

Later Malcolm would remember the brief conversation. I will be safe, not, He will be safe. Is that what she meant?

Bernie was everything PK was not: rootless, boorish, unhelpful, unhappy. Perhaps he lacked a culture to give him support, but in his own mind what he lacked more than anything else was security. But whereas Malcolm's insecurity lay in his mind, Bernie's was more tangible. He had no rights in Kenya as the repeated rejection of his applications for residency confirmed. With no right to residency his work permits would always be temporary. He had no rights of entry to any country save that of his birth, South Africa, and to that he seemed reluctant to return.

The next day he sidled up to Malcolm in the shamba unusually charming.

'Settling in OK, old chap.' The warning signals were already there in the false sincerity.

'Fine thanks. The neighbours are a bit noisy,' replied Malcolm, surprised at his own waspishness.

'Yes. Sorry about that. Been out celebrating.'

'Celebrating what then?'

'Being alive, old chap. Being alive. Well not being dead anyway. I promise it won't happen again.'

'Fine.'

'But you must be celebrating too. I mean a good job in very pleasant surroundings. Not to be sniffed at, no indeed. Plenty of places to see and things to do. I suppose you're finding your way about. A big expense settling in, isn't it? Still, you have all that income from your government building up at home. You can use it to see the sights here. No good it just languishing in a bank account.' Malcolm couldn't see where the conversation was heading. 'You lose a bit on the transaction though. Big financiers get their rake off. Bastards.'

'I haven't thought about transferring money yet.'

Bernie looked about him.

'Well, when you do, have a word with me before you do anything. I might be able to do you a good turn. Your predecessor did quite well out of it.'

'Don't touch it with a barge pole.' Malcolm had asked Rogers about Bernie's proposition. 'It's illegal. Currency smuggling. Yes, you can make some money and there are plenty of people here who will be very pleased to do business with you, but don't expect them to visit you in Kamiti prison if you get caught.'

'He said Shelley had been involved.'

'Mr. Shelley is no longer with us and you need know no more than that.'

'Where is he now?'

'Saudi. No doubt involved in an alcohol racket.'

Malcolm had not seen Rogers quite as acerbic and wondered what story was behind the bare facts.

'Have you ever been to the middle east?' He didn't want to let go of the topic.

'Round it. Over it. Never in it.'

'Where have you been?'

'Got about a bit in the war. India mainly. Too hot and dirty for me.'

'My father was out east. Singapore, I think.'

'That's a nice place. Had leave there once. He couldn't have been there long.'

'No. North Africa later. And Italy.'

'What did he make of it all?'

'The war? He didn't say much.'

'No, I can understand that. Most of it's too boring to tell and other bits too awful. But you get to see the world. I didn't want to go back home. Later we had a spell in Cyprus. Alice and I were married by then. And then this job came up.'

'Have you ever regretted it?'

'No. Never. This is the best place I've ever been. It's been a bit of a challenge though. It's very difficult to change attitudes here. But Alice and I have been very happy here despite our ups and downs.'

It would have seemed that the one person with whom Malcolm would have most affinity would be John Harrington - same nationality, same age group and same experience. But this was not to be. Harrington and his wife were too gregarious for Malcolm's taste. They were away touring, at the coast or in the good life of Nairobi whenever the opportunity arose. The confidence with which they explored the country and the intimacy they shared with each other were beyond Malcolm's reach and his contact with them rarely extended beyond the superficial and fleeting.

'Have you been to the Drive In this week? The Cincinnati Kid. Great film. All about poker. Steve McQueen. Cracking stuff.'

'No. I haven't got the time this week. Perhaps it'll come again.'

'If it does, don't miss it. It's great the Drive In. Can you imagine that in England? Sitting there in the open air, steak sandwiches and chips from the bar, bottles of beer on the facia. Marvellous. And when it rains all those flying ants flying through the projector lights. What a sight. What a hoot.'

'What's on next week?'

'I'm not sure. I think I must have gone for a pee while the trailer was on. I'll ask Teresa. She's got a job by the way. A sort of PA. Personal Assistant,' he exaggerated the two words to stress the title. 'It'll help pay for the next holiday. We're thinking of going up to Uganda. Murchison Falls. We were hoping to go to Zanzibar but the revolution buggered that up. These people. You have to wonder don't you.'

Harrington moved away and Malcolm reflected on the banality of the conversation. Harrington's interests seemed so superficial. He was surprised at the strength of his feeling. He had discovered a loyalty to his new home and he didn't want it treated like a theme park. From this unlikely source a surge of emotion ran through him. A negative emotion perhaps but something visceral at least.

Gitau, the African foreman, was the one who Malcolm founded most fascinating and the least easy to assess. The fact of their differing races tended to cloud Malcolm's judgement. Every attempt to understand was undermined by stereotype, expectation and preconception; Gitau, the man, lay undiscovered. He was an ever-present fulcrum around which the station functioned. At times a buffer between management and workers, at others a bridge between cultures. Malcolm was to grow to respect Gitau without ever being offered enough to like him. He was punctual to work, methodical and meticulous in his book-keeping. He was rarely ill, even bouts of malaria saw him at work. He had a strong independence which raised his lowly role well above servility.

'Can you remember a time before the white men came?'

Gitau felt Malcolm's knowledge of colonial history a bit vague.

'Ah, no. It seems as if they have always been here. My father used to be a soldier with white officers. He used to tell us stories about them. He was in quarters in Nairobi but we lived here. My mother looked after the shamba.'

'So, when did you see your first white man?'

'The Larsen family have farmed here since before I was born so I've always known them. But I do remember one thing. I cannot quite remember how old I was. I must have been five or six. One of the officers drove my father home one day. I think he just wanted to see village life. They were very bored, far away from home. He let me sit in his car. It felt very strange. I seem to remember he drove me a little way in it, but I cried and he let me out.'

'What did you think of him?'

'I could not believe his skin. It was as though he was ill. And his skin had spots on it. What do you call them?'

'Freckles?'

'Yes. Freckles. When he went to the toilet in the long grass all the children crowded round to see if he was white all over.'

'What else?'

He told me his name but I have forgotten now. My mother made him some food but he would not eat it. He did not come back again.'

'And now all the soldiers have gone. You're been given independence now. You must be pleased.'

'Of course. But it was not given to us; we had to fight for it.'

A fierce and brutal decade-long campaign for independence had not long finished and yet it had passed Malcolm by. While the deaths of a small number of Europeans filled the newspaper columns for a day, the callous treatment of tens of thousands of Kenyan Africans barely registered. For the last ten years Gitau and Malcolm might as well have been on different planets.

'Is the country any better off?'

Better for who thought Gitau but tried to be helpful. 'It is too early to say. We need time. But it is changing.'

His father had been killed during the war and his mother had brought up the family under some difficulty. This tragedy had been repeated in the next generation when Gitau's brother had died of drink and Gitau was left to raise his brother's children as well as his own. By the tribal custom the children were all considered brothers and sisters and Malcolm never quite worked out who was in whose blood line. It might be thought that Gitau's remoteness towards Malcolm was a consequence of his father's death fighting for the Europeans. But that would be to underestimate Gitau. His aloofness was a consequence of his wish to set his own standards deferring only to his own gods. No-one, black or white, male or female, young or old could deflect him from his chosen path.

His son, Ngugi, was more approachable. He became a frequent visitor to Malcolm's house, his clothes clean and repaired, his manner respectful but not subservient. He was clearly bright and Flynn's decision to get him into the government school rather than educate him in the mission seemed wholly right.

'Do you like reading Ngugi?'

'Ah yes. I do.'

'But can you read long books?'

'I think so.'

'Read this page to me.' He showed the boy a page from one of his own childhood books in which he had emersed himself years ago.

Ngugi read it fluently, although he took time over some words and others were rendered unclear by his African accent.

'Well done. Would you like to borrow it?'

'Ah. Yes, I would. Thank you, sah.'

'And when you've finished you can have another.' And in three days he was back.

And so Ngugi became a regular client of Malcolm's books. That they gave a Eurocentric view of the world had not occurred to Malcolm who saw them only as the staple diet of a civilised education. Thus, did Ngugi come to read *King Solomon's Mines* and *Robinson Crusoe*. But the extra-curricular education did not stop at reading. Malcolm taught his young pupil card games, like whist and cribbage, and board games involving dice. These he purchased in Nairobi, when Ngugi's appetite seemed endless. As a lonely, if not an only, child Malcolm had not spent much time with other children and despite the difference in their ages Ngugi became his surrogate playmate.

Gitau watched this intimacy from a distance. He had a vast store of botanical knowledge he could pass on, but his son didn't seem to want to know. A gap was growing between them.

Although a near neighbour, Peter Larsen took a while to appear, not finding the artificiality of the station's affairs or the attitudes of its personnel to his liking. Malcolm first met him when Arthur took his assistant to the estate to check up on the development of a patch of coffee that was being used as a control in a real farming environment. The Swede - which is how Malcolm saw him although Larsen himself believed himself a man of Africa if not an African - was about Arthur Rogers' age. He had a wiry frame and his once blonde hair was nearly white. His exposed arms and legs were deeply bronzed.

'I suppose you've come to make a few shillings and then move on.' Malcolm was surprised by the directness.

'I'm not sure how long I'll stay. It doesn't altogether rest with me.'

'None of you lot stay very long. Arthur's an exception aren't you, Arthur.' He broke off to shout at one of the African labourers. His manner removed the need for interpretation. 'These bloody people. You give them simple orders are they don't listen to a word you say. It was a big mistake letting you have Gitau all those years ago. He could keep the buggers in line.'

'He applied for the job. I gave it to him. I'm not sure you could have prevented him coming.'

'Perhaps not. Probably just as well. We'd have come to blows you know. He can be a difficult bastard. Always arguing the toss. I had to pull Ken off him once; he might have killed him. Ken was just out of the army then. Didn't want anybody answering back. Might have got away with it then but not now. Not now. You remember he used to say all this land was his. It was his family's land when the government sold it to my grandfather. I tell you we own this land.' He stabbed his finger towards the coffee. 'The deeds are there in the bank. A thousand-year lease. No question. And anyway, there was nothing here only rocks and scrub. We made it what it is now and we're staying. He used to go on about the hut tax. What's the problem? The government put on a hut tax to pay for schools and such. The Africans needed money. We paid them to work here. Bas. End of story. I don't want lessons in history. We are the only history here. I was born here and I shall die here. On this farm. I'll be buried here too; you mark my words. I'm not letting greedy little politicians rob me. No sir. Politicians? Crooks. You see Arthur. It's all well and good talking about Uhuru. Freedom for who. Freedom for the politicians to make a killing, that's what. You mark my words, Arthur. It'll end in tears. You mark my words.'

Arthur Rogers looking uncomfortable, said, 'Well, it's all a bit complicated.'

'Only if you make it so. It's simple to me. I'm a farmer not a politician. If I don't make a profit these people are out of a job and then where are they? Anyway, enough of that. Can you come over for a meal tomorrow, Arthur, about seven? I think Connie has spoken to Alice. We've got the Erikson's stopping over on their way to the coast. He says the ranch is doing well.' Malcolm was ignored.

'Yes. We're looking forward to it.'

'I see they're having some bad weather in Brazil. Bloody good, eh? Keep the price up. By the way, Arthur, your idea of letting the bushes grow a bit higher isn't working. No. We've been growing coffee here for 50 years and I reckon we've got it right.'

Africans were not the only ones to reject changes Rogers would like to have implemented. Those who worked on what they saw as the real world judged them only as changes not improvements. History and tradition were hard to dislodge.

He looked out over the coffee. He was the third Larsen to farm here and, as he was to say more often than most people wanted to hear, that when his grandfather had come to this valley it was hardly cultivated. He had to haul off the rocks with a mule before the land could be tilled and the coffee planted. Every bush owed its fertility to the Larsen family's efforts. They'd developed this land; it was theirs. The first Larsen had left Sweden in 1919 and never went back except to be buried. Few of his descendants had either and then only as tourists in a foreign land. Two of the children were working in other parts of Africa and the eldest, a son, ran a building firm in Nairobi. The successive generations of Larsen's repeated the tales of hardship their family had borne as if to justify their place in society, but in time their hardships lessened and their status was claimed rather than earned.

Larsen's foreman was a Scot called Ken Forbes. He'd been in Kenya with the forces just at the end of the war and taking his gratuity had settled in Kenya in 1948. His wife and family had returned to the UK when the Emergency began and Forbes was to all intents a single man. The Scot was a different sort of settler to Larsen - a different wave and with different ambitions. What he offered were good practical skills and experience of handling groups of men who were not exactly dedicated to the task they were expected to do. He and Larsen needed each other but neither wanted to be the other, an agreeable symbiosis.

Like Larsen, Forbes was contemptuous of the more recent visitors. They considered the likes of Malcolm to be spoilt upstarts working in an unreal world having reached it with minimum discomfort. They both believed that without men like themselves the country would be nothing and if they went, it would fall apart. Malcolm and his like would traipse home to a comfortable future whilst these two settlers would have to make the best of the mess that was left.

So, Malcolm found himself in a new world. Here his companions had some aspects of a family - close daily proximity, a range of ages, a personal interest in the success or failure of others. But stronger factors kept them as strangers - the transient nature of their residence, the difference of their race, the variety of their earlier lives, the diverse expectations of their futures. And unlike the membership of a family, they came with their separate histories, their attitudes and personalities accepted by the group but not formed by it. They had their own yesterdays, some as complicated and as fraught as his own, and these too were hidden from the public gaze. The country too had its past and like Malcolm was looking to a change of fortune. For it, political freedom, financial security, social progress but above all else the acquisition of dignity. For Malcolm the hopes were not so clear but none the less optimism was edging out trepidation and uncertainty.

NINE

If this disparate group really had been a family, then surely Flynn would have been the favourite uncle. Avuncular, open, supportive, devoid of malice, always there to diffuse the high passions and low despair of others. Malcolm was pleased to receive the invitation to visit the priest, although he had seen him fleetingly on his visits to the Rogers. It arrived via Ngugi's hand in an already opened envelope imprinted Nairobi City Council, the paper taken from a writing pad some wisps of solid glue still sticking to the upper edge. The ink pen writing sure and solid invited Malcolm to Sunday afternoon tea beginning with a visit to the church at 3.00. Ngugi undertook to direct him there, although quite how he knew the contents of the letter was not clear. Nevertheless at 2.30 Ngugi appeared at Malcolm's door, though he had been waiting in Karui's quarters since midday until the time was right.

Inside, the church was as simple as the exterior implied. At one end an altar, just a simple table saved from crudity by an embroidered cloth; on it, two candles in sticks and on the wall behind a figure of Christ on the cross, looking as European as ever. The pews were simple wooden benches arranged in orthodox double blocks separated by an aisle. There were no windows but the top part of the walls, below the roof, were just pillars the large gaps between them letting in the air and enough sunshine to give the room reading light. Depending on the time of day and year these gaps would allow the sun to cast its beams upon the altar - an accident of construction rather than architectural foresight.

Flynn and Malcolm sat on the front pew, in the cool shade and with a slight breeze coming through the open door. Beyond it the strong afternoon sunshine reflected off the leaves of a banana tree casting a sliver of light on the opposite wall.

'How long have you lived here?'

'Oh. Well. Now then. Let me see.' After some silent calculations Flynn said, 'Well, it must be about 15 years at least. I can't think of my own age now nor what year it is. It was before the Coronation anyway. I was here when the Queen's father died - the present Queen that is. She was here when it happened you know. In Kenya. Yes indeed. She wasn't Queen then of course although I suppose she became Queen as soon as he did die. Or does she only become Queen when she's crowned? No that can't be right or there would be big gaps between the reigns without a monarch. And Mr Simpson - we used to call him that just to annoy the English - Mr Simpson wouldn't have been Edward the whatever because he wasn't crowned, was he? Couldn't have these gaps then, could we? Now then the coronation, that was the early fifties, wasn't it?'

'My birthday. She was crowned on my birthday. 2nd June 1953.'

'Well would you believe that. You must be special. Did you get a good present?'

'I got a bike. And ..' Malcolm stopped. The reflected sunlight from the banana tree was flickering on the wall as the breeze moved the broad leaves. Past became present. Flick. Flick. Flick. Malcolm closed his eyes. Go away. Go away. For God's sake go away. But he couldn't escape now and Marion had not let him go.

'Malcolm! Are you alright? You look pale.'

'Yes. Yes. I'm alright. It's just the light.'

Flynn saw what was troubling him, at least he saw the physical cause. He got up and shut the door.

'Flashing light. I've heard it causes epilepsy. Have you any history of it in your family. Perhaps you should see someone. We'll ask Alice.' He took Malcolm's hand in his but Malcolm withdrew from the physical contact. He wanted no contact. Not with the living human present, nor with the dead human past. He had thought he had

104

escaped but she was reminding him of her claims. Go away, Marion. Please go away.

'No. There's no need. It's not a family thing.' He was admitting nothing. 'It's just the heat, the light, the altitude.' He was blaming anything in sight to disguise the thing within him. 'I'm all right now. Go on. Really, I'm all right. You were telling me when you came here.'

'Well, it must have been the forties. Nineteen forty-eight perhaps. Yes. Yes. I remember now. I can remember sitting at the airport and seeing a newspaper picture of Johnny Carey holding up the FA Cup. Yes indeed. Captain of Ireland you know. And there he was holding up the English Cup. Oh, we were so proud I can tell you. There was a lot of anti-English feeling then. I expect you find that strange. That anyone could hate the English. It gave me a fellow feeling with the Africans I suppose. You English have a blind spot don't you. You find it hard to believe that not everybody thinks you are as wonderful as you think yourselves. You're not alone in that, I suppose. Perhaps all nations see themselves that way. Perhaps I've just stated the first law of nationalism. But now I mustn't talk like this. Hate gets us nowhere. I've learnt that at first hand. We must learn to love each other however difficult that seems. Now, where was I? Oh yes. I stayed with a little group of priests at Langata and then all of a sudden, I was here. No time to think about it. There was nothing here then. Nothing at all. Well, the village was here. But no church I mean. And no house. This all came later.'

Malcolm worked out that Flynn must have been as old then as he was now and he wondered how he would have coped with the conditions.

'Has it changed much from when you came?'

'The country? Yes certainly. Then an out and out colony with all that means. It's a nasty thing colonisation. It harms the colonialists as well as the subjects. You wouldn't believe how badly people could behave. Even good people behaving badly. That's very hard to take

105

isn't it, good people behaving badly. Your optimism takes a bit of a bruising. Mine did. But all that is behind us now, thank God. Schools, hospitals, jobs promised for everybody. The future looks very good.'

Malcolm felt he ought not to report Larsen's views.

'But has it changed here? Not so much. I could have sat here at any time in the last 15 years and seen the same things. Larsen's estate was here. Old man Larsen, Lenard, ran it then although Peter was eager to take it on. Oh, the research station didn't come until about 1954 - perhaps a bit before that. Arthur came then. Well Arthur and Alice of course. She's nice isn't she. I often drop in for a chat with her. And a little prayer. And she runs a little clinic here, right here in the church.'

He looked around.

'Anyway, they built up the research station so that was a big change. Then Larsen expanded his farm when coffee became big business. It all gave the villagers some paid work. It changed the culture as well I suppose. Both men and women worked on the estate and, for some, family life was neglected. Some children were left to their own devices, became feral if you like. Traditional values weren't always passed on. Yes, it definitely changed things. Once there was money somebody opened a bar and a lot of the money went there. Before that they used to brew their own so I don't suppose that makes much difference. Now if they die from drink, it's cirrhosis rather than some bacteria in the beer. They have a healthier death now.'

He smiled at his own wryness. Then revising his view of local history, he said, 'So, it has changed hasn't it. I suppose you don't notice things while their happening only when they've happened. And then it's too late to do anything about them. It's like steering a boat. You can slightly change direction and hardly notice the difference but after a while you find yourself not where you wanted to be. I suppose that could be a theme for a sermon couldn't it. Once you sin however small it sends you off course and you end up where you don't want to be. The Emergency had a big effect and I suppose that dominated things for a while. Barbarity became tolerated if not condoned. Good, good people were led astray. People lost trust in each other. I tried not to take sides – see all points of view. I feared that if I was too out-spoken I could be a target because although I am not British, I was representative of the Europeans and had to share responsibility for all the awful things the British Army were doing. Each side had its beliefs and did awful things to support them. I tried to rationalise it, square it with my religious beliefs. But I knew that Christians had done dreadful things over the centuries in support of these beliefs. I must tell you I was in despair. I would have like to have found some simple moral stance within my religion but it I couldn't find it. I was having to make up a morality to fit the facts. So, I often remained silent when my calling demanded I should speak. When I think of the sacrifices people have made for their religion over the years, I am deeply ashamed at my response. But if I had become a martyr I wouldn't be here and now I try to make up for my failings by some dedication, some loyalty to these people. Perhaps you can understand why at times I looked towards Ngai up on the mountain, just like Gitau does, and asked for his forgiveness. It passed, of course. A small incident in the human story but a massive convulsion in mine.'

He paused and looked at the altar but before Malcolm could comment he was back to his story.

'As I say the church wasn't here. I built that. Well, helped build it. We had donations from back home. Little amounts here and there from different parishes. Isn't it a nice thought that all those people making little sacrifices would help build God's house here in the wilds? Just like an army of ants all contributing their little bit.'

Malcolm didn't like to suggest that anthills were vulnerable to being knocked down by anyone who disliked their presence. Couldn't the same happen with his church; one mighty outburst could knock his anthill church over but he didn't think it right to undermine his host's analogy.

'I used to get regular donations from individuals as well. Let me tell you a story.' He gathered himself in anticipation of a tale he knew well. The two men sat symbiotically at ease. The one pleased to have someone to talk to; the other glad to listen and immerse himself in someone else's life without the need to express his own feelings.

'One woman used to send me £20 every year until the church was built. £20 will buy a lot of materials - even now. The cheque was always dated the same each year - the nineteenth of July - she sent it through a solicitor. Everything went through the solicitor, so I don't know where she lived. I used to write and tell her the progress we were making, but her replies were very terse. When I wrote and told her we'd finished it, she wrote back with one request. That a simple sign with a man's name on it should be placed on the wall of the church overlooking the altar. There it is. Up there.'

The two men looked at the sign its string support making an inverted V over a nail.

Flynn continued, 'I had it made in Nairobi. A hardwood surround with the name inset with ivory. A bit extravagant don't you think but not really expensive here. After all we've plenty of elephants. So, you'll see the name of Gerald Daley looking down on all our services. Who he was I've no idea? Daley wasn't her surname. Was it her father? her fiancé, killed in the war perhaps. Perhaps it was a secret lover.' The priest looked impish, 'That would be a bit naughty asking it to be put up in a Catholic church, wouldn't it? People often have little secrets they can't bring themselves to share, don't they?'

It was said rhetorically and Malcolm had no need to reveal his own secrets.

'But why that date? And why here? I don't know. There must be lots of stories like that throughout the world. Separate lives connected by threads. One big network. A web. A spider's web. And sometimes we're the spider and sometimes the fly. So, there we are. Europe is full of churches with brass plates and marble statues. But my church has one sign saying Gerald Daley. Or at least it says that now. Come closer and let me show you.'

He guided Malcolm by his elbow to face the sign and felt the younger man ease away from the physical contact. He stored the action away in his mind.

'Look at it closely. Can you see it?'

Malcolm shook his head.

'When I sent in the request for the plate whoever made it misread my writing and mistook the last Y for an X. Wouldn't be familiar with written names, I expect. It came back as Gerald Dalex. I blacked out the extra tail of the X with some paint so it's spelt right now and it's high on the wall so no-one looks too closely.' He looked over his shoulder as if to make sure they were alone. 'I once called it the sign of the cross. X you see. Cross, eh. I don't think God minded my little joke. Do think He likes a joke? Eh Malcolm.'

He's got a strange sense of humour if he does thought Malcolm, thinking of his sister.

Flynn flowed on, 'Doesn't life confound us even when we have the best of intentions? But why should this woman want this man's name honoured in my church?'

'God knows', said Malcolm instinctively, then failing to snatch the phrase back.

'Yes, He does know. I believe that,' it was said with such simple sincerity that Malcolm almost believed it himself.

'Every year about the nineteenth of July I make the episode the subject of one of my sermons. It's quite difficult to get fresh ideas but this gives a prop. I don't know why she did it. Generosity? Compassion? Guilt? Redemption? A wish to be remembered through him? I don't know. But there is enough there for a twenty-minute talk. I sit here quite often and contemplate this pair. When my imagination is fired up, I can think of her as God, hidden from us in some other place but always there, dispensing her gifts among us. And he is Christ sent by God to live among us. Thankfully I never let these ideas go beyond my mind. They could be misunderstood. I might start a cult and pilgrims would come from across the world to worship at the feet of Gerald Daley. A false god indeed.'

Neither man spoke each with his own thoughts.

'You probably don't realise that when you preach you are not always honest. You're making up things to make people feel better, to be better. You keep your real thoughts to yourself – your ignorance, your ……. doubt. I'm rambling a bit, aren't I? But it's so good to talk with someone. Talking to yourself is a bit repetitive and becomes frustrating. And you're a good listener. Alice too. Bless her.'

'Come on time for tea. I don't have beer here I'm afraid. I used to like a glass of beer but I've stopped now. It would set a bad example. It's hard setting standards for people, you know.'

He smiled wistfully, embarrassed by his own piety. He paused in thought.

'We're all selfish aren't we. Anyway, tea is quite refreshing.'

They walked from the church away from the village and towards his house. Between the two buildings stood a Volkswagen beetle its light blue paint sun-bleached. One wing was a darker colour than the rest. Flynn paused to look at it.

'Very reliable little car. It gets me around to the other villages and into Nairobi. I'd be lost without it. It's like a brother to me. I call it Karl. It's a German car. So, Karl. D'you see? He nudged Malcolm gently in the ribs and giggled.

They carried on down the side of his house and up a short flight of steps to the veranda. From it, Malcolm could see the same view he had seen when he first met Flynn and realised their meeting place was down below the thick foliage at the end of the garden.

'Sit down. Sit down, please do. Make yourself comfortable. Are you feeling all right now?' Malcolm nodded. 'Good. Good. I'll just get it organised.'

He went into the main body of the house and Malcolm could hear a conversation. He returned and was followed ten minutes later by an African woman carrying a tray with a pot of tea and cake.

'Thank you Wambui. Mr Bryant is new here. He's at the station. He works with Bwana Rogers.' He must have told her back there in the house so this was for Malcolm's benefit.

The woman wore a cardigan over her long dress which reached almost to her bare feet. Her face and hands carried very little flesh but the smoothness of the skin suggested she was not old. The scarf covering her hair was knotted at the back and surrounded a light brown face. She nodded impassively and her unresponsive dark brown eyes did not linger on him. She said nothing before withdrawing into the back.

Wambui does not like to speak in English. She's a widow. Her husband, Gitau's brother, died of drink. It left a stain in her life. The family rejected her. They blamed her for her husband's death. She's an outcast now. I gave her refuge. Gitau is bringing up her children,' the staccato sentences, unusual in the priest's conversation, summarised a life. 'Do you take sugar?'

They sat for a while. The priest was unusually quiet and still, gazing into his cup as he stirred the contents. Malcolm surveyed the garden. The trees and shrubs were mature. Below the bungalow were some banana trees masking the rocky land beyond but not obscuring the view down the valley. The frangipani tree close to where they were sitting had deposited some of its ivory petalled flowers on the veranda. He picked up a fallen flower its petals smooth and strong to his touch. He smelled its soft sweet scent. The movement brought Flynn back.

'When I came this was barren. I lived in a native hut until we built this house. I think I planned the garden, but it looks as though it grew like Topsy and none the worse for it. Each plant tells us something. They are undemanding companions.'

Malcolm looked at the banana trees and found no message.

'Why did you come?' seemed a more interesting question.

'I suppose I was called. I had a picture of ignorant natives waiting to be saved through Christ's message. I would be the messenger. We have such simplistic notions when we are young. I'm shocked now when I think of the naiveté and ignorance that brought me here. Rural Ireland is very unsophisticated you know.' He gazed beyond his garden. 'A bit like here I suppose but narrower. Or it was then. When I came, I found them not savage or ignorant although manifestly different. There's a beautiful simplicity in them you know. It makes it very easy to be patronising. And such stoicism in face of hardship and bad luck. There's a lesson for us if we wanted to learn it. I found they didn't want and they didn't need the message I brought although some were receptive. What they wanted were the things I brought as by-products - education, medicine, tools. So, after a while I went through the ecclesiastical motions and helped them with their daily lives. It may be that by my involvement in their life, if not their culture, my message of goodness spreads subliminally. As I told you earlier the Emergency came as a big blow. I couldn't believe that out of such gentle people could flow such barbarity. I shouldn't have been surprised of course. I need only have remembered European history to realise what people can do. Don't get me started on Cromwell.'

Malcolm looked blank.

'But it's any of us. Me and you if the circumstances were right. But to be amongst it was heart-breaking. Thou shalt not kill. Such a simple message. So clear. It made no difference. They wouldn't discuss it and they couldn't stop it. They had no more influence on what was going on than I did. I like to think we are all ashamed. When we are frightened and insecure, we will believe anything, do anything. You and me too.'

'And now? What do you do now?'

'I carry on. I have to stay as I've nowhere else to go. I may not be part of these people but they are part of me. I used to hope great things would happen; now I just pray awful things will not.'

'Perhaps you brought the wrong message.'

'No. No. The message is fine and still valid to all of us. At first, I didn't realise the real message was parcelled up with bright paper wrapping and gaudy string. Made in Europe it said on the wrapping,' he paused, smiling, 'in Latin of course.'

'What did the message say?'

'Just what I'd been taught as a small boy. Tolerance, love, truth, forgiveness, redemption, salvation. We are not alone. God will look after us, come what may. There is hope whatever the present. It seemed clear then, but the longer I was here the fuzzier it became. I thought I knew, but that was only what others had told me. I began to fear they was no message and that was awful. Better to believe there is something worth saying, worth doing, worth passing on than to be left in a void. Don't you think?'

Malcolm knowing his own void couldn't reply. He thought again about praying. If it meant getting down on his knees with hands together, head bowed then no he didn't pray. But he knew on many grey days, grey outside and grey within him, he had said things, done things which expressed his deep unhappiness and his inability to do anything about it on his own. Was that praying?

As afternoon was turning towards dusk both, in their way alone, sat together each with his own thoughts. Malcolm was pleased with his companion's openness and it would enrich his life in the years ahead. This priest was such a simple man. The certainty which annoyed him in other clerics was absent in this man and it made him seem more wholesome if less holy.

'I must go now. You have a service soon I think.'

'I do. I do indeed. Duty calls. Duty calls. Thank you for coming. Come again. You don't need an invitation. Come anytime. Anytime.'

I will. Malcolm nearly added the phrase again echoing Flynn's repetitions but he held back in time.

'Come this way.'

The priest took his visitor down the path at the side of the garden which eventually came out on the road where they had met weeks before.

'Why come here when you get the same view from up there?'

'Quietness. Solitude. Peace. Up there is modern - man made. Down here it's simple and natural. Just me and God. Well gods if you include Ngai.'

Malcolm found the clichés a little sugary but Flynn had a simplicity about him which imbued them with some integrity.

'Goodbye.'

'Thank you'

Malcolm set off but at the bend turned to see his new friend staring down the valley. He followed the gaze and saw the mountain glistening in the setting sun, sharp, permanent, uncompromising, beautiful and for a moment he wondered whether the priest was seeking help from another god and whether it could be a source of his own salvation.

TEN

Arthur Rogers had spent most of his working life at Kimura station. He had been appointed to set up the research station in 1952. He'd come to it via war service in India, a two-year course in agricultural techniques, two years working for a government department and two years on secondment in Cyprus. He had arrived at the beginning of the Mau Mau Emergency and had lived through its carnage. He had found mutilated bodies on the roadside and seen huts burning across the valley. He heard of events that brought no credit on African elders or European powers. Yet throughout this fraught period of African history, he had stuck to his task of building and developing the station. He had recommended to his superiors the research that would seem most beneficial and carried out their wishes even when he disagreed with them. He had appointed and encouraged a series of young scientists to support him through this period. He had taken satisfaction from the academic strand in his work and if he was honest pursued some lines which he knew had little relevance to rural Africa. But he had never lost sight of his prime role of identifying crops and methods which would enhance the lives of native farmers. His relationship with Africans had been paternal; he knew no other way. He did not presume on their culture or question their experiences. He did not try to share their lives nor try to understand their attitudes. He accepted what he found. He was detached although his detachment did not diminish his concern. There were a thousand Arthur Rogers in Africa. Arriving with a flood of ideas and ambitions only to see them disappear into dry African soil. Whilst his own ancestors had bred and refined a multitude of crops in an equable and predictable climate their African counterparts had toiled away in an unforgiving terrain subject to capricious weather and the unremitting attention of insects. It was not surprising that the ideas and practices of these different cultures differed so widely. If Arthur did not understand this when he arrived, he had learnt it long before he was due to depart. He had read that in his many years in missionary work David Livingstone could only claim the conversion of one black soul and Arthur came to understand why that was so. Like Livingstone he did not despair and developed a love of Africa and a respect for the African. As with Flynn, ambition gave way to stoicism and resignation. He found he could not make the significant improvements he would have hoped for and that Africa, though it could be cajoled, encouraged, massaged and manipulated could not be moved from without.

The station had been promoted by a UN agency with some support from the British government to carry out research into how to improve crop growing amongst indigenous farmers. Small farmers had been difficult to influence being unconvinced that the station's techniques were any better than those that had been employed for generations. The chemicals suggested were too expensive and no-one had found a way of providing more rain. Initially the station concentrated on coffee, bananas and maize but now it was trying to encourage the development of a wider range of crops. There were high hopes of selling more produce to Europe - beans being a prime hope. Other agencies were looking at fruit and flowers.

As the task had changed so had his role. Once a research scientist he was now an administrator, accounting for the expenditure, justifying the bids, securing the funding, recruiting the staff. Over the years he had recruited many assistants like Malcolm, their characters and motives as varied as their commitment. To induct Malcolm was a chore he had done many times with little long-term benefit. Most of his staff took two years of the good life and went home to secure their careers; some went elsewhere in search of greener fields both agricultural or metaphorical. As he had grown older his assistants had become relatively younger with expectations and backgrounds that had become increasingly alien to him. And now he was having to Africanise, in his case appointing an African to work with expatriate staff with a view to replacing them completely. The logic was right, the practicalities enormous. Malcolm's post should have been filled by an African but an extensive search found no suitably qualified citizen who would work for the pay offered. Well qualified Africans were rare and the multinational companies were keen to recruit them. After a delay of about six months, it was agreed to look overseas again, possibly for the last time. Malcolm's presence here owed everything to this delay. Without the failure of an important government policy in a faraway land Malcolm might still be back in England.

The Rogers were solicitously friendly but the age group to which they belonged and the habits of a life time in the country excluded Malcolm from their social circle. Arthur found that friendship with the many young people who came and went through his charge brought decreasing satisfaction and what there had been reduced the older became the age gap. The repetitive nature of their arrival, acclimatisation, assimilation and departure discouraged any intimate contact. The Rogers' network of friends flourished well beyond the compound and was independent of it. Alice and Arthur appeared to Malcolm the epitome of calmness, certainty, civility, surrogate parents perhaps in an unfamiliar setting. But just as parents have early lives unimagined by their children so the Rogers had their hidden history which made them what they were.

Alice met Arthur when he was on a post war emergency training scheme and she training to be a veterinary nurse. When he found a post on the other side of the country, she gave up her training to marry him. They put off a family until they were settled and the two years in Cyprus made for more delay. She had wanted to be a mother as long as she could remember. To call it an instinct would be to devalue it. She foresaw and accepted the selfless requirements of motherhood but knew within her were reserves of love that would make a child happy. Not the sugar-sweet love of greetings cards but the love that accepts sacrifice, endures strife and generates patience. When she and Arthur settled in Kimura, they decided it was time to start a family. The day she found she was pregnant was the happiest day of her life She was on leave in England when she found out and was able to share the news with the family and friends that had made her own childhood so secure. When she arrived back in Kimura, she found metal grills on the windows and a shotgun in the living room; the Emergency had reached Kimura. Not long afterwards, the baby girl she was carrying was born dead. They called their daughter Elizabeth. It was a long-standing family name lent modernity by the newly crowned queen. But throughout her long reign Elizabeth II would unwittingly remind them of their loss. They knew the cause could have been the change of climate, the reaction to illness or the stealthy work of hormones, but tucked away separately in both of them was the notion that their child had been dragged from them by the anxiety caused by the conflict around them. Having come to Africa to give, they found it took something from them.

The consequences of the loss meant Alice could have no more children. As will happen she and Arthur failed to confront their loss and their lives became a separate togetherness untroubled by passion but strengthened by devotion. Thereafter Alice was a different woman. Outwardly there was little change and her treatment of friends and visitors was always kind and warm. But she carried her loss inwardly. She could not understand how such a cruel thing could happen. Her life had been full, joyful, hopeful. She was kind, generous, understanding. She was a friend of goodness, a stranger to malice. Had not her whole life been a preparation for motherhood? How could this happen to her? It was so final, so irreversible, destroying continuity, killing hopes. She was not a Catholic but she turned to Flynn for help. He was a frequent caller during her pregnancy, not as a priest but as a neighbour. He enjoyed and needed chatty, bright conversation as much as she did. But later she needed more than fleeting talk.

'Why me, Joseph? Why me? I would have been a good mother. I wanted children.'

'I can't answer that, Alice. A lot of life doesn't make sense.'

'But it's cruel. You can't believe what I feel inside. Why did God allow that?'

Flynn was struggling to sound convincing, 'Perhaps there is an element of chance. Perhaps He doesn't plan things. But He's there when we need Him.'

'I can't talk to Arthur about it. He's quite busy. Anyway, I wouldn't know what to say. It affected him too. I can tell. He's gone very quiet.'

'You need to talk.'

'Yes. I've tried talking to Connie Larsen but she doesn't understand. She says I must pull myself together. But I am pulled together. I'm not a gibbering wreck. But I'm not at ease either.'

'We could try talking to God. Pray. What do you think?'

'I have done.'

'Let's try again. The two of us. I'll try to say something.'

They shut their eyes and clasped their hands. After a while Flynn said, 'I can't find the words you need. Mine are just routine, artificial. Let us each pray silently. It's easier that way because you don't need to make full sentences or know where you're going before you start one. It's a sort of flow of thought. I'm sorry. I feel I'm letting you down.'

'No. I understand.'

But prayer only allowed Alice Rogers to think and this only brought further questions.

Flynn had found it difficult to ease Alice Rogers' melancholy after the death of her child. Then with his spiritual approaches floundering he came up with a secular solution.

'Alice. I need your help. You know I run a small clinic in the church. I can only deal with minor things and I'm not very good with women's problems. I need some help particularly when I'm away at other missions. Could you give me a hand - perhaps two mornings a week? What do you say?' He did not say it might take her mind off things but both understood the implication.

'Well, I do have some medical training - a bit better than first aid. But I'm not qualified.'

'Who is?'

'Let me think about it.'

'I sometimes think I'm not qualified to be a priest. Trained, perhaps. But not qualified.'

'No. I don't need time. I'll do it.'

So twice a week she set up stall on the altar of Flynn's church attending to the doleful queues of villagers sitting on the benches, a sickly congregation for her service. Whether it was God, her new vocation or simply the passage of work-filled time Alice Rogers became reconciled to her life. Her generosity of spirit and her acts of kindness eased her personal tragedy into a corner of her mind. It could not be forgotten but it was at least reduced to the proportion that allows life to continue.

As the years passed the clinic gave a more and more value to Alice Rogers' life. From a mere helper she progressed, by way of Flynn's default, to having full responsibility. She found a real fulfilment in helping others and was able to sublimate her motherly feelings in her concern for other people's children.

But she had an independent streak and was not just content just to follow Flynn's guidelines. She saw how real improvements could be made. In the first instant she got beyond the sticking plaster stage and provided remedies for more substantial ailments. Flynn became alarmed as his budget would not allow her to do what she wanted. But the budget of the research station was a little more elastic and by coaxing Arthur into a little creative accounting her clinic became better able to serve the needs of the village. And as her ability to heal increased so did the attendance at her clinic; but so too did the complexity of the ailments. Proper diagnosis became a problem not just because she lacked the skill but because her understanding of Kikuyu was not good enough to follow the descriptions of the symptoms. Her salvation came in the form of Wambui who knew not only the language of her people but the nature of their illnesses, able to separate the clinical from the social. She already worked as a daily housekeeper to Flynn and her informal secondment to the clinic was a natural extension of her role.

But they became more than a medical team. After each session Alice and Wambui would retire to Flynn's house and drink tea on his veranda. If he was not there, they would enjoy the small talk through which women can discuss the big issues of friendship. And when he did join them, he sat in quiet satisfaction watching the healing his ministry had failed to provide.

Then one day their ministrations took another turn. Wambui had been talking to one of the village women.

'She says she does not want any more children.' Wambui interpreted.

'How many does she have?'

'She says five.'

'What does she think we can do?'

'She says, she knows you can get things to stop children. Her sister in Nairobi told her about them.'

'Contraceptives?'

Wambui looked blank. 'She says they can be put inside you so the man does not know and you don't have children.'

'Tell her we don't have those.'

'She says, all the women want them. They are tired of babies and the men will not listen.'

'Tell her I'm sorry, we do not have any.'

Later over a cup of tea the two women talked the matter over.

'How many children do you have?'

'I have four.'

'Will you have any more?'

'I hope not.'

'Do you use anything to stop becoming pregnant?'

'Ah. No.'

'Does your husband use anything?'

'No, he uses beer. He is usually too drunk to prick me.'

'And when he's sober?'

'I push him out of me before he spills.'

'African families can be very big, can't they?'

'Yes. It is tradition. But it is not good. There is not enough land to feed the extra mouths. We must stop. Europeans have small families. We must learn from you. You have no children. You are fortunate.'

A shiver from the past ran through Alice. 'I cannot have children. That is not lucky.'

'But your husband does not divorce you?'

'No.'

'That is good. He is a good man.'

'Yes, he is a good man.'

'But can you help the women in the village?'

To help women not to have children when she had so desperately wanted one of her own. How could she do that? But there were other problems.

'The Father would not allow it. He says it is against the laws of God to stop people having children.'

'But he is man. He does not understand.'

Flynn understood and he knew what to say as he took a break on the Rogers' veranda.

'It's against the teaching of the Church. It's clear-cut.'

'But a lot of Catholics ignore it,' Alice was determined to make her case.

'That doesn't mean it's wrong,' as was Flynn but less so.

'For a lot of people, it doesn't make sense.'

'I know. When I attend briefings with the bishop in Nairobi we talk about this issue. It crops up all the time. A lot of the priests are uncertain but the bishop sets out the line very clearly.'

'But it's making you look foolish. It's undermining everything else you do.'

'The Pope has initiated a big debate on this. I don't know the details and not much filters down to me out here. There may be a change.'

'So, while you wait can I give out contraceptives at the clinic?'

'No. I'm sorry. I would be failing badly if I said yes.'

'Failing who?'

'Don't you see my dilemma?'

'Yes, I do. Can I give contraceptive advice then?'

'Look. It's not just a clinic. It's a church. I have to say no.'

'But if Wambui and I went to the village huts, you wouldn't oppose that?'

'I can't can I? But please, nothing in the church. And keep it quiet.'

'We will. We don't want the men to know either.' Alice's personal unease remained but a stubborn streak in her wanted to overcome Flynn's doctrine.

And so, the unlikely partnership of Alice and Wambui set out to serve their sisters and each found a deep satisfaction in the task. But the scheme was to end as it began - with a pregnancy.

'Wambui. Are you there?' Wambui had not appeared at the clinic that day and after it was over Alice went to find her.

There was no reply but as she wandered towards the back of the house, she heard a sobbing from the kitchen. She knocked gently on the door and turned the handle. Wambui was sitting at the table with her back to the door.

'What's the matter?' Alice leant to reach her friend. Wambui could not reply but turning hung her arms around Alice's waist damping her dress with tears.

When she had recovered, she said, 'I am pregnant.' Alice remembered her own tears long since relegated to the wings now emerging centre stage.

'Does your husband know?'

'He does.'

But when the baby arrived it was clear its father was not wholly African. To her husband Wambui described how Forbes had found her beyond the village one evening. How he had put his hand over her mouth and pushed her to the floor. It was rape.

Gitau went to see the District Commissioner and the police interviewed Forbes. The incident would have been some time ago and there was no corroboration of the events. Forbes was not charged and the Africans were left to find their own justice. Wambui's husband accused her of lying, of having gone with Forbes willingly. It was known she was encouraging the village women to disobey their husbands and this supported the charge of unfaithfulness. Wambui was banished from the family home; she would be allowed to stay in Flynn's house but could not go into the village. When six months later her husband was found dead, hanging from a tree, Gitau, true to his tribal custom, took charge of her children. Her new-born child, Grace, could not know her father and did not meet her mother confined in a house a short distance from her family home.

Alice continued with her clinics without Wambui's help but the calls for contraception ceased not because a white man in Rome laid down his law but because black men in Africa laid down theirs.

ELEVEN

It was not just people who had substantial pasts when Malcolm arrived. Institutions too had their yesterdays. Larsen's farm had a lengthy history, the research station a shorter one. But others beyond Kimura village had strong roots.

For most of the settlers and expatriates living in the farms and plantations scattered around the area a central gathering point was The Phoenix Club although all called it The Club, eschewing the classical reference. Situated just off the main road to Nairobi, its pre-war buildings were built on the site of a wooden shack that had fulfilled the same function for an early generation of settlers. The original had burnt down under unexplained circumstances. This fire and a deference to classical mythology explained its current name. It was home from home to virtually all the European population of the area. Not to be a member of the club put one outside the social round. Even under independence the membership, legally open to all races, was overwhelmingly white. This seemed not an issue for those who were members nor for those that were not. PK's family were not members but they frequented the Gymkhana Club in Nairobi where attitudes and activities were more in tune with their culture. For club members it was a combination of village hall, leisure centre, library - a secular church dedicated to European values. Thus, it had its golf course - admittedly only nine holes, the extension to 18 inhibited by Independence - tennis courts, a squash court and a swimming pool. The sight of African women carrying tins of water on their heads from the bore hole, walking within sight of the swimming pool and the green sprinklers had that hint of surreal obscenity that only the outsider could see. To insiders it was God's estate.

The shaded veranda echoed to the clink of china. From it could be seen not only the fairway leading up to the final green but also the corrugated iron rooves of the native settlement beyond the boundary from where the water carriers came. The bar and snooker room were attended by uniformed waiters. The lounge tables held the latest magazines. From the walls gazed down the past presidents - all white - all male. Elsewhere gold-lettered boards proclaimed the names of successive presidents, captains and winners, several Larsen names among; even a Forbes crept into the last category. It was a caricature of the upcountry settler club and this was no accident. Its typicality, its convention, its archaic tradition, were essential in reminding its members of culture long dead in the native land still clinging on abroad. Without this heritage the tribe would be defeated. Within the narrow bounds of race, the membership covered the various waves of settlers who had come this way.

The tribal elders were those who had come in the twenties and thirties to convert barren land into fertile pasture. The superficial legal claims to much of this land faded into the background as their monumental tenacity and sacrifice changed a landscape forever. Their descendants, too, inherited the mantle of pioneers although their actions often undermined their status.

Another wave came for the good life in the enclaves of Europeandom the settlers had established as they pushed further and further afield. They were the anti-missionaries - egocentric, self-indulgent, rich and with that disdain for discretion that so disorientated the righteous. Here the leisurely rich seemed not as unhappy as the industrious poor would have liked. That they would evaporate leaving only a wine stain on the floor of the Rift Valley didn't prevent them stigmatising this country for a generation. Through the few that lived on the lasting impression of that era was a confection of expensive dreams and drunken nightmares; exotic parties and erotic pairings filling days with endless pleasure.

They were followed by the clerks, managers and artisans released from a war service that had opened their eyes to a world far richer in every sense than Albion. Here they found a land fit for heroes offering its riches to a wider clientele. They were to make the place work, to harness western technology to somebody else's good.

And latterly came the aid workers, Malcolm among them, less settlers than interlopers, some fuelled by philanthropy, some by a sense of adventure and some by ambitions which could not be satisfied in a more demanding developed world at home.

In The Club, this varied crowd mingled if not engaged, joined only by their race but separated by experience, ambition, need, condition, education and circumstance. Farmers, teachers, engineers, restraunteurs, shopkeepers, builders; all invaders in their fashion. If there seemed a timelessness there was one break where the tectonic plates of history had slipped. Once the language had been as colourful as the flower beds surrounding the veranda. Now, after colonialism had given way to independence, this crude abuse was muted. No one dared upset a nervous government and run the risk of deportation. That some did not wish to cause upset and wished the native governance all success was equally suppressed. The culture then was neutered, left to peter out unhindered but without issue.

It was into this tradition that Malcolm was introduced, proposed, seconded and accepted with little enquiry. All the questions were implicitly answered by the colour of his skin. He was drawn without enthusiasm and with little alternative. His interest in playing Bridge revived and through it he met the women of the tribe who had seen Africa through different eyes. It was difficult to imagine these twin-setted doyens had given birth on their verandas, buried their parents in the bush, and slept with loaded guns under their pillows, their iron wills focusing now only on successful finesses.

He was pleased to find that from this throng came not just the tired bigots their public-school manners undermined by their public lavatory minds but strong individualists with real depth, understanding and sensitivity. It confused him since he had neatly parcelled up mankind to reflect his own limited experience and to satisfy his own preconceived divisions.

The club president, Major Duncan Logan, fuelled his confusion. This first world war veteran now farmed hundreds of acres of coffee, sisal and pineapples. He had developed his estates from nothing enduring the same hardship as the Larsens and PK's itinerant ancestors. With his military moustache, impeccable manners, precise vocabulary, blazer and tie, he seemed to epitomise the officer class settler. Yet his estates had their own schools and clinics, his workers their own allotments and he had been the first to introduce an African to membership of the club. Many ridiculed him, but the current climate subdued any revolt. He became, for all, the acceptable face of post-colonialism and although many rejected his attitudes, they knew they provided the camouflage which blended the whole chameleon clan into the surroundings.

TWELVE

Malcolm's working day ended about three o'clock and the late afternoon gave him long periods of leisure. If Ngugi did not call he could be found on his veranda shaded from the late sun reading and drinking a beer. Occasionally he would lift his head from the pages as the beer made him drowsy and wonder what he had done to deserve this. Was there some demon hiding beyond the compound waiting to take this all away from him?

He looked at Karui taking down his washing from the line and asked himself who had ordained that he should be able to sit untroubled and safe whilst this other man worked a twelve-hour day for one twelfth of his pay. He would have asked Karui had he not been afraid Karui would have known and told him, bringing the house of cards down. Sheer chance had ordained it as it had decreed Marion's condition.

For Karui such thoughts were not necessary. What was happening to him exceeded his expectations too, but when his boss had tired of the lifestyle and sought satisfaction elsewhere, he would still be here, still with the dust and malaria, still with the capricious rains and unreliable infrastructure. While he had no wish to question the fairness of life, his sons might not be as accepting.

'Have you ever done another job, Karui?' Malcolm asked on one such occasion.

'Ah, no sah.'

'How did you come to do this?'

'The British army, they had a camp near my village. I began as a kitchen toto, peeling the vegetables, washing the plates. And I learnt other things too. Then I went to work for one of the officers. Captain Burton. When he went home, I had no work.' So, it was he learnt how to iron and turn beds. It explained too why his culinary skills, though adequate for the lone male, did not satisfy the memsahibs.

'So how did you come here?'

'My brother', Malcolm knew by now this was a vague construct, 'he was building this place and he told me there would be work here. So, I came here and waited to be taken on.'

'What will you do when I go?'

'I don't know. Perhaps you will be here for ever.'

It made Malcolm think. Could I be here for ever? The one man hoped it was possible; the other feared it was unlikely.

But more than that Malcolm began to see how dependent Karui was on him. His family too. How many children did he have? Malcolm didn't know. But for the first time in his life, he understood he had people who relied on him and with that realisation came the understanding that he had responsibilities. This was new.

The next day in the late afternoon as the air was losing its heat, Malcolm strolled up the road to visit Flynn. The older man was usually undemanding, his need to speak proportionate to Malcolm's wish not to. That day he was in a puckish mood and told some racy stories of misbehaviour amongst his fellow priests but with a jolly empathy rather than condemnation.

When Flynn seemed to have exhausted his supply of gossip Malcolm brought up his conversation with Karui.

'I didn't expect to be so well off when I came here. I'm well paid; I can afford a servant. A servant! He's very nearly a slave. I have such power over him. I have to say I'm shocked by it. Why does your God allow such unfairness?'

'Because it wouldn't work if we were all equal. It may only work if its unequal, making us want to make it less so,' came a reply which was as unconvincing to Malcolm as it was unlikely from the pulpit. He wondered Marion's view on equality.

'You mean God, your God, made it unequal - to give us something to do?'

'Perhaps to help test our goodness and suitability for His house.'

'But didn't this inequality bring conflict, unhappiness?'

'Yes, but also compassion, understanding, tolerance, sacrifice. Inequality breeds all kinds of emotion. Perhaps even love flows from injustice. You said yourself you were shocked; you came to a moral view of it.'

'Is that what you tell your African parishioners, that their hardships are due to a decision by the loving God you are asking them to worship?'

Flynn looked uncomfortable.

'When I am with them, I try to deal with things as a find them, to offer some hope and optimism. But within myself I have to try to bring some rationale to it all, to reconcile what I see and what I believe. We all have a need to bring some meaning to our lives. Don't you?'

It was Malcolm's turn to look uncomfortable. 'I just get on with it as best I can.' He was avoiding the question.

'And I expect Karui does just the same. He learnt that in his life there were some things he could do nothing about and learnt to live in their shadow,' the priest clumsily closed the circle of their conversation, leaving Malcolm to remember the shadows cast by his childhood.

The two men paused in their conversation each muted by the world's incomprehensible ways. Their eyes, detached from their thoughts, took refuge in the garden beyond as if some answer might be found there. As the seasons changed so too did the colouring in Flynn's garden. Bushes and trees flowered and faded but there was always something to catch their eye. Malcolm asked about a thick bush that grew at the far corner of the veranda.

'It's beautiful, isn't it?' said Flynn gathering himself for a story. 'It's called Yesterday, Today and Tomorrow. First its dormant, then the buds break into flower, a beautiful deep purple at first, then within a short time change to a soft mauve and finally to a pure white before dying away. You can see them now, all three stages in the same plant. I don't suppose it's exactly three days - yesterday, today and tomorrow - but its close enough. A birth, a brief life nurtured by the warmth of the sun changing colour as it matures and then death. Like a human life I suppose. Not the seven ages, as the man said. But three. We all have our yesterdays, our todays, our tomorrows. Our yesterdays house our regrets and our tomorrows our hopes.

'And what about our todays?'

'They house our confusion, I suppose.'

'Now. Now. Joseph. You're supposed to be a bit more positive than that. It's we unbelievers who are supposed to be confused.'

'Well even confusion can be a positive force. Can stop us being complacent. Can make us think. Think about what is true and what is false, what is real and what is illusion.'

'Perhaps so. And is your bush confused? Does it ever get the colours in the wrong order for example?'

'I don't think so. It has little choice. That's what makes our life difficult isn't it? Choice. It puts so much responsibility on us.'

I suppose we must make the wrong choice more often than not and the regrets build up in our yesterdays, mused Malcolm.

'We're being a bit hard on this plant turning into a metaphor for human life. If it had feelings, it might wilt.'

'It doesn't seem too bothered. Its blooming nicely now.'

'There are times when the bush seems always in bloom although each flower lives only a short time. When one dies another takes its place. The briefness of its bloom heightens the pleasure you get from it. My life here has been very like that. My training was dull and unreal. Then I came here and we built the church. Those first few years, so full of hope and optimism. They were like a rich bright bloom bringing colour into every life I thought. Well, it did into mine.'

133

'But it didn't last?'

'No. It didn't last,' said Flynn flatly. He knew his bloom had faded and he felt the pale flower of death.

'Won't you bloom again?' said Malcolm trying consolation.

'I don't think so. A human life is only one season and I fear we have only one flowering. Some don't even get that, so I mustn't complain.' The human stoic in him came to the aid of the religious champion.

'That's a very sad thought.'

'Sad for me I suppose but if you have faith, you realise that others are waiting their turn. Each will experience the beauty once. Perhaps we don't deserve more.'

'You said, *will - will experience the beauty.* Do we all get a turn?' asked Malcolm, now thinking of himself.

'Only if we sow and nurture the plant to begin with,' said the priest struggling to sustain his own metaphor.

'And those that cannot plant,' said Malcolm thinking first of Marion and then thinking of himself.

'Then others must plant for them.'

THIRTEEN

'Now there's a lucky bastard.' Bernie muttered to Malcolm. They were in the shamba working on some beans as Forbes came to talk to Rogers.

'Why?'

'He fucked one of the local women, the one that works for Flynn. Got her in the family way.'

'Is that lucky?'

'No, but she cried rape - the way they do. The family went to the police. Ken denied it. That big sergeant got it sorted. Told them she'd made it up. Told them to get back to their village and forget it.'

'And that's lucky?' Malcolm carried on doggedly.

'It was just at the time of independence and the old regime was still in place. It'd be much trickier now. He still puts his wick about but he's got to be more careful now.'

It was a topic Bernie knew much about.

Alphonse Bernard was not a happy man and had never been so. He had usually placed self-indulgence on a higher plane than happiness. He had been born in South Africa of a mother of mixed race, part African, part Dutch and he had not known his father. Nevertheless, Bernie would claim him to be part Chinese, part Brazilian. This melodramatic claim to world citizenship, invented in his early teenage years, remained as an embarrassing sentimentality as he grew older. Few believed his story which was part of the embroidery which disguised a childhood that was insecure and loveless. The family home was in a group rather than a community, there being no cultural identity or tradition other than survival. His disparagement of things became embedded in his thinking and his self-worth was lower than was apparent to an observer. He was a very good-looking youth, his mixed parentage a happy recipe, although his subsequent lifestyle and outlook contrived to sabotage his countenance.

As a child he was bright and had succeeded to a university education both of the academic and streetwise variety. Deprived of a cultural background he made up values as he went along and soon learned to exploit which ever individual or group he was associated with at any time. A feigned political righteousness, religious fervour, academic seriousness, sobriety and abstinence of all kinds, dedication, loyalty, sincerity, trustworthiness, light-heartedness. Each to suit the time and place. Some thought him a rogue, some a cavalier, some a friend, some a deceiver.

For a man of his attractive appearance and manner, racial laws were no barrier to sexual contact. Several white women defied the law and the spirit of the time to taste his richness and for some of these the illicit nature of the relationship merely added to its aphrodisiac appeal. One such assignation in the back of a car was discovered by a policeman. An exchange of words led to an exchange of blows. The policeman fell against the fender and was concussed. In a combination of rage and panic Bernie drove over the man who died. His companion knew enough to realise she would rather lose a lot of money getting Bernie out of the country rather than status in the community.

He travelled north and crossed illegally into Mozambique. The purchase of a false passport under a new name got him through several border posts and he ended up in Tanzania where he was granted temporary residence. The poverty and parochialism of Tanzania was not to his liking and he settled in Nairobi. A temporary work permit allowed him to establish his research skills and had eventually brought him to Kimura.

At first, he found a new clientele for his plausibility and charm and there was no difficulty for this cultural chameleon to find his niche in Nairobi's social life. He didn't try to get into the establishment clubs, the drinking clubs on Gulzaar Street and the cocktail bars of tourist hotels being more his style. For a while people of both sexes and all races enjoyed his company and considered him their friend. But they, too, were streetwise and rootless and his novelty would wane. One proposition too many, one more debt unpaid, one more promise not kept, soon saw him displaced as he had displaced others. Now, past 40 years of age, he looked, at best, ordinary and the features he had inherited from his parents now fought rather than complemented each other. Some semblance of curly Negro hair was plastered flat, its darkness contrasting with a skin which was a pasty white refusing to succumb to African sunshine. His declining appearance helped make him a curiosity to be tolerated rather than a jewel to be prized.

'You're due for leave soon aren't you, old boy. I wonder could you do me a favour.'

'Like what?' Malcolm had reason to be suspicious.

'Just take a small package to the UK for me and post it. It'll be addressed. I'll give you some money for the stamps.'

'Why can't you send it from here?'

'Bit of a rigmarole isn't. Customs and so on. And pilfering of course. No, it's a present to a special friend. I wouldn't want it to go astray.'

'Well, I'm not going for a while.'

'There he goes.' Forbes was driving off. 'He's a sad case you know. I see him from time to time. He's usually in the Star Bar with his friends chatting up the hookers. It's a wonder he's still got his health. You're not a Nairobi man are you, Malcolm? Night time, I mean. You must let me take you down there one evening. You'll meet some super people. Smart people. Levers of power. That sort of thing.

You'll enjoy it. I know one or two ladies who'd love to meet a fresh young thing like you. Believe me.'

Malcolm asked PK what it was all about. PK pursed his lips and paused.

'Crudely. It's illegal. It's currency smuggling.'

'Go on.'

'It's illegal to export currency above certain limits.'

'Why?'

'Well, we're into big economics. I suppose otherwise it would create instability in the country.'

'If you say so. Is it a big problem?'

'I think so. It's a good example of the individual against the state. The needs of the community versus the freedom of the individual.'

'Go on.'

'Well, lots of people who live here have amassed big sums of money, usually by hard work it should be said. And because of the currency laws they can only really spend it here.'

'Why should they want otherwise?'

'Security. Hard currency in a European bank is insurance about what might happen here.'

'What could happen here?'

PK gave him an old-fashioned look. 'Who knows.'

'Go on.'

'Well, you're in the reverse position. You have sums of money in England in Sterling which you quite legally transfer here to spend in Kenya shillings. So, a lot of people here would be very pleased for you to transfer your pounds to their English bank and give you Kenya shillings here at a much better rate than you'd get from your bank.'

'Seems a good idea to me.'

'Except it's illegal and you can end up in gaol.'

'Yes, Arthur said that.'

'And some people would say it's immoral.'

'Immoral?'

'The people who suffer, indirectly I suppose, are the Africans. Directly in the end I suspect.'

'So, what's in Bernie's package?'

'Pounds, dollars, marks. Who knows?'

'Where does it come from?'

'Clandestine deals here, with foreign business men, tourists, aid workers.' The last he said sharply.

'Why does he ask me to take it?'

PK placed his hand alongside Malcolm's.

'Colour. Race. You are a nice white British citizen with a passport issued in Britain. I am a brown Asian with a British passport issued here. Who is least likely to be stopped by customs?'

'Me.' Malcolm looked sheepish.

'Exactly. And you'd be carrying out an illegal act on Bernie's behalf, or his friends, some of whom might shop you.'

'Why?'

'Revenge.'

'On, me?'

'On Bernie.' PK has surprised at Malcolm's naiveté. So was Malcolm.

'But you must want to take money out mustn't you. You or your family.' PK shrugged. 'I could do it for you. Not anybody else. I'm going on leave soon.'

PK was touched by the thought. The other face of naiveté he mused.

'Thank you. I wouldn't dream of asking.'

So, these were the people, this was the place, that took Malcolm under its wing. Mainly a community sharing the superficial and fleeting, sometimes a family sharing, not always knowingly, the profound and the sincere. Whatever its history, by the time he arrived Kimura had settled into the patterns he thought to be timeless. And within this world he found a comfortable niche. He convinced himself that this is where he wanted to be and where he must stay. His week days were filled with interesting but undemanding works and the rest of the time in the company of people whose sadness was hidden from him much as his was hidden from them. Tuesdays and Thursdays became bridge nights at the club. Wednesdays had to be avoided to miss the midweek golfers whose conversations he found narrow and manic. On Fridays he could get away early for a long weekend down across the Rift Valley towards Uganda, northwards towards the Aberdares and Mount Kenya and south and east into the game parks.

So it was, his life settled into an untroubling routine; the uncertainties of the past lay dormant. It asked so little of him, physically, professionally, personally. And just as Flynn had not noticed life at Kimura changing about him so Malcolm had not noticed the changes in himself. Each day was one of contentment and contentment does not reveal itself in a spasm but it insinuates itself into the fortunate, soothing the troubled, though seducing the unwary. His past was forgotten. There seemed no reason why this equable life style should not go on for ever.

FOURTEEN

Malcolm's life gradually acquired a gentler more confident mood. The community in which he worked, the country in which he lived, were ignorant of his past and the barrenness of his early life was allowed to recede. Even if this legacy had been publicly known it would have been thought insignificant against the vast and complex backdrop to his everyday life. For him though, it was still there, contained now, muted by more positive experiences, submerged but not suffocated. Marion still sat in her wheelchair her involuntary movements evident in the periphery of his vision. She waited in the wings of his life threatening, as she had done before, to disrupt the public stage. When the time came to renew his contract, Malcolm had little difficulty in deciding to continue the new life he had acquired during the previous two years. Rogers was pleased to secure permission to re-employ someone with experience and dedication to the job. And he had developed a fondness for Malcolm whose self-effacement echoed the fifties orderliness of his life in contrast to other recent expatriates who brought a sixties inhibition which he found unsettling. He feared the appointment of an inadequate local and did not want to face the induction of another raw expatriate.

Malcolm didn't really want to return to the UK on leave but was obliged to spend some time there under the terms of his contract. Personally, he had nothing to return to. Any fragments of a family and remnants of friendship required revival of a life to which, he realised now, he had become indifferent. He feared, too, that his past would re-emerge in surroundings resonant of his childhood. Thus, he told no-one of his return and slipped like a subversive into the land of his birth. Yet as he emerged from customs, he half expected Marion would appear from amongst the waiting relatives in the arrivals area as though she was bound to him as much as she was confined to her chair.

While in the UK he spent his time in a seaside boarding house, cheap enough out of season. To pass the time he went for long walks along the rain-swept and desolate promenade. Here he passed the children's playground, its equipment chained up for the winter. Denied their purpose the swings and slides seemed like relics of a lost civilisation as their skeletal frames scarred the open plane of the promenade. He put his hand on the arm of a roundabout and was about to rotate it when it reminded him of a bicycle wheel. He paused and looked around. Nothing. No-one. Good. Bustling around him the damp winter winds evoked the coldness of Malcolm's own upbringing. And as his body sought the return of African heat so his spirit yearned for a warm comfort it seemed to be denied.

Each day he went to the local library and scanned the papers for reports of life in Kenya. He became aware of what limited a view the press coverage gave, but still devoured every detail however banal. His life was full of trivia - novels which he would take back for Ngugi, TV and, a short bus ride away, a cinema. Here he sought out the films with some tropical connection and wallowed in the dark of the cinema enjoying the vicarious warmth of the screen, wishing to rise from his seat and join the celluloid performance.

Every day was a reminder of how empty a life it had been in England and how much he missed the country of his adoption. Here the rain was sharp and the wind cold; there soft warm rain gave no discomfort and even its dampness could be refreshing. Here the temperature fluctuated, confounding his choice of clothes, as the sun worked hard between the showers; there the warmth of the air and the ground made minimal demands on his wardrobe. On only one day did his birth land leave a mark. One spring day, a late frost brought a tingle to his ears and his breath turned cloudy in the clear air. For a moment, a very brief moment, he regretted not having that experience more often.

But the differences were not just meteorological or geographical. England held the secrets of his unhappy past and threatened to reveal them; Africa knew little of his background and was indifferent to it. He wondered whether to confront those secrets, to diffuse their strength by facing up to them. He could return to his home town unrecognised; this bronzed adult not identifiable with a pasty-faced youth whose public presence was minimal. There was no family there, no family home although someone now enjoyed a well tilled garden, no names on the war memorial. There were school records of course; but these would be inert reports rather than favourable memories amongst the staff. He could visit the family grave, his parents and sister buried together. He could stand before it confronting their names chiselled into the marble, passive labels of lives long ended, their personal immortality not only in the etched letters but just as sharply scored on the spirit of the living him. He could whisper to them of the richness and warmth of his present life and mock their cold responses. He could turn away leaving their bodies to face the overgrowing weeds of their neglected resting place. Perhaps in doing all this he could banish their clammy, oppressive hold over his life. All of these he imagined as he lay in his rented bed hearing the rain driven on his window, feeling the slam of the front door as residents returned late, From where? he wondered, seeing the beams of passing head lamps sweep across his bedroom ceiling like those of an erratic lighthouse. But none of these things he did; a simple cowardice kept him away.

But in keeping away, the power of the past was kept alive in the present. On one of his afternoon walks, a wheelchair turned a corner into his path and he froze beyond the demands of late winter. At first its occupant, wrapped up against the searing wind, was indistinct. It was not Marion but an elderly man, his face reddened in the passing air, a large dewdrop on the end of his nose. He raised his hat in greeting as he passed Malcolm. His pusher, a young woman, hatless but face red with the exertion as well as the weather, added a greeting to which Malcolm could not respond until they had passed beyond him. Then his weak greeting was lost on the wind and he became for this contrasting pair another of the oddities of public life.

So, he avoided the symbolic confrontation with the past which could have been his saviour and kept his mind fixed on the future. Once on a headland high above the frothing sea he imagined himself on the edge of the Rift Valley looking out across hundreds of miles of dry landscape full of life, unseen from that height, obscured by the dusty layers below him. Now it was the relentless rolling of cold salty water that obscured the teaming life below. The vastness of the seascape before him recaptured the insignificance he had felt in Africa and he rejoiced in it. For a stranger the sight of a lone man standing on the edge on a rocky cliff might have occasion concern for his motives. Less of a stranger, who knew more of Malcolm's past, might well have been alarmed. Both would have been mistaken. This man was not in despair. He was in a state of suspended animation longing for the warmth of Africa to revive his dormant feelings of wellbeing. If he was looking at the waves beating on the rocks below it was not because he wanted to join them but because he saw every wave-break ticking off the time on some maritime clock before he could return. Before long he realised the wind in his face was not the warm breeze from the depths of the great valley but hail-pitted gusts which drove the cold deep into his skin. He felt his face frozen for some days afterwards.

The food in his lodgings became monotonous and he sought out some variety but most of the restaurants were closed for the winter. Down a side street he found an Indian restaurant clinging to the edges of solvency judging by its sparse clientele. Over a series of visits, he chose dishes he had had in Kenya, but they were as like those as tinned pineapples were to the fresh ones Karui served for breakfast. The coloured faces of the staff reminded him of the warmth he had left. In conversation he hoped to find they had come from Kenya and they could rekindle mutual memories but they had not and so could not. He wondered what they felt as strangers in a foreign land and whether they had been treated as well as he had. He thought not.

Throughout his two months leave his conversations were short and superficial and for this he was grateful. He resented every syllable of contact with these natives fearing a hook on which the past could reclaim him. Throughout that time, he received no mail, although he had written to Flynn and the Rogers, and received no calls or callers. His landlady, although used to a variety of peculiarities amongst her guests, became at first alarmed and intrigued until, realising no drama was about to unfold, lapsed into indifference. To his fellow residents Malcolm must have seemed odd, rude even. Their polite and anodyne enquiries were dispatched with an unencouraging brusqueness but as none of them stayed more than two weeks the consequences of this behaviour were short-lived. As his leave progressed it acquired the status of a game in which he was charged with revealing as little of himself as he could. The light-heartedness of this approach contrasted with the Malcolm of earlier times for whom the tactics would have been a necessary protection rather than a mild diversion.

To outsiders his daily life might seem odd, even perverse - the single figure on the cliff top, the lone man in the cinema, the solitary diner in the restaurant, all indicative of sadness and sinister to the unknowing. But inside his life was full, of incidents, of experiences, of people which he hoped were the appetisers of his life abroad not the main meal.

So, slowly and uneventfully, his leave passed. Towards the end of his stay, he began counting off the days of his holiday anticipating not just a return to work but a return to life.

FIFTEEN

On the previous occasion, the touchdown at Nairobi had brought apprehension; this one brought relief. The journey had bored him; he knew what to expect. His fellow passengers engaged no interest. In the main they were the inexperienced travellers beginning new lives with a confusing birth; he was the confident, knowing doyen to whom they turned for example or so he liked to believe. All that distinguished them from the passengers of two years previously was a more recent cycle of fashion which determined their clothes. Beneath these they had the same hopes, the same motives, the same anxieties. As it had been for Malcolm two years before, for them the flight would be a memorable event in their lives but for him the journey was insignificant; the arrival everything. That he now could imagine himself as a template for the behaviour of others confirmed the changes that had taken place within him over his first tour of duty.

He was met by the Harringtons who had offered to meet him as they were visiting Nairobi. They would not have been his first choice to greet his return but the convenience overrode the reservations. On the journey up country, they chatted to him and each other but his mind was on the scenes outside the car, joyfully revisited for their familiarity. Colours, contours, vegetation, people, animals, even smells, reminded him of what had become his life and from which he had been temporarily denied access. The Harringtons - they seemed a pair rather than individuals - invited him to join their party at the Caledonian dinner at the club. This, together with Scandinavian night, were considered to be the cultural highlights of the social calendar attracting Scots and Scandinavians from far and wide usually to both events.

The Ministry in Nairobi had not been able to find a suitable replacement for John Harrington when his contract ended eighteen months ago. The country had insufficient qualified people to meet the needs of its burgeoning prosperity. Rogers had pleaded to look overseas again and this was granted. Rogers had persuaded John Harrington to renew his contract after his first tour but this time he could not. The Harringtons were leaving for good and this was their farewell do. All the research staff at the station had been invited as well as friends from Nairobi and beyond. It was not something that naturally attracted Malcolm but he was resigned to being drawn into the event.

Back at the station Karui was there to greet him. The house and garden were well kept as usual. Malcolm looked round to see if anything had changed; to his relief nothing had. The floor was brightly polished, the windows transparently clean, the bed clothes crisp and neat. He found its simple orderliness refreshing as though he had showered off the dust of a journey. And that he did literally as well.

Within an hour Ngugi was on his doorstep. With him he had some of the books Malcolm had lent him during the leave. He wanted to borrow some more and had brought these as a counterweight although he had kept some, he especially favoured. By now he had gone through the small collection of books Malcolm had kept from his childhood and Malcolm had promised to buy some more in the UK.

'It is so good to see you back,' the solicitous announcement a preamble to news of some books.

'It's nice to be back.'

'How are your family?' Ngugi would not understand there wasn't one.

'Fine thank you,' Malcolm didn't want an explanation.

'Was the weather good?' The youngster was reaching the limits of his social conversation.

'It was very cold.'

'Colder than the mountain?' he enquired jerking his head towards the hidden Mount Kenya.

'Much colder,' said Malcolm although he was wrong.

'I've brought your books back.' Ngugi was losing patience. 'I liked the Charles Dickens.' He pronounced the 'les' as a clear syllable. 'I can see the pictures from his words. But the names are so strange not like the European names here. They are odd. When I see one it's like finding a cherry in a cake.'

Malcolm wasn't convinced by the metaphor which he assumed to be remembered from some book. He handed over the new books he'd brought from leave not sure whether he'd brought the right ones. As the young African scanned the titles, the interest in his benefactor's holiday evaporated.

'Ah. Robert Louis Stevenson,' he picked out the syllables of a name he had not seen before but had to be helped with the middle name. 'That is good. Thank you, Bwana Bryant.' With that he picked up his bundle of books and set off down the road to the village. Malcolm wondered whether he would ever see all his childhood books again and decided it didn't matter if he didn't.

In his hut Ngugi took each volume and after reading its title covered it in some grease proof paper that had been wrapped around the bread Malcolm brought from Nairobi - Karui was not the only one to benefit from the leftovers of Malcolm's house. Around each package he put a rubber band, one of the many he had coaxed from Phillip in the office. Each package was then packed into one of a number of biscuit tins stacked on a large flat stone in the corner of the hut. Neither ants nor damp would spoil his library. From a corner of the hut his mother watched him work, recognising each step as a loosening of her claims on his life.

And before the day was out Flynn came to pay his respects. He had news of his own which he wanted to share.

'I'm going to Uganda.'

'Uganda! You mean you're leaving here?'

'No. No. Only a visit. A pilgrimage really. In July Pope Paul VI is visiting the shrine of the Martyrs at Namugongo. I've not seen him but I did see Pope Pius XII in Rome before I came here. Do you know the story?'

'Of you going to Rome? I think you did tell me.'

'No. No. The martyrs. It's awful. King Mutesa challenged some converts to confirm their Christianity on pain of death. About forty or so did just that. So, he killed them. Some were slowly burnt to death.'

'I'd rather you didn't go on.'

'Well, I've got a book on it, if you want to borrow it. Anyway, I'm going with a group of priests from Nairobi. Barry Hames from Dagoretti. He visited me here once. Didn't you meet him? Oh no you were on leave. Anyway, Barry's got a minibus so he's in charge of transport. Someone else used to live in Kampala so he's in charge of accommodation.'

'What's your role?'

Flynn looked bemused, 'I'm not sure. I'd better be in charge of conversation. What do you think?' and the priest laughed at himself.

'Well, you've had plenty of practice.'

'I know you're not religious but let me be serious of a moment. I must go to Uganda, to honour the martyrs. Those men gave up they lives rather than deny the God that I believe in. I hope I'm never asked to do the same. To deny my God to save my life. It makes my little sacrifices here insignificant.'

'Do you really make sacrifices?'

'When I meet some of the boys in Nairobi, when we are planning this journey, I see how much richer my life could have been. And - I have to say it - envy sneaks a look at me. Although curiously as soon as I admit that, then I know it's right I stay here. Lives are ruined by envy. Have you made any sacrifices in your life?'

'No. No, I don't think I have. I used to think I had been sacrificed - my childhood wasn't happy,' This admission, the first to Flynn or indeed anyone, confirmed his growing confidence. 'But when I think of what I have now that seems self-indulgent. I hope your journey goes well. But don't leave here. I would miss you.'

That night Malcolm relaxed on the veranda looking forward to work resuming its comforting regularity. He was relieved it was all there. Supposing Karui had not been there, or Rogers, or Gitau. Supposing it had all evaporated leaving nothing to return to from the emptiness of his homeland. All these irrational fears could be set aside. From out of the darkness came sounds with which he had been familiar. Frogs croaked in their dark holes; cicadas chirruped against the bark of trees, a young goat bleated by the valley stream below; high above, the sky still spread its sparkling blanket of stars. If there were demons out there in the dark, they were demons for all men, not just targeting their ill will against him. The sounds and smells, once strange and disconcerting, were now familiar and comforting, providing the feathers to his nest. Today, content as he had never been, Malcolm was home.

SIXTEEN

Malcolm discovered late in the day he needed a formal suit for the Caledonian dinner. He had never worn one before. Alice Rogers would come to his rescue by adapting one of her husband's. Despite it being one Rogers had had when much younger and reflecting a dated style, Malcolm looked rather better than he felt. With some misgivings about the strength and invisibility of Alice's stitching he drove to the dinner. He was going out of a sense of loyalty to a colleague with no hope other than that the evening would be tolerable.

The Harrington's friends were a mixed lot. A paint salesman and his wife, a nurse, a teaching couple from Western Province down for the weekend, three RAF men seconded as instructors to the KAF at Eastleigh. With the exception of PK, they were all European. The Harrington's had no strong views on race but the notion of friendship with Africans and Asians was not foremost in their attitudes. On their return to the UK, they would regale friends and relatives with stories of this exotic episode in their lives unaware of the richness below the surface which had defined their lives. However, it would have made little difference to their listeners who would quickly bore of these vicarious adventures. For them there would be little difference between the Serengetti and Sorrento.

Through a window to the veranda Malcolm could see the heads of several young children huddled together, jostling for the best view through the lowest pane. Their bodies were hidden in the dark and only their faces could be seen like masks at a Restoration ball. Eyes flashed from one episode to another, the whites highlighted in their black faces by the internal lights of the room, making them look like a swarm of fireflies in the night. A generation ago they would not have been allowed there, beaten away by the sticks of moody askaris. Now their nation was escaping its past, much as Malcolm was escaping his, and they were claiming their innocent and unthreatening rights to vicarious pleasure.

Larsen, his white hair and sober dinner suit marking him out as a patrician, held the attention of a group of men and women. Their laughter was formal and exaggerated to the outsider although in reality the humour was as superficial and harmless as the old-fashioned dances they would soon enjoy. Larsen, with his family and friends, assumed a status in the community which they felt they had earned although the credit might more easily rest with their ancestors. In placing themselves above others they found it less easy to make real friends and as death and emigration took their toll, they found themselves an isolated vestige of past success. Their actions and announcements were no longer be taken at face value and the less favoured among the newcomers took their dumb revenge.

At the bar sat Ken Forbes with his cronies. Their conversation stopped as PK walked by but Forbes jerked his head in a gesture of recognition. He looked self-conscious in his black waisted jacket and kilt, a dagger in his knee length stockings. As he sat and joked with his guests, he saw Larsen charming his group and a sliver of jealousy ran through him before he turned back to the bar.

At the dinner table Malcolm was placed next to the nurse who was introduced. On her other side was an empty chair which had been earmarked for Bernie who had not yet appeared. Malcolm, therefore, had Alison's full attention. Had she waited for him, the conversation might never have got going but after a moment's silence she began a flow of information and enquiry which demanded Malcolm's involvement. She was born in Tanganyika where her parents farmed sisal. She had trained in London and now worked in the Nairobi hospital where she had been for four years. This information she managed to impart with a wealth of anecdote as if Malcolm had asked. Equally she found out about his background as if he had volunteered the information. Marion had not been declared. Enough detail had been given to describe a conventional English upbringing in an ordinary family with typical experiences. Such an interpretation gave a substance to Malcolm's past which fashioned some kind of picture of him even one seen in a distorting mirror one which took the real unbalanced Malcolm and gave him a more acceptable shape.

After a suitable delay following the dinner, a small band began to play. Although all kilted, they began with a variety of standard ballroom numbers which might be heard anywhere from Kensington to Kuala Lumpur. When Alison had asked him in the Ladies Invitation it was with apprehension, he took the floor. To accept or decline would have put him under scrutiny but Alison's firm hand made the decision for him. Though the dance was a slow undemanding waltz it seemed to offer baffling complexity as Malcolm took to a dance floor for the first time in his life and he found it necessary to apologise every half dozen steps or so. After a while he judged the rhythm and despite his concerns about Alice's needlework, he found himself enjoying himself. As with many things in his life he found he enjoyed the experience once it was happening; it was making it happen that was the difficult bit. He found it strange to be holding another body so close to his. His father had held him close once and his mother often when he was young. He had been encouraged to put his arm round Marion for a family photograph and the memory lingered distastefully. Part of Marion's legacy had been an inhibition against physical contact. Thus, to find a firm, strong, mobile female body so close to his was a novelty he found alarming. Marion's motions against his body had been uncoordinated and unintentional; Alison's were rhythmic and sensual. If their faces came close it was Alison who brought them so, not Malcolm. He felt the firm swell of her breasts against his chest. He smelled her perfume and the sweetness of her breath. At the same time, he became aware of the chemical smell emanating from Rogers' dinner jacket. He looked self-consciously over her shoulder and was surprised to find no-one taking any notice of them. Couples clung together in a range of embraces, most coaxing banal responses from their partners. When the music stopped, she thanked him and kissed his cheek, her face damp with perspiration from the warm air. He judged it to be a thoughtful acknowledgement of his discomfort but he was too gauche to respond and she pulled him gently by the hand back to their table.

Malcolm was spared the agony of making more conversation as Bernie arrived by taxi from Nairobi with already too much to drink. He joined the Harrington's table seating himself in the empty chair between Alison and PK. John Harrington introduced him to his guests leaving Alison to the last. Bernie eyed her in a way he thought roguish but to observers was comically lascivious.

'Well, hello, hell-o. So nice to meet you,' Bernie, in his practised lounge lizard voice, mistook the convivial atmosphere for the forced bonhomie of the Nairobi bars. 'Tell me ..... ,' he had forgotten her name already, '..darling. Haven't we met before?' The corniness of his approach and the unsteadiness of his body which caused his elbow to slip from the table caused some hilarity amongst the airmen.

'I don't think so. I'm sure I'd remember if we had.' The cold unoriginal sarcasm from Alison went largely unnoticed.

Bernie paused not sure of his ground. A decade ago, his well-balanced face and twinkling eyes would have made even the most banal conversation seem interesting to most women. Now drink had puffed out his face and veined his eyes leaving him with only Don Juan ambitions that could no longer be satisfied. He looked round the table for another female face to smile at or another male to smirk at. He found nothing of interest and returned his attentions back to Alison.

'Would you care to dance?' Bernie stroked her bare arm with the back of his hand.

'I'm sorry, I can't, I've hurt my leg.'

'How did you do that?' said Bernie reaching for the hem of her dress in an attempt to reveal her thigh.

'Playing rugby,' the corny reply brought guffaws from round the table and put Bernie clearly beyond the group.

'Fucking lesbian,' was the best he could manage and called for another beer.

'OK, mate. That's enough. If you can't watch your language, clear off,' Malcolm wished it had been him but it was one of the airmen.

Bernie focused on him and raised both palms outwards towards him in supplication.

'Sorry. Sor-ree,' he said but to no-one in particular.

He continued to drink and when he stood to go to the toilet he slipped and fell against Alison's chair. Malcolm volunteered to drive him home. With Bernie barely able to walk Malcolm steered him to the car park his farewells to the Harrington's friends necessarily brief. As he pulled away from the club, he heard the sound of a Scottish reel as the evening turned from the sedate musical openers to the more robust dances which were to be the highlight of the evening. For Malcolm it was a relief. He felt he would have been fated to be a conspicuous individual unaccustomed to the steps and rhythms. His gangling ineptitude would have confused his fellow dancers throwing the intricate dance patterns into disarray.

Bernie was unhappily drunk and his ranting prevented Malcolm savouring his unexpected enjoyment of the evening.

'You know my problem? They don't want me in South Africa because I'm too black and they don't want me here because I'm too white. These bastards won't give me a work permit. They want the work for their own people.'

In South Africa his mixed parentage had put him in ethnic limbo and here too he was in the no man's land between black and white, and between an Africa he couldn't leave and a Europe he couldn't reach. Malcolm had heard it all before but now the alcohol marked the usual bitterness with fear.

'Why don't you go back to South Africa?'

The passenger paused, Malcolm not being sure whether he was reluctant to say anything or his mind unable to form the words.

'They'd bang me in prison. I was involved in a scuffle. Someone got killed. It wasn't even political,' he stumbled over the last word and began to hiccup.

'Really.'

'I can't even be a political martyr. Hic. I was with a white woman. Hic. Nobody wants me back. Hic. It would cause them too much trouble. Hic. My family, the police. Hic. Anyone. I'm not wanted there and - hic - I'm not wanted here.'

He had said this tale to so many people, on so many occasions, it had lost its interest and become merely a self-pitying incantation. The detail was correct but his culpability had become muted with the story's repetition. With the jolting of the car on the corrugated road he fell asleep. At the compound Bernie's door was opened by his house keeper and she and Malcolm got Bernie to bed.

In his own bedroom Malcolm discarded Rogers' dinner suit hanging it on the old-fashioned wooden hanger with which it had come. He showered and lay on his bed. From outside familiar noises carried on the warm night air but within his head only the sound of a waltz could be heard.

SEVENTEEN

During his first contract Malcolm had realised how much the work of the station revolved around Gitau. He ensured that programmes were carried out, rotas followed, deadlines met. He was the link between the professional staff and the labourers yet he often seemed apart from both groups. During work breaks he would often sit alone under the big tree in the front square drinking his mug of tea. There he sat with a kind of dignity as much a patrician in his own world as Larsen across the road in his. In reality he needed solitude as other men required company. He did not want to absorb other people's values or share their problems. He wanted to make up his own mind about the world and determine his own fate. In his open-air temple he would turn in the direction of the mountain hidden in its midday cloud beyond the skyline and seek the guidance of his own god, Ngai, just as Flynn turned to his God in the church. For each the guidance was limited.

'How long have you worked here, Gitau?' asked Malcolm one day as they worked in the shamba.

The foreman shrugged. 'A long time. Since it opened. I used to work for Bwana Larsen'

'Do you like this job?'

'It brings me my wages. It feeds my family. Should I want more than that?'

'You have a lot of people to look after. How many is it now?'

'I have four children of my own and five belonging to my brother.'

'Because he died?'

'Yes.'

'I'm told he killed himself.'

'Yes. He was very drunk and hung himself from a tree.'

'Did he drink a lot?' Malcolm's curiosity overrode good manners.

'Too much. He was a troubled man.'

'His wife - his widow - Wambui, she works for the priest.'

'She does.'

'And she does not look after the children?'

'No.' And then before Malcolm could say more, he said, 'It is a family matter. I do not want to talk about it'

Malcolm's questioning was not planned but each answer seemed to provoke a further question until Malcolm knew he had gone too far. He felt shame that his curiosity had turned a gentle enquiry into an intrusive interrogation. He dared not go as far with the father as he had with the son.

'Is Ngugi the eldest?'

'No. There are two older ones. My brother's first daughter is the oldest. She is in England training to be a nurse.'

'Oh yes. Where?'

'Brighton,' he had trouble with the 'r', 'Is that a nice place?'

'I don't know I've never been there. It's by the sea. Have you ever seen the sea?'

'No. I have not travelled far from here.'

'What does Ngugi want to do?'

'Now he says he wants to cultivate the land'

'Like you?'

'Like Bwana Larsen. He is rich. I am poor.'

'And will he do that?'

'He changes his mind a lot. Your books keep giving him ideas.'

'I'm pleased they do.'

'Yes. Education is important'

'He is very clever. He will do well at school. Then he can find a good job. Maybe not on the land.'

'The secondary school near here is not so good. It is a Harambee school. It's only just been built. Sometimes the teachers don't get paid. He may not do well.'

'You could send him to a better school, in Nairobi? He could go to a boarding school.'

'I cannot afford the fees. I have ten mouths to feed.' The older man eased himself away from Malcolm and bent to examine some bean plants. It was a clear sign that the conversation had reached a limit.

Malcolm was bemused although the simple arithmetic of Gitau's salary could not be denied. His own parents had had to struggle but only with Marion and the logistics of getting her around. They had inner struggles too, but they had never struggled over money. It was taken for granted that he would go to school and beyond. It was axiomatic that Marion would get medical treatment and the family would not starve. When he got back to his house Malcolm asked Karui how many children he had.

'Seven', replied Karui, evidently pleased at the declaration. Malcolm divided Karui's salary by nine and marvelled.

For supper Karui had made a chicken casserole with boiled potatoes. Malcolm wondered whether he should ask Karui to share it but settled for leaving a substantial amount in the container. He needn't have bothered. Karui always made more than his boss could eat knowing the leftovers would make a substantial meal for himself. Although he did not steal, neither did he rely totally on the generosity of his employer.

The routine of one lunch time was broken by a loud shouting from the front office. Phillip rushed through to say Boniface had been bitten by a snake. The clerk was carrying the battered body of a brown snake looped over a stick. He had had the presence of mind to kill the reptile so that it could be identified. He and Boniface had been walking behind the storerooms and Boniface had stopped to relieve himself when the snake struck. His flip-flopped feet had been an easy target for the alarmed creature. In the front office Boniface lay, clutching his foot and moaning pathetically. To the onlookers it made an amusing sight but to him it was the prospect of death.

'At least it isn't green,' said Harrington, his crude assessment of danger not fool-proof.

'No, it's an adder of some sort. I think he'll be OK but we'd better get him to hospital. Can you take him?' Rogers asked of Malcolm. Rogers put the snake in a large envelope and handed it to Malcolm. 'Show them this. They'll know if it's dangerous. I don't think it is. It's not life and death. Mind how you go.'

Malcolm drove as fast as seemed sensible wondering why no one had sucked the poison out of Boniface's foot as always seemed to happen on screen. He concluded that it wasn't the lack of medical knowledge but the condition of Boniface's feet that had been the deciding factor.

The hospital staff were waiting for them alerted by a phone call from Rogers. A doctor looked in the envelope and took the snake out. He handed it to Malcolm and bent to attend to Boniface. Malcolm was surprised to find himself holding the snake. Its body was softer than he had expected and he stroked it with his finger. The snake gave a slight reflex movement and he hurriedly dropped it back into the envelope.

As he waited for Boniface to be treated, he was greeted by Alison the Harringtons' friend who was on duty. Her appearance revived Malcolm's memories of the high of their dance together and the low of Bernie's attentions. He explained why he was there. Her bright laughter at the incident made him smile too. Only Boniface, fearing the worst, failed to be amused. A doctor gave him an injection.

'He'll be OK. It's not poisonous; at least not lethally so. It'll hurt for a while and he'll have a headache. I'll give him some painkillers.'

Whilst an orderly was washing and dressing Boniface's foot Alison chatted with Malcolm.

'I enjoyed the dinner although that kind of thing is too serious in a trivial way. And you can get too much Scottish dancing. The Gay Gordons might be all right on a cold night in Invercockerleaky or wherever but it doesn't capture the spirit of Africa. You were lucky to get away. You got your friend home alright?' she asked.

'Yes, after a struggle.' He wanted to say Bernie was not his friend in case Alison thought he approved of Bernie's behaviour.

'He is an odd ball isn't he. We've had him in Casualty a couple of times. Once after a car accident; the other after a fight. Sad really.'

'But you said you hadn't met before.'

She gave him an old-fashioned look. 'He wouldn't have wanted to be reminded, would he? Anyway, one woman's much the same as another to him, I expect.'

'I didn't know you played rugby.' Malcolm had enjoyed the put down.

'You have to learn to deal with drunken men when you work in Casualty. It's the uniform. It either makes them horny or abusive.'

Malcolm took a prudish view of the language and looked at her uniform. It gave a shape to her body as well as an authority to her manner. She was medium build, grey eyes, light complexioned with soft curly dark brown hair.

'What are you doing this Saturday evening?' Malcolm would never have been able to ask this question and he was startled when it was asked of him.

'Er. Nothing much.' It not being his weekend duty at the station he was free but had no plans to go away.

'Do you fancy going to a concert?'

To accept or decline would have been equally embarrassing to him.

'Er. Yes. That sounds nice,' said Malcolm not sure what kind of a concert it might be.

'There's a German touring ensemble at the National Theatre. They're doing various bits and pieces. Some Mozart, some Vivaldi. Oh, and the Elgar Cello Concerto. That might cheer you up.' He didn't understand the irony but the need to be cheered up was a chronic condition.

'I'm not very knowledgeable about classical music. But. Yes. I'd like to come. Thank you.'

She broke off to say something to Boniface in Swahili and turned to Malcolm. 'Fine. We can grab a snack first. The concert is at eight. I've got two tickets. I'll see you at The New Stanley. At the front. At 6.30. Saturday. Bye,' and was off around a corner and out of sight before Malcolm could make any response. And so, with no effort from him he had a date with an attractive woman. He felt a tightness in his chest; it felt as though something, perhaps only blood, had livened a part of his body that had been dormant. It was only excitement, strange to him because he had needed to suppress it in the past.

The journey back to Karima was in silence, Boniface dead to the world, Malcolm alive to something new.

Malcolm dressed as smartly as he could. He couldn't think of a previous occasion when he had been out with a woman as a twosome and he was 28 years old. He had lacked a sexual appetite, the embarrassment of the required intimacy enough to extinguish all lust.

Fearing being late, he had arrived very early and sat near the entrance. He delayed an order for a drink when a waiter approached and looked at his watch repeatedly. Conversations at neighbouring tables caught his attention only momentarily before his eyes returned to the street activity. He'd just returned from the toilet a second time when she arrived. He saw her park and her white dress picked her out as she crossed the street in the growing dusk. He felt his tongue going dry in his mouth and his body shivered with a nervousness he had not felt before. He stood to greet her, to her a rather outdated formality, to him an assumed requirement. He had to cough slightly to free his tongue.

'Hello,' was the best he could manage.

She was ten minutes late but not deliberately so. 'Hi. Sorry I'm late. There's a lorry overturned on the highway - pineapples all over the shop. Well, all over the road anyway. The police had it all under control. I didn't stop to see if they needed a nurse,' her fuller reply eased things slightly.

They ordered drinks and then a snack. Her dress was sleeveless and her upper arms were full and strong, though short of plumpness. He could see an inoculation mark and it added human ordinariness to her attractiveness. Her skin was faintly tanned and delineated the rounded outline of the dress at her neck. She was pretty but lacked the spice that would have made her beautiful. Malcolm did not need to start the conversation. Alison flowed easily from one topic to another towing him in her wake She spoke mostly about the incidents in her hospital life. Even the most gruesome were dealt with in a matter-of-fact way. He was relieved she said no more of Bernie. As she spoke, he watched her lips. They were full and shown off by a bright lipstick that contrasted with her pale skin and dark hair. Male eyes at other tables and with their own companions, sought her out but she seemed unaware of the attention. Her eyes took only Malcolm's and her honest undivided attention prized open many shutters in his mind.

After the concert they returned for a drink. As they walked back Alison held Malcolm's hand. He felt the pressure of her hand waxing and waning as she put emphasis on her words. It was alive and warm and human. He was surprised by the comfort given by this simple action.

At the table she said, 'They were a good group, weren't they?' Malcolm hadn't got a clue. 'Some of it was a bit sentimental, wasn't it? What did you like?'

Malcolm knew but he was frightened by the intensity of his feelings about the piece. It wasn't that he liked it but that it moved him to an unexpected degree. He wondered had she seen him wipe his eyes after it. 'The cello.'

'Elgar.'

'Yes.'

'It's a bit mournful.'

'Yes.'

'Tell me.'

'I can't. It's too .. ,' he was going to say personal, '.. complicated.'

'You cried.' She was not trying to tease him but to tease more from him.

'I had tears in my eyes. Yes,' the admission was cathartic.

'Good. Music is a good for revealing emotions you don't know you have.'

He was close to tears again. Alison watched his face and could not fail to be intrigued by the person behind it. She would have to find out more later but now her stories of school life diffused the emotion. 'I used to play instruments. At home I had piano lessons from an old Greek lady. Madam Ionides. She liked the Madam bit. She had a ruler which she threatened my hands with but she never used it. She was a sweetie really. We both knew I wasn't going to be any good so we just enjoyed it instead. At the end of each session, she would play a piece for me - different one each time as far as I remember. I used to watch her hands, wrinkled of course. When you look at old peoples' hands you can't imagine them wrinkle free. It's as though they've always been that way. And you can't imagine your own becoming wrinkled.' She paused to look at the backs of her own hands. 'I hope mine never become wrinkled. Madam Ionides wore rings that flashed as she played and the fingers were brown with smoking. And when she played fortissimo the candelabra on the upright piano rattled. She was quite lively - like her spirit had wrinkled more slowly than her skin. She lived with a man younger than herself but when you're young you don't notice that. All adults are old. I don't think my parents approved but piano teachers are hard to come by in rural Tanganyika. Her husband was killed by a lion.'

'A lion!' Malcolm looked surprised.

'Yes. I suppose that is a bit shocking. But it sometimes happens. You can read it in the papers often enough. Child snatched by crocodile. Ranger gored by elephant. It is Africa after all. When I was in London three children drowned by slipping through the ice on a lake. Accidents happen. We see the end product in Casualty. How's Boniface by the way?'

'He's OK. He's not back at work yet. I think he's coming back on Monday.'

'And I played the recorder, of course, at boarding school. We all had to play something there. The music teacher was Miss Goodbody. Can you believe it. People don't have names like that do they. Anyway, she did; but she didn't have a good body, if you see what I mean. I think she fancied some of the girls but I don't remember anyone fancying her. Or if they did, they didn't admit it. I graduated to the clarinet but I was useless and haven't played since. But I never lost interest in the music. London was wonderful for that. I used to love the Proms. You could really have a good time. Have you ever been to the Proms?'

'No. I'm afraid not.' He didn't like to admit he'd never been to London apart from his interview and flight.

'Have you ever played an instrument?'

'No. No.' Malcolm smiled at the thought. At the concert he had been as interested in the players as the pieces. He marvelled at the confidence it required to stand exposed in public view, to risk ridicule in the hope of acclaim. For them it had been reduced to a routine job, for him it would have been unrelenting anguish. And for the Elgar he was mesmerised by the soloist who sat producing the most moving sounds. A thousand people, all watching her, sitting alone in the spotlight. He marvelled.

They talked for over an hour and Malcolm felt an easy partner in the conversation. But if he had analysed it, sentence by sentence, topic by topic, he would have found it was Alison that was the dynamo.

'Well, I must go. I'm driving down to Moshi tomorrow to stay with my parents for a few days. I haven't seen them for a while. I want to get going before it gets too hot.' Malcolm thought how wonderful it was to have a childhood you could talk about and parents you wanted to visit. As she stood, she scraped her chair and several eyes were attracted to the noise, lingering on her not Malcolm though he felt otherwise.

He escorted her to her car. As she got in, he shut the door on her too quickly and her white dress caught in it, a small piece sticking out from the door frame. She did not notice and he was too confused to draw it to her attention. She wound down the window.

'Thank you for a lovely evening.'

'Thank you. I enjoyed that,' Malcolm was formal but truthful.

'Well, we can do it again you know,' said Alison her voice showing a hint of teasing.

As she drove off, he watched the white edge of her dress showing clear of the bodywork of the car as it turned a corner and disappeared. He stood for a moment, no coherent thought in his mind. But among the jumble of feelings, he did feel some were new to him.

And they did go out together again. Their meetings in Nairobi became a regular feature of their lives aided by some co-ordinated manipulation of hospital shifts and station rotas. That night marked the start of a battle over Malcolm's life between two women. The one pert, open hearted, eager, the other dead, disabled, defenceless would compete as conflicting influences in the confusion of Malcolm's emotions.

Alison was two years older than Malcolm. She had had many suitors and two lovers. The one in London provided a sad baptism to a life so different from rural Tanganyika and its uncomplicated social values. Brought up in a traditional family and conventional schools, her simplicity and openness had fallen to his big city sophistication. She surrendered to him and he abandoned her. The parting marked her. They were sitting in a small bar. He told her they were finished and got up and left. No warning. No reason. She sat there for a long time unable to accept it, disturbed by its implications, shocked by its brutality. And this from a man she had told the intimate things of her life. Laying naked with him she had removed the cover of her own insecurities, glad to share them with a sensitive lover. Every declaration, every admission, every question weaned her away from secure childhood into his capricious adult world. And he then abused her openness. In her own eyes she was the victim of her own innocence; in his, she was the dupe of her own naiveté. He had begun by piercing her hymen and ended by breaking her heart She trusted no man after that and her confidence was slow to return. Unwilling to socialise she sought her solace in music.

The second affair, with a visiting doctor on a two-year contract in Nairobi, was more cautious and its ending less hurtful. Despite her experience in London, she had supposed herself in love; he considered it only a tropical infatuation as transient as a bought of malaria. She had felt so much surer this time. She was on her ground, not his. She was more experienced and felt less vulnerable; for protection she had developed a sliver of doubt to every feeling and a damper of inhibition to every action. But again, she was deceived and then deserted. Neither of these two men, so different in their personalities so similarly casual in their attitude to her, gave her much optimism for the family life she had taken for granted. If with the first she lost the will to trust a man, with the second she had lost the confidence to judge one. Was it always to be like this? Can't anyone be trusted? Is it always a gamble? For all the passion and excitement of her two affairs she would forgo them both for the serenity and certainty of true loyalty.

Malcolm was not like the other two and she did not see him as he saw himself. To her he was self-effacing not socially inadequate, quiet not dull, restrained not shy. If he was naive and innocent then these were plusses; he had not the guile which had betrayed her earlier commitments. She did not expect to be hurt by him but she did not want to frighten him either. That she saw in him a potential husband was clear to her very early in their relationship but she was experienced enough of things to know not to overplay her hand. She could not bear a third mistake.

EIGHTEEN

All parents know the anxiety of an accident with one of their children. Will its effects wear off or will the child be scarred for life? A broken leg could lead to the loss of a sporting life, an outbreak of measles to sterility, a bang on the head to mental instability.

So it was, when Tom Mboya was assassinated in a Nairobi street, that the world looked on this developing country for signs of damage. Mboya was Kenyatta's heir apparent, in Western eyes at least, although locally there was some disagreement. Did his murder represent a threat to the stability and affluence Kenya had enjoyed in the few years since independence, a melting of the glue that held together different tribes and different ambitions under a firm leadership? Although time would seem to relegate it to a minor episode longer hindsight might see it as a symbol of mutation like the midnight change of one year's diary for another.

Its immediate aftermath caused anxieties throughout all sections of the population. The Europeans claimed a justification for the wilder settler beliefs leading up to independence and looked southwards for a lifeline. The Asians noted history's propensity for the scapegoat and prepared a further wave of their diaspora. The Africans remembered tribal hostilities which had scarred their people for generations and which had erupted during the Emergency but they had nowhere to go.

In their respective clubs Asian and European voices uttered muted fears now fluttering along a social surface below which they had been protected in recent history. Gone the certainties of colonial rule, replaced by an unnerving vulnerability like a scavenger fish in the mouth of a shark. The older members remembered dark days and feared a return of what they had known. The youngsters, untouched by history, feared what they did not know. All feared losing what they had, including their lives. Nights grew darker, journeys longer and shadows more sinister as a brisk wind of apprehension saw people draw on the protective clothes of their own communities. In the African villages a more sombre mood arose. These residents knew what it was like to be the victim of huge forces beyond their control - plagues of locusts ate their crops, violent storms flooded their villages, invisible diseases took their children. No flight was available to them; no benign Western media would show their plight; no law would protect against savagery.

During the Mau Mau emergency the solidarity of the Kikuyu was bolstered by a crude reversion to tribal practice. It was required of them to show their allegiance to the tribe by partaking in ceremonies which by their reportage drew on the darker side of their culture. These ceremonies, allegedly involving the slaughter of animals, the drinking of blood, the swearing of oaths, were always hidden from Europeans and the latter's imagination and expectation of the African no doubt embroidered these events with more savagery than they deserved. After Mboya's death this practice was revived, whether by orchestrated design or local panic cannot be known to the outsider. Its effect was not only to revive for older Africans the nightmares they thought had gone but to introduce a new generation of youngsters who would be drawn out of their accustomed world of transistor radios, Coca-Cola and aeroplanes to a primitive world which had previous only existed in folklore.

Kimura would not be unaffected. It was said that one night a lorry came and took the local men and older boys away to a gathering of the tribe. Phillip of the suit and tie and Ngugi in his shirt and shorts joined together by a collective protective spasm. Even Gitau, usually fiercely independent, could not resist the claims of community and history. Through legend, Ngai had given silent approval. None would admit, even in the most private conversations, that they had been anywhere but their huts, asleep. Some were said to fear going to the ceremonies others to be feared of not going. But for a while panic soaked everybody only to evaporate in another political season.

The disturbances affected Malcolm and Alison too. There had been rioting on the streets; a European had been killed in Nairobi. Malcolm took to picking Alison up from her flat rather than meeting her in Nairobi and it was a measure of her apprehension that she accepted his offers. Indeed, it drew out a more positive and thoughtful side of Malcolm. By now their relationship was steady and monogamous, romantic but not sexual.

One night at the drive-in cinema she asked him to drive her home before the film was over. In the car she said nothing leaving Malcolm unsure of what to say. At her flat they stood in her small kitchen, close but not touching.

'Are you OK?'

'Of course, I'm OK? Why shouldn't I be?' she was unusually curt.

'You're rather subdued.'

'I'm just tired that's all. I haven't been sleeping.'

'There has to be a reason.'

'Does there?' she snapped.

'Yes. You're not usually like this. Is it the hospital?'

She nodded. 'It's just awful at the moment. We're getting a lot of people brought in with machete injuries - deliberate mutilations. It's the unrest that's doing it. All this oathing and so on. I can cope with accidents but this is barbarity.' Her voice was unusually thin and shrill.

'There's not so much you know. Absolutely no trouble at Kimura. You must see the excesses in Casualty but it's not widespread. It really isn't.'

'Yesterday they brought in a young child. It ...... ,' she stopped and started to cry.

Malcolm put out his arms and invited her to him, for once instinct overriding caution. Even he was awake to her condition and her needs were stronger than his inhibitions. She came to him quickly and willingly, pressing against his body, her hair brushing his mouth and nose, her arms encircling him, pulling their bodies tight together. They had not been so close since the night of the dance and Malcolm felt her full female body pulsing against him with the rhythm of her breaths. When her sobbing subsided, she looked up at him, her mascara-streaked cheeks undermining the strength and confidence he had always seen in her.

He cupped her face in his hands and brought his lips close to hers not knowing what to expect to feel. She completed the contact between them. Her lips, damp with her tears, were soft to his touch. She moved her mouth to bring greater sensitivity and for a moment her mouth opened to breathe a warm breath into his. She drew away slowly lowering her head onto his chest leaving his face smeared with her mascara. Malcolm's hands dropped from her face to her shoulders and with a motion that was unmistakably sexual brought them slowly downwards towards her breasts. He was more surprised at the action than she, but she quicker to assess the potential. She pulled away firmly but not abruptly, removing his hands from her body and holding them one in each of hers. She looked him in the eyes.

'Not now. Not yet,' she said and kissed him briskly on the knuckles of his hands and withdrew from him.

Malcolm's was silent. He was savouring what he had just felt and what it seemed to promise. He was conscious of a slight erection. If Alison had won a further round in the battle for Malcolm it was because of her vulnerability and weakness not her strength. She saw the mascara stains on his shirt front and reached to brush them away. The action pressed his wet shirt against his skin.

'You'd better go. I'm on duty at eight o'clock. I need the beauty sleep.'

'Will you be alright?'

'Yes. I'll cope,' she said with mock stoicism. 'But can you come down tomorrow evening? We could go for a meal. I need the company.'

That she would *need* him removed another restraining layer from Malcolm's emotions. 'Yes. Of course. I'd love to come'

And the word *love* stuck with Alison as she let him out the door.

That night in bed Malcolm thought of a woman's breast. This time it was milky white but it moved as rhythmically as the brown one he had seen before. This time the movement was caused, not by a suckling child, but by his own hand and he fell asleep with the motion.

NINETEEN

The idea that he should pay Ngugi's school fees grew in Malcolm's mind until it assumed inevitability but one possible obstacle grew alongside it. How could he offer to pay the fees without offending Gitau?

The catalyst for his action was Bernie who was sounding off about his uncertain future. Usually he was careful, at least when sober, not to expound views of the Kenya government in front of Africans, in case one should report him to the District Commissioner. The belief that some Africans were placed in European surroundings to act as spies was quite widespread. More usual was for some observer to report some half-understood remark in the hope of gaining some advantage for himself or his family. Nevertheless, it fuelled the racial paranoia. Inevitably, it seemed, Bernie was on the wrong side of the racial divide. That day he spoke openly to Gitau in front of Malcolm although the African was merely the reflector through which the European should hear his woes. Whether this was a measure of his belief in Gitau's soundness or a cavalier disregard for his own increasingly insecure position was not clear. He stood in the compound brandishing a pair of secateurs.

'Why can't you give me citizenship?' he snarled at Gitau, as though this simple villager somehow had access to the levers of power.

He continued. 'I was born in Africa. I am African for Christ's sake. I'm not even white.' This last comment seemed odd given his pale skin but he was playing the racial card to his advantage as he had throughout his life.

'You'll take these people,' He looked at Malcolm, 'and they'll go home when they've had the good life. But I live here. It's my home. I belong here.' He produced a gloss of sincerity to suit his needs.

'Without citizenship I've no security. I could be sent back or I could be thrown out. Talk about the devil and the deep blue sea.' His repetitions had an air of rehearsal about them as though he had made up several phrases in private intending to use the most effective but in the passion of the moment using them all. 'I'm in limbo. It's not fucking fair.' Overcome with frustration he threw the secateurs into a row of beans breaking several as it bounced along the soil. He stalked off, his eyes now smarting with tears, his despair, for once, a show of genuine emotion.

Gitau followed the path of the secateurs and after recovering them pruned some of the damaged plants. However, his thoughts were not on the plants. He had said nothing during Bernie's outburst although he understood the other man's plight. He too was in limbo between two things. But rather than being between two places he was between two cultures and both made claims on him. His African tribal past had shaped his values and he understood their potency. Tribal ritual, primitive to the observer, inclusive to the participants, cemented village security. Improbable gods gave protection against capricious climate. Family structures, indecent to Western eyes, provided stability and a prophylactic to misfortune. But these things were past and fading, holding no value for the contemporary generation of his children. The other world was the future of technology, medicine and international trade. It too had its gods and its customs although to Gitau they made unreasonable demands on their followers.

His traditional culture had a dark side too. He had been disheartened by the oathing ceremonies in which he had been involved for fear of retribution against his family. He was saddened that they seemed to drag his people back in time. Whatever the origins of these ceremonies in tribal history they were now tinged with political opportunism. He and his parents had lived out their lives under foreign rule and their tribal loyalties had been instrumental in the survival of their pride, but his children could not go back to that time. They would have to live a different life; he hoped a better life although he had misgivings. He understood that many tribal attitudes would remain with them, some for good, some not. What was almost self-evident was that a modern education would provide the opportunity for that development, but he knew he could not afford the fees and support his extended family.

For Malcolm the fees were affordable but would dent his savings. He had quite a sum of money building up in the UK and he could transfer some out easily. Doing it illegally through Bernie would produce a bonus and surely this was in the interests of everyone; a sickly morality argued an African would benefit. He considered how discreetly the payments could be made. A grant from an agricultural company perhaps; a gift from the woman who donated to Flynn's church seemed ideal but she must be long dead and would Flynn go along with the deceit even though the outcome would be benign. Eventually he decided he could not avoid openness.

Malcolm cleared his throat. In recent days he had created many introductions to this topic and rejected them all. He resorted to directness hoping to minimise the patronisation which was endemic to the act.

'Gitau. I think Ngugi should go to a school in Nairobi. He will get a better education. He will meet people and make friends who will favour him in later life. He will have the opportunity for a better job. I'd like to pay for Ngugi's school fees. He's a clever boy and I'd like to help him. Would you find that acceptable?' the belated question intended to draw Gitau into the decision.

The African's face muscles relaxed and his eyes moistened. He did not want to be beholden to a European, but he had to think of his son too. Pride urged him to reject the offer; parental responsibility made it inevitable he would accept. Eschewing a lifetime of restraint Malcolm reached out and put his hand on the African's arm as though bodily contact would validate his message. Please don't say grateful, thought Malcolm.

'Ah, yes. I would be very pleased for you to do that. Thank you, Bwana Bryant.' The title was common place but, in this context, Malcolm saw a hint of subservience that Gitau did not intend. He wanted Gitau to call him Malcolm but such familiarity was not on the agenda.

'When you and Ngugi have decided where to go we can start the application. Mr. Rogers will advise on the best school. I've spoken to him about it. I hope you don't mind. Philip will deal with the paperwork. The money will be available whenever it's needed.' His terseness reflected his need to explain the practical details he had planned for some time.

'I will repay you one day.' Gitau knew it could not be done but he did not want to acknowledge his loss of independence so did not meet his benefactor's eye.

'I don't want repayment. It's a sort of bursary. Anyway, perhaps one day Ngugi will be rich and he can repay me.'

'I hope so but you know the rich often forget how they came by their fortune.'

'But Ngugi won't. He's a good boy.'

'He is now. He is now.'

'Good that's settled. I was afraid you might reject my offer. Silly really. I'll see you tomorrow.'

'Good night, Bwana. Assante sane. Thank you.' He turned to the distant hills towards Mount Kenya hidden behind Larsen's farm. Up there his god Ngai would have seen his good fortune and must surely have brought it about.

Gitau offered up his thanks, 'Assante sane. Assante sane.'

Ngugi had set off on registration day long before Malcolm woke up. The benefactor didn't see the best second-hand clothes that the family could muster fitting rather less well than Malcolm's dinner jacket at the Caledonian dinner, didn't see the bulging carrier bag with Ngugi's belongings, didn't see Ngugi wearing socks for the first time as he walked down the dirt road to pick up the bus at the junction of the dual track with the main road. And had he seen, he would not have noticed that one of Ngugi's trouser pockets was stitched closed, protecting the school fees from youthful carelessness and prying fingers.

Gitau saw all this as he went with his eldest son to the bus stop. He had warned about alcohol, women and ganga but none had any appeal to this young boy. By the time they did, he would have forgotten his father's words, his actions determined more by promiscuous opportunity and peer group. The proud father had advised that hard work would bring its rewards despite abundant evidence in his own life it might not. As the bus set off for the capital its tyres churning up the dust in the dirt apron alongside the carriageway, he studied the handful of his fellow Africans going about their lives up and down the road, their clothes soiled by the road's dust, their heads and shoulders laden with heavy burdens. He looked into the coffee estate across the road and saw the shirts and head scarves of the labourers highlighted in the green of the bushes. He knew many of them well since he had lived his life in this location. They were good people but they were poor people. The bus had now disappeared over the brow the dust from its wheels beginning to settle in the cold morning air. Gitau turned his head towards Mount Kenya hidden behind the hill line although, at this early hour, free of the cloud mantle which obscured it during the day. He stood facing his hidden altar and addressed its god, Ngai. His silent words would have been spoken anywhere in the world, to any god. He did not ask for everlasting life, a world free of illness or an end to wars. He asked, only, that his family should be successful and that his son, Ngugi, now being driven into adulthood would achieve much but lose little.

Although Malcolm did not see Ngugi leave he did see him return later in the morning. He and Gitau were supervising the planting of a new strain of maize when Ngugi stumbled up the pathway, his still full bag swinging by his side. He stood wretchedly at the gate to the compound, his head bowed.

'What's the matter? Why are you here?' his father asked in Kikuyu. Ngugi replied. Unable to stop his tears, the boy who had left earlier with a first step to manhood was now back as the youngster he'd thought he'd grown above.

'What is it?' Malcolm's ignorance of their tribal language left him in the dark.

'The school would not let him join. He is expected to have a uniform before he will be allowed in.'

'Uniform! You mean blazer and cap?'

'I do not know. He is too upset.'

'You talk to him. Find out what the problem is. I'll go to the kitchen and make some tea. Bring him along shortly.' Malcolm's outrage manifested itself in these brusque requests. Gitau bridled under the instructions but had no other course but to comply.

PK was in the office and Malcolm described the problem. As Malcolm made the tea the two of them could see father and son talking together. Gitau took his son by the shoulders and pulled him to him pressing his face to the top of the boy's head. For a few moments they hung together like models for a Makonde wood carving. Malcolm remembered his father hugging him and him not knowing why. This embrace seemed wholly explicable and he envied their close contact. He looked at PK and the two men smiled self-consciously both touched by the tableau. Gitau stood back and taking hold of his son's hand drew him gently towards the kitchen.

The four sat for a while in silence. Ngugi, his eyes reddened white, switched his attention from the mug of tea cradled in his hands to the faces of the adults around him. When Ngugi seemed to have calmed Malcolm said, 'OK Ngugi tell us all about it. You got to the school, OK?'

'Yes.' the youngster's voice was low and he didn't make eye-contact with his sponsor not knowing if his actions had been a betrayal of generosity.

'And you still had the school fees?'

'Yes.'

'And you've still got them?'

'Yes. They are here.' He patted his secure pocket.

'Did the other boys have uniform?'

'They did.'

'What uniform did they expect you to have?'

Ngugi pulled a crumpled foolscap sheet from his plastic bag and Malcolm looked it over. 'The man at the school said I should have received this two months ago.'

'It would have come here, to our box number, wouldn't it?' Malcolm looked at PK. 'That bloody Boniface.' Weeks earlier the messenger had been caught stealing stamps and opening mail and Arthur Rogers had sacked him on the spot. 'Why did you come all the way back here?' He was going to ask why Ngugi hadn't phoned realising in time Ngugi had never used a phone in his life.

Ngugi shrugged helplessly. 'I didn't know what else to do. It was all so strange. I have never been on my own before.' Malcolm understood what it was like to be alone.

'Can you go back?' Gitau saw a dream ending.

'If I can get the uniform within one week I can be admitted.'

'Right.' said Malcolm we'll soon sort that out. 'PK. You must know which shops will sell this stuff. No, wait a minute there's some addresses on this form. There's one here on Muindi Mbingu Street. Asian. You must know them PK?'

'I know the shop but not the people. They are Moslem not Hindu.' For Malcolm it was an irrelevant distinction. 'It's near the photography shop opposite the market.'

'Yes, I know where you mean. Come on Ngugi. Let's get you sorted out.' He looked at Gitau who looked away. Gitau knew he was poor and most days it did not matter. But on this day, it did. He could not help his son. This European and this Asian could. He knew they would and he knew he would always be in their debt - not in their eyes perhaps, but in his own certainly. His position in the pecking order of power was cruelly declared. It was the same for his country too, free but still dependent. Malcolm, oblivious to this predicament, escorted Ngugi to the car.

Ngugi emerged from the shop with more clothes than were required but Malcolm was not in the mood to be cautious. Had he known the cost in advance in might have been more prudent but the money was not uppermost in his mind. For him it meant a slightly depleted bank balance for Gitau it would have meant several months wages.

Shortly after they pulled up in front of a mature building with a sign indicating the school office. They got out of the car both apprehensive. Ngugi was wearing his new shirt and shorts and the cloth was rubbing against his skin. Malcolm was discomforted in a different way. He was anticipating a looming confrontation and long-standing inhibitions dogged his thoughts. They entered an office in which sat a female secretary behind a long desk.

'I would like to see the headmaster.' There was little sign of his usual reticence; strange emotions were fuelling him now. Ngugi stood a little behind him.

'Perhaps I can be of help?' The secretary sensed the tension.

'I'd like to deal with the headmaster please. There has been a problem.' Ngugi eased himself further behind Malcolm out of her sight.

'I'll see if he's available.' She spoke on an internal phone. 'He's coming now. Would you like a seat?' Malcolm declined wanting to retain a physical equality at least.

The headmaster arrived after a few minutes. He was a tall ginger haired man wearing a check shirt and a tie with some sporting motif. He spoke with a home counties accent.

'Good morning. I'm Trevor Wallington. What's the problem? Can I be of help?' He held out his hand.

Malcolm described the circumstances that had brought them there. The headmaster picked up a clip board from the desk.

'What is the name?'

'Ngugi,' Malcolm said without reference to the boy himself and then realised he did not know if Ngugi had any other names.

The Headteacher ran his fingers down a list. 'Are you from Karatina? Oh, no he's already registered. Ah yes. From Kimura. Paul Ngugi.' On hearing the first name Malcolm looked down at his charge who seemed unperturbed. 'And he had no uniform? Well, that is a requirement as our letters say.'

'Surely it's not essential.?'

'Well rules are rules and we have to obey the Ministry. Indeed, it comes from higher than that' he said, looking knowingly at Malcolm. 'I know it seems a bit strange, but uniforms have great popular support even - indeed especially - amongst the pupils. We think they bring a unity that brings together boys from all the tribes of Kenya. We think it raises pupils' expectations of educational opportunity.'

Malcolm, himself no enemy of conformity, wanted to say what he thought but judged conciliation more productive.

'Well, he's got the uniform now. Everything on your list. He's got the fees. I assume he can be admitted.'

'Of course. Yes, of course' He took some documents from a stack of paper trays on the desk. 'Could you please fill in this form? That's all we need for now. You can sit there.' He indicated a table by the window.

Malcolm stood behind him as Ngugi filled in the form. The boy wrote his name as Paul Malcom Ngugi. Malcolm wanted to question this innovation but saw the simple acknowledgement it was meant to be. He noticed the missing 'l' in the name he had written so often himself. For a fleeting moment he felt a part of himself flow into this youth, chastened but sensitive, whose dark head was so close to his own. Ngugi wrote his date of birth confidently and gave the box number for Kimura station as his home address. His religion was given as Roman Catholic; Flynn's church had staked its claim on the village.

The formalities complete the headteacher put out his hand to shake Malcolm's. 'And what relationship is Paul to you?'

After a slight hesitancy Malcolm responded, 'He's the son of a friend of mine.' Is he, my friend? thought Malcolm. Is he a colleague? a workmate? an employee? No. Today, he was happy with friend.

'Welcome to our school. I hope you'll be very happy here. And work hard of course. I'm sure you will.' The headteacher put out his hand to the new pupil who took it diffidently and, looking up at Malcolm, swallowed hard.

His immediate task accomplished Malcolm returned to his car. As he started it up, he noticed Ngugi, a slight, doleful figure walking with the headmaster towards an accommodation block. The youngster turned and started to make a slight gesture as if to wave, but then held back remembering the presence of his teacher. The pair turned the corner of the block and were gone from sight. Ngugi - now Paul Malcom Ngugi - was entering a new life not knowing what he was facing nor understanding what he would leave behind.

For Malcolm the sudden and sustained emotional charge of the day burst the dam of constraint that had so impoverished his life. He broke down in tears, his head resting on the steering wheel and his chest pumping the air out of his lungs. After some moments he realised he was now crying for himself, for the strong emotion for another person, for the release from years in an emotional straight jacket. As he drove away, he was crying and laughing at the same time. It was joy, simple joy, and he had not known it before.

TWENTY

Within days he had proposed to Alison and she had accepted. She paused in her reply and he choked as it had not occurred to him, she would refuse. But she was being coquettish for reasons she didn't fully understand. They kissed slowly and longingly but no more than that and would share no more than that until they were married. Neither for their differing reasons wished to spoil anything.

The wedding ceremony itself was in Tanzania in Alison's family home. For Mr & Mrs Parkinson, Malcolm was a bit of a surprise, not quite the husband they had imagined their daughter choosing nor one they would have chosen themselves. Malcolm had not realised how much his present personality was sustained by Alison. With her parents he was gauche and clumsy, returning to the awkward introvert that had been in the past. That he knew it was happening only fuelled his anxiety and worsened his performance. With the prospect of being in the nuptial spotlight his insecurities returned. He coped with the routines of the service and seemed a convincing supplicant. As he slid the ring on to her finger he felt, for a moment, he wanted the world to stop as though he had reached some summit of happiness from which there could only be decline. But then another surge of adrenaline hit him at the realisation that this was only a start. The walk down the aisle was a blur and his lack of concentration only fuelled the doubt in the minds of Alison's parents.

The reception put him to greater test. His vote of thanks had been written by Alison; she had the wit not to include jokes, but Malcolm contrived to make even the simplest of toasts sound grudging and turgid. Alison's mother had a sense of foreboding far greater than usual for these occasions. But Alison knew how difficult it was for him and for her, every gaffe, every stumble made her feelings for him stronger. She did not need him to be attractive, to be confident; she really did love him for what he was, what she knew of him not what others saw.

Malcolm had claimed his obligatory leave and their long honeymoon was spent in the Seychelles. Alison knew he was a virgin and Malcolm knew she was not. The consummation was natural and satisfying. She accepted the lack of foreplay and although she did not enjoy full pleasure, she did at least feel satisfaction. For him the sexual act removed from him the need to think, to consider, to decide but swept him along in a flood of instinctive movement. As they became more used to each other's bodies Malcolm gloried in the shared intimacy with another human being and Alison welcomed the shared concern she had not experienced with either of her lovers. Neither had spent as much continuous time in the close company of another human being and their past lives were shared in extensive, if cautious, detail. They went as individuals and returned as partners, more confident in each other's company, more settled in their expectations, more understanding of each other's history, more sympathetic to each other's insecurities. They were not, as yet, alive to each other's weaknesses, conscious of each other's irritating habits or privy to each other's fears. Four weeks together could hardly be expected to reveal those.

Although Malcolm had told Alison about his childhood including Marion's condition, he did not describe the affect she had had on his parents or himself. He did not because he could not find the words to do so. There was a shell around him but what was within that shell knew no description. Hard, dark, cold, silent, frightening, heavy, relentless, lonely, bleak: none of these seemed quite right though all had their place. If he had he been able to describe what he felt as well as what he had experienced then perhaps Marion would have been exorcised for ever. But he did not and one part of his debilitating past, the most significant in its impact and enduring in its effect, was left un-illuminated and un-confronted and so remained a threat. If only Malcolm had understood then that a few moments confession to

186

Alison in the close aftermath of lovemaking might have banished his blighted sister for good. If only. If only. The epitaph of so many lives.

Although Alison continued to work, they lived at Kimura. Wherever they had chosen to live one of them would have had to drive the hour's journey into Nairobi. She was older than him, had more experience driving in Africa and was a better driver. Nevertheless Malcolm, subconsciously assuming the traditional role of husband, worried about her driving at all hours depending on her shifts. Two events coincided to change the course of their lives. Rogers was to retire leaving Malcolm to take his place and Alison would become pregnant.

The Rogers had been planning their retirement from the time of the oathing ceremonies after the Mboya murder took place; the revival of this practice was reminder of the grimmer days of the Emergency. Their plans to retire to the UK were fortuitously completed before Alison announced her pregnancy so Alice Rogers was spared a voyeuristic motherhood.

The couple spent their last few days in the Norfolk Hotel where Rogers had always placed his new charges. On the day of departure Malcolm and Alison came to the airport to see them off. They took Ngugi with them collecting him from his school. For the three males it was a neat but unplanned symmetry of the circumstances in which Malcolm had arrived.

Alice Rogers was openly tearful. She was leaving something precious here, a little bundle, consigned to an incinerator, its short life defining her stifled motherhood. She could not escape the feeling she was deserting her child, that little thing alone in this big world. Nobody but her had known the life of her Elizabeth, not even Arthur. She alone had felt the kicking, sensed the growing power of a new being, endured the pain of childbirth finding there was no life to celebrate. But in her bag, she was carrying something away, not in compensation, it could never be that. But a symbol to sustain memory. In her luggage lay the poker work sign saying *Kahawa* soon destined to succeed *Periwincle* at the entrance to her new home.

Earlier her husband had made his farewells to people, places and hopes in the methodical way he had run the station. Whatever feelings he had at this point of departure were well hidden. After relinquishing their luggage Rogers took Ngugi to one side and handed him a wrapped present. As they separated the old man patted the youngster's head, an action which was as patronising as it was full of genuine affection.

As Alice and Arthur Rogers left the land they had served for 20 years, they felt a glow of pride. They had been some bad times but it had been worth doing; they had lived contentedly and worked effectively; they had given and received in fair proportion. Theirs had been a good life and they could look forward without regret or apprehension.

As the three watched the aircraft take off Ngugi unwrapped his present. It was a well-used copy of *Tom Brown's Schooldays*. Inside the front cover Rogers had written a message of goodwill. Opposite, on the flyleaf, was pasted a label, the once bright colours of its florid design now faded. In a bold copperplate the original hand-written inscription read *To Arthur Rogers of III Albion for a full year's attendance*   *1933/34.*

TWENTY-ONE

Although Rogers had felt Malcolm now had enough experience to take over the station there were other forces at work. Whenever expatriates returned home their place was taken by a citizen as part of a conscious programme of Africanisation. After the Harrington's had left the station was short staffed until the appointment of a young graduate from Makerere University. David Okumo was a Luo from near the Uganda border and in some respects as much stranger in Central Province as the expatriates. He lived in the bungalow opposite Malcolm where the Harrington's had been. His tenure was short lived and after the murder of his fellow tribesman, Mboya, he decided to find work nearer his homelands.

Rogers' fear about his succession was principally that any African appointment might not be on the basis of benefit to the project, but could arise out of nepotism which was beginning to sour Kenyan life as a generation of African administrators found jobs for the burgeoning numbers of their relations with significant qualifications and expectations to match. He therefore employed European nepotism to ensure his succession went to Malcolm; and in this less certain world Malcolm took up post. For Malcolm being responsible for something was to be a new experience. It had not occurred to him that his qualifications and experience might lead to a career over which he might have control and through which he might have influence. On a more mundane level his promotion meant a significant increase in salary and the chance to inherit the Rogers' well-appointed bungalow.

Just as Malcolm had not considered he would assume the responsibilities of a career, so he had never considered the possibility of parenthood. When Alison told him she was pregnant he found it difficult to anticipate the pleasures and thought only of the pitfalls. To be responsible for bringing another human being onto this earth and for its well-being whilst here was very daunting. He thought of Marion and feared a similar fate for his child. Alison was able to reassure him about the health of the baby but his doubts did not wholly disappear when the child, a boy, finally arrived. He had driven Alison to the hospital but lacked the courage to be there at the birth. In the bag she had pre-packed, Alison had put her camera, film already in place so that Malcolm could record the event for posterity. This he did and copies of a photograph of James Haddon Bryant, aged two hours, and his parents spread through the friends and family to announce his arrival.

Malcolm had been born into a world of unrelenting Anglo-Saxon convention which had entered a period of wartime sacrifice which in turn had reinforced the emotional austerity of his own home. In retrospect it seemed a cold black-and-white world and the explosion of colour in the 1960s had put it into even sharper monochrome. His own son's world was so different. Outside a warm bright aspect peopled by different races, the air resonant with different tongues. Inside two parents at ease with each other, uneasy only about their joint responsibility for this fragile being and for a few days overawed, as all first-time parents are, by the enormity of what they'd done.

But outside their family group the world continued to turn, undeterred by the emergence of one new passenger. The baby's arrival coincided with that of a new member of staff. George Kariuki was a graduate of Nairobi university and as a Kikuyu more at home at Kimura than his predecessor. He had had some postgraduate experience in Moscow. Malcolm did not have to meet him at the airport nor involve himself in the initiation ceremonies that had so preoccupied Rogers. His man-management skills were not then to be tested, nor was he distracted from his new life as parent. His new colleague now resident in the bungalow once occupied by the

Harringtons might well have felt neglected had it not been for PK's quiet and competent assumption of responsibility for the smooth operation of the station.

Bernie's decline continued. The injustices of his upbringing and the insincerity of his relationships embittered his mind. And superimposed on it all, the uncertainty of his work permit and, with it, residency. He had tried bribery but the people who could be bribed had no power and the people who had the power saw no point in being bribed by someone who didn't belong when they could be bribed by someone who did. The annual renewal brought closer the day when he would have to move on. He had nowhere to go and no-one to go to; still less go with. For Bernie the options were closing down. An added twist on the rack came with the appointment of George Kariuki. Clearly here was the vanguard of a host of citizens with qualifications at least as good as Bernie's and it was only a matter of time before his permit was not renewed. Rogers' influence could no longer be brought to bear and he knew Malcolm had no pull and was probably too busy with his new baby.

One morning Bernie was found hanging by the neck from a beam on his veranda. He swung very gently in the early breeze and the rays of the rising sun gave length to his shadow, seeming to amplify the movement of his body. The rough surface of the strong twine had bruised his neck but without breaking the skin. His face now had more colour than it had ever seen and by then its blue aspect reflected the blueness of the far hills. In this respect at least he was closer to being home in Africa than he had ever been.

On the floor beneath him lay a whisky bottle, almost empty, lying on its side, the liquid in it like a brown sea without its ship. His housekeeper found him when she came in to prepare his breakfast. As she came from the kitchen, she saw the shadow of his body cast across the veranda floor by the morning sun. Realising he was dead, she stood fearing the moments before he died when twisting and jerking, he might have wished to remove himself from yet another melodrama.

Soon she would take his demise phlegmatically, her sadness at his death a continuation of her sadness of his life. He had been good to her and she had known real tenderness from him. All his anger and violence had been turned on himself.

Turning she looked at his lounge. There were few personal belongings, only the odd carving on the standard government furniture. On the coffee table, near the plate that had contained the meal she had made for him the previous night, were the contents of a brown envelope - his passport and documents concerning his work permit. Looking through them she couldn't find what she wanted. As his housekeeper she knew where to look and going to the top drawer of his dressing table she felt beneath the paper lining for a passbook its folded card once stiff and clean, now worn and stained. It was his university student card. Inside it bore his picture as a young man, the face full and confident, the camera accurately catching the slight arrogance in his smile. Beneath the picture his name, his real name. She put it inside her blouse next to her warm bronze breast. She would keep it to show her son when he grew up. He would like to know about his father.

Malcolm had the responsibility of dealing with the aftermath. He and Gitau cut down the body, the latter efficient and calm in comparison with Malcolm's inexperienced efforts. The older man had had to cut down his own brother from a tree near the stream, one foot bleeding all over Gitau's clothes from the wounds inflicted by wild animals. That his brother had died by hanging was incidental, it was the drink that brought him to death, and his life that brought him to drink. When Gitau first discovered the body, he had had no knife with him and he had had to go back to the village before he could cut his brother down. The children had followed him back and some of those who watched the mutilated corpse being manhandled to the ground were watching their own father. For Bernie there was no blood and the removal by two grown men was relatively easy. The only audience was the housekeeper who stood in the shade between the veranda and her quarters and just behind her, peering from behind her dress, her small son. She would not tell him that this man had been his father.

The police were informed. They searched his papers but found no trace of family details only a Mozambique passport which turned out to be forged. In a severe commentary on his life, all that remained of him in death was false.

'Mr. Bryant, I have to ask you some questions.'

'Of course.' Malcolm found himself staring at the detective's turban rather than looking in his eye.

'How well did you now Mr. Bernard?'

'We were colleagues. We worked together here. Lived next door. Six or seven years I expect. Why?'

'Did you have any business dealings with him?'

'Business. I don't understand.'

'Mr. Bernard was known to us as a minor criminal.'

'Criminal? Bernie?'

'Did you have any dealings with him over currency?'

'Currency! Oh that. He did approach me once.' The detective wrote something in his notebook and Malcolm feeling he was incriminating himself didn't know how to proceed.

'It's a serious matter, Mr. Bryant. It can't be dismissed.'

'I had no dealings with him.'

'What about your colleague, Mr. Patel?' Malcolm froze. PK? Surely not. And yet.

Mr. Patel must answer for himself but I would be very surprised if he was involved.' Malcolm felt a pang of disloyalty but justified it in defence of his family. And himself.

'And what about Mr. Shelley?'

'He went years ago. Before I came. I didn't know him.' Malcolm wanted to say more to separate himself entirely from this affair. And from PK too? He didn't know. He'd never been involved with the police before, never knowingly talked to a detective. And despite his innocence he felt himself being dragged into guilt.

'Yes, I know but was there any gossip about him. About him and Bernard.' Malcolm's mouth was dry.

'I never heard any.'

'Never?' The Sikh had a high-pitched voice and Malcolm found his own voice going to a higher register as he became more anxious.

'Never.'

'Have you heard of a man called Hancock, Alan Hancock?'

'No.' Malcolm was pleased to be able to give a truthful answer.

'What about Shah, Bobby Shah. He had a filling station in Westlands.'

'Yes, I know him. I buy petrol at his garage. I haven't seen him for a while though.'

'Mr. Shah is no longer free to sell petrol. Did you exchange currency with him?'

'No.'

'Pay for your petrol in sterling perhaps?'

'No.'

'Your predecessor, Mr. Rogers, did he ever talk about these things?'

Arthur. Surely not Arthur. Yet he seemed to know about the practice. 'No certainly not.' A lie but a justified one he thought.

'I didn't think he would be but we have to explore every avenue.'

'Look, why don't you look through my bank statements. I'll get them for you.'

'There's no need Mr. Bryant. We already have.' He smiled, friendly he thought, but to Malcolm it seemed sinister.

He stood up to leave. 'Well thank you Mr Bryant. I hope I won't have to trouble you again.'

'That's all right. I'm surprised you are so interested in Bernie. Mr. Bernard.'

'We're not that interested in him as such. In fact, we know more about him than he knew about himself. He was small fry. Out of his depth. But he knew other people, powerful people, important people, people who used him. That's who we want. I'm sorry I can't say more. But you will let me know if you hear anything, anything at all, won't you?'

Malcolm recalled how when considering how to get money for Ngugi's school fees he had contemplated doing a deal with Bernie. He had not been involved though not out of rectitude, but merely lack of opportunity. His stomach churned at the thought.

Malcolm watched the car arc round the square to return to Nairobi. As it accelerated across the dry ground its wheels squirted clouds of dust which settled on Bernie's cook and her young son sitting in the shade of the tree.

That night after supper Malcolm told Alison about the interrogation, which it what he felt it was.

'You came across Bernie before I did. Did you hear anything about him?' He was the interrogator now.

'No, not a thing.'

'And you didn't have anything to do with him?'

'Me. No. Of course not.'

What involvement with Bernie she did have, she did not tell, could not tell. Not without losing what she had gained. Not that it amounted to much. She had been in her kitchen preparing some drink for James, Karui was off duty. Bernie came to the kitchen door. She had invited him in. When her back was turned to him, he put his hands around her body and began to fondle her. She pushed him away but not immediately. For a fraction of a second, she yielded, her body aching with the boredom of motherhood, her spirit dulled by the routine of marriage succumbed to the capricious lust that both fuels and destroys human relationships. But then she turned on Bernie and slapped his face. It was such a little incident, not worth declaring. And like many small incidents this was too important to confess, too damaging to share, best left to be eroded by time.

TWENTY-TWO

Malcolm's assumption of managerial responsibility took place against a sea change for centres like Kimura. Many officers of Rogers' generation were retiring from government service. At the same time the international aid agencies were re-examining the direction of their resources. Identifying Kenya as a country finding its feet, they decided to withdraw some support on the assumption that the local government would fund activities it determined to be of greatest benefit. The effect was to make redundant the type of research Kimura was undertaking. The success of cash crops drew attention away from the growing need for subsistence farming to meet a quickly growing population. Whereas Arthur Rogers had been able to devote his energies to developing Kimura station Malcolm had the unenviable task of managing its decline. Only the remuneration of a senior management role made it tolerable.

In the first few months of marriage Alison continued to work in Nairobi. Apart from the travelling her main task was to modify the domestic arrangements in which she found herself. For several years Karui had been, with Malcolm's happy acquiescence, the lord of the household. Now his powers would be shared, even subordinated. At first the relationship was strained as each jostled for the upper hand but it soon developed into a confident partnership. Karui's initial scepticism about European women gave way to admiration when he realised Alison was a child of Africa conscious of its moods and practices. She spoke fluent Swahili and understood village life; she understood the afflictions he suffered, from malaria to melancholia. Of course, she had her own way in the house and her own standards in the kitchen but Karui would soon see these as his own. She taught him how to cook new dishes and he boasted of his prowess on his periodic visits to his village.

The move to Roger's house was a further feather in his proprietorial cap. The new sign *Nyumbani* near the front door meant as much to Karui as it did to his employers; it was his home too for most of his life. He was a happy man. He had been employed for five years now and there seemed more in prospect. He had used his wages to put a corrugated roof on his family house so that his family would be safe and dry. He had been able to buy more seeds to plant in the shamba his wife would cultivate in his absence. His children were healthy and the older ones were in school. Life was so good to him; he was a lucky man.

The arrival of James clinched his acceptance of his new boss. During pregnancy he fussed and cosseted Alison. It was likely that Karui spent more time with Alison in her one pregnancy than with his own wife in her seven. When James first arrived home Karui offered the present of a *kikapu* from his own wife. This strong carrying bag at first held the nappies and milk bottles which accompanied the family on its days out but as James grew older it would hold the host of small toys he accumulated in his bedroom. Its robust construction meant it would linger in the family effects long after its utility had faded with its colouring. That Malcolm and Alison would see Karui as part of their family would be to overstate the case; he found it easier to see them as part of his.

If the unexpected assumption of managerial and responsibility presented Malcolm with a challenge, so parental responsibilities changed his life as well. The position as sole expatriate in charge of inexperienced staff with high expectations demanded more of his time and energy than he would have wished but he tried to bear his share of family commitments. The latter were in theory shared with Alison but his preoccupation with work meant he became very much a minor partner in the bringing up of their son. Her personality and nursing experience meant her husband's weaknesses were not a serious handicap. When not at work he shared the chores of parenthood and in so doing shared the unexpected joys as well. Singing songs and changing nappies did not reflect the Malcolm in his twenties. This new man had a new slant of life and he revelled in it.

In the evening he would sit on the warm veranda cradling the floppy body of his newly-washed powder-smelling son whilst Karui prepared the dinner and Alison bathed away the day's dust. He would feel the increasingly firm grip of the infant's fragile fingers on his own calloused hands. Then he would suck clean the minute digits lest they capture any germs from his soil-ingrained skin. And in those moments of gentle inactivity his mind would float through time imagining the past and anticipating the future. Back to his own father holding him, before the war took him away, unaware that soon Marion would mar their serenity. Did his father have the feelings he felt now? Why shouldn't he? Forward to when James might have a sister of his own. Oh, that she should not be like Marion. Back to the garden which provided the rare closeness with his own father. What did his father hope for him then? Then forward to this little mite growing strong into manhood satisfying all the ambitions of old-fashioned unperceptive adults. No failure this boy, no rebel either. (How awful if parents saw the future; would they could avoid the mistakes or compound them into even greater tragedy?) He would be surprised, and pleased, how easily he thought of James and his well-being and not just wallow in his own satisfaction.

And then the child in bed, he would dine with Alison, her fresh-washed skin flavoured with a subtle perfume. Her body was plumper now under the influence of age and childbirth. But her fuller face still retained its character as her body retained its promise. She would suck his fingers now, not to protect his vulnerability but rather to disarm his strength and release the juices of seduction. Then they would sit listening to their growing record collection of classical music. Alison's modest collection had expanded as she introduced her husband to a greater range. He knew little of the composers but found their music could describe his innermost feelings where words were inadequate. Or perhaps they would sit on the veranda whilst Karui cleared away the dishes and tidied the kitchen. Here they would talk the matter-of-fact talk of everyday, knowing they would soon be lying in their bed their bodies coiled in sweaty lovemaking undoing the toilet of dusk.

Not all days were like this; they rarely are. But they are the days to be remembered. Not whole days, not real days, but fragments of many days blended into a season. They are condensed here, denying their effect on Malcolm. Contentment, however long lived, passes unobserved; it is passion and tragedy that capture the attention.

When Malcolm first came to Kimura, he unavoidably joined a family, the Rogers, the Harringtons, PK, Flynn, Gitau of course and even Bernie, people thrown together only partly by choice and getting through the days, good and bad. There were not the ties of blood, but his own blood ties had given him little satisfaction. One by one they had flown and now it was PK's turn to go. The loss of his most experienced and closest colleague would add to the burdens of his professional life and impoverish the personal one. PK's relatives were spread all over East Africa and the coming of Idi Amin to Uganda made them reassess their future. The Asian diaspora took him to the UK although many of his family thought Canada a more inviting prospect. When it became clear PK was leaving for ever, Malcolm recognised the important role this man had played in his life. PK had been reliable and unflappable making few demands on Mr. Bryant, the manager, or on Malcolm, the man. At the same time Malcolm never felt he altogether understood a man with whom his contacts had been formal, conventional and undemanding. PK had been a cultural yo-yo in his life. At one moment the dapper, cultured, civilised Aryan sustaining him in the face of a disorganised and unreliable African system, the next the inscrutable Asian deploying an exclusive cultural and religious barrier to real contact. It was not PK that oscillated only Malcolm's perception of him.

After PK had gone, he realised how much PK had given him and how little he had returned. Before Alison he had been invited to many ceremonies at his family home - religious, cultural, social. The wedding presents for he and Alison were lavish. And when James was born the smallest version of traditional dress for a Hindu boy. It would remain in its presentation box, an unused reminder of different days, like the boxes of cutlery old people retain, items still wrapped in tissue paper, leaving butter un-spread, fishes un-filleted and cups un-stirred. James would never wear it. It was too big when it was given and when he was big enough it had been forgotten, tucked in the wardrobe with the zebra-skin cigarette box and the soap-stone napkin rings. All these things, together with Karui's *kikapu* would linger in the family, kept for fear of throwing something more important, if less tangible, out with them. And on his first birthday another present and by the time of his second PK had gone; only a card this time. Only a card! PK had remembered and would remember always.

And what had Malcolm given in return. Some gifts of course, PK's father enjoyed malt whisky, the demands of Hinduism a little more elastic away from India. So, duty free Glenfiddich solved a problem there. And for his mother, flowers. English pastels in welcome contrast to strong African colours and Indian garlands. So, some gifts had been made, as though it mattered. Malcolm would not understand it was not a trade-off. One gave for its own sake not for want of return. Reciprocal giving, like an English Christmas, was too ingrained in Malcolm for him to understand.

But these were only the tangible things. Down the years PK had given Malcolm insights into his religion and culture not as a lesson in comparative religion but as a civilised interchange of experiences. Not that it had been much of an interchange with PK doing much of the explaining. Malcolm's responses had always been counterpoints to PK expositions. He was intrigued by the relationship between husbands and wives; PK remarked that spouses came to love each after the marriage not necessarily before and the guidance of parents laid the foundations for that love. Malcolm wondered who would have arranged for him to marry Alison; not her parents for sure. PK was given no insight into Malcolm's values or his people's. Malcolm had not done so because he thought them universally understood, accepted and acceptable with the same arrogance and ignorance as the missionaries and settlers before him. PK was saddened by his response because he knew from personal and historical experience how much this English man would leave misunderstood.

An older, more reflective Malcolm would understand these things a little more clearly but only when he returned to his untutored homeland and encountered an ignorance cruder than his own. In time he would become envious of PK, his extended family, his secure religious beliefs, his cultural richness; none of these things he had himself. After PK went, he kept in touch and in doing so kept open a link that he would value. His ultimate absence was more noticed than his sustained presence

As the old family diminished a new one took its place and the domestic life of the Bryant family (how Malcolm cherished that word) settled into comforting and sustained bliss. But as its members grew closer together so it became more exclusive the main victim being Flynn. At first the priest made regularly visits to the bungalow taking late afternoon tea with Malcolm leaving only when Alison arrived back from work.

Then James's arrival provided a further barrier to their close friendship. Sitting on his veranda overlooking the valley, he would conclude he was resentful of the grip that Alison and James now had on his long-standing friend. It was not a reasoned or justified response merely emotional. They had pushed him to the rim of Malcolm's life. That this should be unsurprising and understandable did not diminish the feeling for Flynn. The priest in him found shame in this response; the man in him, levered into isolation, found sadness. Nevertheless, he continued to visit and when James was born his visits became, for a time, daily. Dressed in a cloak of pastoral interest he knew the wellspring was a need for a shared joy, even if it was vicariously enjoyed. But as it became clear his visits were not needed, not by the family at least, they became less frequent and he was forced back to his pastoral routine - a rudimentary clinic after breakfast, school lessons in the church in the morning, visits in late afternoon when the heat of the day had eased. He had wondered whether Alison would have helped with the clinic taking Alice's place as smoothly as Malcolm had taken her husband's. She was after all a nurse and knew Africans well. She would have been invaluable. But the invitation was not made and the offer not volunteered. Perhaps there was stubborn pride on his part, perhaps thoughtlessness on hers. But these two Europeans - well-disposed though they were to Africa - failed to give what they had in abundance to a people who had overwhelming need for their support.

The images of the Pope's visit were paling with the passage of time. But it had brought more than religious ceremony. Unknown to Flynn it was the catalyst which might have a longer-term effect on his life. In the background the bureaucracy of the church brought its ponderous light to shine on East Africa and there took place changes, of emphasis, of direction, and more significantly for Flynn, of organisation. The Kimura mission and its satellite parishes did not meet the needs of the new country. It was suggested they be disbanded and reassigned to larger missions. Flynn's Society accepted the proposals and Flynn was asked to leave his post. At first sight it gave him the opportunity to leave his isolated home and enjoy a richer life elsewhere. But he could not leave Kimura, not now. He was devastated and pleaded to be allowed to stay, putting forward objections which were as spurious as they were personal. Nevertheless, he won a small concession with big implications for him. He would be allowed to remain at Kimura. The price for permitting this was that Flynn had to lose the other parishes and run

Kimura on a much-reduced income. In return he could remain in his house, with his church until he died. He accepted the proposals with a mixture of regret and relief. He sold his car and cancelled his phone link; with these major expenditures gone he could get by but at the cost of being even more confined to Kimura. He did not find it a high price to pay. He was over fifty years old and had no real links elsewhere. The village would become his sole life. But because of that he became more dependent on those who lived there. The fact that his great confidant Malcolm had his attentions drawn elsewhere made the changes more difficult to accommodate.

Meanwhile the life of his friend was changing too. If Flynn had to cope with the retrenchment of his pastoral role, then Malcolm was having to cope with a diminution of his research activities. The effect on Malcolm of the changing role of Kimura was to leave him with fewer resources and staff and required him to undertake partial responsibility for projects elsewhere in the country. Increasingly he found himself away from home much more than he would have wished. Gradually home life became Malcolm's sanctuary from increasing difficulties elsewhere and in consequence he took from it when he might have been giving to it. He still found in Alison the perfect partner. She was able to understand his difficulties and talk them through with him. She was desirable and responsive in the bedroom and she raised James with all the affection and guidance that could be expected. She did none of these things for duty but because she enjoyed every moment of her family life. But life at Kimura was not stimulating and Malcolm's increasing absence threw her life into a dull routine. As James grew older, a toddler searching for speech, she hired Bernie's ex-housekeeper, Hannah, as an ayah to give her some private time. Instead of giving her fulfilment, this private time made her realise how narrow her life had become. The compound was now a male preserve and although Connie Larsen would invite her to visit, she felt little in common with a woman of an older generation and a less liberal view of African life. Alison began to feel a desperate need to escape the compound. Increasingly she spent time at the Club, taking Hannah and James with her.

It was here, from an opponent on the Ladies' Squash ladder, she learnt of the vacancy back at the hospital. Following up a hint she went to talk to a friend in administration and although she had not previously made up her mind to return to work, once she got into the wards again and felt the buzz of hospital life, she knew she wanted the company as much as the employment.

Malcolm had some unease because it shifted responsibility for James a little more on to him. But he wanted her to be happy and understood that personal fulfilment might not come from motherhood alone. He remembered his own mother's life being smothered by the needs of Marion and in the end, he accepted the need for Alison to regain some of her independence. He would not have wanted to prevent it but he was concerned for his son. However, the terms of Alison's employment meant she could avoid shifts when Malcolm was away and he knew James would be on the compound close to his work should any emergency arise.

So daily life took on a different shape. In Alison's absence Hannah would often bring the toddler into the compound to share his Daddy's work. Here the little boy would meet Gitau and begin to see him as some grandfather figure. From him he learnt simple tasks and some words of Kikuyu. A plot was established in the allotment which was James's plot which he tended like the adults. Gitau and he would discuss the best way to treat the plants. The older man seemed to have a patience and serenity that Malcolm found difficult to emulate. He seemed to have a fund of games, songs and stories that were both African and European. Once he was surprised to hear his son singing *Frere Jacques*.

Had Malcolm been more perceptive he might have noticed that it was Gitau that stimulated his son's imagination, solved his problems, soothed his upsets. He, the father, was being bypassed. The little boy would have welcomed Gitau singing him to sleep at night but Alison knew from her own childhood the limitations she should place on non-family members. Within the house she re-established the blood family in the life of her son, a need to which Malcolm was oblivious.

But if Gitau was innocently usurping Malcolm's role then his son, Ngugi, would increasingly look to Malcolm for his stimulation. As a young boy he had a voracious appetite for reading albeit of a rather dull and traditional English style. Now as a young man his tastes were more sophisticated. Suddenly more substantial European authors sustained his interest. He devoured Thomas Hardy with the tales of rural simplicity striking a chord of familiarity. Malcolm's library had long since been exhausted but both Rogers and Bernie, in their different ways, had left behind unwanted reading matter. From Rogers, Ngugi found Jane Austin and Agatha Christie and from Bernie, Buck Rogers and Ernest Hemingway. Alison had a richer store. From her boarding school education and tedious night duties she had garnered a catholic collection from which Ngugi hand-picked at his pleasure.

But it was not just literature that grabbed his attention. His involvement with geography and history was routine; he learnt by heart the names of rivers, mountains and capital cities. He could recite the names of the books of the Bible with no regard to the pointlessness of what he was doing. He was competent at science. In biology he eschewed the practical knowledge his father had in abundance, in favour of Malcolm's explanation of diagrams and tables. He lived his life through the passive medium of books and did not question the validity of what he was being taught in his Anglocentric school.

Life in the Bryant household achieved a stable amalgam of personal fulfilment, adult pleasure and family activity. Evenings were spent together in the undemanding surroundings of their simple home and they would play records on the stereogram they had had as a wedding present from Alison's parents. On one gloomy moment of reflection, he wondered whether they were metamorphosing into Arthur and Alice though the presence of James soon banished the shadow.

Nairobi was a source of culture and entertainment. They had some friends from Alison's hospital life but their family life seemed to provide most of the stimulation and satisfaction they needed. Holidays were at the coast or with Alison's mother and father in Tanzania. These gave Malcolm chance to spend more time with his family. He and James would chase the crabs as they raced up the beach from the onrushing tide. They would lie on the sand, Malcolm holding his son tightly, and let the warm surf wash over them. As each wave retreated it dragged the particles of sand over their skin and Malcolm felt as if it was dragging from him all the strain and dullness of working life. Once he imagined, the dancing particles pricking his skin and pulling from him all the poison of his past leaving a purified person behind. In the evenings he and Alison would sit on a beach veranda watching the waves sparkle in the moonlight as they broke on the distant reef. Above a canopy of stars provided a benign shelter.

Publicly it was she who took the limelight. She was friendly and interesting, she could flirt whilst promising nothing, she could tell jokes as well as take them. And her partner Malcolm was seen as an accomplice in this behaviour; his reticence a counterweight to her gregariousness. And he was pleased to be seen, not in her shadow, but seeming to sustain the limelight. Privately she radiated light and warmth too but here a gentle glow. She coaxed responses from her subdued partner like encouraging a timid tortoise to put its head out of its shell. She did not fear what was hidden from her. She knew Malcolm was not full of a twisted bitterness waiting to express itself through violence, perversion or infidelity. That he was consumed by a neutralising blight she understood full well and had done so when they were married. She had taken him for better or worse and she understood she would not find it easy to edge him towards comfortable normality. But to a large degree she succeeded. In the rockery that was his past took root small plants; optimism here, contentment there, some pleasure, some love, some concern for others, some declarations of feeling. And she was the one who through her perseverance, good humour, kind thoughts, fed and watered this covering which hid the jagged outlines of the past. That she was the wellspring of this change was indisputable and, as will happen, he took its continuation for granted.

And so, on one night at home they sat close together on the settee after another of Karui's suppers. Outside frogs croaked, cicadas chirruped, cautious animals slid and loped their way through the bush. Inside Malcolm and Alison sat listening to music stroking each other's skin to acknowledge the mood of each piece. They played the Elgar which Alison had bought for his birthday, the rich aching sounds filled the room and swept out into the big sky beyond. As Malcolm knelt on the floor his head bowed, his face hidden on his wife's lap she felt his warm tears soak into her dressing gown and she stroked his hair more a mother than a wife.

When it had finished, his face was still buried in Alison's lap and she felt his lips move against her damp clothing.

'That frightens me.'

'Frightens you. Why?'

'It gets deep inside me. I'm not in control. It sets off emotions. And not soothing ones.'

Alison waited for him to go on.

'It echoes inside my body although it's my head hearing it. I don't want to cry, but it makes me and I don't know why I'm crying. It's as though the bow was being pulled over every nerve inside me.'

'But you wanted me to play it.'

'Yes'

'Do you know why?'

'Yes,' but he said no more.

They sat silently for a while. The one unsure of what questions to ask, the other frightened of questions he did not want to answer.

Wanting to avoid an unwelcome questioning he asked, 'Did Elgar write much else?'

'Oh yes but not much after that one.'

'Why?'

'He said he was exhausted, by the war'

'Which war?'

'The first world war.'

'What did he do?'

'I don't know. His wife died not long after and he lived for another fifteen years.'

'All alone?'

'As far as I know.'

'How awful.'

'Yes'

'You seem to know a lot about him.'

'I read it on the album sleeve as we were listening.'

'And I thought you were clever.' He pulled her close to acknowledge her cunning.

She wanted to understand and tried again, 'Why did you cry when it was playing?'

He couldn't avoid a response and tried to be more forth coming, 'Because the early part sounds like what I used to feel all the time. I can't describe it in words but if you want to understand listen to the start. I'm sure it's the cello as much as the music.'

'But it brightens up doesn't it. It's quite hopeful at the end. Are you hopeful?'

'Yes. Yes, I am' he had paused before reply but there was no doubt. He hugged her again, his arms linked beneath her knees pressing his face in the groove between her thighs. It was as well he did not know the cello player was confined to a wheelchair or his response might have been less positive.

'Time for bed.'

Later they lay, her back curled into his chest, his face hidden from her view. She reached her hand back to stroke his thigh but she felt no growing erection against her buttocks.

She turned her face so he could see her profile. 'I love you,' she said.

The woman found that easy to say; the man, especially this man, could not say the words. He kissed her cheek and she felt his warm breath in her ear. She dropped her face back to the pillow and they lay close until sleep prepared them for another day.

TWENTY-THREE

Even days which end awfully must have begun normally. Jack Kennedy and Archduke Ferdinand presumably had the usual breakfast. The citizens of Hiroshima packed their briefcases and made out their shopping lists.

And so, too, this one day began normally in the Bryant household. Malcolm Bryant shaved and looking in the mirror he saw the reflection of a normal thirty-six-year-old man, his face tanned under a tropical sun, his hair conventionally cut and parted, his eyes clear after a full night's sleep but darting from their origin as if reluctant to maintain contact. It was a comforting sight; his own image brought no surprises, made no judgement and reflected the emotional neutrality that defined his life. He felt reassurance that the night had taken nothing away. He had seen the first thirty knowing years of his life grind from miserable childhood, through anxious adolescence and enter numbed adulthood. That his was minor suffering in the whole scale of human experience did not make it seem less unfair to this one individual. But now those three decades or so had given way to a plateau of deep contentment, he might have said joy and happiness if his earlier life had not made him a stranger to such emotions. He had a wife and child both new enough to engender simple love; he had a job which gave him a sense of fulfilment; he had a life style better than any he could have invented. All of these held his past at bay, a personal history which was still present in the shadows of his mind. He knew how fortunate he'd been. Deep inside he could acknowledge all this luck; but he just could not express it in any public way. For him no emotion however deep, however sincere, however inspiring was allowed out; all remained mute inside him. This was the legacy of an earlier life which mutilated the later one.

But he had a saviour; his wife Alison had become the articulation as well as the catalyst of his emotions. By default, on his part and by instinct on hers, she fuelled the emotional life of them both. And as if that was not enough, they had produced a healthy, happy child who coaxed from each of them waves of parental love. If this situation had remained his life might have continued with a normality he thought beyond his reach; but it would not.

'I think it's going to be very hot today.' Malcolm was looking out from their veranda. From his breakfast table he could see the valley losing the early morning mist that had gathered in the hollows and around the shrubs of the rough African landscape.

'You must remember to wear your hat, James.' Alison brushed a light quiff of hair, brown like hers, from the toddler's forehead.

'And Daddy,' the words came through a mouthful of toast.

'Yes. And Daddy,' his father confirmed the importance.

'What are you going to do today, James?' Alison changed the subject.

'First I'm going to water my plants.'

'It's better to leave the watering until the end of the day, when the sun's going down,' said Malcolm, the scientist, wanting things understood.

'Why?'

'Well, the water evaporates in the hot sun.'

'What's 'vaprate' mean?'

'Well. Um. The sun boils the water away like steam.'

'Does it cook the plants?'

'No, it's not that hot.'

'So why do I need a hat?'

'Because your skin is very tender, very soft, not tough like a plant.'

'What's 'tough' mean?'

'Hard. Come on it's time for me to go.' Alison signalled the end of the conversation. James turned his empty eggshell upside down in its cup so that Karui would think he had not eaten it.

'I'll be back about four Karui. I'll bring some fresh fish from Nairobi,' she addressed the cook, who had come to clear the table.

'Yes, madam. Come on James you have not eaten your egg.' He feigned surprise when James smashed the upturned shell with his spoon. 'You are deceiving me!' Neither tired of this almost daily routine.

After breakfast Alison left for work on her day shift as a casualty nurse in Nairobi having ensured the three-year-old James, was dressed and ready to spend the day with his ayah, Hannah. From the front steps of their bungalow Malcolm watched Alison's car disappear beyond a patch of maize leaving a plume of dust to resettle in the growing heat. He set out the few short steps to the office of the agricultural research station where he spent much of his working life. Behind him James, with Hannah in tow, jumped into the sunlight kicking the soft dry murram into small red clouds which settled on his plimsoled feet. Under the big tree he looked around to see what would capture his capricious attention that day. Thus, all three members of this family left their bungalow to start another normal day.

Now, nearing midday, Malcolm brought himself upright arching his back against the strain of bending over the coffee plant he had been examining. He picked at the centre of his floppy hat and raised it vertically from his head then wafted it up and down to cause the air to circulate. He used his forearm to wipe the sweat from his brow. The sun was at its hottest although its effects were ameliorated by the high altitude of the hills above Nairobi. He looked around at the plots of plants in the fenced compound. Maize and bananas, tea and coffee, beans and peppers each to their own segment, each tended with a care they could not expect in real farms and plantations. In a neighbouring plot Gitau was putting a compost on selected plants. Elsewhere workers under his command dug and cut to order. Malcolm found a pleasing orderliness in all he saw. The plots were carefully delineated with hose pipes squirming along the paths between them like elongated snakes rising to clutch the mouths of several standpipes. Neat rows of plants were clearly labelled, the soil between them clear of weeds. The high wire fence surrounding the compound was free of gaps which would have allowed the entry of wild animals. The labourers worked conscientiously any slackness bringing a sharp Kikuyu rebuke from Gitau. In five minutes, they could break for lunch. Another day moving with easy routine made Malcolm feel at ease.

He looked to see if James was in sight - his son often came into the compound to tend the little plot that Gitau had made for him - but there was no sign of him. Perhaps Hannah had taken him into the cool of the bungalow beyond the station office or perhaps they had gone up the road to the village where Gitau lived, to play with the local children. There they would have chased the chickens and fed the goats, sat in the shade of the huts and nibbled roasted maize, sung the native songs and played their childhood games. Wherever the toddler was he would be cared for; only accidental harm might come his way.

The equatorial sun, vertically above Malcolm, cast the smallest of body shadows on the red soil. And his life seemed shadowless too. It had not always been so. His earlier life had been full of shadows, threatening, enveloping - cast by the cold light of a blemished upbringing. Now these shadows had been banished by the brightness of his current fortune. Yet at these times human beings are at their most vulnerable, fate at its most cruel and as that day's sun turned towards night so his personal shadows were about to return.

'Bwana Bryant. Bwana Bryant.' Phillip the office clerk, came running from the rear door of the office. 'Mrs. Bryant has had an accident. She is in the hospital. They have just rung me.'

'Is she badly hurt?' Images of a patient going berserk with a panga struck at Malcolm's mind.

'They didn't say, but they want you to go.'

214

'Which hospital?' He realised the possibility of confusion.

'The Kenyatta. Where she works.'

'I know. I know.' Malcolm's rude impatience a sign of his anxiety.

He rushed to find the ayah and James. He ran through each room of the bungalow calling his son's name, part in frustration, part in fear; but the boy was nowhere to be found. Their absence and his anxieties produced a confusion. He stood on the steps and shouted again.

'They will not be far away. I will look for them. You go.' Gitau was waiting outside in the open area outside the bungalow.

'Yes. You do that. Thanks.' He raced back inside to find his car keys cursing their absence from where he thought they'd be. He jumped into his car and left clouds of murram dust behind him as he accelerated towards the main road. The rear end swayed in the dry dust and the car rattled as he drove too quickly over the corrugated dirt road.

On the main road to Nairobi, he saw the country bus at the side of the road by the Changa bridge. Its side was severely damaged scarring the idiosyncratic message on the paint work. As he sped past the bus, he did not notice Alison's car in the ravine below, its roof squashed to the level of the bonnet, the body bent into a slight V. If he had, he would have known she was dead. As she had approached the bridge the oncoming bus veered slightly to one side. Her car glanced off it and into the containing wall of the bridge from which it catapulted onto the rocky river bed below. It was not death at the claws of a wild animal, a poisonous snake or a virulent illness; nevertheless, it was a death that Africa knew well.

The usual insouciance of Nairobi's drivers and pedestrians did little to ease Malcolm journey to the other side of town. The major landmarks were not hotels and mosques but donkey carts and buses. He left his car on the spot marked for the use of ambulances and ran to reception. He was invited to a side-room and to sit in a chair in

215

front of a desk. The tubular steel frame of the chair bowed slightly and the slats creaked under his weight. He scanned the surface of the desk, a blotter, an empty document tray, a tubular container of ball point pens, a circular stain where a hot mug had stained the varnished surface its outline highlighted by the reflected sunlight from a window - all neutral indicators of the day's events. His mind, usually dull and slow, leaped from thought to thought; the heavy breathing left by his dash from the car heightened his anxiety. Within seconds fearful impatience had brought him to his feet, the chair creaking again in response. Beyond the desk a door opened.

'Mr. Bryant? I'm Dr Khan. I'm sorry to have kept you; we've been very busy in casualty.'

The doctor was a young Asian, his sparse moustache adding to his apparent youth rather than offsetting it as he had hoped. His white coat was open to reveal the bright white shirt and neat trousers beneath; his plum-coloured tie was held in place by a gold pin. His name badge was obscured by the flapping lapel of his coat. Malcolm would not have noticed it had it been visible. His enquiry was as business-like as the dryness of his mouth would permit.

'Where is she? How is she?'

The pause told him more than he wanted to know. The doctor's face was thin and his eyes deep-set. He squinted slightly under the strain.

'I'm afraid she's dead. I'm so very sorry. You'd better sit down'. For the doctor the situation was not new although he was sufficiently inexperienced for the sincerity in his voice to be real.

For Malcolm the situation was far from routine. He sat heavily and the chair groaned beneath his weight, its feet screeching as they scraped the plastic tiled floor. He leant forward clutching his knees, the rivets in the chair straining as he did so. He had expected some injury. He had even prepared himself for something serious; but not death. His thoughts raced. The recognition of a horrific act which could not be undone filled his mind. There was no going back; no starting again. It was final; it was permanent. She was gone. His hands seemed unresponsive, moving to some unspoken agenda from face to lap to each other. His normal thought processes stopped. Fears, plans, comments, people flipped in and out of his mind in a confusing jumble. His eyes were open but saw nothing in the room. Images flashed as though a dozen slide-projectors were randomly turned on in his head. No. No. No, said his mind, his mouth unable to follow. On the very occasion he needed to turn to his beloved Alison, his irreplaceable Alison, for support and guidance she was not there. Alison. Alison. Alison. There was no-one there. He was adrift again and the darkness of the past gathered to return.

'How did it happen?'

'She was involved in a car accident at Changa bridge. She was wearing her uniform She was coming on duty, with me as it happens. She was well liked here. I did my first shift here with her. She was very helpful and kind.' The words, true but insignificant, washed over Malcolm. The young doctor thought of saying more: of conversations about Moshi where they both had relatives, of England where they had both studied, of her sensitivity when his mother died, of her presents for his younger sister, of her spontaneous and sustained sympathy with all the distressed attenders at casualty, of her friendly professionalism. But he judged such thoughts, real and important though they might to him, were out of place now. 'She should be identified. Would you like a cup of tea first?'

'No. I want her.' He checked. 'I want to see her now.' The doctor's voice had re-coordinated his senses. Shock had stemmed tears but his voice was dry and rasping. As he stood the chair creaked again the noise ricocheting across the thoughts of both men. He put his handkerchief, sodden with tears, back in his pocket.

They walked down several corridors. Malcolm wanted to run but he didn't know where they were heading and he was limited by the speed of the doctor. He brushed against people, staff and patients alike, as he pushed down the corridor. Turning a corner, he fell into an incoming wheelchair and bumped his shin cutting the flesh under his trousers. He glared at its occupant half expecting Marion to have returned to remind him of life's capricious harshness. No. No. No. Not Marion. Surely not Marion. Please not her. In his fluster he could not summon an apology to the bemused elderly Asian lady. The mortuary sign put a formal signature to what he'd already been told. Inside the temperature was appropriately low and it calmed his brain as it cooled his body. The solitary bed covered by a sheet mesmerised him. The two men stood either side of it like theatregoers awaiting the curtain to go up, bound to silence by a deferential ritual.

'Are you ready?'

Malcolm nodded. The doctor pulled back the sheet slowly to reveal her head and stood back. Malcolm gasped as her face was revealed. She was badly bruised. Her dark hair once lively and springy was plastered to her scalp; the lips usually red and welcoming were now a dull purple. An earlobe was torn as her earring had been ripped away and the cotton wool plugs in her ears were stained. Below a not quite closed eyelid he could see a crescent of blood red eyeball. He knew it was a face that would not greet him again. The skin had no bloom, the lips no twitching sign of sensuality, the ears deaf to his sighs of satisfaction, the eyes blind to his condition. The lifeless form had been anticipated by his brain but was unexpectedly shocking to his eyes.

'She wouldn't have known anything about it. She died instantly,' the doctor lied conveniently ignoring the moments between hitting the bus and crashing onto the rocks below.

To Malcolm it was inconceivable that this inert body was all that was left of one who had brought such life to him. For him Alison had been responsible for the creation and release of intense feelings. Heightened happiness and pleasure had come to one who had spent most of his life repressing those things which distinguished him from an animal. His feelings were intense now but not those he had grown used to. There was no control now, no stifling of embarrassing action.

Now he felt himself sliding down a slippery walled well rapidly leaving the daylight above. He wanted to scream but his hand was clasped tightly over his mouth. He wanted her back; he tried to will her to life, to drag her into existence again. He reached down for her body pulling it to him moaning her name over and over. There was no aroma of the scented morning soap only the smell of antiseptic wash, no comforting embrace from her arms which hung stiffly at her sides. The body was heavy and unresponsive only confirming her death not denying it as he wished.

His dry sobbing seemed unstoppable, but conscious of the doctor on the other side of the bed a flood of convention calmed him. As he let her body drop the sheet fell away from the bed revealing her full nakedness. Her torso was badly gashed, the slashes across her breasts held with crude stitching. Her dark pubic hair sat in silhouette against her pale belly. Those secret parts of her body, promises of intimate passion stood revealed in insult to their usual privacy. Her left foot was missing, the stump covered by a crude dressing. He turned away, shocked, his mind racing uncontrollably. He tried to get away physically and stumbled to the corner of the room trying to disappear into the non-existent gap at the junction of the walls and the floor, to slide into the fabric of the building like the wall spiders seeking refuge behind the skirting board in their home. Some instinct made him sink to the floor and pull his knees up to his chest, to reduce his body to nothing.

The doctor, familiar with death but uncomfortable with life, reached for him but withdrew his gesture in respect of some professional ethic and reflexed into his public manner. Malcolm now lay in a foetal ball in the corner of the room sobbing but crying no tears. His head was pressed onto his knees each eye-socket engaging a knee cap. He spoke her name over and over until each repetition grew softer and then stopped. Later he would relive this scene, his actions a deep embarrassment to his conventional mind, but now discretion, control, predictability had evaporated in the face of absolute despair.

The doctor again stooped to help him to his feet. He led Malcolm, still shaking and mumbling, to a washbasin in the corner of the room. Malcolm looked in the mirror the abnormal version of his own face reflecting his deep breaths. The contented image he had seen in the shaving mirror that morning had been replaced by one which was raw, uncontrolled and embarrassing. He filled the washbasin with cold water and bending over used his hands to dowse his reddened face and eyes. The water, ice cold to his burning skin, damped down his emotions. The effect was to restore order to the proceedings in a way which reassured the normal Malcolm. He rested his hands on the edge of the basin his rigid arms supporting his upper body as he kept his face downwards away from the mirror. He held himself in that position as his breathing slowed. Drips of water collected on the end of his nose and pattered into the water below. His eyes read the name of the basin's manufacturer and the Hot and Cold on the taps.

Dr Shah held out a towel. As Malcolm dried his face a long-standing inhibition filled the gaps inside him. His thoughts and feelings, fragmented and wild a few moments ago were corralled into a more submissive form.

'I'm sorry,' he said to the doctor. Apologising! For his wife's death! For normal human grief! Yes. For Malcolm deep emotions, revealing emotions were not for public display. They were secret, private, personal. To reveal them merely put him in the public gaze, in the childhood spotlight with Marion. That must not happen.

By now the doctor had replaced the sheet over Alison's body replacing her individuality by a crude outline. Malcolm glanced at it as he moved away, its neutrality a minor comfort. In the doorway he paused standing in silent formal homage to the body much as mourners leaving a funeral service respect the casket. He didn't want to leave the room recognising that even that simple action only reinforced the inescapability of his loss. Yet what else to do? Outwardly he was calm and controlled, all the anguish had been screwed into a tight ball which lodged inside him far from public view. The doctor took him to a small office across the corridor. The doctor went about his business. 'Mr. Bryant. I have to ask you. Can you identify the body you have just seen as that of Alison Jane Bryant?'

No. No. No. That was not my wife. She is full of life, of promise, of gaiety, of generosity. What I have just seen was nothing like her. His slow, mournful analysis anticipating the years ahead.

'Yes'. The public Yes of admission and the private Yes of acceptance.

'We shall miss her. She had a way of making the world seem brighter.' Khan avoided a longer catalogue of her virtues.

You saw that too, thought Malcolm surprised she would affect others as she did him. But you are only losing a member of staff, he thought uncharitably. For you she will be replaced, another name on the payroll, another person in the canteen, another uniform by the bedside. For me she was irreplaceable. What am I to do now? It felt strange to have logical thoughts after the confusion.

Malcolm left the office rejecting all offers of help - self-sufficient again. Nevertheless, the doctor accompanied him to the entrance neither man finding anything to say.

Dr Khan held out his hand but Malcolm had already turned away. Good bye. I'm sorry. So sorry. Be careful. The words were formed in his mind but there was no chance to say them as his proxy patient hurried to his car.

Malcolm's car was facing the hospital entrance and as he sat in it, he saw a wheelchair abandoned by a departing patient. There was no one in it but for Malcolm it was not empty. In it he saw Marion staring back at him with the images of the past staking a claim on the future. As he left the car park the sun was gaining speed in its descent to night and the shadows of the buildings strafed his way. But it was other shadows that he feared and his homeward journey contained the seeds of an ungainly reversal of the journey that brought him into the warmth of the last few years.

TWENTY-FOUR

It was no normal day now. Alison was dead. Gone. For ever. This day now acquired an unwanted status in his life. It was scored into the annual calendar of his life eclipsing all others.

Malcolm remembered that journey home from the hospital not because of its geography but because of having to drag his attention back to the routine of driving and away from the frenzied anger at being deprived of Alison. He felt his brain being clamped, incapable of rational thought, nor indeed of selfless consideration. He was not thinking of her, her family, their son; only of himself, his loss, his anguish, his emptiness.

At the Changa bridge a handful of people stood looking at the wreck below. He pulled up short of the bridge. From a brow above the gully, he could see Alison's car. Some children were sitting on the rocks beside it, just distant from it, enough to portray apprehension. One boy threw a stone into the gap left by the broken side window and it clattered inside the battered shell. The sight of a toddler among the group evoked James and he drove off.

When he came to the station he pulled up under the tree in the middle of the square. He got out of his car, his trembling now a physical reaction to his experience. There on the steps of the office was James.

'Daddy.'

The boy came running towards him the ayah bringing up the rear, Gitau hovering in the background. Malcolm stooped slightly, intending to pick the boy up. In doing so he saw his own hands the palms open towards his onrushing son. He knew these hands had not long held his dead wife. If there was any of her blood on them or on his clothes it could not be seen. But Malcolm knew they were tainted

222

with her death. With his actions all instinct in the panic, he withdrew his hands and shouted.

'No. No. No.' Just one small word, open to so many interpretations.

He was not rejecting his son, or at least not wanting to. He just did not want to envelope him in her death. If that was how it seemed to him it was not how it seemed to his son. The boy cowered away. He was not to understand. He stood for a moment. His face, unmistakably Alison's, crumpled into confusion. Eyes that had been confidently quick, froze into bewilderment and the face around them set like a photograph. It was an image that remained in Malcolm's mind always and many unsettled nights would revive its accusing stare. Turning, James ran barefooted past his ayah to Gitau.

Malcolm would rationalise the incident by saying he was too unclean to pick up his son. But this event would haunt his mind and echo through their future relationship. He could not decide whether his reaction was purely clinical or whether it was emotional as well. He feared that at this point he had rejected his son deliberately. That this child, their child, was too potent a reminder of what he had just lost. That rather than compensate for his loss the presence of this child would exacerbate it. In darker moments he feared the child's emotional demands on him would only push him deeper into the state from which he had been rescued by Alison.

Such intricate thoughts were beyond the young James Bryant. He had sensed there was something wrong from the behaviour of Gitau and his ayah. His father had returned in an odd mood too, and just when James had run to seek the uninhibited comfort that physical contact brings to children, he was abruptly and woundingly rejected. It was no surprise that this little boy, the placid routine of his life crudely jolted, would see the world a little differently from that day on and viewed his father more circumspectly too. The sudden absence of his mother would be puzzling but not frightening; he would be unhappy but not scared. It would be his father, still present, who would trigger the insecurity. This man who so far had been placid, loving, reassuring had turned on him like some capricious dog. And just as some children who are bitten by an animal lose the confidence to offer a stroking hand so he too would hold back some part of himself from this suddenly strange adult. It was that one moment, innocent in its genesis but indelible in its effect, that laid out the relationship between father and son. No. No. No. If only it had not been said. If only.

Malcolm frightened by his son's reaction, followed him. He crouched to bring himself level with James sitting on Gitau's knee on the steps of the office. The boy withdrew slightly into the African's enveloping arms turning his face away from his father, his running nose leaving a wet streak across the African's shirt.

'Mummy's dead.' James pulled closer to Gitau's body.

It was what he had to say. It was what had to be said. But there had been no preparation for it, no explanation of death, of its finality. He wished he could mention heaven. There would have been some easy comfort in that. To equate Alison's death to that of a goat whose body they had found one day in the bush would have been unacceptable too.

He put out his hand to touch his son in an attempt to reverse the rejection he had just instigated. The young child pulled back further into the arms of the African leaving his father alone, the act of rejection conjoined. Once again father and son failed to draw close.

Gitau looked over James's head at Malcolm his eyes wet with sorrow for them both but could do nothing. He held the child but knew the father needed help too. Malcolm had just lost his wife and might have lost his son too. It was he who needed the physical comfort of another human being. The son only sensed, but the father knew, he understood the awful finality of what had happened. But no succour was available to him. He was alone but not as he had been before. Before Alison he knew no better than his youthful emptiness but she had shown him companionship, emotional depth, joy. His loneliness now could be contrasted with the rich expectations of life her presence had given.

He raised his eyes and looked into Gitau's. There he saw reflected his own grief, his own helplessness, his own despair. The African closed his eyes and as he did so tears flowed down his cheeks highlighted by his dark skin and fell on the hair of the boy cradled in his arms. Malcolm reached out his hand not sure if he was trying to touch the boy or the man but it got no further than half the gap between them before he withdrew it. He stood up and turned to walk back to his bungalow. He ordered Karui to wash the car, meaning the seat and steering wheel which he felt had been contaminated. Instead Karui washed the outside body of the car as he had always done. Understanding the importance of the occasion he cleaned every cranny until the body shone even in the shade of the tree but the infinitesimal remains of Alison's body remained untouched. It did not matter; the gesture was more important than the reality.

Inside the house Malcolm put his clothes in a pile on the bedroom floor and showered rubbing his body over and over again. He was puzzled by the gash on his leg and then remembered the collision with the wheelchair at hospital. Marion. Marion. Marion. Not you. No. No. No. But she was back, in his head, regaining the space that had been conquered by Alison. No. No. No. He scrubbed the small wound mercilessly, the physical hurt some crude antidote to his emotional pain. Having put on new clothes he sought out Karui who was in the kitchen. From the window he could see his son still sitting on Gitau's knee the old man singing softly as the two rocked to and fro. His stories and explanations had no more meaning than Malcolm's crude objectivity but they were to comfort the bruised infant.

Malcolm told Karui to throw out the discarded clothes. Later he would demand them back and burn them himself knowing that through Karui they would be worn by someone else. He did not want Alison's death to linger anywhere.

Later Malcolm put James to bed both wary of each other. He had feared his son would not leave the refuge he had with Gitau but the toddler was too tired to reject the comforting folds of routine and Hannah carried him back to the family home. She made towards the bathroom.

'No. Hannah. Thank you. I'll see to him. Come on James.' And his son came, not calmed by soothing expectations but subdued by undemanding habit. Malcolm took his hand. Father and son were not reconciled but at least reunited.

He watched as James played boats in his bath and became irritated by the time it took to do what, for him, was a simple routine task. His mind wandered despairingly through the day's events his thoughts interrupted by nautical collisions and war like noises. When the boy finally got out of the bath, he handed Malcolm the towel and Malcolm realised his son expected to be dried. This was a task Alison usually undertook and the requirement for him to do it only highlighted her absence. He was conscious of his son being close to him, that his young body yielded and stiffened in turn as the drying took place. He felt the rounded bones of his shoulders, the xylophone of his ribs. He eased the towel between the boy's toes as the youngster sat on the bathroom stool. He had done the task before but it had greater meaning now. When he had finished drying him, he offered James his pyjama trousers and the youngster slid off the stool straight into them. In doing so he stumbled into his father's arms. Malcolm felt the damp hair against his neck, smelt the recently soaped skin, and sensed the slight quivering of his naked body as the boy shivered in the comparative cold out of the warm water. The contact lasted for a split second before the boy squirmed away to get his pyjama top. In Malcolm's tired eyes this act of simple innocent childish routine was interpreted as an act of further rejection. But the whole encounter had been virtually silent; James made splashing noises with his boats;

Malcolm had given simply instruction but neither had really spoken to the other. They had been physically close but had not hugged. This was Malcolm's fault; he was the mature adult. He knew it was a missed opportunity and regretted his reserve thereafter. But he could not do it; couldn't let go; couldn't risk the embarrassment, couldn't lose the control. And in failing he might have lost his child.

In bed Malcolm told his son a sanitised version of how Alison had died. He told, rather than explained, that they would not see her again. His son listened absorbing a totally new and dramatic reality into his psyche. Malcolm tried to think of some nursery rhyme to sing but every time he began, he choked on the notes. James, exhausted by the heightened emotions of the day, soon slept, the tiredness of his young body stronger than the confusion of his immature mind. Malcolm sat for a while looking at the sleeping face its form reminding him more than ever of his lost wife.

Whilst this was going on Karui and Gitau were sitting under the tree in the compound. Their rural African lives forced them to confront death more than others elsewhere. Death by disease, death by malnutrition, death by predator, death by political act; all had borne heavily on them without lessening their distress at its effect. They shared their knowledge of the day's events and in the telling shared their grief.

As Malcolm came out of the boy's bedroom, Karui told him Gitau wanted to see him outside. It was a quiet African night, a quietness that can spell intrigue, peacefulness, loneliness according to the mood of the listener. Gitau was standing in the darkness of the square, his face lit by the light from the kitchen window. Malcolm stood on the top step looking down at him. The two men looked at each other separated by height and distance but other things too.

Tears ran down the older man's cheeks his eyes reddening. He said nothing, in words at least, but his very presence was significant enough. Indeed, words would not have been necessary. Had they not been separated by a flight of steps, had one not been the European boss the other the African employee, had they not both been men then the consolation of physical contact would have been possible and helped them both. But these two simple human beings were, not unwilling, but unable to find mutual comfort because of an inherited legacy of expectation. Each wanted to reach out to the other and neither could. For Malcolm held back his tears, an English stoicism prevailing over other deeper feeling. But for him the reticence was not just cultural it was personal and deeply ingrained. Part of him wanted to reach out to this man, to cling to him as his son had done, part to enjoy the same security and part to cement the common humanity they shared despite a gulf of race, of experience, of outlook, of position. But he couldn't; Malcolm had rebuilt his shell. He could not display the public emotion his condition required.

They turned, having said nothing but shared something even if it was only an appreciation of their emotional inadequacies. They returned to the familiarity of their own homes. Each would put his own interpretation of the incident and both would have an understanding of its value. That these differed did not matter.

Back in the living room Malcolm noticed the wedding photos on the bureau and saw her parents. The realisation that they did not know, startled him into sense. Consumed with the importance of her to him, he had overlooked the importance of her to them. Someone had to tell them. It could only be him.

He wanted the ringing tone to go on; for there to be no-one there, to postpone the painful contact. Mrs Parkinson answered but he couldn't reply. The slight anxiety in her voice as she repeated her greeting forced him to speak. The words were the only ones his brain could create.

'It's Malcolm. Alison's dead.'

They stood, hundreds of miles apart, unable to continue. Eventually Malcolm described the circumstances, the factuality of the reportage making it easier to speak. Dull routine came to his rescue. The phone went dead. Later Mr Parkinson would ring back and

Malcolm would repeat his report, the two male voices disguising from each other - and from themselves - the extent of their owner's loss, the matter-of-factness of their dialogue their support for masculine convention. It was agreed her parents should come at once and stay in the empty bungalow. It had been unoccupied since Bernie's suicide. Malcolm thought it best not to tell them that.

Whilst this telephoning was going on Flynn reached the edge of the compound, brought by news from Gitau. His initial motivation was compassion but on his walk from the village this became sanitised by parochial duty. By the time of his arrival at the compound he could bring himself to go no further. He couldn't face the emotional turmoil it would entail. This was too real, not like the rituals of church services which he could carry out by habit and he had lost the will to face it. He had encountered death and tragedy many times and with his comforting religious balm had brought real comfort. But to this man, his friend, he could say nothing. Malcolm did not believe the message Flynn would give. For him to try would be an insult to his friend. So, what could he do, what could he say? He concluded he had nothing to offer. He stopped at the edge of the square just outside its light. And much as he was excluded from the illumination so he felt excluded from the lives within it He looked at the house and knew that the people within it were self-contained and his arrival would be an intrusion. He had nothing to give and if that became apparent, to him the priest, it could undermine his own belief. He turned, believing he had not turned his back on the world but that this part of the world had turned its back on him, not because he wasn't wanted but because he wasn't needed. He shuffled up the darkened road helped by the moonlight but moving more quickly than was prudent. He reached the door of his church and let himself in. Kneeling, he said his formal prayers but thought more deeply too. He looked up at the Christ figure discernible against the white wall.

Why? his voice was silent although the words clearly articulated. Why do you let me fail? I've tried to carry your message and your burden faithfully. But I couldn't do it. Not all of it. Not all the time. Not on my own.

He paused in the praying position not expecting an oral reply but hoping some idea might enter his head which he could interpret as a divine message. Nothing came. Flynn wept that day too, but it was not Father Flynn crying for one of his fellow human beings, it was Joseph Flynn crying for himself. He got to his feet using his knee as a lever to support his ageing body. The unrelenting stoicism that keeps most of the human race from despair would rescue him too. As he rose, he saw the sign dedicated to the mysterious Gerald Daley.

'Well now. Gerald,' he now spoke aloud a soft echo from the stark walls shadowing his voice. 'Do you have a message? Can you give me hope?' He stood for a moment in the silence not expecting a reply. He looked around the simple room. People came to it every day seeking something, sometimes from the god and sometimes from the man. And now the man who was supposed to have answers could find none for himself. Without sunlight and without people the room seemed to have a cold sterility, which made the lone man yearn for company.

He closed up the church again, the key in the lock echoing in the empty building. When he returned to his house, he found Wambui on the veranda sitting in one of the wooden chairs facing the mountain whose glacial peaks glistened in the full moon. She, too, had wept; for her at the thought of a child losing its mother but now her cheeks were dry, her face impassive. Neither spoke and he sat in the chair beside her. He, too, looked at the mountain and addressed its god, Ngai. Ngai was as silent as his own God but at least he faced the silence with another person.

Back in his own home his friend had his own cloud of isolation. Malcolm sat for a while in the bedroom which only this morning had been shared. The furniture which then seemed the natural touchstones of their daily lives now seemed like pieces on a stage set, devoid of ownership, defined only by shape. Her night-clothes lay on the bed, hastily discarded by her, but now neatly folded by Karui on his daily routine. He stroked them against his cheek and felt their fragile silkiness against his skin. He could smell her body on them and he gasped at the air to suppress any sobs. He picked up her lipstick from the vanity table and unscrewed the cylinder. As the two parts separated the lipstick fell across his hand marking his palm with a bright red line. It looked like the wealds and gashes he had seen on her body and he wiped it off in panic. He wanted to destroy all her belongings, to rip the clothes to shreds, to trample the makeup, to burn her books and magazines. But he wouldn't have known where to stop and he was liable to destroy not just what was hers but what was theirs and ultimately himself. And whereas many men would have allowed their feelings, of anger, despair, loss, to burst through into frenzied physical action, Malcolm's instinct was to repress them forcing them deep into himself keeping the passive bodily image which had protected him against embarrassment throughout his life. He looked in the dressing table mirror at his own image; it stared back impassively strengthening the stronghold on his emotions. He turned away from it wearily and said her name silently.

Alison

In order to escape the tangible triggers of memory we went to sit on the veranda. Once bright metaphors became sinister and threatening. The shadows produced by the bright moonlight seemed to become the shrouds of past lives. The bleating of the goats became the shrieks of spirits endlessly wandering the dark world beyond his garden. The blanket of stars, whose sheer scale he had once found exhilarating, now became a sieve through which life was sucked into eternity. That they would one day absorb him froze his mind. But his death was not the only thing he feared. There was, too, the time before it, until today so full of hopeful life, now reduced in an instant to barren expectation. As the air cooled with the onset of night, it was not his body he felt growing cold but an icing of the spirit. He had been thrown back into his own emotional ghetto and he did not know how to escape from it on his own. Before there had been Alison; twelve hours ago, they had sat breakfasting on this same spot at the start of another normal day. Now she was gone, completely and finally. No more prefect days. He struggled to think what day it was. When his mind acknowledged the date, it became another milestone - tombstone - in his life. There it would lie with the memorised record of others, his own birthday, hers, James's, Marion's, the battle of Trafalgar, the bomb on Hiroshima. Her death joined them, fixed into the annual calendar to remind him ever more of her life and his loss.

Karui came to see if he wanted anything. He did not say what he wanted to say. He might have been able to convert his confused feelings into Kikuyu but not into English. The links were too complicated, too premeditated. Malcolm declined and sent him off duty. There were words of course.

'Goodnight, Karui.'

'Goodnight, sah'.

The same words as spoken on any other day but on this special day their tone was soaked in desolation. So many normal words used on this day of searing abnormality. No. No. No.

It was not Malcolm, but Karui, who got drunk that night sitting alone in his cabin. A lonely, intense, quiet drunkenness leading to a sleep which quelled all demons. The demons had time to spend on Malcolm instead. He lay in their double bed but occupied only his half of it, pushing her pillows off when they confirmed her absence. Her scoured the walls of their bedroom the surface as stark and unrewarding in the moonlit walls of Flynn's church. That night again he thought of a female breast. This time its creamy whiteness was crossed with a jagged gash leaving the flesh exposed. It was not pulsating comfortingly; it was cold and still and it would not let him sleep.

TWENTY-FIVE

The following morning Flynn appeared at the bungalow. He had slept little and had been praying in his church since dawn. The bruising of his faith the previous evening had troubled him much. He realised how untested it had been in recent years. He duty now was to support a fellow human being in his darkest hour and this he had done for his African flock for decades. Now it was a fellow European that was in need and he wondered if that made any difference. Had he become insulated from the emotional aspects of his parishioners' trials? Instead of offering brotherly love to the Africans had he merely given paternalistic protection?

He was in better spirit now the sun had risen. If Brendan Behan was a daylight atheist, then Joseph Flynn could be a daylight believer. For the both of these Irish men the night would bring doubts. Here in the sunshine some purpose could be discerned. If he could not offer the conventional comforts of the church, he could offer the informal support of common humanity.

Karui was in the kitchen as the priest approached the house. His head was still muzzy and his mouth furry; both would clear as the day progressed. His spirit, the one that took him through the tests of life, would take longer to recover from the previous day. He showed Flynn to the veranda where Malcolm was toying with his breakfast. James was sitting with him, seemingly unaffected by the previous day's events. Flynn stroked the boy's head as he passed behind him. James ducked his head to remove himself from the contact. The priest sat in Alison's chair now surrendering its ownership and looked at Malcolm strangely uncertain about conversation.

Flynn began conventionally, 'I am so, so sorry.'

He reached to touch Malcolm's hand lying on the table but Malcolm withdrew it.

'I've prayed for you. I'm suppose you think me foolish. But I get help that way and we all need help. It's awful thinking there is no help to our desperation,' the priest was speaking to Malcolm but thinking about himself as well as his friend.

Despair is certainly what Malcolm was feeling. During that night he had revisited his cold upbringing and how Alison had brought a warmth which had transformed him. Now that warmth was disappearing and the cold fingers of the past had already touched him, numbing the joyousness he had begun to take as normal.

'Thank you.' The simple reply seemed best and he was not seeking some philosophical discussion like the ones they had shared on Flynn's veranda in the past.

'Did you sleep?' the brevity of Flynn's enquiry was unusual.

'No.' Then remembering the moment he had woken up and found the bed empty beside him, the missing pillows making his aloneness even more stark, Malcolm added, 'Yes in the end.'

'She was a fine woman.' To describe her in more detail, to fashion adjectives which failed Malcolm's test of her importance would have been unfortunate. But Flynn was not thinking that deeply. He was trying, only, to keep a flow of words between them.

'Yes'.

For both men conversation was inadequate. Both needed to hold each other and expunge their grief with tears. Neither could manage it, inhibited by James's presence and by their own staid conventions. Malcolm turned his face away from the table to prevent tears. His son looked up at him his head to one side, one eye closed to see against the sun shining low in his face.

'I cannot talk much now. I'm too confused. I have to go to Nairobi and make the funeral arrangements and I've got to pick up Alison's parents. Can I come and see you this evening?'

'Of course. Anytime at all. Can I do anything?'

Yes. Yes. Bring her back for me. I want the warmth of her, a weary thought not said.

'No. No, thank you. There is nothing can be done. You cannot bring her back. Even your God will not bring her back.'

Malcolm had intended tired irony but to Flynn's confused mind it sounded like sarcasm. But he had not lost the capacity to forgive. Then turning to more practical things Malcolm said. 'Yes, there is something. Here are my insurance documents. Can you contact the insurers, report the accident and see what should be done about the car? You can use the phone in the office. And can you just be around?' he looked at his son.

Flynn was pleased to have a concrete job to do. 'Yes, I can see to that, leave it with me. Don't you worry about a thing. I've got to go back to the church first but I'll come straight back. I'll see you later. Bye James.'

The little boy had been listening to the conversation but not part of it. Now given attention he dropped his head back to his breakfast plate. He didn't need either of these men today; his daily routine with Hannah and adventures with Gitau would be quite enough.

The priest left to walk back to the village. Today he did not notice the buzzing insects, the raucous birds, the high clouds feathering a clear blue sky. His head was bowed. Today, and not for the first time, he carried another's burden; that he did so out of his duty rather than the other's need was not the issue. How long would he have the strength for this he wondered.

'I've got to go shortly. I think you should stay here with Hannah and Gitau. I'm going to fetch nanna and granna.' The two names the boy had for his grandparents brought a hint of warmth to the barren explanation. Malcolm thought about explaining that these two people were Alison's mummy and daddy, that they would be upset as husband and son had been. But he had no idea what concepts James had of the relationship nor how to put it into words. He was conscious how little he had talked to his son as opposed to reading him stories or giving him explanations and instructions. The shortfall was too big to make up today.

They walked out to the car and Hannah appeared from the kitchen to take charge of James. Karui watched the group his eyes red from a night of alcohol and tears. Malcolm unlocked the car door and turned to say goodbye but James was already running to the rear of the office where he had seen Gitau heading for the allotment.

At the hospital Malcolm sat in the office signing certificates and forms. The almoner advised on a suitable undertaker and made the arrangements for the body to be collected. Alison and he had rarely discussed wills and funerals, these seeming far away possibilities in their minds but he knew Alison wished to be cremated. He read his copy of the autopsy. Its medical jargon neutralised any trauma the description might contain so he missed the significance of the sentence It is likely she died instantaneously. He saw the implication much later when he reread the account. Likely? Likely!

There was one passage he did not miss. Alison had been two months pregnant. He wondered why she had not mentioned it. Perhaps she wasn't certain, but surely, she would be after two months. Perhaps she wanted to tell her mother first or perhaps she was holding it back conscious of the pressures of his working life.

As he left the hospital, the doctor he had seen yesterday rushed past him alongside a trolley. On it a young girl was connected by tubes to various pieces of equipment. He glanced up to avoid a collision but did not recognise Malcolm. Malcolm watched the trolley surge down a corridor its path another journey from light to dark, hope to despair. Yesterday, Today and Tomorrow.

Alison's parents, John and Hilary Parkinson, were both second generation settlers having come to Tanganyika from Northern Rhodesia to establish a sisal plantation. With the tenacity to tame barren land and the luck to catch a global demand for the product they had become wealthy. Their needs and aspirations were simple, some might say narrow. Their chief pleasure was in their daughter. True, with no son, they did not expect the farm to stay with the family but nationalist ambition would discourage them from an extension of their tenure. They took the easiest solution and sold out at the height of the market. Not being citizens, they had no rights to remain but were staying as long as they could. Their wealth and their British citizenship would keep them secure in a poor foreign land.

Malcolm's agricultural background might have enabled him to take over the farm but by the time he had married Alison the farm had long since been sold. They had finally approved of the match seeing Malcolm's quietness as an antidote to their daughter's gregarious behaviour which they could not help but equate with licentiousness. Her period in London had caused them great disquiet and even Nairobi, though nearer home, was still stamped with the stain of Happy Valley-ism. They knew nothing of her affairs thinking her lovers merely boyfriends. Like many parents they fondly imagined their daughter to be still a virgin, to them still holding pigtailed innocence.

He saw them emerge from the baggage area seemingly older than he had remembered. They looked around more used to seeking their daughter's face and taking some time to see Malcolm even though his face was a minority white. They stood for a moment all uncertain whether to embrace or not; in the end neutral formality prevailed.

The sheer mechanics of getting their luggage to the car and of negotiating the exit to the airport muted the conversation and stifled the emotion. The drive around the outskirts of Nairobi and up the Kimura road was more difficult. Long silences separated bouts of cliched questions and evasive answers. The scenes along the road, captivating to newcomers, were routine for these experienced residents.

As they crossed the Changa bridge a recovery truck was reversing to the edge of the ravine. Flynn's Catholic contacts had found a garage owner and secured some speedy action. The unfortunate consequence of this was the highlighting of the site of Alison's accident. If Malcolm had had any thoughts of not showing the Parkinson's where their daughter had been killed, they were undermined by his friend's efficiency. He slowed and explained but did not stop. In his mirror he could see Mrs Parkinson turn to look out of the rear window.

James was waiting when they arrived. The dust from the car would have been seen long before the vehicle came into view and Hannah had put James on alert for its coming, encouraging him to stand in the branches of a frangipani tree as a lookout. The many branches of the short tree made ideal footholds and were strong enough to take his small weight.

The youngster hugged the older people with genuine warmth and recognition. Like all grandparents, their manner held less tension than those of the intervening generation. A frangipani flower had fallen inside James's shirt. The hugging squashed it against his back and he squirmed away to remove the damp remains. Neither grandparents nor grandchild would mention the person who linked them.

They took afternoon tea on the veranda. When a tea cup rattled against its saucer as a shaking hand sought to bring them together it was Mr Parkinson who was the cause. Karui was more smartly dressed than usual sensing the importance of the occasion and remembering older European women's sharper interest in protocol. None of the eaters was aware the fruit cake they were eating had been made by Alison on the day before her death, but for Karui it was a suitable present from their dead child.

Afterwards Malcolm took his in-laws to the bungalow across the square. James led the way with a confidence borne of familiarity of the compound which was his world. Hannah stayed in the shade of the tree in the square not wishing to visit again the scene where her lover had killed himself. She still lived in the servant's block and had been allowed to do so even though she had, for a while, lost her official links with the station. Malcolm had always avoided the decision to ask her to leave; a sin of omission for him, an assumed charity by her. She had nowhere to go; she was not of the village and for reasons best known to her would not return home. Nairobi was a possibility but there only slum life would provide shelter and prostitution provide food. Even here some men from the village had offered her money for sex; for a while she resisted. Now she was employed again, but for how long? In Malcolm's life Alison's death meant one thing, in Hannah's quite another. The unemployment which might flow from it could mean a sort of death too; that of independence, of integrity, of self-respect.

The Parkinson's unpacked while Malcolm took his son back to their home to have his supper and go to bed. As Malcolm sat on the veranda watching James play bread soldiers with his boiled eggs, he remembered he had forgotten he had promised to go to see Flynn. There would be no opportunity today so he told Hannah go to Flynn's house and tell the priest he would come up for afternoon tea tomorrow. In the meantime, he would bath James and put him to bed.

Further up the valley the old priest receiving Malcolm's message left his veranda where he had been waiting for two hours and walked down to the rocks at the corner of the road. He stumbled slightly over the uneven downward path at the side of his garden. From the shadows of the house Wambui watched him go.

At the corner he sat on his favourite rock and could just make out the mountain in the dying sky its snow cap caught by the setting sun. He looked up to where the stars were multiplying in a sky now losing its blue daytime fullness and easing through paleness to a black ceiling. At times this sky would display sparkling diamonds of light in a soft warm protective surround. But tonight, it was a hard metal hemi-sphere the stars searing exits from a hellish inferno beyond. Fear not comfort was its message. The quiet of the nightfall, the high barrier of the heavens and the distant walls of the valley made Flynn feel insignificant. He prayed that evening, not sitting rejoicing at the peacefulness of it all but head bowed, hands clasped tightly, eyes closed against the world, fashioned into a small aloneness. He was praying to his own God but was comforted that Ngai was looking down on him.

Malcolm had given no thought to what he and the Parkinson's would do in the days before the funeral. They had been little time to think and, so far, all their activities had been conditioned by practicalities. At dinner the previous evening Alison's parents said they wished to see her body. Malcolm had been unprepared for this already concluding that the body that lay on a hospital slab had little to do with the person he had known. Her body had been a pleasing aspect but it was her spirit, her confidence, her understanding that he had loved and they had been swept away in the ravine.

By phoning the hospital he found the body had been removed to a chapel of rest and it was here that the three mourners went. Malcolm did not want to see his wife's body again and he remained near the door as her parents looked into the casket. He tried not to look at their distress, the way their reserve crumbled into deep sobbing. Two bodies, initially separate and upright, hung together in inelegant and heaving embrace. He envied them their physical contact.

They lunched in Nairobi. Little was said or eaten. For a while Mrs Parkinson, seeking the blame for the loss of her daughter, had thought Malcolm should not have let her go back to work. She had not voiced this but kept it as a secret sour judgement. By now the irrationality of the argument had blunted her accusation and she knew Alison was strong enough and independent enough to make her own decisions and Malcolm far from being a culprit was a compliant victim of the whole affair.

When they had driven into Nairobi, Malcolm had indicated again where the accident had taken place but had not stopped merely slowing as much to save their own skins from the oncoming traffic as any salute to Alison. Now on the return he stopped just short of the bridge on the top of the hill which contained the ravine. He pulled off the roadside forcing the pedestrians to walk on the road itself or on the rockier surface beyond. Several muttered their objections but their complaints went unheeded by the car's occupants. From their position they could see the rockiness of the ravine although not the stream itself. Nor could they see the paint marks on the rocks where Alison's car had been winched up before being taken to the scrap yard in Nairobi. They would not see either, just as the scavengers had not, some of Alison's personal belongings that had got lost between the rocks of the river bed, a small address book, a set of keys, a tube of lipstick. Here they were to lie undiscovered slowly decaying in the hot sun and the torrential rain, the dying tentacles that tied her life to others.

That afternoon Malcolm kept his appointment with Flynn. The priest talked but not of any consequence. His habit of lengthy and often interesting discourse was letting him down. But he knew that any conversation however superficial was better than the prolonged silence he knew Malcolm would withdraw into. He understood Malcolm would reject prayer but could find little substitute to this ritualised grief.

After tea the priest suggested they went to the rocks. As they descended the path Malcolm looked back at the veranda and more precisely at the bush beside it - the Yesterday, Today and Tomorrow tree. It was in bloom but if some were the blooms of yesterday none were the blooms of last week and none would be blooming a week from now. The two men had spent many hours discussing this tree over the years and it had become a useful metaphor for much of life's birth and decay. Now it held a more personal essence.

'We are like those blooms, aren't we?' Malcolm's question not wanting an answer. 'Even after we're born, we lie in a bud waiting for some calling, some stimulus to bring us to bloom, some warmth to bring out our rich colour. And then our life is full and fulfilled.' The clumsy alliteration unintended and unnoticed 'But it won't go one for ever. It's a short life. Shorter for some than others. And then only the dead head remains.'

Flynn nodded and looking beyond the veranda to the cross on the roof of his church nodded again and sighed, 'Yes'.

The priest recovered from the melancholy first. His ability to see his life in a wider context saved him. 'Yes. Yes. But there are always new buds coming through to brighten and enrich the world.'

The fate of world was not at the forefront of Malcolm's mind. He was concerned only for himself and he felt himself dying. The two men, the older one bruised but resilient, the other battered and resigned, continued the journey to their open-air shrine. Here they sat mostly in silence. Flynn had lost his usual loquacity and spent more time thinking of himself than his vocation would have approved. A slight chill as a cloud passed in front of the rapidly lowering sun brought both of them to action.

'I know that any help I can give will not be enough but you must find some comfort and I may be the only one who can give,' Flynn was right even if impertinent to say so. 'Don't forget James will need you. You might find giving help to him is a way of getting help yourself.' The priest was thinking of himself again.

Malcolm was about to admit he might be incapable of giving anything to his son but the thought was too despairing to utter no matter how close to the truth it was. The priest wanted to reach out a hold Malcolm to him realising the close physical contact with another human being was often better than words. A professional caution came over him. The action should come from Malcolm. Malcolm oblivious to the possibility turned to go.

'Come whenever you want. I'm always here,' called Flynn after him. Always here, he said to himself.

As if the act of walking had set his emotional preoccupations aside, he realised the kindness Flynn had shown. He turned to say thank you but the priest had turned away to face the mountain and was sitting with his face bowed. Without saying anything Malcolm continued home. As he passed the village Ngugi approached, not now a ragamuffin but a mature teenager in shirt and slacks. The quality of his clothes, though unremarkable in Nairobi, made him seem here a stranger out of his usual habitat.

They shook hands and Ngugi expressed the sadness he and his family felt putting into language what his father had felt unable to do. Malcolm learnt that Ngugi was finishing his Higher School Certificate - English Literature, Economics and History - and was hoping to go to university although the finance would be a problem. Malcolm had continued to pay Ngugi's school fees and the young man was hoping that by bringing up the matter of university fees now Malcolm might entertain the idea of paying these too. That Alison's salary would no longer be available, that he might have to pay fees for his own son and that he had not given a thought to his future plans deterred Malcolm from any commitment.

For the funeral Malcolm wore the suit in which he had been interviewed for the overseas post those many years ago. He had worn it to his parents' funeral too. There had been no occasion to buy another and it was rather tight on his ageing body.

At the chapel of rest, he had placed a flower in the casket with Alison. It was a bloom from the Yesterday, Today and Tomorrow tree and it was now bruised after being carried in the suit pocket. He had thought of putting it in her hand but a cloth revealed only her face. He placed it against her face tucking its stem inside the surrounding cloth. There it held, its colour contrasting with the, now artificial, paleness of her skin. The mortician smiled professionally as he closed the lid, the screwdriver for securing it already in the pocket of his black jacket. Unknown to either of them the flower, disturbed by the movement of the coffin, would fall from its resting place long before Alison's body succumbed to the flames.

The service was functional, conducted with dispassionate compassion by a cleric who knew none of them. As the casket withdrew behind the curtains Malcolm did not cry, he had already reverted to the man he used to be. He did however think of the two-month-old foetus dying before it had been fully alive - before it could be unhappy Malcolm decided.

There was a buffet meal at the hotel where Malcolm had stayed on first arrival. George Kariuki had brought Ngugi and Flynn. Malcolm noted how confidently Ngugi took his place and contrasted him with the urchin who took to the streets on his first day in Kenya. He conversed with the Parkinson's but his colonial education was so far in advance of their colonial experience that no real dialogue took place.

James without Hannah or Gitau to turn to had to rely on his father. He filled his plate with food from the main table and brought it over to his father for explanation of its content. In doing so he spilled bits from the plate which his hands were not quite strong enough to keep level. It was his first experience alone and he would find the world did not always behave as he wished.

That night at Kimura Malcolm and the Parkinson's discussed the future.

'We will make an annual allowance for James's education and upkeep until the age of 21. Should either of us survive to that time we will review the position. Should we both die our estate will go into a trust for James to be available to him in two instalments at 21 and 25. Our solicitors in Moshi will handle everything.' Mr Parkinson had taken refuge in this planning which had occupied his mind and blunted his feelings. The arrangements appealed to Malcolm too and he saw nothing unnatural or unsatisfactory about not being directly included.

Mrs Parkinson had some proposals too. 'We want to create a small memorial to Alison but we're not sure what to do. The way things are going there won't be many people left in Africa who'll remember her. Apart from you and James, I mean,' she concluded hurriedly. Her assumption they would remain there went unremarked.

An inspiration took hold of Malcolm. 'Alison and I have been sponsoring Ngugi - the young man you met at the funeral - through school. He's a very clever boy who should go further - university I mean. You could set up a trust in her name to support him. I think Alison would have liked that.' He had no idea where the thought came from nor whether Alison would have approved but he took pleasure in the sleight of hand. Though not an initiative the Parkinson's would have made left to themselves, they had been sufficiently impressed with Ngugi's cleverness they saw the merit of the proposal and acquiesced.

'Yes. Good idea. I like that. I'll see to it.'

'Yes. Alison would have liked that.' Mrs Parkinson presumed as much as Malcolm but took shelter in the certainties of the two men.

Malcolm did not feel he had exploited the Parkinson's any more than they had exploited Tanganyika. The appropriateness of the outcome seemed to far outweigh the machinations that brought it to life and Malcolm felt a rare glow of satisfaction.

It was agreed that Alison's ashes would be scattered on the Ngong hills overlooking the Rift Valley. It was a decision which was profoundly moving as much as it was sentimental. There seemed no long-term future for the Parkinson's in Tanzania and yet Alison belonged nowhere but Africa. The day before the parents left, the three drove up to the top of the Ngong Hills overlooking Nairobi on one side and plunging into the Rift Valley on the other. They left the car and, carrying the casket that contained Alison's ashes, walked self-consciously and guiltily to the down slope of the hills. In the distance stood a Masai man and youth tending two cows. Their presence only fuelled the guilt of the three Europeans. This was Masai country; were they about to defile it? The three sat on the same boulder hoping their actions would be hidden from the native inhabitants. Malcolm unscrewed the top of the urn and passed the container to Mrs Parkinson. She leant forward to pour the ashes over the ground and Mr Parkinson griped her arm to stop her falling down the steep slope. His unexpected action caused the smooth urn to slip from his wife's grasp and it fell forward to the edge of the hillside. There it caught a rock and catapulted over the edge. Gathering speed, it rotated in the air scattering Alison's ashes as though in a Catherine wheel. Her remains far from being discreetly scattered on the ground were spread more effectively over Africa than had been planned.

The three people reached after it but could do no more than watch their beloved Alison catch the swirling wind and float away high over the Rift Valley. Mrs Parkinson collapsed in tears into the arms of her husband. Malcolm too had tears in his eyes as a piece of dust lodged under his eyelid; even in death Alison contrived to affect him. The lid of the urn was to become one of those possessions he dared not throw away.

After composing themselves the three mourners returned to their car and the two Masai watched them go before returning to their vigil. The wind scattered Alison's ashes far across the landscape. Ashes to ashes; dust to dust. She returned to the land into which she was born leaving Malcolm alone.

TWENTY-SIX

The following years were barren ones for Malcolm. It would not be a complete return to the anguish of his youth since Alison's effect on him would never completely wither. James, without the warmth of his mother and with the coldness of his father, grew older with important elements of life missing. If he was not damaged, he was bruised. For a few years he found a gentle security and love with his ayah, Hannah, and from Gitau who was able to stimulate and encourage the boy more than his own father. The relationship between this young child and two people of a different race was considerable and their mark would always be on him even if he did not recognise it.

When Malcolm had sole charge of James the club was an easy solution to leisure time. Here father and son were showered with genuine concern and sympathy. Many of the older members had experienced tragedy. Logan, the President, was patiently solicitous. He did not discuss the loss of friends in wartime, the death of a son in the Emergency, the passing of his own wife through cancer but if he saw Malcolm, he always stopped to pass the time of day, his conversations unfailing polite and discreet. Unlike Malcolm his sadness did not turn him in on himself but caused him to seek compensation in the well-being of others. It was a compassionate instinct rather than a philosophy and it had no name. Nor did it have a precise origin but grew and developed in the man as he passed through life.

At the first Christmas the usual card, from the Hindu to the atheist, arrived from PK. Malcolm remembered that he had not told PK of Alison's death. He wrote back and received PK's reply by return. The letter was in precise and impeccable English and through it, with its perceptive phrases, came a touching tribute to Alison's personality. Malcolm saw his wife through the considered eyes of another, confirming his loss.

At seven James went to a preparatory school in Nairobi where he boarded with other expatriate children. What had been until then an emotional distance between him and his father became a geographical one too. He would return home in the school holidays where his attachment to Gitau and Hannah would wither. Hannah had been sacked when James went to school but Malcolm allowed her to continue living in the servants' quarters with her son. Then one day Hannah left. She told no one of her going and it was recorded only by her absence. She disappeared starting a life that might have little significance other than its end. Gitau remained, indispensable and indestructible. He understood the changing needs of the growing James and did not resent the boy's declining interest. But he did see the growing white male eroding the openness of their relationship. At this he was sad although his feelings were not directed at James personally; he was merely a symptom. Constancy, continuity, certainty were victims of this modern age.

As James made friendships at school, he accepted invitations to stay at friends' homes during the holidays. Malcolm acquiesced, accepting that Kimura had little to offer, but gloomy in the thought that other people's homes seemed more attractive than his own. If there was an upside it was that the routines of his life would not be disturbed and he would not have to entertain James with trips to Nairobi and beyond. The cosy and unchallenging routines of his life would not be disturbed.

The three years until James was ten were a period of stocktaking for Malcolm. He had no wish to seek other female friendships. Sex was an irrelevance. What Alison had brought was more than that; it was a liberation of his whole being from the stagnation of his upbringing. It could never be repeated and he would never recover from it being snatched away from him. If his abstinence was complete one incident might have blemished his record. One day not long after

James's departure for boarding school he was sitting at his desk in the main office. He was beginning to feel the loss of James's company and this increased his feeling of loneliness. He saw Hannah cross the square moving slowly in the afternoon heat. She was no longer the slim girl he had first met but a woman with a full body. As she climbed the steps the movement gave her body shape and strength. Malcolm remembered, long ago, her gentle undulating breast and for moment he longed for her. Not for sex, though some strong conditioned drive might deny that, but for comfort. He wanted that warm body to pull itself around him burying his head as he felt only live human sensation. He recovered; it was an illusion. He said nothing; he did nothing. By coincidence he did not see Hannah again for that was the day of her leaving.

He continued to go to the club but he was not the same person there that he was before the accident. Then, he was the gauche young man, patronised by his elders for his inexperience, disparaged by his peer group for his un-athleticism. But Alison's death had changed his status completely. The tragedy had given him a gravitas that brought respect. Obviously, it was thought, one who had so suffered must have some character, some resolve, even some longings, that less suffering people could not have. Gaps opened up as he approached the bar, heads nodded in solicitous greeting, even the staff seemed more attentive. He resumed bridge playing and here his delay in playing a card was not taken as naive uncertainty, but as thoughtful deliberation calculated to bring home a trick.

He certainly had female attention. The doyens of the settler generation, aware of the cruelties of African life, enquired sensitively and caringly of his health. Younger, less thoughtful women, married and unmarried, tested his availability, not that he had good looks but because they believed, or wanted to believe, that deep inside this man who had suffered so much there must be some dark and exciting feelings waiting to be laid at a female breast. Silence became strength, moodiness became emotion and daydreaming became thoughtful

250

detachment. So, to the outer world he grew but in his private world he shrivelled. He declined invitations, to the Caledonian dinner and elsewhere. He shunned gatherings that had no specific purpose. He conversed when approached but chose to sit at the end of the veranda drinking afternoon tea defying all but the most persistent of social animals.

But to make it all bearable there was Flynn. For three years these two men, so unlike in many ways, leant against each other for strength. Removing one would have the other fall. Several times a week - they had to actively avoid making it every day - they shared their private time. Malcolm showed his friend how to play cards - whist, cribbage even brag. Once they decided to make a bridge partnership but despite all the theory and tortured rehearsal never felt confident to tackle bridge night at the club. They took to days out in Malcolm's car. A day at the races recalled Flynn's childhood; his father had been a betting man but he would not bet himself. They went to the open-air cinema and sat enraptured at the celluloid adventures.

Earlier in their lives they had discussed the big issues of politics, religion and philosophy - big in their minds anyway. But now wearying of the irreconcilability of their views and worrying about the inadequacies of their own beliefs, they lowered their sights. So, in a sense their lives became more trivial and in consequence they were more at ease in them. The Yesterday, Today and Tomorrow tree brought forth succeeding generations and grew to the height of the veranda. The two men referred to it less often, avoiding its implications for their own mortality. Their friendship had never been declared but was real enough. Whether they would have been friends in a wider circle was not asked by either of them. Here they were forced, by circumstances, into each other's orbit and each found his own satisfaction in it.

Malcolm's professional life was coming to an end here. The agencies gave notice of the withdrawal of funds and the station closed.

Even though this was predictable for many years Malcolm failed to acknowledge its reality nor plan for its implementation. Eventually he accepted he would have to return to the UK and was lucky enough to secure a lectureship in tropical agriculture at one of the many new universities that had sprung up. James would come with him to attend boarding school in the UK and through this their dual existences would run parallel.

The closure of the station shocked him. At the end only he and Gitau were running the experiments. Gitau would have a month's notice and two months wages and Malcolm had to break the news to the labourers. At first, they all reported for duty and did nothing. After a few days of absurdity Malcolm told the men to go as soon as they arrived to work. The plants grew untended. Gitau and Malcolm would watch them through the wire mesh fence. It occurred to both of them that their efforts over the last few years had been a waste of time. The meticulously weighed fertiliser, the measured watering, the detailed record keeping, all these things that underpinned the importance of their own jobs had been a waste of time. And for how long? Had such a project ever had any effect on the life of the country? Were thousands of small farmers doing exactly what they would have done without the benefits of this research. They declined to decide the issue lest it diminished them.

He delayed telling Karui because he knew he was not just sacking his long-standing servant he was probably ending his employment for ever. He needn't have been quite so bashful, as Karui knew on the grapevine as soon as Gitau did. He had known Karui for a long time, but never met any of his family. His daily companion had been greying when he first arrived and now his hair was nearly white. The tribal scars so glaringly evident at first had long disappeared from notice as the man's personality outgrew his aspect. There was no final speech, no leaving present, no glowing testimonial. The low key of the dismissal suited them both. Malcolm gave him six months wages and shook his hand. What else to do?

And on Malcolm's last day on the station a man arrived from the ministry. Malcolm, anticipating his coming, had meticulously locked very door, labelled every key, crated all the research records and turned off the electricity generator which provided power for the buildings and pumped water from the bore-hole. Climbing into his car he dropped Gitau off at the village and went to take his leave of Flynn. He did not say formal farewells to either of them dodging the emotion of the occasion. They were both coming to the airport so he reasoned it should be delayed until then.

On his way back he stopped in the road alongside Kimura station for one last look. He would not know that Karui, with his own secreted key, had let himself back into his quarters and would remain there hoping for something to turn up. There was no tap water and no electricity but, although he had grown used to such things, their lack was no great privation to a man whose village, high up in the Aberdares, had neither.

To Malcolm it was deserted. All the life, and death, it had seen. All the energy, the dedication, the kinship, the achievement - solid virtues so often overlooked in the diary of a life - all gone now. Where? He drove off down the dirt track failing to ride the ridges in his eagerness to get away, straddling the dual track and out onto the main road to Nairobi.

He could not fail to cross the Changa bridge. Was he to stop, to get out, to revisit Alison's accident, to mourn her death, to honour her life? He had visited the scene on the anniversary of her death each year. On the first occasion he felt he ought to commemorate it, social convention rather than need. There was no grave, so a visit to Changa bridge was all that was left. And it became a habit, no more than that. Each year resting his arms on the wall of the bridge he stared into the ravine. It seemed unchanging but each year had eroded the few tangible remnants of Alison's life trapped below its rocks. On this last passage he chose, yes chose, not to stop. Such decisions, each both big and small in their way, are no better made by careful deliberation than by casual instinct. And that is what determined his action that last day.

He had sold his own car and the hired one he had been using was picked up from the hotel where he spent his first night in Kenya and where he would spend his last. It had been an emotional day. Kimura station was no more; the freight handlers had arrived, only an hour late, to claim the bulk of his belongings. James had arrived at the hotel delivered by the family of a school friend. He would have liked the comforting symmetry of being in the same room as the one he spent his first night in, but he had been allocated a twin room with James.

In the early evening they sat at the outside tables, Malcolm with his beer, his son with a cola and crisps. The father's mind was full of memories but empty of expectation. Years before he had sat here, a single man not fully developed, at the start of a new phase of his life and with no idea of what the future would hold. Looking back, it had held so much drama, not the drama of international incident or public recognition, but the quiet hidden play of family life. The joy, the satisfaction, the hope of this time had been substantial although they had been overshadowed by Alison's death. He had wanted the good bits but life had given him the whole package. There was no point it wishing it had been different.

If he had arrived alone, he was leaving with something significant. His son might carry those qualities Alison had had in abundance; they could still live in him. But what else did this young person carry? He had had to take the full package too and all its contents had made him what he was now. James toyed with the large moths and beetles as they attacked their table lamp, offering them crisps in flight. His face, lit from different angles as he ducked this way and that, showed Alison in every aspect. After a while Malcolm became mesmerised by this hypnotic effect which took away his disorganised thoughts of the past and delayed the need to consider the future. They went to bed at the same time, late for the one, early for the other.

Back in their room they were as physically close as they had been since James had been a toddler. Yet they skirted each other not intentionally but habitually. If only Malcolm had been able to say something profound and sincere, to reach out and touch his son, to turn the physical contact into a conduit for his emotions. But he couldn't do it and the two climbed into their respective beds as remote as they had been before. Both slept well, the father tired with the full emotions of the day, the son in childish ignorance.

The days leading up to the departure had been full of the rituals all returning expatriates face - the exchange of addresses, the farewell suppers, the prolonged emigration procedures, more buff forms, credit control. At the last, came the final farewells, stretched to the near unbearable by airport delays. Flynn was there to see them off and the priest had brought Gitau with him. They had set out early to ensure the succession of buses they needed to catch would deliver them in time. Gitau had no prospect of work now the station had closed and would have no paid work for the rest of his life. He was beginning to go grey and bald. His tidy raincoat covered clothes that Malcolm guessed were not his own.

James could give no more than a formal farewell to Gitau, what they had shared conveniently shelved in his hidden mental archives. The European boy fashioned by an expatriate school life and threatened by his own hormones betrayed the intimacy of his African childhood. Gitau, though not surprised, remained disappointed by an indifference which was alien to his culture but which he feared would run through his people like the diseases of long ago. His own son, Ngugi, had begun to display this and had begun to seem uncomfortable in the village when home from university. He was now in America on a scholarship in Business Administration and his father wondered what cultural disease he would catch there.

As the plane left the tarmac Malcolm looked beyond his son in the window seat and saw the setting sun scatter shadows across the brown landscape. It soared above the Ngong Hills. Was Alison watching, tears in her fragmented eyes? The plane banked towards Europe. As it did so he saw the snow-capped peak of Mount Kenya flash in the sunlight. Ngai was looking down on his people and guarding their interests and offering hope. In an instant all would disappear as the plane burst through a bank of cloud into the bright clear sky above. The man and his son were taking their memories with them. Those of the first would crystallise into crude forms and hurt his emotions with their sharp edges, those of the second would diffuse into the melting pot of adolescence. The origins of the memories were the same but they would not be shared.

TWENTY-SEVEN

The inactivity of the flight allowed the trauma and distress of the previous year to crystallise into deep trepidation about the future. During those twelve months his daily routines had blurred the apprehension that had inhabited him. But here in this cocoon, only his mind had anything to do and the boredom of the long flight gave no barrier to his unease. When he had left, nearly twenty years ago, he had hoped to be leaving behind the legacy of his childhood. The focus of his unhappiness, his sister Marion, had been metaphorically stranded on her island birthplace leaving him unburdened in the lands beyond. This image, simplistic as it was, was a potent one which he had clung to for many years. But now he was returning to Marion's realm. Was she still there to haunt him, to undo all the good done to him and for him by his new home and by Alison? He was not the same man. With maturity and security, he had learnt to face his demons down. But his personal aid workers - Alison, Gitau and Flynn - were not with him now. Could he keep his strength without them and with the lengthening shadows of middle age even now dogging his mind as they snagged at his body. He had left so much behind. Two men, Gitau and Flynn, with whom he had shared so much, he might never see again. He realised, too, the home comforts he was leaving. Now there would be meals to cook, clothes to wash, floors to clean. Where would the time come from? That these activities would provide a cycle of work which would blot out his unhappiness was not then apparent.

For a younger man this change of direction might have been welcomed, presenting a challenge and an incentive. For Malcolm it meant neither of these things. His change or direction had not been sought; it had forced itself upon him. He did not need an incentive and he was too old to relish a challenge. He was afraid; afraid of returning to an academic life that might have left him behind ignoring the real-life lessons of his African experience. Even more afraid of an expected loneliness. He had over time and often with Alison's help overcome his unease in human company. Now he was going to have to meet new people at ease in their own world and all the inhibitions of his earlier life returned. His preoccupation with his own insecurities robbed him of any thought about his son who would have to find his own salvation. It never occurred to Malcolm that James might be the means of retaining his confidence and refreshing the influence of his wife. But James, his potential life jacket, would float away on the swells of life.

Delays in Rome had pushed their arrival into day time and the descent into London accelerated his despair. The bright sunshine above the clouds giving way, after a period of misty gloom, to the more persistent graphite-grey of a damp English day. The rooftops and roads darkened by the rain gave no welcome only a mute acceptance of another intruder from above.

PK was there to greet them. He had left for the UK when his family no longer felt secure in Kenya. For him it had been an unwelcome if not unexpected interruption in his life. His people, like those in any diaspora, had retained a protective strand in their social culture that anticipated upheaval, an abandoning of territory, a loss of security, a diminution of status determinedly won from nothing. They would move with a collective sigh and start again seeking acceptance, suspicious about assimilation and fearing envy.

PK and Malcolm had been very close in the early days. Malcolm's relationship with PK had been a counterpoint to that with Flynn. Whereas Flynn was relaxed, open, imaginative and iconoclastic, PK was altogether more restrained. Both he and Malcolm were closeted in their own worlds, PK in his cultural compound and Malcolm in his emotional stockade. Their friendship was cordial, formal, restrained not like true friendship which is unguarded and capricious. Their greeting was a handshake not a hug neither man looking for more. Their formality spared James his adolescent blushes as he stood, an appendage to the reunion.

PK drove them to the hotel he had booked for them and arranged to meet for lunch the next day before delivering them to the station for their onward journey.

James, not quite old enough to want or to be permitted his own freedom, sat with them in a pleasant restaurant transformed from a failed dress shop by a theme which caused no offence or attention.

PK was working as a booking clerk with British Rail, his Indian qualification and African experience disregarded. He and two brothers had taken over a chain of laundrettes which they hoped would lead to a bigger undertaking. Malcolm marvelled silently at this stoical adaptation in life style which for PK was unremarkable even satisfying.

As the restaurant filled up, he became aware how their table seemed to attract the attention of fellow diners. Looking up from his meal he would catch eyes being averted. It made him feel the centre of unwanted scrutiny. He had had that experience many times in his childhood when Marion's condition had had the same effect. There was no overt hostility, no obvious repugnance but eyes were drawn to her and by proximity to Malcolm. To his young eyes he, not Marion, was under the microscope. He imagined every conversation at every table was directed towards him and he had nowhere to hide. His pimpled face, his ill-fitting clothes were magnified by this attention. Life was singling him out from much needed obscurity because his sister dribbled and gurgled in her wheelchair. He wanted to shout out that she was not his sister, not the same genes, he was not abnormal. But he didn't. He could only shrink into the smallest body space he could create, keeping his face down above the plate in front of him avoiding, if not ignoring, the fellow eaters.

Today he realised that he was not the centre of attention. PK with the only brown skin in the room was now the magnet. That he was simply the thing in the room that was different did not dispel Malcolm's suspicion that his friend was the object of hostility, of sly comment, of conjured disdain. That these people, tired of shopping or bored with their companions, were aimlessly scanning the room finding PK a mild curiosity did not occur to Malcolm. He saw them as the same insensitive spectators that had seemed to blight his childhood. He had forgotten how he had stared at the beggars on his arrival in Nairobi. Within minutes he had cast these innocent eaters as racist bigots. Had he been capable of expressing outrage Malcolm would have stood up and harangued the diners although the effect on James might have replicated his own condition. He did not stand up but did what he always had and withdrew into himself. PK could not be blamed for seeing his reaction as disinterest.

Malcolm's interpretation of all this left him distressed. His African experience had seemed to pull a veil over a past in which he had felt exposed, ridiculed and condemned to being an outsider. There in the warmth, his past was unknown; he had been welcomed and been loved and had loved. The attitude of these diners seemed to wipe that all away. He looked at the door into the street and felt it an offered only an avenue back to his former misery. He excused himself and went to the toilet. The room was small and dank; the tap in the wash basin dripped. Malcolm went to the head-high window and looked out. Below four black youths lounged at the street corner swaying and bouncing to their radio. Their self-centred exuberance untypical of the black youths of Nairobi, their body language a threat by its inhibition rather than its intent. Bonds of tribe, of culture, of community had been snapped during their ancestor's itinerant past leaving flamboyant bravado to mask the gap. Beyond them ugly buildings rose from littered wasteland; their rooftops above were back-dropped by large rain clouds. How unlike the past twenty years. Gone the warmth, gone the innocence, gone the simplicity.

He turned the tap in the washbasin and scooped handfuls of cold water over his face bumping his head on the contraceptive machine on the wall. After drying himself with paper towels he returned to the table avoiding the eyes of diners as he emerged from the toilet door.

He found James and PK deep in conversation and re-experienced the envy he felt for those who could so easily engage with his son. They settled the bill and PK dropped them at the station to catch their train to a new destination; for neither would it be, or could it be, a home.

The university had arranged temporary accommodation in a house near the campus and it was here that Malcolm and James went the next day. The spare furnishing and spartan decoration reminded Malcolm of his first days at the station at Kimura and caused him no concern. He acquired a car and a bank account much as he had done in Nairobi, but this time he needed no minder.

James was to attend a boarding school. They had discussed the possibilities some months before. James sensed he would be alone whether he stayed with his father and attended a day school or if he boarded. The mutual indifference between father and son reduced any sadness in living apart and if they were to admit it was welcomed by both.

For James boarding school was a salvation. With his father he displayed a diffidence which seemed hereditary. But at school it was his mother's qualities of self-confidence and gregariousness that shone through, although he had little memory of her and would not have known the gifts she had left him. He found secure relationships with staff and pupils; had modest success with photographs in the school magazine and learnt when to be guarded and when to be uninhibited. He thought little about his father and when he did, thought little of him. He grew up with no real role model and so all the skills he developed were acquired rather than inherited. In a small way he had broken the cycle into which his father's life was turning him. That his rootlessness was reminiscent of Bernie's led to the possibility he would be left with no moral code, exploiting when he was strong and being exploited when he was weak. That he would end up killing himself like Bernie, seemed unlikely. Away from his father James grew into a sensitive and resourceful human being who was capable of sincere and lasting relationships. Only one side of his being remained undeveloped; his relationship with his father.

Malcolm was a little apprehensive about returning to academic life after such a gap. The university department had valued the practical experience shown in his application and wanted him to boost the utilitarian configuration of its staffing. In his earlier incarnation as a lecturer Malcolm had found it difficult to stand up and talk in front of a group of other people. He surprised himself by electing to do it but it had been a line of least resistance. Now his age and experience allowed him to engage in the task of teaching, if not with enthusiasm, then at least with competence and assurance. His insecurities could hide behind his seniority and his lectures would pass without serious exposure to challenge. His students valued his understated style and solid knowledge. In his tutorials, away from the spotlight, he showed a genuine concern with their difficulties in stark contrast to the attitude of some of his less-sensitive colleagues.

After a few months Malcolm moved into a two bedroomed house smaller than he could afford but as big as he wanted given his need to look after only himself. It was here he unpacked and displayed his few personal possessions. Many barely saw the light of day before being put at the back of a wardrobe when it became clear how out of place there were in his new home. There would be found the zebra skinned cigarette box, the soap stone napkin rings and the warrior shield. And with them more personal things whose presence jarred more because of the memories they revived than their aesthetic weakness - James's Hindu outfit, Karui's kikapu and the top from the urn of Alison's ashes. They would lie hidden year after year occasionally uncovered in the search for something else. And with their revelation small hooks of memory snagged in Malcolm's mind exciting feelings he had managed to subdue.

It was here he came after a day's work. He cooked in his small kitchen and sat in his front room reading or watching TV. He employed a cleaner, who he saw rarely, to do the routine household tasks. He found new walking opportunities in the distant hills but he could not find the enthusiasm to seek out a bridge club. He feared his mind was no longer sharp enough to work out which cards were in whose hands nor challenge opponents more proficient than those at the Phoenix Club.

For Malcolm it was years of solitude, his life reduced to routines. He was not unhappy but then happiness is something he had never aspired to. He was not fulfilled but then he never sought high achievement. He survived without distress and for him this was enough.

Although he kept in touch with PK and Flynn the other players in his African story faded away. The Parkinson's, now in South Africa, visited England rarely. Arthur Rogers had a stroke and when Malcolm visited him, his old boss could not remember him. Alice took great care of him, too glib to say he was now the child she never had. After a while he heard no more of them, his cards and letters unanswered.

He took holidays within the UK, James showing the usual truculence of a young teenage boy. But otherwise, father and son lived separate lives. Had they ever been together in any meaningful sense it could be said they grew apart.

James returned home in the holidays although as he grew older, he found other places to go sometimes alone and sometimes with others. He would reappear unannounced at the family house much to Malcolm's annoyance. He was not displeased to see his son but the unexpectedness of his appearances disrupted the predictability of his daily life.

Malcolm had never been able to relate to his son as he had wished; the weaknesses in himself had always prevented it. Deep down he did love James with that unconditional love lucky parents have for their offspring and he anguished over his son's present happiness and his future prospects. He just couldn't find it in him to declare it. They had never hugged to assuage a common sadness. Their conversation had rarely gone beyond the superficial. Perhaps all fathers and sons are doomed to be strangers. Male expectations might require they both hold back the openness which might make them really close. Strong on genes but weak on bonding; if that is the theory then these two were prize specimens in its supporting evidence. And on the one occasion when he could have broken his own suffocating bonds and joined with his son, he had failed to take the opportunity. He felt he had failed James and feared that his inheritance to his son was not genetic, that it stemmed from how he behaved towards him, that it was not inevitable. With perception, sensitivity, patience he could have avoided it. But that assumed he had power over his own condition and he did not.

With his mother dead and his father deadened James had had to develop without the emotional touchstones that comfort and unify most families. Yet the start of his life had been normal even promising. Somewhere in Malcolm's belongings there was a photograph of the three of them, taken by a nurse soon after the birth. In it, James was lying asleep in Alison's arms, her sweated hair the only sign of the struggle that brought him forth. Malcolm, too, was sweating but not from effort or emotion, only the heat of an African summer. If only Alison had lived it would all have been different. If only. If only. He had always thought he loved her and after her death realised and regretted how rarely he had said so. He hadn't needed to engage with her; she created all the emotional warmth in their lives. Why she put all that effort into him he couldn't imagine and what did she get in return? Not that it was an effort for her. Her openness and energy flowed spontaneously and freely sweeping everyone with them. It was so natural and so comforting. All that they shared came from her; he felt he had given nothing. Her death left a gap which filled with nothing more than the trivial detail of everyday living, an emotional black hole which held all feeling tight at its centre. Nothing could get out and all that came in sank into its sterile core. Within its orbit his son grew up in its stifling coldness.

TWENTY-EIGHT

For a decade Malcolm passed an undemanding academic life and an uneventful personal one. His waking life was determined by the triumvirate of working day, weekend and holiday. The first was the easiest to deal with as it had a predetermined shape which required little choice. Rising to the alarm call and the standard toilet, the conventional breakfast with the morning paper launched his day. Leaving the house, he would pull the door beyond him and pause at the top of the three steps to the small front garden. Before descending he would turn to the front door and push it to ensure the lock had engaged. A fifteen-minute walk brought him to the campus and five more saw him in his office. The timetable on his notice board defined his working day. Lectures were delivered correct in detail and interesting in delivery. Students' work was marked assiduously, assessments given rigorous attention. Evenings began with a simple meal with TV or crossword filling the time until sleep. Occasional visits to the cinema varied this pattern.

Then technology brought a new and pleasing aspect to his life. The development of computers filled his time more readily and without threat to his personality. At first it was an unstated requirement of his job but in the machine, he found the perfect foil for his attention. The computer was predictable, made decisions but eschewed judgement, gave numbers but not values. By spending many hours at home his lecture notes became more detailed and his presentations were supported by graphics of varying designs and colours. He had grown used to his own controlled face in the morning mirror now he had a neutral picture on his computer screen.

Weekends required more effort. He forced himself to drive into the surrounding countryside and walk or view whatever the guidebooks suggested worthy. Once he saw the local theatre were

266

presenting Hedda Gabler a play he had seen with Alison so many years before. He stood in front of the theatre looking at the advertising photographs disturbed by a real choice. Should he go to see it, sit alone amongst couples and groups. Would he be able to sit through it? Would he need to scramble along the row in mid-performance unable to remain with the memories, stumbling over the feet of incensed customers? The imagination of such a scenario quickly made up his mind and he passed onto to do his weekly shopping. His house had a small back yard and in the right weather he could sit within its containing walls. On clear days he felt the warm sun on his face and with eyes closed relived times long gone. And in those evenings, he could see the clear sky and its ceiling of bright stars. He knew little of astronomy but was content to think of them as the same stars, in the same positions, relaying the same messages they had done a lifetime away. But the coolness of English summer nights soon took him indoors before the memories became too intense.

In holidays time seemed unending and the lack of structure unsettled him. He found time to visit PK in London and was overwhelmed by generosity and memory. Often James was home from school and joint activities were undertaken as a matter of course. He saw more films and drove greater distances than he would have wished but it was a price to be paid in order to think himself a good father. But it was duty not devotion that drove the events. Once they went to a museum of photography and wondered at his son's intense interest. He stood behind him as James looked at the various exhibits and demonstrations himself interested more in his son than the displays. He realised how tall his son had become, taller he thought than Alison and destined to be taller than him. He saw a strong upright frame and tried to pull his own stooping body more fully. He saw the hair youthfully luxuriant on the shoulders and sensed the thinness of his own. But all this was external. What was inside he wondered? Was there constrained confusion as in his weary self or well-balanced uncertainty carrying his son from experience to experience?

'Isn't that just marvellous?' James's eyes were bright with enthusiasm and the words came from Alison's face. His father didn't respond at once. He had his own feelings. 'Just marvellous.' That was a phrase she used a lot. The view from the top of Mount Kilimanjaro they had climbed together, the lioness and her cubs in Amboseli Park, the Ngorongoro crater, the Seychelles beaches of their honeymoon. They were just marvellous she had said. Had those words stuck in her son's head too? It was unlikely; it is hardly a rare phrase; one he had not heard elsewhere. But it was her face using her language and it clutched something inside her husband's being.

'Yes,' the staccato response all Malcolm could generate.

The son's response was too intense to be ignored, 'Yes. Yes. It's just marvellous.' And the words unsettled the father.

This lifestyle may seem drab and soulless but it suited Malcolm's temperament and he found a certain contentment in its cloying routine. Each year he received Christmas cards from Joe Flynn. Each one contained a little essay about his life in the past year, about the church, the village and sometimes national politics but never the things that were really dear to him - those he could not speak about. Through them he learned of Ngugi's progress. The youngster he had supported through school had some important job in government although he couldn't remember whether it was political or professional. His father, Gitau, was still living in the village and had acquired a new wife some years younger than himself. Larsen had sold up and gone, south of course; there was no word of Forbes. There was no work to be had now. The youngsters were leaving the village for Nairobi returning only when injury and pregnancy turned their world around. Malcolm wondered about the station, his house, the club. He wondered too about the country; a fledgling independent state as he knew it, now an established country its initial optimism dowsed by pragmatism, its fabric now eroding under incompetence, nepotism and corruption. Malcolm had kept the cards, building up a collection, each successive year showing the deterioration in Flynn's handwriting which reflected the passing years - the passing years for both of them. And although they all made searching enquiries about James's progress none mentioned Alison. Nevertheless, she was part of past days and she infiltrated every sentence.

Early retirement brought this era to an end and unexpectedly fashioned a significant episode in his life. There is a belief, to which many of us fall victim, that present unhappiness can be relieved by revisiting scenes of earlier contentment. Such a belief, so strong in its conception, so disappointing in its execution, certainly inspired Malcolm. The notion of going back to Kenya, on holiday, was not suddenly born in Malcolm's mind but took root and grew over many years. Alongside it the idea that James might come with him surprised him. It was not a conscious intention to revive the family connection although he began to contemplate the possibility. It just seemed right they should go together there, as they had lived together there. The final stimulus came from the shop window of a travel agent he passed on his shopping expeditions. He merely glanced at the window but the one word, Kenya - bright red in some large exotic font - leapt out at him. He didn't stop but went on to pay his newspaper bill. Whilst waiting, the advertisement agitated his mind and he returned to the agency for further details. At home over a cup of coffee - it was the Kenyan which he bought out of loyalty rather than taste - he took in the possibilities and his grand plan emerged.

James agreed to go on holiday with his father but without overt enthusiasm. To spend a week in close proximity with his father did not seem immediately attractive but he recognised the opportunity for photographing new and more unusual images. He had now left school and following a course at the college close to his father's home. The course had a strong photographic theme and indeed he would not have

269

embarked upon it had it not. The other elements, of media studies and art, did not hold his interest to the same degree although they were tolerable enough. He had not decided how he would use his skills in later life - a magazine photographer perhaps. It was this youthful uncertainty that both pleased and dismayed his father. His photographic experience had been almost completely in the UK and the challenge of new lighting conditions intrigued him. At home it had become harder to find novel and interesting areas without employing contrived angles or lenses. Having appreciated the photographic potential his anticipation wavered when he remembered he was reviving memories which had a thread of tension running through them. They were not memories recalled with comfort, but those that lurked in the subconscious waiting to unnerve a settled existence. He knew there was a person, whom he remembered vaguely, but whose dominance came from her absence. He understood she was his mother, but he only knew the simple genealogy of the connection not the complexity of the relationship. He had no feelings about her but knew she represented some cloud over the family life. The facts were simple but this was not analysis but memory. He knew, too, that there were bright toddler images which promised this cloud was an aberration of his childhood rather than the essence of it. But he knew these positive images had come from outside the family and not within it. Although it did not dominate his life it made him suspicious of the background that formed him.

If his motives were simple and selfish, those of his father were altogether more complex. In his hours of solitude, he could not prevent his mind returning to that time which had been the peak of happiness in his life. However much he pondered on these wider issues he could not escape the fact he wanted to go back to recapture those beautiful days when Alison was his keeper, friend, lover, inspiration, guide. Before her and since her there had so little joy. At heart, he knew it would fail as strongly as he knew he had to do it.

He met PK again the day of the flight. His old friend would run them to the airport. They, too, exchanged Christmas cards, Malcolm recognising no incongruity. They met quite often in the last decade. Malcolm's visits to London and meetings with PK's family being highlights of his calendar. He could never bring himself to invite PK to his own home. The two had not seen each other for two years now. He saw in his old friend the ageing he knew was in himself but could not see. PK was successful in business and had become very plump, his once springy hair now thin and grey, fashioned to his scalp. He had his own children, two girls and a boy.

'Don't you ever want to go back?' asked Malcolm.

'We can't go back. We never contemplate it. We are resigned to moving forward. Anyway, we are settled here.'

'You were settled there,' countered Malcolm.

'We are settled wherever we are. We do not live in a place. We live in a community.'

'It's been quite the reverse for me. I've always lived in a place never lived in a family. Well hardly ever. We were a family, Alison and me. And James,' he added quickly, remembering his son's presence then and now. He surprised himself at the public admission and took it as a sign of the significance of what he was doing. He wanted to conjure up some more memories to reassure himself about his own.

'Have you heard from anyone there lately?' PK had not. 'I wonder what became of the station.' He paused. 'And Gitau. He was a fine man. He didn't seem typically African.'

'None of us is typically anything. It's only other people's judgement that typifies us,' said PK starchily.

'What do you remember, James?' he said asking the question Malcolm had tried to avoid.

'Not much,' said James deflecting his own thoughts as much as PK's enquiry.

271

What he did remember of infancy was an early blur that he did not wish to focus. What he remembered of daily childhood life was, for him, unremarkable. To him beetles, paw-paws, snakes, roast corn, violent storms, torrential rain, ant hills, poverty, early death, dusty roads and all the variety of Africa were his childhood worthy of no more comment than double decker busses, motorway signs, TV, morning newspapers and computer games. When it was convenient for him to do so he did remember Gitau, although to remember a poor African was not encouraged by the values of his school friends later nor helped by the distance of time and place now. But how could he forget a man who had been so close to for some much of his childhood? He remembered the smell of his body, the roughness of his legs. He remembered the brown stains on his teeth, the redness of his eyes, the darkness of his skin, the tribal scars on his face and for all of these Gitau had a story. He remembered the games they played, the songs they sang. But aside from this detail his all-embracing memory was that Gitau had never neglected him; he answered his questions, bound his wounds, shared his curiosity. Young James would rejoice in all these things but modern James could not. In part he was denied by the gaucheness of youth, but in the main he feared that too close an analysis might bring comparison with his own father who had managed to give only a fraction of the attention Gitau had. And in addition, in one dramatic day had turned him away. Gitau's scars left by his father were on public display and represented belonging, security and continuity. James's, on the other hand, were hidden and reflected rejection and panic. Perhaps, in the future, these secret memories would be revealed, whether to lover or therapist time would tell. But they were not going to be told today, not to someone he barely knew and certainly not to his own father.

'I'll send you a card,' volunteered Malcolm.

'Better send it early otherwise you'll be back before it arrives.'

As the plane stood on the end of the runway waiting the signal to take off Malcolm anticipated the seat pressure on his back as the plane surged forward. If for most of the passengers it was a hidden force projecting them forward, for Malcolm it was projecting back.

There was no Lake Victoria this time, the plane going direct to Nairobi. From his window Malcolm saw the white buildings of Nairobi in the distance interrupting the flow of the African plain. Below him were the Ngong hills. He leaned across James to get a better look. For a fraction of a second, he hoped to see Alison. For longer he did wonder how far her ashes had been blown by the warm thermals over the Rift. He thought of his dead wife's warm body now reduced to dust and did not register he was pressing against the warm body of his son.

TWENTY-NINE

By now, Malcolm's memories of the Kenya he'd lived in had been sanitised and romanticised. In his mind the country had a predictable, consistent and equable climate; daily life passed effortlessly; city life was orderly and unchallenging; people were invariably courteous and happy if not always dependable; the past laid a comforting solid foundation and the future seemed optimistic. Compared with England it was a sea of tradition and tranquillity. The assault on these cosy illusions began at the airport which now seemed like most other international airports - efficient, air-conditioned, chrome and plastic. After the entry formalities, better organised than he had expected, he was met by the courier, a brisk and friendly African woman.

'What is your name please?' Malcolm savoured the accent he had not heard for some time.

'Bryant. Both of us.' The courier looked down her list and ticked their names.

'Ah, yes. Have you been to Kenya before?'

'Yes.' Malcolm was reminded he was a stranger here; his memories had no claim on today. 'Yes. We've both been before.' He eschewed any explanation.

'Come this way. There is a coach waiting.'

She escorted them to their coach parked in a carefully laid out carport. Cars eased their way in and out of regularly marked bays. It was quite unlike the melee of former days.

Malcolm had taken the road from the airport to town many times and there were few surprises. The countryside seemed drabber than he had remembered and the children did not wave at the coach as it passed. Had wonder been eradicated along with TB? Scenes and landmarks jogged his memory but his mind rejected the images it saw.

There was an unreality, it was a faded newsreel the colours muted; such were the romanticised pictures his mind had catalogued.

James was disappointed with what he could see. His clouded childhood memories had been more of rural Kenya with a garden watered and tended into a comparatively luxuriant playground. Tourist publicity, too, had implied a greenness that was not evident through the window. The route did not pass through the town itself and the clean, comfortable, air-conditioned bus left Malcolm detached from the world in which he had lived his life. Nearer to the town the central reservations were cultivated flower beds rather than the sparse dusty display on the outskirts. Eventually the bus brought them to a modern many-storeyed hotel on the edge of the town centre and looking down on it from a hill.

Their room was world standard tourist. The twin beds had no mosquito nets. The toilet flushed effusively as Malcolm tested it. The cold water from the tap felt good on his face which had acquired the dust his mind had removed from memory.

From the window they could see over the city. Tall trees and taller buildings stood out above the rooftops. A slight haze - part pollution, part heat - hung about, reducing the brightness of the afternoon sun. Malcolm stood looking out, trying to identify the buildings and with each sighting associating some episode of his life. After a while he became aware of James's impatience.

'Let's get into the sunshine.'

'Take a hat. And some sun-cream.'

'Yes. Dad. I know.'

'I don't want your holiday spoilt by sunburn that's all.'

'And we don't want to spoil your holiday either, do we?'

Malcolm couldn't decide whether it was adolescent sarcasm or touching concern but chose the latter.

The corridor, the lift, the lobby could have been anywhere. Only when they left the cool of the building into the part-shaded garden at the rear did they feel in Africa. In the centre of the garden was a large swimming pool and around it the standard tourist apparatus of sunbeds and tables shaded by thatched parasols.

The two men, for this is how the world saw them, wandered around the pool to the shade of a large tree which, although rooted beyond the wall, spread its branches to give a natural shade to one corner of the garden. The afternoon sun seemed to pierce their skin and the relief of the shade was welcome to bodies long used to a cooler, damper climate. Malcolm sat in a canvas chair beside a table first shaking off the droppings from the branches above. He put on his newly acquired sunglasses and then almost immediately took them off again seeking the brightness of sunlight denied to him by the darkened glass.

James peeled off his sun-top and walked to the edge of the pool his body paler than others around but only by a few days. Malcolm watched his son dive into the pool with a youthful confidence he could not recall having himself. His son's body was strong and spare and to someone other than his father, enormously attractive. Malcolm had never been proud of his own body. It seemed to have developed the diffidence and wretchedness of his personality. His walk was a modest shuffle rather than a confident stride. His eyes darted suspiciously, unable to hold a steady gaze. His son had none of these mannerisms. Malcolm supposed this confidence and athleticism came from Alison. He wondered whether James had inherited anything from him and if so, what he would have chosen it to be. He concluded he knew none of his characteristics he wished to pass on. Here he was, with a son who seemed not of himself, in whom he had shown little interest and who seemed disinclined to share his life with his father. They might as well have been separated at birth. It was no fault of James's that on one level they had been distant from not long after that.

Malcolm's musing was interrupted by a waiter who enquired whether he wanted a drink. He resisted the temptation to reply in Swahili although he wanted to use the language he'd acquired incrementally so long ago. In the weeks leading up to the holiday he had invented little episodes in which he had been required to carry out a sustained conversation in his adopted tongue. The waiter seemed to have no more connection with the villagers with whom he had conversed in his plans than his hotel room had with a mud hut.

As he was ordering, James's head appeared above the edge of the pool. His strong dark hair - Alison's hair - usually full and falling over his face, was now plastered down as he swept his hand backwards over his wet head. But without his luxuriant curls his face took on a different shape, sharper, less strong. And in it, Malcolm saw his own face, or at least that face of his that peered from the photographs in his passport. This was his son. It was him, Malcolm, too. A strong emotion tugged him deep inside. It was no stranger to him; it was the love of his dead wife. Yet it was not the image of her face that had aroused it, not the echoes of her strong and happy voice, not the warmth and comfort of her body. Its catalyst this time was his living son now in front of him, real, tangible, close. The feelings rampaged deep inside him their unexpected genesis making him confused. Overcoming a choked throat, he asked James did he want a drink. He did. As the waiter moved to the open-air bar James slid back into the pool.

When the drinks arrived, James joined his father in the shade, the loss of sunlight bringing no discomfort, although the water evaporating from his skin lent some coolness. He wrapped himself in a towel. Neither man spoke but each sensed that here was an opportunity to communicate. Neither was indifferent to the other at this moment but neither could find the words which would begin a sincere conversation. Malcolm cleared his throat after the emotional effect of the last few moments but said nothing. James cleared his throat of the chlorinated water before he attacked his drink.

'Don't get cold. Not at the start of the holiday. That wouldn't do.' The father's words were genuinely concerned but directed with a cheerful formality at someone five years younger than the son beside him.

'No Dad.' The reply showing exasperation at an overprotective parent. 'I'm fine, honestly.' The follow up was more balanced. 'Are you OK? You look a bit confused.' It had taken the younger man to reach beyond the surface sensing some adult fragility he did not understand.

'Yes, thank you. Tired after the journey, I expect. I'm not getting any younger.' He paused momentarily and as if released began to talk about the tree above them, the flowers on the fence across the pool, and a gecko on the wall to their right. His language was a little stilted with the hint of the lecture amongst the phrases. James watched his father, understanding that this man was talking to him about these things rather than about these things to him. He asked a few inconsequential questions but his delivery was laboured. The conversation soon slowed as both men dozed, suffocated by the heat of the day, the tiredness of their journey, and the banality of their conversation.

After dinner they decided to walk into Nairobi in the evening air, dark and warm though cooler than the day. The city centre shops were closed and only the tourist stalls and street sellers enlivened roads whose politically modernised names jarred on Malcolm's memory.

They stopped and looked in the window of a photography shop its vast range of goods from the far East protected from the street by a heavy grill. James's passion for photography held them there for some time the younger man dodging about to get a better view through the tight grill; the older man watching his son's face illuminated by the light from the brightly lit interior. The youth's hair hung about his face obscuring it as he bent forward but just occasionally, as he looked upwards to the higher shelves, it fell back revealing the face that Malcolm had seen emerging from the pool earlier.

As they stood, a lone beggar shuffled across the street his one leg balanced by a crude crutch on the other side. He came to a stop behind James and held out his hand to Malcolm. The light from the window, there to highlight many thousands of pounds worth of equipment, put this hunched figure in a bright spotlight, a spectre haunting their affluent lives. James, intent on the window, had not seen him arrive and stepping back to look at some items on the top shelf bundled into the man knocking him over. Both men reached to help the beggar to his feet. The sparse body was light and fragile to their touch. Their hands seemed to grip fleshless bones beneath his old clothes and they could not avoid the smell of his body. Several pedestrians had stopped to watch as the three men became a trio in a theatrical round. One retrieved the crutch which had fallen into the gutter. The watchers' eyes seemed to stare accusingly. Malcolm spoke to the man in Swahili and gave him some money not quite knowing or caring how much he was giving, his action fuelled by embarrassment and compassion. Father and son felt their departure might imply fleeing and reinforce their guilt and so they stood falteringly. Soon the crowd dissipated and the two tourists detached themselves and moved away.

'Sorry, Dad' James was shaken by the experience but his father had taken any initiatives needed. Through an instinctive reflex, and unexpectedly to both of them, Malcolm put his hand across his son's back and squeezed the side of his neck reassuringly. He removed it more quickly than he should and the contact was transient. For James the sensation remained long after his father had removed his hand and it was more than skin deep.

By now the darkness, which earlier had seemed warm and comforting, now seemed oppressive and threatening as they made their way back to the hotel. As they passed the park, they were suddenly surrounded by half a dozen youths whose menace was palpable, their dark skins making them threateningly anonymous in the poorly lit street. One of them waved a knife at the pair. James eased behind his father's shoulder.

'Give. Money. Dollars. Watch,' the staccato words aimed at unknown nationality.

Malcolm said something in Swahili although some Kikuyu words infiltrated the content. His naiveté about modern African street life subdued fears he might have felt in similar circumstances in central London. One of the youths behind the leader began to laugh and two of the others broke into smiles. The leader looked bemused and snarled at his fellow thieves. Malcolm spoke again and the tension eased. He showed them his watch. It was at least twenty years old and had to be hand wound. They lost interest in that. He took some money from his back pocket and gave it to the lead youth. He spoke again and the leader replied sullenly. Then the group moved away and were soon gone down a side street into the night. The two Europeans looked at each other bemused rather than shocked although each aware of the potential danger.

'Well. Well.' Malcolm recovered first.

James looked at his father. 'What did you say?' his voice thin with apprehension.

'I told them we were English not Americans and so we were poor. They thought that quite funny.' He was lucky that such ironic insights were alive and well in the middle of Africa. 'I told them their mothers would be ashamed of them behaving like this but I doubt they're from a village, so family pride may not mean anything. I suppose they've spent all their lives in the shanty towns of Nairobi. I think they were impressed I could speak their language and I suspect they feared some trouble if I had local connections. We were lucky. They were sober and not desperate. Come on, let's get back to the hotel.'

Malcolm had lost little. Much of his money had been given to the beggar earlier. But although he and his son were unharmed,

Malcolm was upset. He had been used to walking around Nairobi without any fear and had known so many Africans who despite gross inequalities of wealth and influence harboured no ill will towards him and indeed were almost universally kind and gentle. Although he did not feel the loss of his money, he did feel a greater loss of innocence. As Malcolm dwelt gloomily on this, he remained unaware of what he had gained - the sneaking admiration of his son. Twice that evening his father had taken the role of protector; twice son had felt a security in his presence. There was something between them that had not been there before but Malcolm was denied the comfort of knowing of its existence.

THIRTY

Long before coming on holiday, Malcolm had arranged with his old friend Flynn, the priest, that he would come up to Kimura to visit. With no car Flynn would have found it difficult to come down to Nairobi and for Malcolm not to visit Kimura would have been unthinkable. It had been his home, the centre of his world. If there was to be a focus to his holiday it had to be a return to the surroundings that had meant so much to him - first a secure freedom, then a loving passion and then, it had to be faced, a crushing tragedy followed by a long desolation. These episodes, kind and cruel, defined the middle part of his life putting the emotional sterility of his early life into retreat. It was this return he yearned for and feared. Never go back, he said; I must go back, he said too. He liked to think James would have come too, if not out of nostalgia, then at least out of curiosity.

He had also arranged to meet Ngugi, who was now a senior civil servant. Flynn had ascertained the department address and an inconclusive correspondence had been left with Malcolm agreeing to come to the ministry and make an arrangement to see Ngugi when he arrived in Kenya. The correspondence, whose tone was formal but not unwelcoming, made it very clear that Ngugi's plans for the period of Malcolm's holiday would be uncertain. Ngugi had appended a hand-written greeting which Malcolm took to be an attempt to sweeten the sterility of the typed page.

Malcolm had replied giving the dates of his stay but there had been no reply to his suggestion that they make contact early in his holiday. So, on the first day of the holiday, he decided to track down Ngugi combining his search with a little sight-seeing in the capital. James, after the previous night's experience of Nairobi, preferred to stay at the hotel enjoying pool side life and trying to photograph a gecko.

The hotel courtesy bus dropped Malcolm outside the ministry, a new building with large glass doors embossed with the national symbol. Beyond the reception desk stood a security guard clearly well-armed. At the desk Ngugi explained his mission to a receptionist. She relayed the facts through a phone. As she was speaking Malcolm weighed up her smart uniform, her straightened hair, her bright red nails and lipstick slightly garish against a dark brown face. He remembered the village girls of her age beating the maize into flour. He wanted to believe she would be happier working in the shade of a tree outside her hut rather than here in the air-conditioned cleanliness of a modern office building. Did she really want to swap the joyous camaraderie of village life for one which many Westerners seemed glad to get away from? If he had asked, she would have told him without any doubt that that is exactly what she wanted.

'Mr. Ngugi cannot see you now. He is in a meeting. His secretary is aware you might be coming and suggests you come back at 4.00?'

Malcolm was slightly taken aback. He had expected Ngugi to come rushing down to see him immediately. His image of Ngugi as the grateful village boy was hard to eradicate. That his protégé was now a top civil servant with a strict diary of important meetings, not the urchin of old, was difficult to accept.

'Yes. Of course. I'll come here, shall I?'

'If you report to me, I'll tell him you're here.'

'Thank you.' Malcolm was too restrained to be a bigot yet something deeply ingrained in him - a paternalism seemingly inescapable in the expatriate - could not readily accept a middle-aged European man being told to report to a twenty-something African female.

With time on his hands, he resolved to have lunch at the hotel where he had stayed those many years ago. He strolled past buildings he knew well, down familiar streets with unfamiliar names and arrived at the hotel early. Rather than go in he decided to wander up towards the supermarket where he had shopped and where he had seen the legless beggar. Was he still there? Which was most awful; that he had died a lonely death or had spent the last twenty odd years enduring his degrading ritual? Was his back still straight? Were his eyes still clear? How many times had he changed the rags which protected his hands from the hardness of his crutches?

He was not there. The road was now metalled, the roadside paved. Outside the supermarket, now extended into adjacent buildings and modernised with plastic frontage, there were stencilled parking bays for cars. But no beggars. James looked around searching for something to remind him of the old order. He went into the supermarket and stood door-side of the cash desks. It was less of a warehouse now and more like the sanitised small-town supermarkets of Europe. Thus, it held no interest and he wandered out.

Even the hotel had changed. The aviary in the square outside of the rear had been replaced by a circular bar with the drinks' optics fastened to the trunk of the central tree which was decorated with spears, arrows and shields. This remnant of another age, many ages, surviving still because of the shade it offered. Despite the warlike decoration the bar was called The Rafiki Bar - Swahili for friends. He rejected the bar in favour of a place in the sun. He sat outside at the front and ordered a beer and sandwich. The world passed by as before but not the same world, at least in his eyes.

Most of the fellow diners were African. He wondered if they knew they were sitting where, seventy years before, European police had fired on a group of protesting Africans, killing many. He wondered if it mattered and decided it did not. Harry Thuku and his supporters were cast into history and frozen out of contemporary life as much as the Tolpuddle martyrs back home.

At the end of the veranda sat an elderly white couple, resident in Africa rather than Europe from the colour and texture of their skin. Both were formally dressed, reflecting the conventions of a past age, but seemed at ease in their attire. She had a white skirt with a dark blue blouse topped by a string of pearls; he wore a jacket and tie his white hair pressed flat to his head. They both had cigarettes, the white smoke curling against browned fingers. They said little to each other and watched those around them with a detachment which seemed to an observer like disdain. They fitted a stereotype which Malcolm applied thoughtlessly. To him they lived a little English life resisting the call of the homeland until civil unrest or serious illness took them back. Enjoying British citizenship and enjoying not being in Britain. That it might one day have been Alison and him did not enter his mind. That these two might have given unstintingly to the substance of this land and were now enjoying a languid retirement on its surface seemed unlikely to Malcolm, showing a touch of cynicism which was untypical. Two African youths walked past the hotel hand in hand in traditional friendship, their baseball caps a salute to the present. They walked slowly in the midday sun and their flip-flops flip-flopped on the hard surface of the pavement. Their quiet conversation was interspersed with gleeful laughter. The male European made a comment to his wife.

To fill the afternoon, he took the tourist trail, disappointed by how the simplest structural changes had robbed most of what he saw of the landscape of its familiarity. The Indian shops in Bazaar Street seemed less well stocked than he had remembered. Hessian sacks had given way to plastic bags and the aroma of exotic spices to diesel fumes.

At the ministry he reported to the receptionist.

'Hello, Mr. Bryant. I'll tell Mr. Ngugi you're here.'

She announced his name as though he had been the most important visitor that day although he could not see her notepad below the reception desk reminding her of his name and motive. Her smile revealed teeth brilliant white against her skin and he saw the gaiety of the village girl he wished her to be.

Malcolm waited on the plush mock zebra-skin settee until a door opened along a corridor and through it came a sturdy, well-dressed man. It was only when he spoke that Malcolm recognised the person he had not seen since he was an unsophisticated youth.

'Hello, Mr. Bryant. How good to see you after all these years.'

The voice was cultured and confident. Once again Malcolm was disconcerted by the change in their relative status. No longer an African boy with a European man but a holder of significant power and authority with a minor visitor to a foreign land. The former dressed in a dark lounge suit, a smart tie against a white shirt with gold tie clasp and cufflinks; the latter with summer shirt and slacks, his pale skin and pastel clothes mocked by the sharp black and white stripes of the settee. They shook hands. Their eyes met as strangers, a slight reserve shading each gaze.

'Hello .....' The European paused. He wasn't sure what to call the African. Ngugi didn't seem right; that belonged to the village.

'Paul. Please call me Paul.' It was what he had been called in his formal life ever since he first registered at secondary school. All the boys seemed to have an Anglicised element alongside their tribal names and he'd heard Flynn talk about St Paul.

'How long are you here? Where are you staying? Are you alone?'

The questions were routinely polite; the answers routinely absorbed. Malcolm had given all this information in his correspondence.

'Would you like a drink?' he asked and barely giving Malcolm chance to respond with a nod of the head went on. 'There's a nice bar a few doors away. I've been cooped up here all day. Come.' The last word an invitation with the hint of an order that the supremely confident can imply.

As they turned to the door a man who had been sitting in the foyer leaped to the door. He didn't usher them through it as Malcolm expected but went first into the street and after scanning it turned and nodded only then holding the door open for them.

'My bodyguard,' explained Ngugi.

They sat at a table in a small first floor veranda overlooking the street. The bodyguard waited in the shade on the pavement opposite.

'Do you need a bodyguard?' asked Malcolm.

'Not really, but he needs a job. He is a cousin. We all have so many relatives. He likes to act the part. I think he's seen too many films. He is my chauffeur as well and much more useful in that role.'

A waiter approached. Ngugi shook his hand and their brief conversation Malcolm recognised as Kikuyu. Malcolm agreed to a beer. The older man did not know how to proceed. He had expected to know the man he was facing and yet he seemed a stranger.

'You've done well. You must be a very important man.'

'There were opportunities for people like me. My American qualifications have usually impressed the people who matter. It's not easy to run a developing country and the turnover of government staff is high. Most want to work for the multinationals. A young man who plays his cards carefully can make out.'

Malcolm didn't warm to this man; he seemed too pleased with himself. Had this man been a top civil servant in London he would have been impressed and deferential. But he knew this man's background, seen him dressed in patched clothes, seen his bare feet, knew his father had worked under him. His mind articulated the idea *under him* not *for him* or *with him* even if his brain did not form the words. He wanted him to be the village boy he knew, to restore their relative status. He felt only the wish and the underlying hypocrisy went unnoticed.

'How is your father?'

'He is well for his age. He still lives in the village but he's staying with me at the moment. He's recovering from a small operation on his eyes.'

'Do you have a family?'

'Two girls and boy.' He took the wife as axiomatic.

'I hope you will come and see them and my father too. We're having a little gathering on Sunday at lunch time. Can you come? I hope James will come too. I haven't seen him since he was very small. Is he like you?'

The question stung Malcolm more than it should have.

'Yes and no,' he said defensively, taking comfort from how unlike Gitau, Ngugi was.

Malcolm remembered he had to get the courtesy bus and gave this reason for having to go.

'No. Stay. I'll drop you off at the hotel.'

Although the first two words contained the seeds of orders they were said in a much more friendly way and Malcolm was content for the conversation to continue.

As the beer took its hold and the conversation ranged over their common and separate histories Ngugi became less and less formal and Malcolm saw the youngster he had once known. The smiles became laughter; the formal posture gave way to the more languid mannerisms of the market place. The alcohol had closed the difference in their ages and positions and eased the reservations in their minds. A third beer was suggested but both men recognised they should move on. Ngugi called out to the chauffeur who disappeared towards the ministry. The waiter brought a bill that Ngugi signed, brushing away Malcolm's attempts to pay.

'You'll pay for it anyway. Through the UN or the World Bank.' Ngugi had meant it as a wry aside about world politics but Malcolm thought he saw a gleeful assertion of privilege. Each man had misjudged the other.

The chauffeur appeared in a black Mercedes which pulled up in the street outside. Malcolm had never been in such a car seeing one only in newsreels. As they departed at his hotel Malcolm remembered he didn't know where Ngugi lived.

'I'll send the car for you at 11.30 on Sunday'. This solved the problem.

The Mercedes drew smoothly away. At various times in the past, he had seen Ngugi as a sort of son for whom he had usually felt duty and occasionally affection. This had embarrassed him as the thought often occurred that he had done more for Ngugi than his own son. Rationalising it, he decided he had discovered Ngugi needed his help and he had been able to give it. Now that Ngugi did not need him, he felt his emotional attachment had withered. Now that Ngugi was strong, independent, and influential, Malcolm's importance was insignificant.

He ascended the hotel steps and sought the way to the pool to find his real son. Across the pool he saw James with a group of youngsters of his own age. He noticed the confidence and pleasure that his son showed in the presence of these strangers and felt empty that he had never had, might never have, that simple relationship with him. And so, his lonely muddled sadness was increased by his son's simple enjoyment with others.

Malcolm's needs were fairly prosaic; he wanted a beer. As he drank, he looked down at his body slumped in the pool side chair. Underneath his holiday shirt, now open down the front, his frame was podgy with the unmistakable hairy signs of age. He convinced himself that inside he did not feel his age; he calculated he might have another thirty years to live. The immediate prospect was one of relief until he realised those three decades might be spent not just alone but in loneliness.

He looked up to seek his son whose interests were more convivial. James was in the water now, his head just showing next to another which Malcolm recognised as a young woman his son had been talking to the previous day. The sun had gone down behind the hotel wall and the residual glow from the sky outlined their heads against the water like two balls floating. Malcolm saw he and his son like this, bobbing on the surface of life, near but unconnected, kept together by only the weak force of their family history. The two youngsters did not swim but talked, spurting out any water which lapped into their mouths. Malcolm hoped that James would not lead a lonely life, that any damage done to him would only mar their relationship and not undermine his son's relationships with others. He need not have worried; beneath the surface they were holding hands, connected incognito.

Malcolm walked to the edge of the pool. At that moment his son, by accident (by design thought Malcolm), turned his head away and made to swim across the pool. The girl looked at the father and smiled, slightly embarrassed as James's departure left her alone. Her hair robbed of its style by the water and her face clean of make-up gave her a childlike look which made James's interest seem perverted. Malcolm smiled back faintly and nodded. She turned to follow James and Malcolm walked up the concrete steps from the pool avoiding catching his arm on the cactus at the bend. At the top he looked back and saw again his son in his world, envious of it because he was not part of it and sad because he had not created a parallel world for them both to enjoy.

In his room he looked out over Nairobi, the lights of its buildings beginning to highlight the onset of night. It was unfamiliar. He thought he knew it but it was no longer his home, its infrastructure had been transformed, its values had changed, its heroes were different. Whether it was this thought or the tiredness after a day in the heat or the effects of the beer he could not tell but he fell asleep on his bed.

His sleep that night was restless. His sun grilled body grating against the sheets was not the only barrier to rest. His mind was raw with emotional friction. Nearer dawn, with the sun providing light, he saw his son in the next bed soundly asleep. The young man's body had absorbed the day's sunshine with little adverse effect; his mind too was unaffected, at this age at least, by insecurities other than those of growing youth. Malcolm wondered about his son's dreams. Were they about that young whole body that had been beside him in the pool? The two women in Malcolm's life were both dead. The one, a cause of his inadequacy, had been mangled by unrelenting genes and unforgiving history and had left him scarred and vulnerable; the other, his potential saviour, mangled by accident and machinery had at least left a gift but one he could only observe and not enjoy.

THIRTY-ONE

Malcolm stood on the steps of the hotel filled with on old impatience. It was 11.45 and Ngugi had promised a car at 11.30. Such a delay had been a common feature of his earlier life here but recent exposure to European promptness had overtaken it. It had been a difficult enough morning with James only truculently agreeing to come with him to Ngugi's. Malcolm realised he could not demand that his son should come; he had to ask him. He would have pleaded if necessary but there was an equability in both of them that did not require such melodrama. Malcolm had not analysed his feelings on this matter; he just wanted his son to be there when they visited Ngugi and his father; father and son, son and father. It was a comforting symmetry departure from which would make him feel conspicuous. The previous day they had safaried into the game parks and in a clumsy attempt to bond with his son he had taken off his shirt and stood bare-chested alongside James in the open topped minibus. Now his skin itched with sunburn adding to his discomfort. The sun tending to its height increased his annoyance and he stood a concentration of hot irritation in a world of languid acceptance.

James, less demanding, was sitting across the road on a low stone wall beneath the shade of a tree. Spasmodically he squinted through his camera lens but saw little to enthral him. Those shots he did take were routine and dismissed as soon as they were taken. He had not wanted to go to Ngugi's. He did not remember, or rather chose not to remember, him nor his family. He had no wish to visit an African household even though he knew it was not a mud hut. Besides he had hoped to go with his newly acquired friend, Sara and explore Nairobi without adult guidance. Sara's parents had not been sounded out on the enterprise so his disappointment at not being able to go was disingenuous. Moreover, his memory loss was spurious. There were, tucked away inside him, many memories of African childhood - feelings, colours, smells, incidents, people. But he chose to relegate them to the unremembered - much as early school memories of fear, of incontinence, of loneliness - lying in wait to surge out at some unexpected and unwelcome moment. And persistent among those memories was that abnormal day, he did not know the date, he did not know how old he was, he did not know the details of what had happened. But he knew something had happened back then in the confusion of childhood. He could not know then, but may have realised since, that it was the day that set his father and him on separate lives. To the detached adult observer, it was the day his mother died. But he did not see her death, only later missed her life. He did remember adults around him breaking from their normal manner - crying, wailing, shouting, silent. He remembered, too, his father - he knew it was his father - no longer the quiet unthreatening presence in his life. Now wild, tear stained, frantic, shouting at him. No. No. No. A small word which on that occasion was filled with the ferocity and anguish of despair. For that small boy there had been a sanctuary. A strong gentle man had taken him on his knee and sung him the songs of comfort in a voice holding a softness which belied his own rough life. But this young man had diminished that experience and that man within his formal thoughts. Below the surface, however, the African's gentle strength still remained, that strength that had given a safe retaining wall against the flood of insecurity.

The sun was beginning to stake its claim over people's lives. Passing cars whisked the dust from the gutter and it hung in the air for longer than seemed gravitationally possible. James focused on the hotel frontage alongside which was a bar raised above ground level its roof covered with brightly coloured trailing plants providing shade for those beneath. It was beginning to fill up as the midmorning drinkers were joined by early diners. Sara came down the steps with her parents. Her hair was carefully arranged and a light make up drew her youth cleverly into womanhood. Her slim body was covered by a white cotton dress which revealed her neck and arms. In her hand she carried a straw hat. As she descended a group of men at a bar table leered down at her but the presence of her parents inhibited any overt comment. She didn't see James as he snapped her. This time his only interest in shape was in hers; this a memento not a folio item. As soon as the three had rounded a corner the large black Mercedes drew up outside the hotel ignoring the parking restrictions. The bar drinkers understood its importance and although drawn to its appearance were sufficiently aware of governmental sensitivity to keep quiet.

'You're late,' protested Malcolm to the driver. It was the same man as yesterday, his screen stereotype further enhanced by the cigarette clamped between his teeth. He shrugged; his eyes masked by the ubiquitous sunglasses. 'Come on James.' He spent his annoyance on his son.

They drew smoothly through the Sunday traffic, the air-conditioning protection against the drowsy world outside. Past the park and up the hill where the roads became quieter and were lined with large bungalows, most set back behind walls and railings, guards on the gates. Down a side road and then another and then stopping in front of some large ironwork gates with metal sheeting preventing passers-by seeing what was beyond. An armed man slid from between the gates now part open. He walked to the car and peeked unsmilingly at the passengers. Ignoring the driver, he went back and opened the electrically operated gates. The gravelled path swung round to the right and passed in front of the main door of the bungalow before swinging round in a loop on itself. The door opened before they got to it and a man with a white robe and red fez welcomed them in. Almost immediately Ngugi appeared carrying a baby. 'Welcome. Welcome. Come through.' His enthusiastic greeting seemed genuine enough.

I'm sorry we're late, Malcolm had rehearsed as though it was his fault but Ngugi beat him too it.

'I'm sorry the car was late. The driver did not arrive here until 11.30. Some excuse about family. You Europeans often enthuse about our extended families but you don't know what a trouble they can be. Or how big.' He paused to let them follow the servant and, as James passed, Ngugi said, 'You must be James. You've grown since I last saw you.' It was the opening gambit from older to younger anywhere. 'Do you remember me?' he continued.

James did not like to say No and mumbled something about jumbled memories of many people. He would not admit, and tried not to admit to himself, that he had clear memories of some things and some people. That which he did remember did nothing to encourage deeper recall. If he did remember Ngugi he could not connect him with this man, his sun top with African motive revealing a gold chain about his neck, his well-cut slacks hiding the scar on his left calf, a legacy of cutting his leg on some corrugated iron sheeting as he ran from Larsen's dogs after one youthful venture to a forbidden place.

They went through a central corridor out onto a wide covered veranda and there a group of black faces. A loud African shriek and gales of laughter were the last sounds before the presence of newcomers was noticed and brought a reverential quiet.

'This is my friend, Mr. Bryant.' Ngugi hesitated before continuing. 'Malcolm. And his son James. I will bring them round to meet you all. Grace, will you look after James?' This he said to a young woman. The two Europeans went their separate ways. Ngugi took Malcolm to one end of the veranda.

'Let me take you to the most important one first.'

It was Gitau. Not the erect patrician he had come to rely on but a shrunken seated figure. He was wearing a formal dark suit and tie. His scrawny neck surrounded by a shirt collar too big for him gave him the look of a tortoise. He wore glasses with one lens opaque and his head fell to one side as he used the other eye.

'Jambo, mzee,' Malcolm greeted him in the way he used to defer to his wisdom now deferring to his age. 'Habari leo.'

The old man smiled just enough to show welcome. His one eye seemed to focus on Malcolm's face.

'Mzuri. Mzuri sana.' His voice was thin and dry now but his reply was garlanded with a giggly laughter. 'It is nice to see you again. Bwana Bryant.'

'How are you keeping, Gitau?' asked Malcolm reiterating his earlier greeting this time in English for no reason other than he did not know what to say. Malcolm wanted Gitau to call him by his first name but even though this man was twenty years his elder, he had still been addressed by him deferentially. Malcolm had still addressed him by what he took to be the older man's first name. It was too late to change now and both men remembered their common past with an affection and mutual respect which went beyond the labels they attached to one another.

'As well as can be expected,' came the formulaic reply rather less positive than his earlier simple Swahili response. Then with warmth 'Well enough to remember you with pleasure. Not much is left of those times. I am the last of my generation. Ngugi's mother died some years ago and all my brothers and sisters and cousins. They died in Africa, still African.' His one eye moved to Ngugi registering a little hardness.

'I'll bring him back to you later. He must meet the others.' said Ngugi pulling Malcolm away. 'He's a very proud man. Very fond of the old ways. He can't accept the changes. He's more concerned with what we've lost instead of the things we've gained. He still lives in our village. He has a wife, much younger, who cares for him.' The hushed, staccato explanation hiding an embarrassment at the tension.

He was introduced to Ngugi's wife and two children, elder sisters to the infant son they had seen earlier. The wife, Elizabeth, was bright and friendly, her body turning to plumpness under childbirth and good living. Her daughters had the slender form she had once enjoyed and which had attracted Ngugi to her. Malcolm wondered had they ever pummelled corn but decided they had not.

He could not remember Ngugi's elder sister, Rose, but then realised she had been training to be a nurse in England. Her hair was straight, so straight it might have been a wig, her hands bejewelled, her body encased in a flowing robe and an expensive perfume. Her husband was small but solid, his neck tie straining at his bulging neck. The couple were overdressed for such on occasion and their manner followed that ostentation. Malcolm felt uncomfortable with them but stayed long enough to ask about Rose's experiences in England. She was too polite to give a frank account. He suspected his unease derived from them being rich and successful - he had a motor franchise for the whole of Kenya. Malcolm had usually known Africans as poor and disadvantaged hoping to gain a better life. His vision of the African was patronising, a mixture of innocence and ignorance, and he couldn't accommodate the equality he had played a part in creating.

In the meantime, James was being taken around the group in the opposite direction. Grace was Ngugi's cousin. Her mother was the woman, Wambui, who worked for Father Flynn and whose husband had killed himself in shame leaving Gitau to bring up his family according to custom. When Malcolm first met the village children she had been slung in a shawl over the back of an older girl. By the time she could walk and become independent Malcolm's attention to Alison kept him away from village life, only Ngugi being the link. She had the physical grace of younger Africans. Her skin was pale brown and her eyes were a greyish-green. It needed little insight to see she was mixed race although James, accustomed to a less uniform Britain, didn't give it a thought. She took little time with her relations and invited James to see the garden. They spoke, as modern youngsters can, about a cosmopolitan world as familiar to them as it is alien to their parents - films, music, personalities, scandals. Grace was older than James but retained a simplicity which brought them closer in temperament.

The garden was well kept and well stocked so that James had much to photograph. A cluster of frangipani trees latticed against a bright blue sky would earn him third place in a competition later although a close up of Grace's hand with a huge beetle on it, the pink of her palms disguising her race, was his favourite. The view from the veranda was not susceptible to photography. To the living eye its panorama towards the Ngong Hills displayed a delicacy of colour and gentleness of contour. The heat haze produced a dazzling effect which turned it into an impressionist picture. But the dust in the air frustrated the most refined film. The time to photograph Africa is when the rain has damped down the dust and brought out the colours to their most arrogant.

At last Grace brought James to Gitau and the two youngsters sat each side of him. The old man put his hand on James's. The top of it was dry and wrinkled, almost cracked, and James feared its touch but the palm was soft and gentle. His good eye searched James's face.

'I cannot see so well now but you look very like your father.'

James was taken aback. It had never occurred to him that he did, nor did he recall anyone saying that before. But then few people knew them both well enough to say so. Gitau could see his mother too, and more strongly, but was understanding enough not to say so.

'Do you remember this?' The old man began to sing - one of the songs he had sung to James as a youngster. His voice was cracked now and his breath did not allow him to touch the notes fully but the gentleness remained. James remembered the tune but was not prepared to admit it. Once these words had united a mature African man and a young European boy. Now these same lyrics separated, by embarrassment, the old man and the youth whose emotions were still held in the dying days of adolescence. The African held James's hand seeing the body of a babe he had once comforted. The European chose to feel no more than a wrinkled brown hand touching his pale skin. Feeling slightly repelled by the touch of a failing body, James withdrew his hand.

'You have seen a lot of changes.' James's formal and unimaginative question changed the level of the conversation.

The old man cocked his head and squinted at James. 'When your father and I worked together, life was good. We helped the farmers with our work. The ordinary people were better for our labours. I was proud to serve my people in that modern way.' There was the hint of a sermon. His one brown eye, veiled grey with age, moistened slightly as he brought back the past.

Malcolm having tired of Ngugi's friends joined his son. Grace made space for the two Europeans to sit either side of the old man whose old mind had relished the opportunity to reminisce.

'My grandfather told me he remembered the Europeans first coming to our area. He told of the wondrous things they could do although I know from my own life much of it was very ordinary. He said they thought everything the Africans did was wrong - their agriculture, their religion, their clothes. He told how they took the communal land and built farms, how they taxed the Africans to make them work on the farms. Yet his son, my father, idolised them. He joined their army and learned to fight. Can you imagine? One generation goes out to fight with spears and arrows, clad in animal skins, flitting from bush to bush. And the next is parading in smart crisp uniforms, rushing across the landscape in vehicles and firing guns. He tried to teach me what he had learnt - the discipline, the routine, the cleanliness, the obedience. He sent me to a mission school and I learnt to be a good Christian. And as a good son I believed and trusted him. Then one day he did not come home. He had been killed in Somalia, fighting some other Europeans in another part of Africa. I decided that if Europeans had to go to a foreign land to fight each other then perhaps they don't have the answers to everything. I understood that some of the things Europeans did were good and some were bad and my task was to tell the difference. I decided first that since their god said THOU SHALT NOT KILL but they killed, then their god must be wrong. I knew their god said THOU SHALT

NOT COMMIT ADULTERY but their servants knew that's just what they did. So, I went back to Ngai on the mountain and felt much easier with him.'

Ngugi hovered anxiously. 'Time to eat. Father, Grace will bring you something from the kitchen.'

'Tell her I want prawns,' he said rolling the African r, 'and tell her to wash them.'

He would not normally eat fish but they were like the grubs which he used to fry on a tin sheet. Although they were not hot, they did have their own salt, tasty for an old man.

'Perhaps the only good things the Europeans brought was prawns.' His laugh became a cackle. He looked at James and the youngster smiled back across the divide, each seeing his own humour in the remark.

'Did you get on all right with Grace, James?' asked Ngugi.

'Yes, she's very nice.'

'She remembers you as a toddler when your ayah brought you to the village once.'

'I don't remember that, I'm afraid.'

'She's always had a special place in our family.' He looked at Malcolm knowing he knew the story of her birth.

'A gift from God,' Gitau interjected.

'It was clear she was only partly African and father explained this to the other children by saying she was a gift from god. He didn't say which god,' Ngugi explained

'Ngai, of course. Who else? You think I'm foolish.'

'Well, she was a gift from someone but it certainly wasn't god' said Ngugi sullenly.

'All parents invent stories to explain things to their children. What will you tell your children when I am dead? That I am in heaven I expect.'

'All right father. That's enough of that. You're embarrassing Mr. Bryant.'

'Embarrassing you, you mean.'

'Come on Malcolm, you too James. Let's get something to eat.'

The food was served to the side of the house under a permanent awning. A full range of meats, several salads, sauces and pickles, rice and a curry. The food was served by uniformed attendants who came round topping up glasses with beer or fruit juice as the meal progressed. James and Grace sat on the wall around the veranda and behind them the toothless old man champed his prawns and maize meal and just occasionally stopped to giggle.

After the meal Malcolm and Ngugi walked around the garden turning to look at the house. Malcolm remembered the ragamuffin who came with Rogers and was the first African whom he had met after stepping from the airport. He recalled the youngster whose liveliness and curiosity so much needed a good education. He recollected how he had helped to get the boy through school and through university. His pride was paternal not only because Ngugi had metamorphosed into a second son - a first son he sometimes felt - but also the enlightened European had raised the noble savage above his ignorance. He felt no shame at this last thought although had he been more reflective, he might have been at least embarrassed.

'You've done well. Your father must be very pleased.'

'Yes, it's all come good,' Ngugi said not mentioning his father.

Malcolm had hoped for a word of thanks at that point. In his view the boy had only prospered because of his magnanimity and he resented Ngugi's lack of appreciation. Ngugi talked with a pride that stopped short of bragging how he had risen though the ranks of the civil service to his present post. He acknowledged it was relatively easy to do. He was bright, well qualified and many of his peer group were in business on their own account or with the multinationals to be bothered with government.

'Come let me show you something.' Ngugi took him by the arm into the house and through to an office near the front door.

'Look' He pointed to the top three rows of a bookshelf at the books Malcolm had given all those years ago. 'I still read them now. Whenever I go on a trip abroad, I take one of these to read.' He took one down. It was Wuthering Heights, a book that had once belonged to Alison when a school girl. Malcolm hoped Ngugi would not hand it to him or open it even. He knew that inside the front cover in Alison's teenage writing was her own name. Ngugi put it back on the shelf, his eye caught by another. It was 'Robinson Crusoe'

'This was one of the first books you gave me. I used to read it to the family. We thought a man called Friday very funny. We called each other names. Mother Sunday, Sister Wednesday.' He paused. 'Life was beautifully simple then. When we look back, we see the things we've lost.' He saw a slight movement of Malcolm's face muscles. 'I'm sorry. That was thoughtless.' He turned back to the shelves.

'I don't take this one.' He'd selected the copy of *Tom Brown's Schooldays* that Rogers had given him. 'It's a bit old fashioned, isn't it? But I can't throw it away. I liked Bwana Rogers although he was old-fashioned too. There was a straightness about him. He didn't judge as much as you, younger ones. He treated me like a boy not an African boy.' The observation surprised Malcolm. 'Do you have contact with him?'.

'No. He died a few years ago. A stroke. I think Mrs Rogers has died too.'

They reminisced about the station and village life. Malcolm mentioned Flynn.

'He's still there,' volunteered Ngugi.

'I know. I'm going up to see him tomorrow. I'll hire a car.'

'There's no need. My chauffeur is taking father back to the village tomorrow. He could take you as well. He'll be coming back to Nairobi to pick me up at five. Use him for the day.'

'Thanks. That would be a big help.'

'Don't worry he won't be late. He's dropping me at the office at 8.00 then going to pick up father. He'll be at your hotel at 9.00. European time, I promise.' His light irony teased the Western obsession with punctuality.

Picking up James from the end of the garden he went to say goodbye to Gitau but the old man was fast asleep. His mouth was open and a paper serviette was still tucked into his shirt to protect his suit which hung loosely, disguising his frail body underneath. The contrast with the picture of a robust Gitau running the garden plots with clinical routine was hard to take.

Turning to Grace, still at James's side he said. 'I expect I'll see your mother tomorrow. I hope she is well. Do you have any message for her?'

The young woman's eyes clouded, their greenness assuming a hint of steely grey; a rush of blood turned her golden face to bronze. She hesitated. 'No. No message.'

Malcolm looked at her but she had turned away. He realised at once his blunder. She was the child Wambui had had by a European. She could not see her mother. She had never seen her mother even though they had lived close together. Wambui was under a sort of house arrest in Flynn's bungalow. He couldn't take back what he had said to the young woman and to try to make amends might only make things worse. She was moving away from him now into the seclusion of the house. She took with her the burden of family duty leaving Malcolm ashamed at his clumsiness.

As they returned to the hotel Malcolm reflected upon the day. The surroundings had been impressive. He was pleased for Ngugi for whom he now had affection. Perhaps he was more pleased for Gitau for whom he had respect. He reflected too on the family strains. Gitau and Ngugi ill at ease on modern Africa; father and son not fully together. And then Grace and her mother, once close geographically but separated by some other gulf. It did not resolve the gap between himself and his own son but it did remind him that in the tension between the generations his problems were not unique. That there was a lot of muddle and unhappiness around brought him a perverse comfort.

THIRTY-TWO

The next day saw Malcolm waiting for the car on the hotel steps in bright early morning sunshine. The prospect of this day had stuck out from the plateau of his expectations as few had done before. It invoked so many memories his brain could not begin to give order and shape to them.

To capture the day, he borrowed James's camera and this was now slung over his shoulder. James had reluctantly agreed and showed his father how to set the speed and focus and explained the functions of the various buttons and levers. He overestimated his father's understanding and the latter nodded in mute incomprehension. Finally, he got James to select a setting which seemed most likely to meet the lighting conditions he would experience and vowed not to change it.

That James would not be coming with him was a source of tension between them. He had implored his son to come, going beyond the mild request he thought adequate. In planning their holiday, he had taken for granted that James would want to visit his old home and had built their joint pilgrimage into their itinerary. But somewhere washing around in James's mind was an unfocussed anxiety which ruled this visit out. Now a spurious lifeline came his way. Sara was spending the day by the pool. She had invited him to join her and hormones had a stronger pull than homage.

So, Malcolm waited alone, the anticipation of the day muting the disappointment at his son's refusal to come with him. This time the car was not late and he got in the rear seat alongside Gitau, the old man dwarfed by the cavernous interior. The car, cool and powerful, insulated them from the busy streets and soon took the road to Kimura. For Malcolm old familiarities returned. The road, newly resurfaced, sliced through land variously cultivated with maize and

305

bananas in patches separating larger expanses of coffee. On the far hills beyond the plantations, little clusters of huts could be seen, the heat blending them into the landscape. Little seemed changed out here in the country. The women labouring under their bundles of wood, the young girls balancing cans of water on their heads, the young boys directing goats with long sticks and the men strolling unconcerned through this activity might have been the same people who trod this road a generation before. That was not so. This was a more numerous, more seasoned, more disappointed generation and their prevailing feeling was not optimism but betrayal. But all this lay below the level of tourist interest.

The Changa gorge was spanned by a new bridge, wider and more substantial. In England such improvement might have arisen after a series of road accidents, a public outcry, a petition, meetings with ministers and eventually action. Here it might have something to do with one powerful man enhancing his standing in his own area. Malcolm could not avoid looking out of the window at the ravine. He managed to avoid any public emotion. It burst out when the old man put his hands on Malcolm's arm and squeezed it gently. Malcolm sucked in air a handful of times to choke back any sobs. The driver looked in his mirror and turned uncomfortably back to the road.

The turn off for Kimura brought another change. The road once dirt, was now solid tarmac and would be so right up to Gitau's village. When they came to the agricultural station where the two men had worked together, Gitau ordered the driver to stop. The heavy car pulled off the tarmac onto the dirt which had been part of the compound of houses, churning the dust with its wheels.

'Come,' said Gitau, 'let's remember the old days.'

Malcolm and the driver helped the old man to get out of the car. He took Malcolm's arm and said something in Kikuyu to the driver who moved away.

Malcolm had glanced at the buildings before turning to help Gitau and had been shocked at what he saw. The bungalows, once regimentally clean and well-kept but with their original starkness mellowed by plants and weather, were now seedy and neglected. Peeling paint and broken windows gave an air of dereliction yet the buildings were occupied, as young children milled about and older faces peered from windows. The fences and car ports had been demolished to feed the food stoves in evidence outside some houses. Down one wall - of his first house - a broken gutter had leaked rainwater causing a brown stain on the once clean surface.

Gitau clutched Malcolm's arm as he walked slowly across the compound. In the centre of the square remained the old tree under which Gitau had taken his routine breaks from work. Here he and James played their games - Gitau the RSM drilling his lone squaddie, Gitau the native chief and James the intrepid explorer paying his respects. Now in the shade of its branches sat several old men. Gitau greeted them in Kikuyu. Although he could not remember much of the tribal language - what he did, not going little beyond greetings and instructions - it was clear to Malcolm from the body language that these were people who knew each other well. Gitau pointed to one of them. He had enlarged ear lobes, the hanging flaps tied like shoelaces. His shirtless body revealed breast bones standing proud of the skin in the V of his knitted jumper.

'Njage used to work at the station. He remembers you.'

The African's face had aged too much for familiarity but the earlobes were a distinctive and memorable feature. Malcolm stooped to shake his hand and remembered a Kikuyu greeting. On this, the men's faces became more animated and their replies indicated friendliness even though they spoke too quickly in their tribal language for Malcolm to follow. He added something in Swahili which all understood.

Malcolm and Gitau left the group and continued across the square.

'Are you surprised? Disappointed even?' asked Gitau turning to face Malcolm's old home.

'At the shabbiness, the decay?' Malcolm nodded. In his planning for this day Malcolm had imagined himself returning to his family home and standing in the rooms in which he had lived with Alison. Nothing would have persuaded him to do it now.

'What did you expect? Did you expect these people to ignore these dwellings with the shelter they provide? Did you expect them to polish the floors, paint the woodwork?' Gitau's voice was tinged with an unusual sharpness.

'No. I suppose not.' He recalled he had not polished the floors or painted the woodwork either.

'What happened to Karui? Is his still here?'

Gitau shook his head. 'About a year after you left, he went back to his village. There has been no word since. He was older than me and I'm only just alive.' He chuckled as he put his head on one side and looked at Malcolm with his one good eye.

The buildings would eventually stand as ruins in the relentless grip of the African vegetation which had been stripped away to build them in the first place. Malcolm recalled the country walks of his student days occasionally coming across derelict cottages tucked away in woods, their roofs missing, walls tumbling, brambles trailing across what once had been living rooms and kitchens. People had lived in them once, had been born and had died, had hoped and despaired, had rejoiced and mourned. This was no different except the buildings before him now had been part of his life and in their decay, he could not help but see his own.

Ahead was the office from which the toddler James had run to greet him on that fateful day. Gone now the imprint of his feet on the fine dry soil; now remained only memories chemicalised into Malcolm's brain, a bewildered infant face becoming accusing under his own interpretation. The two men skirted the building both privately aware of its significance. They walked behind the building to the plot where they had worked together for so long. The wire fence remained. Where it was damaged tree branches had been used to fill the gaps to keep out animals. Malcolm rested his palms against the fencing his fingers poking through and clutching the wire. Inside, the ground was still cultivated. Few signs of the variety of crops that had been grown for research now only the staples of daily life and no sign of James's personal garden. At least some part of the past remained and food was growing here. Not with the precision of earlier days but as a wayward allotment. Malcolm stooped to pick up a plastic marker tag caught in the base of the wire mesh fence. Immune from decay it waited for future archaeologists to identify its meaning and deduce what had gone on there. Malcolm could not make out the writing which had been blurred by many seasons. He slid it in his pocket, a souvenir much more valuable than carved napkin rings or hide covered drums. How odd that this souvenir of Africa was made in Northampton.

As they returned across the square, one of the group of old men spoke to Gitau in Kikuyu and responded again when Gitau replied. Whatever he said the whole group nodded assent and Malcolm felt the paranoia of the foreigner denied an access to language. He remembered he once gave these people orders and paid them money so that their families could eat. Now he had no power over them and their permanence and solidarity were giving them power over him.

Gitau explained, 'He said, he wished the Europeans were back. Then, they had work and food and justice. They looked after us like good parents. I told him that if you had stayed, we would be children for ever. He said children are usually happy - only grown-ups are sad.'

Malcolm smiled, the grim smile of regret. He had shared an era with these old men, there had been a kind of kinship - patronising perhaps - but with the link of shared optimism. Their nation had gained independence, their children would be free. And that seemed to have gone, eroded by factors beyond their control, though perhaps within the control of their children. Today, like their fathers and grandfathers before them, they sat in the dust under a tree protecting themselves from the sharp sun but denied the hope that life might be better for them tomorrow.

Malcolm and Gitau returned to the car. As they approached the car the driver appeared from one of the buildings and dispersed the several youngsters who were playing around the open door of the ministerial limousine. Malcolm remembered he had James's camera and for a moment thought about capturing the scenes they had just seen. Almost immediately he rejected the idea. Better a hazy memory of a rich interlude than a photograph of this present reality.

They drove up the road to another surprise as they approached Larsen's farm. The once well-tended coffee bushes had risen unpruned and between them the weeds had grown to match their height. The gates to the farm were closed and padlocked. Beyond the gates it was clear the farm had been neglected. Weeds had intertwined themselves through the chain link fencing allowing an insipid flower to catch the sun. As the car stopped at the gate two large dogs emerged from an outbuilding and bounded snarling to the gate. They snapped ferociously at the limousine. A man emerged pulling on a dishevelled uniform top. When he saw the car, he rushed to pull back the dogs returning them to the building and stood in the shaded doorway. To one side of the gate where Larsen had had an elephant's skull was erected a signboard which read *Kimura Coffee Co* with a Nairobi address and box number.

What happened? It's growing wild. Back to bush.'

'Yes. It is'. Malcolm had expected a tone of regret but thought he heard satisfaction. He wondered whether Gitau's accent had misled him.

'What happened to Larsen?' inquired Malcolm knowing the Swede had left the country.

'He has gone.' came the terse reply and then something in Kikuyu to the driver who started off.

Malcolm gazed out of the window. The land seemed so barren compared with England's greenness. Yet people lived in it, raised children, tended crops, their ambitions blunted by its harshness, their characters shaped by its severity. Soon the car pulled off the road into Gitau's village. The modern machine was incongruous in the rural setting, its precise lines a contrast to the disjointed surroundings, its value an insult to the surrounding poverty. There were more people around than before and some of the newer huts had corrugated iron roofs and brick walls. A few of the traditional huts remained, Gitau's among them. The bar was still there but inside an oil drum of locally brewed beer had replaced the crates of commercial beer of Malcolm's era. The loss of the research station and the coffee estate was felt throughout the village and its inhabitants were returning to less costly and more risky practices. As always children and chickens ran about the open spaces looking for anything of interest. Malcolm seemed to remember the children of his time would wear old uniforms, often khaki shirts and shorts, looking like dishevelled boy scouts. Now T-shirts were the order of the day their modern urban slogans and designer motifs mocking the rural innocence. One boy had trainers - not a pair but two of different designs.

The driver got a small suitcase from the boot and took it into Gitau's hut. Moments later a young woman emerged. She was introduced as Gitau's wife and Malcolm assumed the baby on her back was Gitau's but nothing was said.

'Will you take some tea?'

Malcolm declined Gitau's invitation. He had always found it difficult to eat or drink anything prepared in the villages although he had never come to any harm. 'I've arranged to be at Father Flynn's for lunch,' he reminded Gitau. 'I'll walk' He addressed the driver, 'I'll be back here at four o'clock'.

He'd forgotten how hot the African sun could be and found the journey more tiring than he thought. If he left his sun hat on, he sweated, if he took it off, he burned. Nevertheless, it was a nice change to walk on a country road - no pavement, no street lights, no shops - only miles of open country showing a natural if not picturesque aspect. The dry-season dust had settled over the countryside making it seem drabber than he had remembered, like an old photograph faded by chemical decay. Flynn too would be decayed he feared, fading into the sparse surroundings that had shaped his adult life. Malcolm marvelled at his friend's commitment. He had known few churchmen but had nevertheless tended to cast them all into the same jaundiced slot in his perceptions - vicars, priests, padres, imams, rabbis; it made little difference. But Flynn was exceptional; no flummery for him, no easy platitudes, no false piety. And it was this place that made him different; this was no place to pretend, not for 40 years.

Malcolm rounded the corner and saw the handful of trees still providing shade from the sharp sun. But now they shaded not just a handful of rocks but a rough wooden bench beneath which grew coarse grass protected by the bench from a variety of feet and host to many insects. Then turning towards the bungalow, he could see its roof edging above the wispy grass and spreading over the highest ridge the Yesterday, Today and Tomorrow plant. Once he had seen it, a small shrub struggling against the drought and heat. Now it proclaimed its triumph. Malcolm's heart leapt and he wanted to run.

The narrow path to the priest's house was slightly overgrown but did not obscure the view of the veranda on which sat his old friend. He was motionless as if dead. As Malcolm approached a low voice spoke from the shadows of the house. Flynn's shoulder twitched and he looked intently into his garden. He did not see Malcolm until he was quite near the bungalow. He rose from his seat as Malcolm approached. He paused with slightly bent back as he got used to being on his feet. Finally, he straightened expelling a noisy breath as he did so. Malcolm put out his hand formally, not sure if the friendship they had once shared had lasted. The priest went as if to hug his guest but ended up grasping his hand in both of his, holding it without shaking.

'Hello, my friend. How good to see you.'

'And you too. It's been a long time, Joe. You've not changed.' Malcolm said but meant the opposite and forgot he had changed too.

'You're alone. No James?'

'No. I'm afraid he wouldn't come. Nothing to do with you. Other things I suppose. He's at a difficult age.' The untrue cliché all he could think of. 'I'm sorry,' Malcolm spoke the truth.

'Come and sit down. You look as though you need a drink.' Flynn called in Kikuyu to the rooms beyond and a voice replied monosyllabically.

Malcolm looked out from the veranda up the valley. There was no sign of the mountain. In the heat of the day the cloud and dust had gathered around it to disguise its precise outline usually only visible at dawn and dusk. The garden was fuller and more mature. Trees were higher, foliage thicker both combining to fence in the garden. Some bougainvillea provided vivacity among the more delicate colours of Yesterday, Today and Tomorrow, tumbling down to form a curtain at the end of the veranda.

'I see the blossoms still keep coming,' Malcolm was referring to the plant that had teased their imaginations so long ago.

'Yes. Yes. Birth, life and death.'

Wambui appeared with a tray on which was a jug of lemonade and two glasses. In a European setting Malcolm might have risen to greet her. Here her status as an African woman servant seemed to absolve him of normal courtesy. She too had aged, her face showing no emotion through its wrinkles.

'I saw your daughters yesterday. Grace seems well. And Rose. She has prospered.'

The woman nodded but said nothing and placed the tray on the table between the two men. The ice jingled in the glass jug as she set it down. She withdrew and Flynn poured the lemon drink in each glass.

'Good health.' The toast seemed incongruous given the beverage.

'She is still with you then?'

'Wambui? Yes. She's been with me a long time.' He paused. 'It must be twenty-five years. Our silver wedding.' He became embarrassed when he realised what he had said. 'No, it's more than that. Thirty at least since she first came to work here. Oh, hasn't time flown'.

'I have never seen her outside of this house.'

'No. This house has been her life for a quarter of a century. During that time, she has never gone beyond its boundaries. To my knowledge anyway.'

'That's extraordinary. Her family only live a few hundred yards away.'

'Yes.'

'But why?' Malcolm knew pieces of the story from many years ago usually from male gossip. He knew little of the woman at the centre of the episode.

'She had a baby which wasn't her husband's. This was realised after the baby was born when it became clear its father was white. The family took tribal advice and expelled her.'

'The baby was Grace,' Malcolm was confirming not asking.

'Yes. Wambui's husband, Gitau's brother, banished her. Men have a lot of power in family affairs. She had nowhere to go. She was already working for me and so she stayed here and has been here ever since. We get along OK. Once you get behind a person's religion or nationality .. ,' he paused briefly, ' .. or race, and find another human being, things are quite different. Her husband hung himself in the end, though it wasn't the rope that killed him but the drink. Gitau brought up Grace and the other children.'

'I was told the father was Forbes.' Bernie had told him the history once, delighting in the misfortune of others.

314

'She told the family that Forbes had raped her,' Flynn agreed reluctantly.

Malcolm remembered Larsen's foreman, Ken Forbes, as a Scot who had come to Kenya with an army gratuity and drifted around accumulating the farming skills that brought him to work for Larsen. Divorced, he spent much of the time at the Phoenix club or in the bars of Nairobi. He seemed a harmless enough man, though not one James would have wanted for company. His jokes were the stuff of bars and barrack rooms, his stories inevitably consisted of someone else making a mess of something. He had offered to supervise the staff on the station for the few days after Alison's death and his wish to help seemed genuine enough. Gitau had indicated help would not be needed and the animosity between the two men might have been the explanation.

'But surely she wouldn't be banished because she was raped. African history is full of tribal wars with women taken as prizes. It wasn't her fault'

'Her husband took up the case with the DC. Forbes denied it. The police investigated and found inconsistencies in her story. They concluded she had made up the story of rape. Her husband believed it was Forbes and that she went with him willingly, perhaps for money. Gitau's brother was badly damaged by drink even then and Wambui says he was not a proper husband.'

'And they chucked her out.'

'They have a strict moral code to follow just as I have.'

'But you took her in.'

'I am supposed to show compassion and forgiveness. I followed the church's teaching. So, she came to live here. It was a place of refuge which the church can provide.'

'But it was you that provided the refuge, not the church.'

Flynn nodded. 'But the church guides me.'

'What happened to Forbes?'

'Nothing then, but about five years ago he was found murdered on the estate. He had been badly mutilated, slashed with pangas. I didn't see the body; Larsen took charge and it was all hushed up. One of the villagers told me Forbes was alive when he was found. It must have been an awful death.' He held the cross on his chest.

'Revenge? For Wambui?'

Flynn shrugged. 'There are many rumours. It was the time when a company was trying to buy out Larsen. He wouldn't sell and perhaps someone was trying to frighten him off. If so, it worked. Within six months Larsen had sold up and gone to South Africa.'

'But why has the estate been neglected?'

'It's a mystery. The sign went up. The guards came in and then nothing. I can understand some African coveting a prosperous farm but then neglecting it makes no sense. No sense at all. Let's have lunch'. Flynn was glad of the opportunity to close the conversation.

Inside the talk was less personal with Flynn wanting to know about contemporary UK, politics, sport, the Royal family. They reminisced and discussed past acquaintances they neither wanted to remember, important only because they linked the two men. Wambui delivered the courses in silence. Each time Malcolm turned to her with some polite comment on his lips he was deterred by her impassive features. Although lined, her face was strong. Malcolm wondered about her giving herself, willingly or otherwise, to a European and he wondered about the European too.

Coffee on the veranda nearly lapsed into a siesta.

'Let's go to the corner view. I haven't been for some time now. It's getting a little too far. I used to go to be alone; now I only feel lonely. You can help me.' Flynn grunted as he struggled to his feet and reached for a walking stick hooked onto the back of his chair.

The walk there showed how frail Flynn had become but after a few stops they got there. Flynn rattled his walking stick in the undergrowth beneath the seat to scare away any snakes. They sat in the shade of the trees gazing at a scene that had not changed. The mid-afternoon sun glazed the hills and buzzing insects amplified the silence induced by the heat. Not much conversation flowed each man retreating into torpid introspection.

Malcolm looked at his old friend. He was fatter now, his hair thin and white, edging greasily below the edges of his straw sun hat, his sunburnt skin shaded with red as if at odds with the climate. He kept dropping to sleep jolting awake as his body began to fall from the seat.

Conscious of the time Malcolm woke his old friend who had dozed off. The older man widened his eyes to shake the sleep from them and Malcolm saw again their sharp greenness. He realised he had seen those eyes before and a huge truth took him.

'Grace is your child. Isn't she?' The words were out before he thought of the consequences.

The priest, only recently woken from slumber took time to reply.

'Yes. *Yes.*' The first word a soft and tentative admission, the second a firm and defiant affirmation. He clung to the cross around his neck.

It seemed impertinent to ask more and Flynn was not ready to declare. Malcolm took in the extent of what had been revealed. Flynn had broken the vows which had underpinned his whole life. What would the parishioners at home who had given their shillings to build his church have thought? Malcolm had no difficulty in forgiving his friend; he understood only too well the despair of loneliness. As an atheist it was easy for him to forgive. But what about Flynn's God? Did He forgive his errant disciple? He looked at the clouded hills and wondered what Ngai would have made of it too.

Flynn felt elevated by the revelation and understood, as he had not done before, the power of confession. Previously it had been a ritual in which he had played the formal role of sounding board. Now he understood its cathartic effect. All that had gone before could be re-evaluated. Wambui had come to work one day in a state of deep distress. Under the influence of drink her husband had abused her more than usual and she could see no future beyond this torment. Tearfully she clung to him her tears soaking the shoulder of his shirt. Flynn drew her to him with human understanding and against the firm advice of his tutors long ago. When her sobbing subsided, she drew away from him but her eyes met his and they both knew something serious had happened. Their physical union followed naturally and Flynn was pleased with its simple pleasure. Only later did he experience the awful guilt of his act. And thus, Grace was conceived and Wambui lied to protect him. Flynn knew the religious crime he was committing but he was not in the bowels of Mother Church. He was in a foreign land, remote from institutional scrutiny, with only this one woman for his human consolation. He thought God would condone it, might bless it even. He was a kind, loving God. Surely, he didn't want to inflict unhappiness. After a while such thoughts faded. What had happened, had happened and could not be undone. Indeed, the fact of his sinning seemed to add to the happiness of his life. As a priest - a pure priest - he was separate from his fellow human beings, remote even. But once having sinned he became one of them, joined their flawed company and rejoiced in this communion of error. But this had remained undisclosed to the world beyond his house. Once he had feared its revelation would be his downfall. Now it was known he felt relief and joy.

'Does Grace know you are her father?'

'I don't think so. Only Wambui would know and she hasn't met Grace since she was banished. Grace would have been about a year old. Isn't that cruel, not to be able to meet your child even though she lives only a short distance away?'

'But you met her. You saw her in the village. You spoke to her, your own daughter?'

'Yes. Such torment. I would see her, a happy child, playing with her brothers and sisters, growing up into womanhood. I saw all these things but could never hold her to me, sit her on my knee and sing her songs, caress her in times of unhappiness or fear. She would call me Father as they all do. And I would hear her say that word but could not call her daughter. Do you know those pictures of our Lord sitting with young children on his knee? He could do that with strangers, but I could not do that with my own child. Sacrifice takes many forms. I suppose it was a punishment for my sin. We usually see punishment as something done to us, a calculated act by a higher authority. But very often we punish ourselves, haunted by our own actions, frightened by our own weaknesses. And perhaps that is a greater punishment.'

Malcolm knew the anguish of separation from a child. He and his son were distant too. Was there no catalyst that could unite these two fathers with their children? A deeper realisation dawned. Had Forbes been killed in revenge for a rape he did not commit? Wambui's lies and Flynn's silence may have led to the death of an innocent man. Malcolm would not know that Flynn understood this and daily anguished over his beads. He would not know that this simple man could not even discuss this prospect with Wambui, although surely, she knew too. Malcolm reached out and touched his friend on the arm

'We must go back. Take my arm.'

They returned slowly to the house stopping occasionally to regain strength. Near to the house they looked at the foliage over the veranda roof. As always, their interest centred on the Yesterday, Today and Tomorrow.

'It looks like it always did - some buds, some blooms, some deadheads - but they're not the same. Only the overall picture looks the same but the individual flowers come and go. I bloomed once. I built a church. I converted unbelievers. I brought relief and hope into suffering lives. But now I'm just a deadhead. The blooming can be so intense but the deadness is so long. So long.'

'But Grace is blooming now,' Malcolm responded, glad to lighten the mood.

'I hope so. I hope so.'

'Do you know what they call her within the family.'

'I've no idea.'

'A gift from God.'

Flynn stiffened. 'From God. A gift. Really. Oh. How wonderful. How wonderful.' He took out his handkerchief and blew strongly into it.

'Do you think they meant your god or Ngai?'

'I don't think it matters.'

'I've intruded a lot. I shouldn't have done. I'm sorry.'

'No, it's all right. I've hidden a lot from you over the years. I think you understand why. It's easier to talk of these things nowadays. Morality has been redefined so often I'm not sure there are any sins left, certainly not many I'm likely to commit. At times it's been very lonely here particularly after you left when the station closed. And then Larsen went. I could have gone home except this is my home if the word has any meaning. And I wouldn't have left Wambui.'

Malcolm realised that Flynn's separation from his daughter would have overlapped James's birth and childhood. And throughout that time his friend, his dear friend, could only experience true parenthood through vicarious association with Alison and James. He could not reveal his feelings; they were bottled up inside him. Malcolm thought how much more they had shared than he realised. He looked again at the plant that had produced so many imaginative ideas over the years. He took James's camera from its cover and not daring to adjust the settings further, pointed it at the veranda roof and pressed the shutter button. They climbed the veranda and found lemonade awaiting them.

'I've never asked God to forgive me, only to understand. Can you imagine anything so absurd as to ask an omnipotent being to understand?'

'Does He? Understand, I mean.'

'I have to believe so. If he doesn't, Hell is going to be very crowded.'

'But He sent you a gift. Grace.'

'Well, He sent a gift but not to me. I've always thought of Wambui as my gift. No, Grace is for others to enjoy.'

'And what of the future? What will you do?'

'I shall stay here where I belong. It's not the same as it was. I do not have the energy to teach the youngsters. Anyway, there is a new school near the main road. Ngugi got it built, I think. I still give services but attendance is not like it was. The church is decaying - the building I mean. I try to keep it in shape. I'm still paid by the society - not much, but I have few needs. I shall be all right. I'm not alone.' He remembered a little plan he had hatched. 'Talking of loneliness reminds me. I have had one other companion all these years albeit a rather quiet one.' He took something from the shelf beneath the coffee table. It was the sign with Gerald Daley's name on it. 'This fell down the other day. The string holding it had crumbled with age. A bit like me, I suppose. When I go Gerald will be left quite alone and I wouldn't want him to experience that. Will you take this sign with you and give him some company in your own home?'

Malcolm nodded acceptance and brushed the surface of the sign clean, the stray tail of the Y now less hidden by the sun-faded stain revealing the X beneath.

When it was time to go the two men stood facing each other. Each understood the other had led a life which had been denied richness by massive burdens, the one carrying the unyielding responsibilities of priesthood the other the unrelenting legacy of childhood. Briefly their lives had blossomed and they had seen the potential which others seemed to enjoy effortlessly and continuously. Both had fallen back into lives in which routine had been the only defence against abject despair. It was not clear who made the first move but in an instant the two men clung to each other in a ragged but sustained embrace. It was not the embrace of love or sex but the clinging together of people frightened by their individual insignificance each conscious of his failings and living life in their shadow. They hung together rejoicing in their partnership, at least their desperation was shared. They parted both slightly embarrassed by the intimacy of their act but each soothed by the tensions it released.

Malcolm bade farewell and despite offering the old man a place to stay if he came to the UK, he knew he would not see this friend again. Both knew it, but with uncomfortable civility chose to ignore it. Flynn watched his friend go until he disappeared at the end of the path. He turned towards his chair to find Wambui taking his arm ready to see him safely seated and looking down the valley. She stood behind his chair resting her hand on his shoulder. He reached his own arm across his chest and placed his hand over hers.

Malcolm hurried down the road looking at his watch realising the four o'clock deadline was near but arrived in plenty of time. Gitau was there to see him off.

'Does Grace ever visit here?'

'No.'

'Does she not want to see her mother?'

'No.' Again there was no explanation

'It would be nice if you could find forgiveness for Wambui. I think it would be nice for Grace to have a mother to confide in.'

'It has been too long. The sun has dried the emotion out of it. It is best to let things be.'

'Will you do something for me? Will you see Flynn is looked after?'

'Of course.'

'Will you visit him for me?'

The response was delayed, 'Perhaps.'

'Goodbye Gitau, Take care of yourself.'

'Goodbye Bwana Bryant. I am old. Time will take care of me. And Ngai watches. You are still young. Who takes care of you?'

Malcolm had no answer. He shook the old man's hand, a simple gesture safe in both their cultures and got into the car. For the second time he left a man he would never see again although with Gitau there was not the sadness. Gitau would live out his life respected by his family, enlivened by his friends, secure in the culture into which he had been born. In as much as it makes sense to say so, it would be a natural life ending in a natural death.

The car created eddies of dust as it pulled from the village onto the tarmacked road. Malcolm looked ahead ignoring the waving children behind. On the road he studiously avoiding looking across the square to the research station. Years before he had driven along this narrow road believing it to be the last time. This time he was older and the act had an irretrievable finality about it, a feeling which seemed to permeate so much of his life now. Back on the main road he wanted to burst into tears but a lifetime of stifled emotion held them back.

As the car crossed the Changa bridge Malcolm told the driver to stop on the other side. This was not spontaneous and his plan to do this might well have heightened his emotions all day. Life with Alison had been a wonderful supporting sea of reassurance and understanding on which he had floated gratefully. He knew that if he did not stop here now, he would never have the chance to do so again and he wanted to confront his loss. He needed to revisit the scene of his wife's death much as the family of murder victims need to confront the killer; not for revenge but to remove an unseen and irrational presence which would otherwise infiltrate their lives for ever. They needed to exorcise the culprit so that their emotions could linger on the victim. He walked back to the centre of the bridge. For him the ravine below had been, still was, an abyss into which had poured his only hope of a fulfilled life. As Alison's blood had poured over the rocks below, the colour rushing with it was not just her

323

lifeblood but the colour of the flower that had been his life. He had been a deadhead from that moment.

He became aware of a young girl peering over the bridge with him. Her school uniform hung loosely from her shoulders over a slim body. She stood on naked tiptoe to see what Malcolm was looking at, her calf muscles taut under the strain. Seeing nothing she eased back and looked at Malcolm.

'Jambo. What are you looking for?' Malcolm supposed she meant looking at but her actual words were apposite.

'I was looking for something I lost a long time ago.'

'Down there?'

'Down there.'

'What was it?'

He couldn't explain and sought to change the subject.

'What is your name?'

'Miriam' came the soft reply her accent blurring the syllables.

For a moment he thought she had said Marion and the cruel coincidence was too much so that the dam that had kept his emotions in check all day gave way. He rested his forehead on his angled forearms which supported his bent body on the rails of the bridge His shoulders heaved as he sobbed uncontrollably. Marion had dominated his youth. He thought he had left her behind in an England of long ago and that now she was so distant as to not to touch him. Yet she seemed to re-establish herself, here on the bridge, here at the scene of his great loss, her voice echoing from the stones below mocking his life. Eventually he recovered enough to return to the car leaving a small African girl bemused and a little frightened. The driver waited his arrival concerned that his passenger's distress might be attributable to him and anxious not to be late in picking up his boss.

The car dropped Malcolm at the hotel, the driver unresponsive to his thanks. His day had been filled with emotions whose intensity and concentration he had rarely experienced, disappointment at the station, sadness at Flynn's bungalow and despair at the bridge. He wanted James desperately. He wanted to hold him like he had held Flynn and tell him how much he loved him and how much he needed him. Had James been there with him on the bridge he might have done just that, but now he would do no such thing. During the journey back the barrier was rebuilt; routine life had restored its constraining bonds.

He found James at the pool side away from the hotel. He was lying on a sun bed with Sara on one next to him. A single large towel covered both their heads and they carried out a hidden conversation of the kind youngsters consider innocent and their parents deduce cannot be.

Malcolm sat at a table and ordered a beer as soon as a waiter appeared. He sat drinking looking at his son's legs and feet which occasionally jerked upwards. The beer was almost finished when James emerged and seeing his father, came over. He decided his father looked distinctly odd but put it down to the effects of sun which had noticeably burnt his face.

'How was your safari?'

Malcolm wasn't sure what to say.

'It was memorable,' he said at last.

'You didn't take many shots,' said James examining the counter.

'No. Just the one. There was nothing much I wanted to record. What I want to recall is in my head.'

James had no inclination to ask any more and his father had no wish to say more and the conversation died. The son returned to his friend; the father ordered another beer; they were still close but separate and unsharing.

THIRTY-THREE

It had been a disturbed night. The events of the previous day tumbled through Malcolm's mind and combined with the heat to prevent solid sleep. Questions were asked, repeating before any answers were given. Words interacted with images. Body reacted to mind.

He asked whether Flynn could love Wambui as he had done Alison. Was race, culture, expectation no barrier? How did a religious man cope with the killing of an innocent man for fathering a child which was the priest's own? Did Wambui's presence ease the loneliness Flynn must have felt or merely highlight his isolation? What was Wambui to him? - loving, gentle, supportive, passionate? To Malcolm she was a spectre emerging from the darkness of the kitchen and yielding no emotions. Yet she shared Flynn's life day after day for twenty-five years. He felt himself not to have slept at all but he was woken from slumber by James in the next bed.

'Thank heavens for morning. You've been talking in your sleep most of the night.'

'What did I say?' Malcolm was fearful of revealing anything of himself. He had not slept in the same room as anyone else since Alison's death except with James on their last night in Kenya.

'Nothing much. Not sentences. A lot of mumbling. Plenty of sighs and groans. Did you know you snored?' To a friend he would have reported the farting.

Malcolm relaxed.

'Who was Marion?' The son was half hopeful of discovering an old flame or indeed a new one.

Malcolm went cold. He didn't remember dreaming of Marion at all. 'She was my sister.'

'You've never mentioned her before.'

'She was older than me. She died long before you were born, before I came to Kenya. She was ....,' he wanted to avoid handicapped and all the questions that might follow, '.... unwell all her life. It was for the good that she died'.

The cliché choked him. She did not know whether it was good for her or not. What he meant was: it was good for him. It shamed him that he always found her a burden, his childhood and adolescence muddied by a sister who was an outcast. He dismissed the thought that without her he might have been unhappy anyway, that she was just an excuse. Perhaps there was no one to blame; except there's always someone to blame if you look hard enough.

'You don't talk about your parents either. What were they like?' The small bedroom gave an intimacy these two did not normally share and James reacted to it with an ease his father could not muster. Malcolm wanted to do better than a cliched put-off but his image of his parents had atrophied into the adolescent judgement of them as accomplices in Marion's blight on his life. He had not tried, or allowed himself, to see his parents as much Marion's victims as he was. They were adults so they had to be to blame; they had power; his young mind decided. Even when he became a parent himself, he did not revise his judgements. James's childhood was equable and the youngster made so few claims on his father he had little cause to see that parenthood was often a burden, that parents could be the subject of the child and might have no more power to affect the world about them than their offspring.

'I suppose they were rather dull. They had their hands full with Marion. I suppose I felt neglected.'

'Awhhhh,' came the teasing reply from James to his father's self-pity.

Malcolm gave a slight smile conscious of the difference in perception of the two men. He was grateful for the pricking of a self-indulgent bubble. He felt lighter. His son wondered if dullness was inherited.

The invitation to Ngugi's two days before had thrown their crude itinerary out of gear and at breakfast they considered their options.

'What's planned for today?'

'Aren't you going with your girlfriend?' He had meant girl friend but it was too late.

'She's not my girlfriend,' said James meaning it. 'They're going up to Treetops for two days.'

'That'll be nice for them. It's a bit contrived but a pleasant enough experience. He remembered a story about the Queen being there when her father died but rejected telling it, seeing it as the remote history it was to his son, like Everest and Stanley Matthews.

'Tomorrow I'll take you up country. We'll hire a car and set off early. There are some sights you must see. No people to meet, I promise, but lots to photograph. I'll keep it as a surprise.'

'OK. Sounds good.'

'But there's still today to take care of.'

'Isn't there a snake park?'

'Yes. You might be disappointed but it's as good a way as any at getting close to snakes.'

He considered telling the story of Boniface and the snake bite forgetting the incident led him to Alison and all that followed. He avoided the story sensing his son did not want more reminiscences.

'I can go on my own then I don't feel pressured over time. I might get some good shots. The skin has a nice texture.'

'It's softer than it looks. You may get to hold one. There used to be some crocodiles there. Their skin is quite different. Don't you remember we used to take you there?' the question flowed out without thought. The *we* struck them both. James saw his father turn his eyes away from him but this time did not feel rejection but a slight pity. He did not understand his father's manner but he recognised there was something to understand. They never talked about Alison. There were plenty of photographs of her in albums and in frames about the house. Husband and son knew who she was but never referred to her. Although she was the physical link between them, she reinforced the emotional gulf that separated them. James formed a question about his mother but his father continued the conversation.

'Well, you go there and I'll look in the bazaar and the market for old times' sake. I'll meet you in the New Stanley at lunch time. It's opposite Woolworth's on Kenyatta Avenue. Take the map. Be careful.'

The warning irked James. At his age he did not understand the fear of parents losing something as precious as a child however old it was. For Malcolm to lose his son after bringing him out here would have been unbearable. Not in the city where he had lost his wife. As James zigzagged his way between the breakfast tables to the exit his father watched him, the capricious dagger of coincidence threatening his peace of mind.

In the city centre Malcolm stopped to examine the wooden carvings of the street sellers. The main attraction of the stall was its position in the shade of a building and, declining *a good price* for a lucky bracelet of genuine elephant hair, he turned to view the busy street. Across Kenyatta Avenue between some palm trees, he saw Paul Ngugi coming out of the doorway of a window-fronted office with two other men. The three men shook hands with each other and separated. Ngugi crossed the wide avenue, unknowingly towards Malcolm, but on seeing him greeted him warmly.

'Good morning. Did you enjoy your trip to Kimura? It's changed, hasn't it?'

'Flynn is still there. At least that hasn't changed.' He didn't mention Wambui. 'You'll know Larsen's sold up and gone.'

'I think he'd had enough.'

'Enough intimidation, do you mean?'

Ngugi paused before replying, 'The climate wasn't with his sort any more. The current turned against him.' The metaphors amplified the iciness in his voice.

'I must repay you for the use of the car and your hospitality the other day. Can you and your wife come to dinner at the hotel? This evening perhaps?'

It was a genuine wish to repay a social debt but he couldn't disguise from himself the opportunity it would provide to find out more about events at Kimura.

'That would be nice but Elizabeth is away up country at her family's. She's taken the children. But I'd be delighted to come. I'm tied up early evening. Would eight o'clock be OK?'

'Fine. Eight o'clock it is. I look forward to it.'

Malcolm stood watching him go. He was sturdily built, running to fat with good living, well dressed, smart without being ostentatious. Behind him followed another man, the chauffeur, now in bodyguard mode. Malcolm waited until the pair had disappeared down the street and then crossed the avenue to the office Ngugi had just left. A board outside listed a dozen companies resident there. The address was the same as the one on the board outside Larsen's estate but *Kimura Coffee Co.* was not listed. In the small foyer, he told the receptionist he had promised a friend in the UK to find some details of local businesses in horticulture he hoped to do some promotion for and asked for information. She went to several filing cabinets and produced a range of leaflets. Beyond her on the desk beside a filing cabinet was a filing tray labelled *Kimura*. She did not take anything from it. He scanned the brochures.

'Nothing on coffee?' he enquired.

'No, we're strictly vegetables and flowers.'

If she blushed her skin colour hid it and her face gave no flicker of response. Malcolm admired her professionalism.

As he sat waiting for James he skimmed through the brochures. The various companies were subsidiaries of a group called KENTRAD. One brochure featured the parent company, listing its directors and managers with their photographs. One was Lawrence, not now recognisable as the little brother who had trailed Ngugi around the village at Kimura, but one of the men who had emerged from the office half an hour ago. Malcolm didn't see James approach and was startled as he pulled back the chair next to him.

'Lost in thought, Dad. Nothing new then.' The finishing tease pleased Malcolm who took it as a sign that his son was not overawed by him, an indication that he was seen as another human being who might have a sense of humour tucked away somewhere. He smiled but said nothing not wanting to begin a speculative trail about things his son cared little for.

'I've just met Paul Ngugi. I've invited him for dinner at the hotel tonight.' James seemed indifferent. 'He's a very important man. A top civil servant.' Malcolm's irrelevant description failed to impress his son.

'More of the old days, I suppose.'

'Are you enjoying this holiday?'

The father was seeking a more positive response in another direction.

'Yes, better than I thought. I had expected you'd want to drag me everywhere with you.'

'Wouldn't you have wanted that?'

'No. This was your life not mine. I was here but not part of it. It's pretty meaningless to me.'

'Do you remember much of Kimura?' He had wanted to say 'of your mother' but couldn't realise the wish. He feared his son's memory would lessen the status he had given her.

'Not much. Bits and pieces. Faces and bodies but not names. I remember Gitau now I've met him again but he didn't linger before as a person, a body. I remember him as a presence; he seemed to be always there, even in bed at night. I remember mother vaguely and I remember the accident. Lots of crying. Everyone crying. Except you. You only shouted.'

Malcolm was surprised by the openness of the response and disappointed with its casualness. He'd forgotten that James hadn't lost a mother as he had lost a wife. He, too, remembered the shouting and his son's response.

'I suppose I frightened you with my shouting. I didn't mean to. I was upset. You can imagine'.

'I can see now how difficult it must have been. I can't remember what I felt then.'

And although that was true, he did know something important had happened then, something that couldn't be described in words. But he didn't blame his father for it, at least not now. But what had he felt in the interim? He was too young for that sort of introspection.

'I don't think you've ever mentioned your mother before.'

'It's never seemed appropriate. You didn't seem to want to.'

Say it, for Christ's sake say it, Malcolm said to himself, Couldn't. Not: didn't want to. Just couldn't.

The conversation was cathartic but he could say no more. He felt like some confused interviewee; bursting with things to say but uncertain of the propriety of saying them. The dam held. Even action was stifled. Most human beings would have managed something, a touch on the shoulders, a little punch of affection to the arm. But not Malcolm, not here in the open. People would have looked. Marion was in her chair beside him.

'It was a long time ago. Best to forget,' spoke uncomplicated youth.

No. Not a long time ago. It seems it was only yesterday and yet it was my Today. It was the highlight, the blossoming and you missed it. You only caught the twilight, but all this said silently.

THIRTY-FOUR

That evening Malcolm showered and dressed before his son. He and James had spent the afternoon by the pool. Malcolm tired after his restless night had fallen asleep and woken to feel his skin burning on his bare chest. Wisely he'd sat in the shade to begin with but the sun had moved round making his body vulnerable. James had been next to him, his lightly bronzed body contrasting with Malcolm's reddened skin, scored by paler lines where the sun had failed to reach between the folds of his flabby body. Now with his burnt skin, slightly eased with some cream, dragging against his clean shirt, he stood on the steps waiting for Ngugi. It was so nice to be in the evening's darkness and still feel warm. He watched, with a practised voyeurism, the comings and goings before him.

Moths and beetles flew around the lamps marking the hotel steps occasionally banging into the glass shade and ricocheting back into a frenzied orbit. High above them, an aeroplane, fuelled by kerosene not the capricious spirit of instinct, speared its path between the dark earth, speckled with man-made light, and the black sky, sprinkled with the pinhead fire of the stars.

Groups of people emerged out of the gloom further down the street, preceded by their conversation, to take their place in the affluent brightness of the hotel. Darker figures passed on the opposite side of the street, ones and twos glancing at a building they would not enter, barred not by law or custom but by poverty and circumstance. In their gloomy world resentment grew like a mildew without the excuse of colonialism to explain their downside of inequality. Malcolm thought of his beggar, out there in the excluded world if not dead. It's the best thing really, he intoned in silent irony.

The black limousine pulled up and Ngugi got out of the back his rear emerging first, his head still inside. From the back a girlish laugh and some words. Finally, words to the driver who seeing Malcolm drove quickly away. Ngugi turned and almost walked into his host. His breath smelled heavily of beer and cigarette smoke hung about his clothes. He looked confused.

'One of the secretaries,' he said by way of explanation, but highlighting his guilt. 'Just giving her a lift home. Sorry I've had a bit too much to drink. Had to stop off for a drink with some business men.'

'KENTRAD business?' enquired Malcolm.

Ngugi flashed a look of alarm and confusion but before he could reply Malcolm led him up the steps. Ngugi tripped against one of them but steadied himself on the rail.

The atmosphere at dinner was a little icy. Malcolm declined a drink and Ngugi followed suit aware of his condition. The conversation ranged over American life and education, international politics and finance, native culture, commercial fish farms in the Rift Valley, the problems of rearing children in the modern world and the impact of computers on employment. The one area they did not tread into was the one they had in common - Kimura. On that subject Malcolm had much to ask and Ngugi had much he did not wish to answer.

James found it rather boring and retired to bed as soon as seemed polite, which was rather earlier than the adults thought. The two men remained at their table drinking coffee, the room slowly emptying around them. Soon they were alone, uninterrupted apart from the occasional solicitous enquiry from a waiter who would like to have finished work.

'Why did you buy Larsen's estate?' asked Malcolm abruptly.

Ngugi looked at his host icily

'I didn't. Civil servants are not allowed to trade.'

The response was curt, formulaic but quickly given as though it had been rehearsed in anticipation. His mind was clearer now, focused by the danger inherent in the question.

'But your brother did, on your behalf,' guessed Malcolm.

'What's it got to do with you?'

The question was ignored.

'Why did Larsen leave?'

Malcolm was browbeating this senior civil servant fuelled by a sense of injustice.

'I've told you he'd just had enough. He didn't like the idea of Africans running the country.'

Ngugi dare not say nothing, which might imply complicity and guilt.

'But his family had been there for generations. You've heard the story often enough. He was always going on about it. They took barren land and, in the end, it was one of the most productive estates around. You don't just leave that because of politics in Nairobi.'

'He was persuaded to sell. He got a fair price.'

'What other persuasion was there?'

'What do you mean?'

'Who killed Forbes?'

'How should I know? He had enemies.'

'In your family?'

'If you're talking about Wambui that's none of your business. The police decided Forbes had no case to answer. You're surely not suggesting that the police, all good British chaps, were wrong.' The sarcasm was evident.

'Forbes was killed, nastily, and shortly afterwards Larsen sold up. Aren't they connected?'

'I know nothing about it.'

Neither man was in control of the conversation which was like verbal table tennis. Each volley was instinctive and unrehearsed with neither man wanting to fluff a shot.

'But your family own it now.'

'So?'

'So, why let it go to rack and ruin?'

'It's our land. We can do what we like. If we want to let it return to the scrub it was before Larsen's family came, it's our business. Not yours.'

Ngugi was seething now. His words admitted an involvement but it was not clear from his tone whether *we* meant the family or the nation.

'You're an outsider. You have no power now. You've got nothing of value here.' Malcolm thought of the ravine beneath the Changa bridge on the Kimura road. 'You Europeans make me sick. You're happy for us to run our own country provided we do it according to your standards. We won our freedom remember not our licence. You made us learn Shakespeare in our schools and find you know nothing about him. You teach us the ten commandments in our churches and all the time you're fucking your best friend's wife. And you still want respect and thanks.'

The diatribe put Malcolm on the defensive.

'I gave a lot of my life to help you develop,' said Malcolm limply, Ngugi in the ascendancy.

'You didn't give. You were paid. You went away with a lump sum after a good life in the sun. You had servants. You didn't exactly make a sacrifice.'

'But you've done well too. You had a good education and you've prospered. I like to think I helped there.' Malcolm was beaten.

'Aren't you a bit presumptuous. It was me sitting up till all hours writing essays, learning poems, doing sums, not you. You add up all the school fees you paid for me over the years. It was a fortune for me but for you just like buying a new car. You did not buy my life with those fees. If you think that, you can have the money back now. It's nothing to me. I've probably got it in my wallet now.' The last claim seemed improbable but Ngugi's anger took him beyond rationality.

'Because of your business interests?' was Malcolm's final lunge.

Ngugi looked at him coldly quite sober now and conscious of the lurking waiter.

'I am a civil servant. I have no business interests.' Ngugi was in control. He got up and offered his hand. 'Thank you for all you did for me Mr. Bryant. I hope the rest of your holiday is enjoyable.'

The grip was limp and formal. Watching him go Malcolm was stunned by the implications of what he had wheedled out. The ragamuffin he first met twenty-five years ago, was now a powerful member of the establishment, embroiled in major businesses contrary to the laws of the land, implicated in the death of a European and if the contents of his limousine meant anything, cheating on his wife. Malcolm would have another restless night.

THIRTY-FIVE

They arose very early and took the hired car out along the road towards the Rift Valley and Uganda. Malcolm had promised his son an orgy of sightseeing to complete their holiday, though he had a selfish motive too. For his son a journey through the photographic highlights but for him a pilgrimage to his own holy places. The modern car pulled effortlessly towards the peak of the escarpment which plunged into the floor of the valley. Malcolm contrasted its performance with his less reliable models of earlier days. He remembered minor breakdowns and accidents and created a catalogue of misfortune which placed him amongst the hardy pioneers of a long-gone age. He smiled to himself as he recognised his pretentiousness. At the highest point he stopped the car and took James to the viewing point overlooking the vast valley.

'When I first saw it, was when I first experienced awe. It added to my life. I was so joyful. I couldn't speak. And whenever I came this way, I stopped here just to recapture that first moment. And I always could. I showed it to you once when we were off to Kitale on holiday. You were not walking then so I don't suppose you'll remember anything but I wanted to share it with you.' James was surprised by his father's lyricism and was pleased there was more feeling in him than he had assumed. 'It's so unlike anything I had seen, so huge. And it's got grandeur. It's frightening too, in a way, because it makes you feel so small. You can try some shots but you may be disappointed when you see them. The size of the valley, the dust and haze, the huge distances will defeat your camera. Better to put an image on your memory than a photograph.'

This homily didn't deter James who focused and refocused and scanned far and wide. As he did his father gazed into the valley. Somewhere in there, was his wife's ashes deposited much further

338

south but blown and scattered over a wide area. He thought of her watching over them as Ngai watched over his people? Could she see her baby son now reaching to manhood? Would she see father and son together? Was she in the air they breathed now, returning to her son, entering into his body and resting there as he had rested in her? He shivered as he accepted that Alison was dispersed into this wide space never to return. Never. To hope otherwise was sentimentality. But sentimentality is a stronger force than many more noble ones and an idea overwhelmed him. If she could not re-join him, then he could join her.

'When I'm dead, I want to be cremated and I want you to scatter my ashes over the Rift Valley. I don't know how you'll do it - a helicopter perhaps. It's probably illegal but you'll find a way.' He gave no reason for the blurted request.

James paused in his work and looked at his father. To talk about death is a serious matter concentrating minds and shedding pretence. He had never thought of him as being dead - that didn't happen to parents. Though his mother's death had occurred it hadn't happened to him. His father, over fifty, became older in his eye, became more vulnerable. And this vulnerability brought forth a flush of concern, falling short of love, but strong enough to see his father anew. Perhaps the great valley seized on some faint signal and echoed it back, louder and more intense. James felt himself grow out of the filial shadow into an open equality. Before he had felt his father cold, indifferent, reserved and this lack of emotion had made him seem strong. Now he saw him a little differently. Whether it was a look in his eye, the tilt of his head, a tone in his voice, a tiredness in his frame, James recognised his father's deep sadness. And, in doing so, shared some of it. Behind the facade was some strong poison, chronic and corrosive. He didn't understand it, didn't know its causes and didn't fully realise the distress it caused his father. For an animal he might have felt pity, for a human being compassion but this was his father and the word did not exist to describe his feelings about him. He understood they were not separate units on this earth although their daily lives might suggest otherwise. They were linked in an unending chain of evolution and shared, without choice, so much because of it. And then from deep within him, where conscious thought has no power, where genes and environment fight their battles, an icy reaction filled him. He could not bring himself to tell his father what he felt. There was some blockage preventing outward expression of inward feelings. He couldn't find the words, couldn't make the actions and it frightened him because he understood it came down the blood line, only a small trickle in him but perhaps from a vast reservoir in his father.

'Yes. OK Dad. I'll do that,' he said and meant it.

Malcolm returned to the car whilst his son snapped away, the outline of his body pausing and moving from shot to shot. On finishing a reel of film, the young man, older by more than the last few minutes, returned to join his father, now a companion in fate rather than a fellow traveller in time.

'Wow. That was just marvellous.'

They descended into the valley, past the small chapel, around the winding road to the flat floor below. Then they turned back on themselves, climbing by a different route up the escarpment but now into the depths of the Aberdare forest. Periodic stops were made to photograph the luxuriant vegetation, the panoramic views and, with some discretion, the local inhabitants. By midday they were tired and pleased to stop for lunch. Malcolm had been determined to avoid the tourist spots and had paid for a cool box from the hotel. The two men sat, away from the roadway in the cool under some trees, eating their sandwiches and fruit and drinking their beer. Around them the forest, with its bamboo bushes and trailing creepers linking tree to tree, brought them as near to primitive jungle as they would see. They sat, twentieth century noise eliminated, with only each other for company. It seemed so long since they had been in each other's company without the distraction of others. Each formed thoughts they wanted to express but neither brought them to articulation. But they were closer now and both in their way felt it. The brittle harmony of their picnic was ended with intrusion of two baboons, attracted by food rather than any tenuous evolutionary kinship with the two men, and they continued their journey.

By late afternoon both men were tired of travelling although they were still a long way from Nairobi. They stopped in a tourist lodge and took their beers to the tables outside. James did not realise the visit was not accidental. After a while Malcolm told his son to look behind him. James scanned the trees and bushes alongside the small river but could see nothing.

'No. Up there,' said his father.

High above them the cloud was breaking up and through the gaps could be seen the sharp outlines on the big mountain highlighted against the rich blueness of the evening sky. As they watched, the clouds cleared completely and Mount Kenya stood dominating the surrounding land.

'I wanted you to see that but I couldn't be sure it would appear. I said nothing in case it didn't. You can photograph that and not be disappointed.'

James took several shots but was frustrated at not being able to get closer or see a different aspect.

'It's sometimes called the Mountain of God. According to local belief up there lives the god, Ngai, who looks down on the land below and protects its inhabitants. It's a comforting thought although he wasn't much protection against the Europeans, or drought or illness for that matter. We tend to ignore the fallibility of our gods.'

'But the country came back to the Africans in the end, didn't it?'

'I suppose so, but it took a long time. Most of us don't want our gods to play the long game. We want the benefits of our worship now.' He continued, 'Gitau believes in Ngai. He believes all the values of his people are handed down from the mountain top. He believes and it gives him comfort. I suppose that's enough.'

He wondered why people needed gods. They don't really want the morality, the codes of behaviour, the ethics. They just get in the way of living. No, it was so that they were not alone? Loneliness was a terrible condition as he knew from personal experience. And so that they will never be alone, thinking of his own mortality and glad his son was young enough to dismiss its implications. He had no god himself. Religion had not been part of his family culture and the experience of Marion belied a loving god. He wanted comfort in his life but had never sought it from a supreme being. And because he had never sought it, he had never found it and his life had been clinically, icily stoical. Apart from that brief interlude when warmth, passion, companionship had made all thing bearable and most things joyful. It was brief, cruelly brief. With Alison's death he returned to a world as cold and barren as the mountain top above him now and there was no god in it to give him comfort. He wondered if James believed in God. He had not been raised to it at home but all his schools had preached the Christian cause. He didn't want to ask his son about his religious beliefs in case he had none either. Strict atheism becomes bearable if others retain a flickering faith; a canopy of belief comforts believers and nonbelievers alike.

The journey back to Nairobi was taken in the dark and James slept for most of the way occasionally roused as the car rattled across the railway line that crossed and recrossed the road. His father, dull but reliable, steered them home his eyes focusing on the road ahead fearful of a large animal or unsteady bus appearing within his headlights. Much as he had loved Alison, he did not want to join her as a motoring casualty and he had an obligation to get his son home safely to carry on with his life. The headlights illuminated the road just ahead but beyond their range, was darkness. It was metaphor for

Malcolm's life, a dull and uninspiring aspect with no apparent long-term future.

THIRTY-SIX

They sat in the hotel foyer, bags firmly secured, tickets and passports checked, times confirmed, waiting for the call for the courtesy bus. The requirements of the departure overtook the regret of a holiday over. James was talking to Sara and her parents who were returning on the same plane. Malcolm sat apart, watching the activities around him.

Two uniformed attendants stood guard over the group's luggage passing comments with other hotel staff who flowed in and out of the foyer. Malcolm overheard and understood the joshing taking place in Swahili. Pockets of tourists, some drawn together by common experiences in the past week, stood waiting, impotent to affect the schedule, habitually executed by the tour company. Outside the early morning sun was heating the front terrace, its brightness silhouetting the main door turning those who entered from distinguishable human beings with race and personality into anonymous blackened outlines as they passed inside.

Then some call, unheard by most, galvanised the expectant passengers into action. They trouped outside only to find it a false alarm. With much resigned but light-hearted grumbling some stayed put on the steps until their travelling clothes made for discomfort in the sunshine. Some returned inside; some sat at the umbrellaed seats spread along the terrace fragmenting their unity amongst those already seated there. Finally, a call, this time correct, which signalled the start of a journey from bright colours and dry warmth to dull grey and cold damp. The bus pulled onto the main highway its central reservation and edges flush with bright colour. It turned down the airport road scattering a flock of small birds that rose skyward towards sky occupied by bigger ones.

'Vultures?' inquired James.

344

'Storks,' replied his father.

Eventually they reached the head of the check-in queue and with relief turned towards departure checking they still had their hand luggage. Almost immediately they came face to face with Ngugi.

'I didn't want you to go without saying goodbye. I tried to meet you yesterday but you were not around. I think I owe you an explanation. I found out your flight from the hotel. Shall we find somewhere to sit?' The sentences followed no coherent logic and could have been spoken in any order.

James was clearly more interested in Sara and made his excuses.

'He seems a fine boy. You must be proud of him.' The tone was conciliatory if not friendly.

'Yes. *Yes*.' The second with more emphasis.

'Sons sometimes have difficulties connecting with their fathers. My father was very firm in his beliefs and makes me feel I've failed him.' Malcolm noted the duality. He felt he had failed his son; this man felt he had failed his father.

'But you've been very successful.'

'Yes, but he thinks I've paid a price.'

'How?'

'In abandoning the old values.'

'And have you?'

'Have I abandoned the values or paid the price?' he asked rhetorically. 'Both and neither I suppose. You can't abandon the values that make you part of something. They are like tentacles. Your acceptance or rejection of them is irrelevant. And we're all paying a price, all the time.'

'What binds you?'

'Family obligations certainly. We all have a duty to support our families which can be very big. The more successful you are the more you're looked to for support. My father had four children; his brother had five. Straight away that's eight others looking to me for help. Now there are their children and then their spouses and their families. It's endless. They want money, they want education, they want jobs, they want medical treatment. That's why I need to have business interests to meet their needs. Most of my family have jobs with my firms or the ministry; you've met the chauffeur.' It was like a confession.

'Aren't you acting corruptly? Aren't you undermining the country you're supposed to be building?'

'Yes, but I can't help it; it's what my culture expects of me. If I didn't put my family in, someone else would place theirs. It wouldn't make much difference to the country but it makes a lot of difference to my family. I suppose that offends your sense of fair play.'

'In a small way I celebrated your people's freedom and welcomed your opportunities under independence. I don't suppose I came here to help you; I just wanted a job. But whilst I was here, I convinced myself we were building something. Something better.'

'History will see it as better.'

'A lot of your people don't see it as better. Some think they were better off under the Europeans; a greater fairness and more stability. Others think your government has the wrong set of values but they're not encouraged to say so.'

Ngugi looked uncomfortable.

'Give us time,' it was a lame reply and he knew it.

'How long will you need?' this a genuine enquiry.

'You boast of a thousand years of history. They weren't all progress. You gave us too many burdens to carry. Unlike my father I admire the Europeans; I want to select the best from them. I want your advice and like a child I want your approval. But don't judge us by your standards or else we'll always fail, like son's fail their fathers.'

'Why did you buy Larsen's farm?' and before Ngugi could deny it. 'Well alright, why did your brother buy Larsen's farm?'

'We... ,' this admitting his complicity, '... bought it for my father. We thought it right he should own property in his own homeland where he had worked on the land all his life making it more fertile. We wanted him to get his reward.'

'So, you frightened off Larsen by killing Forbes.'

'We acted through agents. Some of them may have had a grudge against Forbes; he abused a lot of women. He couldn't keep his mouth shut in the bars.'

'You had a grudge too.'

'Yes, but I wouldn't kill him and I didn't have him killed. After all he was Grace's father.'

James thought about telling him that Flynn was Grace's father but felt he had no right.

'Why won't Grace visit her mother?'

'When Grace was born the family concluded that Wambui was to blame as much as Forbes, so in our eyes she was disgraced. She deceived her husband to sleep with another man. She was an outcast. Perhaps it was harsh but once the family had made that decision no one felt able to change it. Anyway, she was cared for by Flynn and it ceased to be an issue.'

'That was a bit hard on the woman. It's not unusual for men to cheat in that way. Do they suffer disgrace too?' He caught Ngugi's eye before the African looked down. 'I think her mother would like to see her. And the Father, too.' He was pleased with the ambiguity.

Malcolm had no reason to believe this, but it would have eased a situation with a simple sentimentality which human beings feel hard to eschew. However, the thought died there.

'Why is Larsen's farm abandoned?'

Ngugi laughed ironically.

'The best laid plans. We bought the farm in my father's name and then told him. It was a surprise present. We arranged a big family gathering - all the children - and we presented him with the legal documents. We were so pleased with ourselves. It's such a simple pleasure doing things for your parents when they are old. Anyway, he signed the papers and took possession of the estate. But then he refused to farm it, demanding it be used by the village people. He said it was their land until it was taken by the Larsen's and the people should have it back. We put guards in to keep the people out hoping he'd change his mind but it just dragged on. We never resolved the squabble and now the land is used by nobody. And do you know, he relishes the situation. He seems delighted that the land is returning to what it was before the Europeans arrived, wiping out the efforts of three generations of Larsens.'

'Do you understand him?'

'In a way I do. It's reversing an injustice. It's having control over affairs. Establishing the right of Africans to do what they like with their own land.'

'But?'

'But you can't do that on a national scale. The Europeans brought roads, railways, medicine, lots of things. We could decide to reject them but that would be perverse. I can understand what it symbolises and when I'm up in Kimura I sometimes look at the estate and think. Yes. Yes. It brings back our dignity and some little sinew in me twangs with recognition and sympathy. Then I get back to Nairobi and the office and the minister and the aid agencies and the shanty towns and I see it as not noble but self-indulgent. But the whole scale of national activity it's neither here nor there. It's just an issue between me and him.' The younger man's eyes moistened. 'I have always loved and respected my father even now when he doesn't understand the demands modern life make on me. But for a while you were like a second father; that's a much easier idea for an African than for a European. You paid my school fees; you helped my further education, but you didn't leave me with your burden to carry; my real father did. When I tried to give him something back, he rejected it. Can I be blamed for feeling he rejected me too?'

It was Now Malcolm's eyes that moistened. Across the lounge he could see his own real son, as distant emotionally from him as he was physically. Was this son carrying a burden - of emotional starvation, of stunted ambition - that his own parents had handed to him? Did this son, too, feel rejected by his father?

'Can I ask one thing of you?' pleaded Ngugi. 'Don't ever judge me. Because if you do, it will be a harsh judgement and you will be wrong. You don't understand the values that support me and suffocate me at the same time. The chance of birth put me in a society torn between rural poverty and technological wealth, between a leisurely secure village past and a high-speed uncertain global future. I can barely cope with that. If you judge me, I will fail as I fail in my own eyes every day. Rather than judgement I would like understanding of my predicament and love, too, if you can give it.'

Although it was not intended the last phrase stung Malcolm. The conversation paused and each sensed it was time to leave. They bade each other cliched farewells and the African walked away. No bare feet now, no second-hand clothes, no innocence. Just grown up and like his country, bewildered by responsibility.

The sudden surge at the start of the runway brought its usual anxieties. The passengers yearned for the safe rise of the nose leading to the upward rush which reduced houses to sugar lumps. The country spread out beneath them - brown earth criss-crossed with dark roads and pale paths. The wing dipped as the plane banked and gave Malcolm a last look at Nairobi its white modern buildings scorning the swamp from which it had grown. In the distance the peaks of Mt Kenya stood proud of their enveloping curtain of cloud. Below a whole country got on with life with only a passing interest in the capsule above. Malcolm had arrived as a young man when the country had started to bloom. Was it still blooming now or had the stains of decay already entered the petals?

In daylight flight was too high to afford views of the land below and, tiring of the film, Malcolm dozed off. A clicking noise woke him with a start. Seat belts were being fastened in response to the illuminated sign. He glanced out of the window to see the plane dipping down towards the cloud layer. It entered slowly flitting through cloud banks which subdued the sun sometimes obscuring it. It did this with increasing frequency in its descent before finally succumbing to the misty gloom of the main cloud layer. He wondered if slow death was like this. Small and irregular losses of consciousness before a final oblivion. Death was not here. The plane dipped below the cloud exposing southern England's heavily cultivated land, green meadows and brown ploughed field almost indistinguishable under a grim sky. James, beside him, blinked his eyes in mock tiredness.

'That was a good holiday. Thanks Dad.' Once they had landed and free to separate this might not have been said but here with them unavoidably in close proximity it came out.

It would have been nice to think it was *good* for the reasons he had intended. But he expected it was *good* because of sunshine, photographs, Sara, swimming and not because they had spent more time together than they had before as independent people. For Malcolm, too, it had been *good*. He had felt closer to people than he had for some time - not just James but him certainly.

Malcolm reached out and put his hand over his son's on the arm rest between them. He felt a slight reflexive recoil and removed his hands mistaking his son's adolescent inhibition for filial rejection again. He had been close to his son during the holiday but he seemed fated to sense rejection even when none was intended. He assessed the prospect for his future life. He felt able to spend the next few years not in total emotional isolation but with some hope that he would see his son's life blossom before him. He understood that his own parental behaviour had bruised the bud but saw, too, that his son's life force had contained and overridden that weakened start. James could survive and prosper. He could make friends, take lovers, live free of guilt and burden. Whether he would, depended less on Malcolm than on James himself. Malcolm, the father, could put his burden down now.

THIRTY-SEVEN

The sound of a door opening woke Malcolm from a dream, its images crumbling as his brain reassembled his thoughts. He gathered his senses slowly as the nurse pulled the medicine trolley in behind her. It caught the door frame and then cannoned into the metal plate protecting the bottom of the door, rattling all the pills in their plastic containers. It took a while for him to remember where he was. The black woman confused him for a moment. She was not like the Kikuyu women he remembered - they small, knarled and bronzed; this one plump and very black.

'Time for your pills, Mr. Bryant.'

'Assante sana,' he said. It was Swahili for thank you. He couldn't concentrate his thoughts but he knew he'd got something wrong.

'Sure. Anything you say.' The nurse put the pills in his mouth and held the cup of water to his lips cradling his head to the upright. 'Sure thing.'

The institutionally painted walls, the washbasin in the corner, the spare furnishing focused his mind. This was where he had been for some weeks now. Weeks? Or was it months? He couldn't remember.

Malcolm did not want the pills with their associated side-effects but neither did he want the pain they were designed to subdue. The rare type of melanoma was well advanced and he had little illusion, despite the prevarication of the doctors, that the pills were not prescribed to cure him but merely to make his death less unpleasant. Skin cancer, probably brought on by exposure to intense sunshine, was a cruel enough fate. That it might have developed during his visit to Kenya with James was doubly so. He had wondered about the mechanism of its contraction. Was it a slow assault on the skin cells or was there one moment when it took root? If so, when was that?

352

Lying by the pool watching James? Walking up to Flynn's house? Or at the moment he took the photo of Flynn's veranda? How cruel that would be. He relived his whole holiday not in reviving happy memories but as a clinical safari trying to work out the very moment when his illness had taken hold. He had had plenty of time to do this in the months since the diagnosis. How could he spend so many years in the African sun without harm, only to succumb after a few days' exposure?

He swallowed the pills without objection. The water was welcome in a throat dry from sleep.

'Thank you,' he said at last. His outward courtesy reflected his inner helplessness. 'I'd like some more water, please.'

'Sure darling. Sure thing.'

The nurse left, easing the trolley carefully through the doorway. It was only when she had gone, he noticed his son was in the room. James looked good as most young people do by virtue of their youth; a tall slender body, strong lively hair which was tousled rather than unkempt, easy balance; skin and flesh complementing bone and sinew without the battle between them that develops in later life. His brown eyes, set in light olive skin, showed assurance emerging from youthful uncertainty. Malcolm looked at his son getting a sense of pleasure from his outward looks. He had always felt uncomfortable with his own body. From childhood he remembered being sickly without being sick, perhaps the outward signs of his inner turmoil. His body had conspired with his emotions to set him aside from the world. His son's good looks and confident manner contrasted starkly with the twitching greyness of his own youth. But what was below the surface? Was his son blighted too? And did he, the father, blight him? Did he pass on the legacy through his genes - unwillingly, unwittingly perhaps but as surely as we pass on red hair and big noses. Their mutual holiday seemed to suggest James had survived relatively unscathed but Malcolm, ever the pessimist, found it difficult to believe.

'Hi Dad. You OK'

'So-so'. The truth would not do. The whole process was one of lying - the doctors to the patient - the patient to the family. In the end it was the lies that told the truth. He blinked and shook the sleep from his head. 'I must have fallen asleep.'

'You were asleep when I arrived. I didn't wake you. Were you dreaming?'

'Yes. How did you know?'

'Look at your paper. It's all crumpled up. It looks as though you've been fighting it.' His father nodded in acknowledgement. 'About Marion?'

His father looked startled. 'What makes you think that?' His tone was unusually abrupt.

James shrugged. 'You dreamed of her when we were on holiday. Do you remember? I just - sort of - thought... I didn't mean....' He was surprised by his father's reaction.

Malcolm nodded. He did dream of her a lot, more often than he would admit but he had little choice in the matter. He looked at the opposite wall, feeling a coldness in himself. Seeking warmth, he looked up at his son and smiled self-consciously. He began to raise his hand towards his son's hand in a gesture of reconciliation but pulled back almost immediately. As so often in the past his instinct was suppressed, held down by some weight, suffocated by some stronger influence. He was blighted - always had been. Some of the richest joys of life had been denied him. He could express opinions but not feelings, have encounters but not relationships, make acquaintances but not friends. He was adequately equipped to deal with surface contacts with the rest of humanity but his ability to develop deeper emotional ties was severely limited. Every exposure to the uncertainties of close human contact and commitment drove him back into the safety of his shell. In there, a wealth of human emotion passed him by. It stemmed from childhood of course. There was a reason, an excuse, a justification. There was a cause. He knew it; he could identify it precisely. But he couldn't overcome it. Just couldn't. Once, life had offered him amelioration of his condition if not escape from it. And having offered it then took it away again. Even now his contact with his son - his only child - was terse, cold, detached.

'Journey, OK?'.

James had travelled across town from the flat he shared with three others in his college year group. Despite studying in the same town as his father - he never thought of it as his home town, this a concept he had not developed - he chose to live outside the family home. Most parents would have seen this as a natural step for an emerging adult and many would be relieved at the prospect. But for Malcolm Bryant it seemed a harsh confirmation of how his son was rejecting him.

'Not bad. Bus seemed to hit every light at red. There wasn't much traffic, so it wasn't late.'

His father had lost track of time and focused at the clock on the opposite wall to reorientate himself.

'You sat upstairs I suppose.'

'Yes,' came the sheepish response. His African childhood had rarely offered the other world detachment high above street level and in England he sought its changing panorama with childlike enthusiasm. His attire was determinedly studentish but this image was severely dented by the Marks & Spencer carrier bag hanging from his right hand. On other occasions the bag would have been that of some record store or flagrantly upmarket shop. This one was not a symbol - just a container.

After a slight hesitation, which suggested an uncertainty about how best to proceed, Malcolm followed with, 'What's new?'

'Not much.' And after a pause when neither seemed at ease, 'I'm trying a different film for my next assignment.'

'A different speed?' His father knew enough to ask the questions that might show an interest if not a knowledge; but he would not have known the consequence of any answer.

'No, just a different make.'

355

The banality of the conversation was recognised by both of them but neither knew how to change gear.

'What have you snapped lately?' The *snapped* dated him and amplified his detachment.

'I got some good shots of trees in last week's snow. There's something thrilling about the world being reduced to two colours. The prints always seem clearer and the lack of colour seems to add a dimension to the picture when you'd expect it to detract.' He found more to say about his passion than he could about his father.

Malcolm was taken aback by this opinion not just because of its content but because it had been expressed at all. His mind told him it was an opportunity to respond but his voice couldn't join it. He said nothing. This mature adult remained neutered.

'Will you put them in your folio?' This an inspired link between his interest and his studies.

James took a moment to accept the relevance of the link. For him it was more than an interest, it was a passion at times bordering on an obsession. He would have taken the photographs with no motive at all and would have taken many more had he not run out of film.

'Yeah. I think I'll do a piece on colour versus monochrome. All the best photographs are black and white. It's odd how such a big technological development like colour should produce less-satisfying results. I think the full range of colours blur an image whilst the black and white carve out a stark outline of the real object. The sharpness of the image seems to intensify your assessment of it. The lack of colour adds to our appreciation of it.'

Malcolm struggled to respond. 'Is that true?' he followed up limply.

'Truth has nothing to do with artistic appreciation'. The animated comment was not a proper reply. Malcolm was taken aback by the snappiness of the statement but didn't show it. He considered whether James had said anything original or profound, or was just indulging in student speak. He was surprised to find he couldn't decide but grudgingly conceded that the spontaneity of the response suggested some instinctive belief.

'I've been looking at a new camera'

This brought back Malcolm's attention. 'Oh?'. He didn't know whether this was just conversation or an invitation to help buy the new item. He wouldn't have minded the money but would have preferred to give advice, opinion, approval, encouragement even though, in his case, their value would have been spurious. 'Will that help your studies?'

'Perhaps. There's something missing from my shots. I can't tell whether it's me or the technology.' He wanted to explain more but wasn't sure what to say and he guessed his father's responses would not have been helpful.

Malcolm's interest in and knowledge of photography was very limited. Unusually, he had not had a camera when working in Kenya, although he had come to regret this as, back in England, his memories of his everyday life abroad began to fade. His conversations with James on this matter held no great interest for him other than the conversational links they maintained with his son.

'What have you brought to show me,' he said indicating the bag.

'Nothing recent but I've brought the ones I took in Kenya. Just as you asked.'

'Thank you. I'd like to see them again. There's one I'd like to keep here.'

'Yours is in there but I hope you'll look at mine as well.' he said handing over the bag.

'Yes, of course. I thought yours were generally very good and some were beautiful. I saw in them a world I knew but just now I need to see what I chose to photograph. It was a little special to me'.

James gushed inwardly at his father's compliment. Malcolm would have been overjoyed at his son's pleasure but it remained hidden from him. James's reticence about expressing feeling was not a natural reaction but was conditioned by his uncomfortable relationship with his father.

As Malcolm disgorged the contents of the bag, the atmosphere noticeably lightened as though the actions of opening, selecting, viewing held less tension than did conversation. He sorted through the prints his fingers not nimble enough to stop a few sliding onto the sheets. James patiently put them back in place. Malcolm looked only cursorily at the pictures that recorded their holiday or rather James's version of it. He noted some very good shots of trees and buildings but the animal shots were routine tourist. He had seen them before and had used them to jog his memory in his search for the source of his illness. At last, he came to the one he wanted. Placing it to one side he dutifully scanned the rest of the packet - mainly snakes - and rejected the remaining packs. He looked at the picture intently. It was technically a good print but that only served to highlight his memory of the real object - the Yesterday, Today and Tomorrow plant over Flynn's veranda. The pastel-coloured flowers stood out clearly against the green foliage. Pregnant buds and withered heads mingled among the blooms. A corner of the picture had caught the sky, its bright blueness emphasising the brilliance of the day already captured in the colours of the flowers. This sun, bringing life and splendour to the picture, was the very thing that had terminally damaged Malcolm.

How cruel, he said silently and then again. How cruel.

James remained silent. He had seen the print often and noted his father's sustained interest in it. The subject matter left him puzzled.

'Joe and I spent so many happy hours teasing ideas from this bush. He would see the flowers as human lives waiting as buds in God's bosom, flowering in His world and returning to Him in the fullness of time - individual lives coming and going in an unrelenting flow of human life. But between us, they took many forms, nation states, popular singers, world religions all forming, living, dying.'

His fatigue meant he could not complete the sentences without pausing for breath and now he took a longer break. His son, distressed by his condition, could find nothing to say and waited for him to continue.

'Later, after your mother died, the game became too painful. Life with her was my Today - warmth, brightness, colour. And with her death I started to die too.'

He moved his hand to touch his son - hugging was beyond his strength now - but James was beyond his reach and the contact was left unmade. He needed another long pause to find the energy to say what he wanted.

'Afterwards our conversations were more sombre. We were a strange couple. We had so little in common, he being a believer and me not. Yet we were so close. Our loneliness brought us together I suppose. Close together but still with our own pocket of loneliness.'

'When I've gone will you write to let him know? There is no one else left to do it. You'll find his address in my papers.'

It had been a bit like a marriage at times. There had not been sex, of course, but a sort of love based on mutual respect and understanding. And it was a marriage of continuing choice by equals not binding agreement between players. How awful for people to live together bound only by contract, but lacking the personal bonds of wedlock. That his own marriage might have developed like that did not occur to him. For him it would always have been the idealised version he had known in its short life.

'You were too young to see all that. But all the years you have known me I have been dying. I should have given you more. I wish I could have given you more.' He wanted to say more but kept pushing up against his emotional block and he had not, now, the strength to break it. 'I hope you were not damaged by that.' His voice trailed into tearfulness as he remembered he had prayed for this to be so. To whom, to what he did not know but he couldn't deal with it himself.

This sparse declaration had brought an intimacy between father and son more intense than they had known before. Simply words, easily spoken were all there was and all that was possible now. The shadow of irretrievable death heightened the sincerity of the moment. Malcolm had no strength now to hug his son and his son could not bring himself to hug his father. His father's body was fragile and repugnant with its illness and his own youthful inhibition made physical contact unthinkable. Once again Malcolm had death on his body but now the death was his own and the rejection came from his son. No. No. No.

His life was running away from him; he had no control over the time scale. He wanted to hug James to him, to beg his forgiveness, to explain everything so that his son would understand. He did not have the strength, physical or emotional, to do it. He sank back into the pillows his body as starved of substance as his spirit. All conversation stopped as each man quelled unmanly feelings. James blew his nose discreetly as his father wiped his nose on the sleeve of his pyjama jacket.

James cleared his throat. 'Shall I put this up where you can see it?'

Malcolm nodded. James took the snap of the veranda roof and clipped it into the frame of his mother's photograph already on the bedside table. It occupied the bottom half of the frame. Malcolm looked sideways at it. Alison's truncated face looked over the top of the photograph like some giant peering over Flynn's veranda.

'Did you love her very much?'

Malcolm was taken aback by the directness and naiveté of the question.

'Yes,' he said in reflex. It was a small reply to a big question.

James understood his father was dying. He knew, too, he should feel an obligation to stay with him but he was afraid to be there when his father died. Already he had become conscious of his own mortality and wanted to escape from this realisation.

'Well, I must be off now. I'm off down to see Sara. I'll see you tomorrow. Will you be alright?' James suspected he would not see his father alive again and yet he was leaving him. He did not do so because he was without feeling or care. He was not damaged but he was frightened, the normal fear of death, new to his youthful mind, unsupported with the stoicism and familiarity maturity brings. And to stay would mean confronting things alone.

'Of course,' said Malcolm. He had no control over things but he would be fed, he would be taken to the toilet, he would be brought newspapers. He would have the company of the nurses, the doctors, the cleaners. He wondered what James felt about Sara, whether they were in love. James might have said *yes* confusing love with infatuation and curiosity but he was a long way off finding whether he would or could love anybody. The young man left the room closing the door with a touching gentleness. Outside the door he stood for a moment his head pressed against the frame. He needn't go to Sara; he could go back in. But that night he and Sara were to spend their first night together. Two days ago, they had made love for the first time. He had tried many times before but with a maturity and control he did not have, she deflected his attempts. That night, in his flat, she had relented, giving way, not to his strength or passion, but to his helpless weakness as he anticipated his father's coming death. His tears disarmed her and with unexpected simplicity they made love. With that threshold crossed the wish for a night together seemed inescapable and they arranged to go to Malcolm's house where James's bedroom would offer them privacy. He could give up that opportunity and stay with his father. If he went to Sara, they would make love, would lie together, touching and stroking. He would feel her warm body against his. They would talk, telling and teasing, exploring and explaining. He would hold her firmly to him and she would be thrilled by his strength as he with her gentleness. Tonight, he might cry in her arms at his father's plight, his tears a signal of his humanity as precious to her as his virility. If he went back inside to his father, he would sit physically remote, left alone with his father's life as his father lapsed into unconsciousness, waiting the final moment. After a moment, he raised his head and walked hurriedly down the corridor leaving his father to die. With Sara he would not be alone.

EPILOGUE

The frail figure of a man lies in a hospital bed. He is near to death. Above him a ceiling fan cools and clears the malodorous air. Click, Click, Click. He is thinking about his wife long since dead. He can see her in a photograph at the side of his bed, her face partially obscured by another print. She had given so much to him but what had he given to her? He had needed her. She had given to him - light, exuberance, security. And he had taken these in like a thirsty man. But they had been all one way, he thought now. The value of his relationship with her had been measured totally by how she had enriched his life. It occurred to him he might have given her nothing. And if he had given nothing, how could he have really loved her and how could she have loved him. Love had to be two-way, giving and taking, sharing. Love was not inherited; it had to be sown and nurtured in each life afresh if it was to be harvested. It seemed only unhappiness could be handed on. But she knew he couldn't give, surely? He was not selfish. He wanted to give but the ability to do so was squeezed out of him in childhood. By the time he met her, failing to give was subconscious habit. She had been able to take from him what a well-rounded human being could give by instinct.

He begins to panic. What if she had tired of him? Had she tired of him? Had she found somebody else? The baby! She was pregnant when she died. She hadn't said anything about it. Could it have been some other man's? The awfulness of this prospect engulfed him. He had taken solace in the fact that in his miserable life there had been one short period when his life blossomed. He'd taken it as axiomatic that her life had blossomed too. How could it be otherwise? He looks at her photograph again. Without her full mouth and rounded cheeks, now hidden by the photograph, her eyes lack warmth. They are isolated from the rest of her features like a component in a police identikit picture. With his judgement fractured by his illness and medicine, her eyes seem to accuse.

He reaches out to remove the print, to see once again the full faced portrait behind. His hands, mottled with the brown spots of ageing, are trembling with emotion and frailty. They knock against the frame and it falls to the floor sliding away from him. The inset print flutters to the ground and lies face downward on the tiled floor hiding its kaleidoscope of purple, mauve and white. The writing on the back is now exposed – Yesterday, Today and Tomorrow. The glass splits open but is held in place in the frame. A large crack disfigures his wife's face as the frame comes to a halt facing him. Beyond it his eyes see the wheelchair there to take him to the bathroom. His eyes focus feebly on it. Is it empty or is there some vague shape slumped in it? He can't decide. The room seems cloudy. He croaks a word, a woman's name. He closes his eyes and his head drops to the pillow in its final action. Above him the fan continues its rotation.

Click. Click. Click.

Printed in Great Britain
by Amazon

78346347R00210